The Language of Conferencing

Eija Ventola
Celia Shalom
Susan Thompson
(eds.)

The Language
of Conferencing

PETER LANG

Frankfurt am Main · Berlin · Bern · Bruxelles · New York · Oxford · Wien

Die Deutsche Bibliothek - CIP-Einheitsaufnahme

The language of conferencing / Eija Ventola...(ed.). - Frankfurt
am Main ; Berlin ; Bern ; Bruxelles ; New
York ; Oxford ; Wien : Lang, 2002
ISBN 3-631-36048-7

With financial support by
Kultusministerium des Landes Sachsen-Anhalt
and the University of Salzburg.

ISBN 3-631-36048-7
US-ISBN 0-8204-4729-3

© Peter Lang GmbH
Europäischer Verlag der Wissenschaften
Frankfurt am Main 2002
All rights reserved.

Printed in Germany 1 2 3 4 6 7

www.peterlang.de

ACKNOWLEDGEMENTS

Many of the papers published in this book were first presented at the symposium "English as a Conference Language: Linguistic Pros and Cons", organised in January 1999 in Wittenberg, Germany. This symposium offered all participants a forum for fruitful exchange of ideas and views. Thus, my first thanks go to the institutions that financially supported that symposium: Martin-Luther-Universität, Halle-Wittenberg, Verein der Freunde der Martin-Luther-Universität, Die Leucorea Stiftung and Die Deutsche Forschungsgemeinschaft. Secondly, I want to thank my students, Antje Dittrich, Friedrike Langer, and Ina Ruppelt for their great assistance in organising the symposium and for so diligently looking after the participants.

The publication of the book has been supported by Ministerium des Landes Sachsen-Anhalt and Paris-Lodron-Universität Salzburg. I wish to extend my sincere thanks to these institutions and of course to the publisher Peter Lang, and its representative Dr. Karin Timme from the Berlin office. I would also like to thank the following people, who have significantly helped us, the editors, at various stages with the work involved in producing the book: Antje Dittrich, Cassily Charles and Dr. Anja Schwarzl. Moreover, I want to thank the writers who submitted their interesting papers for the volume and made the whole effort rewarding and hopefully worthwhile to many readers. Last but not least, my thanks go to my co-editors, Dr. Celia Shalom and Dr. Susan Thompson, who, even in the times of production stress, kept the positive attitudes and good humour which kept us all going until the book was finished.

Eija Ventola

TABLE OF CONTENTS

Part III

INTRODUCTION

The original impetus for this volume came from a symposium in January 1999 titled 'English as a Conference Language: Linguistic pros and cons', organised by Eija Ventola at the Martin-Luther-Universität, Halle-Wittenberg in Germany. The symposium was intended to address the clear neglect of conference language by applied linguists in the field of English for Academic Purposes (EAP). This neglect is particularly striking in comparison with the attention paid to written academic genres such as the research article. The symposium gave a welcome opportunity to individual researchers working in various academic institutions across Europe to come together and share their interests in the field of conference language. Several participants at the symposium, together with other researchers in the field, have contributed to the present volume. Our hope is that this collection will give a 'state-of-the-art' view of linguistic research into conference language as well as encourage the development of research into a key group of academic research process genres.

The contributors to this collection draw on a wide range of influences and approaches, such as the approach to genre analysis associated with English for Specific Purposes (ESP, including EAP) and the work of John Swales, systemic-functional linguistics, socially- (rather than philosophically-) oriented pragmatics, and social constructivism. These different traditions share a fundamental interest in how texts are situated within particular social, cultural and/or institutional contexts, how they derive from the goals and purposes of particular discourse communities, and how these contextual features and communicative purposes are manifested in the language choices of the enacted text. Deriving from these approaches, certain important concerns are shared by contributors to this volume.

Firstly, there is an emphasis on the importance of studying conferences as a social event comprising interrelated genres. These arise in a particular context, and the unfolding of their generic structures cannot fully be understood without taking that social context into account. Several of the authors in the volume seek to relate the values and practices of the discourse communities to the generic, register and discourse features of conference genres, and aim to see how social context systematically influences the linguistic and semiotic choices made during conference presentations. For example, many contributors are interested in the influence of social contexts at the macrolevel on how social action is organised in stages, and which relatively stable generic features can be found in conference genres. The range of different conference events and disciplines covered by the chapters in this collection allows for some key shared generic features to emerge. However, contributors also stress the importance of taking into account the views and attitudes of the academics who listen to and produce these genres.

In focussing on spoken conference genres, the volume offers a good counterbalance to the abundant body of research and published literature on written academic and scientific genres (particularly within systemic-functional linguistics and ESP genre analysis). Written academic genres are usually approached from the synoptic, 'text-as-product' point of view. However, analysing spoken conference genres forces analysts to consider simultaneously the dynamic, 'text-as-process' point of view. Thus, a second shared concern of several writers in this collection is to offer a complementary view to the relatively stable synoptic view of conference genres outlined above. They stress that conference genres, particularly because of their nature as primarily spoken and often spontaneous or quasi-spontaneous events, are essentially dynamic in their unfolding, and in some respects therefore relatively unpredictable. Speakers must make linguistic choices on a moment-by-moment basis in response to the developing and changing context of situation, not least during discussion genres. This dynamism poses specific challenges for conference participants, particularly those who are novices or non-native speaking (or both).

Thirdly, the predominance of face-to-face spoken interaction in conference genres raises a related concern of contributors to this volume: the importance of interpersonal management and politeness features in these genres. These issues arise throughout the entire conference event, for example, conference presenters need to establish and maintain a rapport with their audience, while conference discussants must deal with potentially face-threatening acts as they arise during interaction. These pragmatic demands are primarily satisfied through the use of pragmalinguistic strategies which are very different from the politeness strategies employed in written research process genres such as the research article.

Fourthly, this collection contains analyses of data from conferences in several different European countries and different fields of academic research. This range of information allows for a more comprehensive view of conference language than has been possible so far, and some extremely interesting findings emerge. For example, some contributors compare generic choices across different fields, and their findings suggest academic discipline or field can have a significant influence on generic expectations and linguistic choices.

Finally, contributors to this volume all share an interest in the pedagogic implications of their findings. Chapters discuss issues such as raising learner awareness of how different conference genres work, and helping novice conferees, usually working in a second, or even third or fourth language, to understand how language choices are motivated by the communicative purposes and cultural expectations of a particular discourse community.

The papers in this collection broadly fall into three areas. The volume opens with chapters by Ventola, Shalom, Räisänen and Rowley-Jolivet, which in their various ways examine the conference as a whole and consider both the role of conferences within the larger framework of research communities which control them, and the systems and networks of conference genres. The middle group of chapters (Tervonen, Heino & Tommola, Thompson, Frobert-Adamo, Charles & Ventola, and Webber) each deal with one particular aspect of the conference, be it a particular conference genre or a particular discourse feature of a conference genre. The final section of the volume contains chapters by Vassileva, Yakhontova, Slepovitch, Banks, and Ventola, which discuss issues of language code and intercultural variation relating to the use of English as a conference language, particularly the problems that this raises for novice non-native speaking academics.

The first group of chapters, then, focus on whole conferences and their component genres, and propose approaches to analysing their characteristic features. Each of the chapters discusses an approach to understanding how a conference can be viewed as a system of interlinked component genres. These approaches may be seen as broadly complementary, though, as indicated above, there are differences in the traditions followed by the writers. Ventola compares and contrasts a rhetorical and a systemic-functional genre-oriented linguistic approach to describing the language of conferences, arguing that a linguistic approach can offer a deeper and more powerful explanation of conference genres. However, she contends that our linguistic tools for analysis are not yet sophisticated enough to deal with the multi-modal and interlinking nature of conference genres, and proposes analytical approaches to deal with this problem, in particular the concept of semiotic spanning. Shalom's chapter introduces key concepts in the analysis of conference genres, and discusses some of the kinds of genre knowledge which conference participants are required to have in order to function successfully. Not least among these is the ability to make situationally appropriate choices at an interpersonal level. Her chapter argues that the acquisition of community-specific genre knowledge is the key for the novice researcher's success. Like Ventola and Shalom, Räisänen highlights the need to consider the conference as a system both at a macro-level, situated within its larger context of the academic forum, and at a micro-level, examining how each conference genre is interlinked with other related genres. Rowley-Jolivet is interested in the conference as a macrogenre serving the communicative needs and purposes of its community. She explores the scientific conference paper from a social constructivist perspective, focusing on its role in the 'life of a fact'. She argues that the conference paper fills a vital mid-way point in the development of knowledge claims, lying between the informal beginnings of the claim in the research lab and the polished final version as displayed in the research article.

The next group of chapters each consider some particular discourse feature of the conference presentation and conference presentation discussion, such as discourse markers, politeness features, and the influence of mode (linguistic and non-linguistic). Contributors argue that these features are central to understanding the communicative purposes and rhetorical patterning of the genres. Tervonen et al. examine the types of metadiscoursal language used in conference presentations. Metadiscourse forms a significant element of the presentations which they analyse. Interestingly, they find that text-structuring metadiscourse occurs less often than hedging and interpersonally-oriented metadiscourse, though they stress the analytical problems in teasing out these different aspects of metadiscoursal language. They argue that this predominance of evaluative and interactional metadiscourse can be linked to the face-to-face nature of the conference presentation.

Like Tervonen et al., Thompson focuses on the interlinked interpersonal and text-organising aspects of the research presentation. Thompson's chapter investigates how academics in the fields of applied linguistics and science present their research story in conference papers, and compares this with the presentation of the same research process in research articles. The analysis focuses on how far presenters use a narrative mode of development to tell their stories, and finds a complex picture whereby narrative is used in the presentations, though it is by no means the dominant mode, and varies according to academic discipline. Frobert-Adamo's chapter continues the theme of interpersonal management in conference presentations by examining the possible roles of humour in presentations. Her study is based on interviews with academic informants in a number of different countries about their perceptions of the use of humour in conference papers. She argues that humour can be seen as a type of hedging device, establishing a 'buffer' between presenter and audience, and that, although humour may superficially appear to be time-wasting, it can in fact save time by providing a short-cut to the audience's better understanding of the topic or of the presenter.

Charles & Ventola focus on an as yet relatively neglected area of conference presentations - the interrelationship between the spoken and the visual information in the presentation, in this case the switching of modes between the prepared talk and the illustrative slide show which accompanies it. They argue for the need for a multi-modal type of analysis, and provide both a synoptic and a dynamic analysis of the generic structure of the slide show element of the talk. Drawing on Ventola's approach to semiotic spanning (see Ventola's first paper in this volume), they argue for the importance of a dynamic approach to genre description, not least to enable novice academics to appreciate how the genre actually works as the discourse unfolds. The issue of dynamism is also addressed in Webber's paper, which offers an analysis of the discussion phase following conference presentations, in this case in the field of medicine. Like a number of earlier chapters, Webber is particularly interested in the interpersonal aspects of communication, emphasising the particular face problems for both presenter and discussant which are inherent in post-paper discussion, problems which are only aggravated by the unpredictable and dynamic nature of the interaction.

The final group of papers share an interest in the intercultural and educational implications of the increasing domination of English as an international conference language. Vassileva examines the use of various kinds of speaker-audience interactive features (personal pronouns, rhetorical questions, direct address, etc.) in the conference presentations of Bulgarian academics speaking in English. She relates these interactive features to the types of discourse acts in which they occur, and discusses 'deviations' from native-speaker norms. The chapter considers some implications for successful intercultural academic communication and for the concept of an international academic discourse community. Yakhontova's chapter investigates the contrastive styles of conference paper titles in English and two Slavic languages, Russian and Ukrainian. She links these differences to variations in cultural expectations about the role of titles and to prevailing ideologies lying behind these cultural expectations. Her chapter raises the important issue of how far non-native speaking academics should be expected to fall in line with Anglophone practices, and she argues for a sensitive approach to raising awareness without imposing alien conceptualisations and strategies. Slepovitch presents a case study of a course in English as a conference language which has been developed at a university in Belarus. He outlines the main features of the course and presents examples of students' presentations. Slepovitch discusses the vital role of academic speaking skills in English in a country which is developing a new role within the international economic and business community.

Banks investigates the perceptions of French scientific researchers relating to the use of English as a conference language, and in particular their attitudes towards being expected to communicate in English at academic conferences and their opinions of how well-prepared they are to do so. The findings underline arguments put forward by other writers in this volume that there is still a long way to go in developing appropriate and effective means of training non-native speaking academics to communicate appropriately in English at academic meetings. Banks shows through the use of a questionnaire survey how French academics perceived their linguistic difficulties. Ventola's paper complements this by showing how such difficulties became issues of language code and codeswitching during a conference where both German and English were used for communication. If the choice of the official language(s) has not been clearly defined for the conference participants in advance, negotiating the language of papers and the interaction during the discussion may become a recurrent issue as the conference unfolds. Furthermore, codeswitching makes comprehension of papers and discussion difficult for monolingual participants. Lastly, the paper illustrates that, in spite of linguistic difficulties and codeswitching, participants from different cultural backgrounds do pursue successful meaning-making and understanding, for the benefit of sharing and construing scientific knowledge.

A key aim of this collection was to signal and start to remedy a situation in which there has been little sustained and coherent research into academic conference language, particularly in comparison with written academic genres such as the research article. It may be argued that written genres carry more weight in the academic community, but as contributors to this volume have found in talking to their informants, conferences are undoubtedly important events in researchers' lives, and form a crucial element in the development of their research profile. Novice researchers need to acquire knowledge of how conferences and their component genres work if they are to become fully-fledged members of their discourse communities.

Several contributions to this volume deal with the issue of cross-cultural and cross-linguistic differences in conference language. All contributors subscribe to the view that further research into the language of conferences is essential if we are to help both native and non-native speaking researchers make the most of the conference experience. Underlying these issues, however, is the increasing dominance, whether we like it or not, of English as the language of international conferences. The implications of this apparently unstoppable trend will continue to raise uncomfortable questions for the international academic discourse community.

WHY AND WHAT KIND OF FOCUS ON CONFERENCE PRESENTATIONS?

Eija Ventola

University of Salzburg, Salzburg, Austria

Abstract – This first chapter explains why linguists and applied linguists have become interested in conference presentations and their language. Traditionally this field has been considered to be closer to the interests of rhetoricians, and indeed, as the chapter will show, traditional 'Public Speaking' and modern 'genre-oriented' linguistic approaches to the study of discourse share some interests. However, it will be argued that the linguistic approach offers us more powerful tools to explain the complexities involved. The chapter focuses on conference presentations, and the discussions that follow them, as social events and discusses them from the point of view of genre and register theory. It further expands our perceptions and understanding of what conferences are, how conference papers are semiotically and linguistically realised, and how they link up with other discourses before, during and after the conference event through 'semiotic spanning'.

1. Written vs. spoken academic/scientific genres

An *academic/scientific research paper* is today treated by linguists as a *genre* in its own right - as a text type whose characteristics are defined by the experienced members of the discourse community. The term *genre* is here used in the Swalesian (1990: 58) sense as

> a class of communicative events, the members of which share some set of communicative purposes. These purposes are recognised by the expert members of the parent discourse community ... This rationale shapes the schematic structure of the discourse and influences and constrains choice of content and style.

Thanks to the work of Swales and other linguists and applied linguists, we have come to understand the linguistic characteristics of written research papers better, in terms of the ways the relevant discourse societies expect papers of these kinds to be realised (see e.g. Hinds 1987; Eggington 1987; Dudley-Evans & Henderson 1990; Ventola & Mauranen 1991; Swales 1990, 1996; Ventola 1992, 1994a, b; 1995; Mauranen 1993). In particular, the typical linear global *generic structure* of INTRODUCTION ^ MATERIALS & METHODS ^ RESULTS ^ DISCUSSION ^ (CONCLUSION)[1], found, e.g. in experimental research papers in

---

[1] The sign '^' indicates the sequencing; the parentheses the optionality of the element.

the natural sciences, has been extensively covered both in theoretical linguistics as well as applied linguistics (e.g. in writing instruction books: Murison & Webb 1991; Swales & Feak 1994). Similarly, the linguistic realisations of the typical written scientific/academic texts have received a considerable amount of attention (e.g. Halliday & Martin 1993; Martin & Veel 1998; Mauranen 1996; Ventola 1994b, 1995, 1996).

Our linguistic knowledge about written academic genres is thus more advanced and explicit than it is about the spoken ones. The relatively more dynamic nature of spoken academic discourse has presented a greater challenge to linguists working within a genre-approach. We find that discourse analysts have for the major part been interested in various genres of conversation and their linguistic realisations, both everyday and institutional (see van Dijk 1997a, b, for present interests of discourse analysts), but hardly at all in the academic context. The fact that writing differs from speaking has been discussed by linguists; the linguistic differences between spoken and written modes were the focus of early 'register theory' (e.g. Gregory 1967; Gregory & Carroll 1978; Halliday 1985) and later on in systemic-functional theory, where both register aspects and genre aspects are taken into consideration (Ventola 1987; Martin 1992; Eggins & Slade 1997). But there have been only a few studies that have focussed on conference language (and most of these as late as in the 1990's, e.g. McKinley & Potter 1987; Ventola 1995, 1996; Shalom 1995, 2001; Thompson 1997, 1998; Thompson & Collins 1995; Rowley-Jolivet 1998; Räisänen 1999). Furthermore, the implications of this research on mode differences have not yet greatly filtered into the teaching of 'conference presentations' nor the materials used: for example, by 'Public Speaking' approaches. Thus, if one looks for guidance in preparing a conference talk in instruction books within 'Public Speaking' – the traditional field for training speakers – the books seem merely to give vague impressions of the variation of modes and their significance and effect on the linguistic realisations in talks, as shown below:

> It may be tempting to have the full text of your presentation written down. All you would have to do then is read it out. You wouldn't need to worry about forgetting the words and you could look at the text rather than having to face the audience. Not a good idea... *Written language is not spoken language. Unless a text is skilfully prepared, it will be difficult to read and will sound unnatural* (Rigley 1996: 80; my emphasis).

The point is that although linguists and applied linguists have researched and discussed the role of differences in genre and register variables in written vs. spoken mode to *some* degree in *some* discourse types, they seem to have done less work on the genres of speaking in academic/scientific environments; for example on conference presentations and their discussions. Further, their work on genre and register differences and the mode realisations seems to have had little influence on instruction offered by the traditional field of 'Public Speaking', as shown by the quotation above (see also Section 2 below). Merely stating the difference in mode is not sufficient – speakers must also be shown how they could/should vary their linguistic and non-linguistic realisations when mode changes are necessary in various speaking contexts. From the linguistic point of view statements like the one offered in the quotation above seem unmotivated and unsophisticated. 'Public Speaking' has a long tradition in the art of rhetoric and training speakers to deliver speeches. Therefore, it may here be worthwhile to look at the nature of the instruction in this rhetorical tradition in some detail, in order to see if linguistic research and linguistic instruction to conference presentations could benefit from 'Public Speaking' and whether rhetorical and linguistic approaches could fruitfully combine and complement each other. During the course of this chapter it will become apparent that the rhetorical and the linguistic traditions share the notion of genre and its unfolding as a typical generic structure. Yet, as will be discovered in Section 2, the notion of genre in the tradition of 'Public Speaking' is more intuitively based and largely lacks sophisticated linguistic advice on how to manipulate language. Thus, instruction books on 'public speaking' seem to help the presenters of scientific/academic papers at conferences only superficially. A more comprehensive approach is needed to describe these global, very often mass events of present day academia. A proposal for such an approach will be offered in the later sections of this chapter.

2. Help for Conference Presenters from 'Public Speaking' Manuals?

When we think of scientific/academic conference presentations, we may very often think of them as occasions of 'Public Speaking'– a tradition of speaking that goes back to Aristotelian rhetoric and the notions of 'Speaker', 'Speech', 'Audience', 'Occasion' and 'Effect' (de Vito 1978: 25). The basic prescription behind the Aristotelian notion of public speaking is that the speaker ought to construct his/her speech purposefully, keeping in mind those different audiences and occasions that demand characteristically specific talks, especially when certain effects are the goal of the speeches. This view is naturally not very far from the modern Swalesian notion of genre (see above), and no doubt the modern conference presenter may learn considerably from various instructional literature on 'Public Speaking'. Throughout the years the field has turned out numerous instruction books aimed at the general audience on how to construct speeches effectively according to the Aristotelian parameters. Just to show the development of these kinds of instructional books on 'Public Speaking', and to compare their instruction to today's conference presenters' situation, needs and goals, I shall cursorily review the contents and aims of four such books: one by

Cox, aimed at law students, from year 1867; one by Griffiths, intended for the general public from year 1935; one by Mears, also intended for the general public, from 1982 (a completely revised edition of his 1957 instruction book); and lastly a book by Rigley, intended for business speakers, published in 1996.

2.1. Public Speaking in the 1860's.

The book by Cox, *The Arts of Writing, Reading and Speaking in Letters to a Law Student,* from 1867, is interesting. It gives us the sense of training an academic community into the 'Art of Speaking' in general terms as well as in their professional field and makes us consider the modern needs of specialists in various academic fields. One interesting point Cox (1867: 189) emphasises is that "[T]he *Art of Speaking* is based upon the Arts of Writing and Reading". I shall elaborate upon this further below, when introducing how conference presentations, too, link with other texts before, during and after the conference ('semiotic spanning', Ventola 1999). Cox's remark also serves as a necessary warning to all public speakers to prepare themselves well in advance. The speaker must plan an outline in his mind and then put it on paper (Cox 1867: 218). Cox speaks of the importance of articulation, levels of loudness, voice quality, posture, gestures, etc. connected with the delivery of the speech, all factors that conference presenters of today also have to consider, but factors which in linguistic research have received less attention. Here, then, we have fruitful contact points between the two fields of 'public speaking' and 'linguistics', whereby the latter might benefit from the experience of the former.

The basic generic structure for a speech that Cox gives is very simple, that of BEGINNING ^ MIDDLE ^ END (Cox 1867: 238). His advice concerning its realisation is also very general in nature. The BEGINNING is "designed to attract the attention of the audience and excite their interest in what you are about to say" (Cox 1867: 239). The MIDDLE "must be logical ... Your aim is to convince and to persuade" (Cox 1867: 239), but he acknowledges how hard it is to give advice on the construction of this section so that it applies to all speeches: "I can do little more than attempt to throw together a few practical hints what to do and what to avoid, leaving the substantial structure of the work to your good taste" (Cox 1867: 239). His END, also called PERORATION, gets most attention. He suggests that speakers are well advised to write this section, rather than deliver it freely and emphasises that this part

> should not be the summing-up of your argument, but rather the pointing of it to its purpose ... the concentrated sum of all you have sought to urge ... Its object is to excite them [the audience] to acceptance of your argument ... a Peroration should grow in power and brilliancy as it advances, until it culminates in a climax (Cox 1867: 242-3).

Having given this general introduction to the global construction of speeches, Cox treats the following genres in more detail: the oratory of the Pulpit (sermon), of the Bar (in court), of the Senate (Parliament), of the Platform (speeches for the constituency) and of the Table or Social Oratory (dinner-table talk, toasts, etc). The first genre is discussed for the sake of noting some rhetorical means in the construction of speeches, whereas the other genres are seen as truly necessary speech skills for lawyers practising their profession and advancing in their career. The discussion is, however, very general and the linguistic advice minimal. There are no examples of speeches, except for the Platform speeches, where Cox illustrates this genre with speeches that were written for the stage: Brutus' and Anthony's speeches from Shakespeare's *Julius Caesar*.

2.2. Public Speaking in the 1930's.

Some seventy years later, Griffiths' book, *Speech Making* (1935), although more detailed, does not bring forth much more useful information about the generic and linguistic realisation of 'giving speeches'. The book first focuses on the phonetic level. Griffiths discusses in more detail than Cox, e.g. voice, the articulation of consonants and vowel, pitch, intonation and speed, the significance of pausing and emphasis, and gives practical exercises for training these production features of speeches. He then turns to the non-verbal aspects of giving speeches and speaks of the importance of posture (stance), gesture, and facial expression. Next follows the preparatory work of giving speeches, taking notes, reading for the speech. Like Cox, he advises speakers not to rely on inspiration when delivering speeches, but on careful preparation through reading and note-taking and organisation of thoughts. The organisation of the speech is expressed by Griffiths (1935: 29), again like Cox, in terms of a three-part global generic structure, although his labels slightly differ from those of Cox's ('/' indicates functionally similar labels):

1.   INTRODUCTION / EXORDIUM / PROEM
2.   DEVELOPMENT / MAIN BODY
3.   RECAPITULATION / ENUMERATION / PERORATION [2]

---

[2]   Griffiths (1935: 28, 32) bases his global structure elements on Marcus Fabius Quintilian's (a famous Roman teacher of rhetoric) structure of speeches ('/' indicates functionally similar labels):
   1. EXORDIUM / PROEM / INTRODUCTION
   2. STATEMENT OF FACTS / NARRATIO
   3. CONFIRMATION
   4. REFUTATION
   5. RECAPITULATION (summing-up) / ENUMERATION / PERORATION (appeal to emotions).

Naturally, this kind of general structure does not help the speaker a great deal. Therefore Griffiths (1935: 37-43), more than Cox, gives individual examples of the structure and further introduces a 'rhetorical tree' as a device which helps speakers to organise and keep the global structure in mind as well as the main points within each of the global elements. His rhetorical tree is meant both for producing and analysing speeches. He (1935: 38) writes: "A good speech charts easily." His example of a rhetorical chart for the topic 'Games' is given in Figure 1.

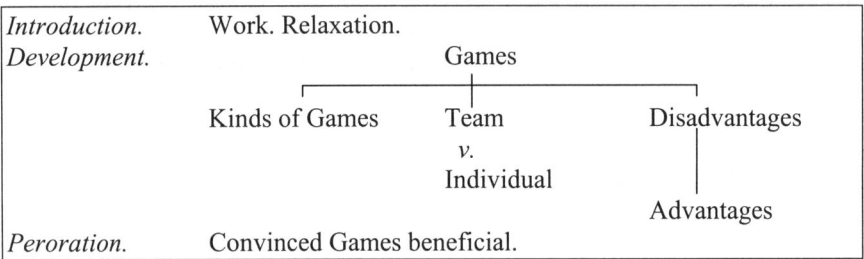

Figure 1: The rhetorical tree structure for a speech on 'Games' (Griffiths 1935: 38).

Griffiths recognises the same fields as Cox within which training in 'Public Speaking' is important, and adds the business field.

> The Platform, the Pulpit, the Courts of Law, Government (Local and National) are the present main professional outlets for speaking in public, but there are also speeches to be made at weddings and dinners, the average standard of which is generally negligible. From the business point of view, secretaries of firms, directors, and others who are obliged to address meetings must have a command of voice and English, and be able by consecutive construction to reason and impress (Griffiths 1938: vii).

His examples of rhetorical tree structures are however not from these professional fields but represent more general genres, like stories, toasts, prayers. Only two further specific context genres are discussed: the political debate and the meeting. None of these examples even come close to explaining what goes on in such complex social events as academic/scientific conferences. Moreover, Griffiths' linguistic advice consists of merely simplistic, normative suggestions on how to use certain phrases. They ultimately leave the conference speakers in awe when it is time to give the presentation.

2.3. Public Speaking in the 1950-1970's.

Mears' book, *The Right Way to Speak in Public,* was originally written in 1957, but went through a complete revision twice in 1974 and in 1977, and the last version was reprinted in 1982. The gap between it and Griffiths' book is thus nearly forty years. What has changed? Does an instructional textbook for 'Public Speaking' at this stage better meet the needs of conference presenters? A quick analysis of Mears (1982) seems to suggest that this is not the case.

Mears (1982) first offers a discussion of the techniques speakers can use to develop ideas for speeches, especially if they are not experts in the subject matter. These techniques are similar to exercises that are frequently used in process writing approaches: e.g. mind mapping or listing. An essential next step is the logical organisation of the ideas, developed into main ideas, subheadings, and further research in the matter. This he calls 'developing the frame'. Table 1, developed from initial ideas on the topic of 'coal fires', illustrates his notion of a frame.

COAL FIRES	
Main Ideas	Subheadings
1. Practical Thoughts	(a) Warm and comfortable. (b) Smoky and dirty. (c) Makes work. (d) Extravagant (coal bill links with next
2. The Coal Industry	(a) What is coal? (b) How do we get it? (c) Conditions in mines. (d) Miners lives.
3. National importance of coal	(a) Size of industry. (b) Basis of electric generation. (c) Value of by-products. (d) Its use in industry.

Table 1: Mears' (1982: 27-8) example of a 'Frame'.

This frame structure illustrates the topical organisation of the middle part of the talk. Similarly to his predecessors in public speaking, Mears (1982: 14) considers speeches to be schematically constructed of the generic structure elements of APPROACH ^ MIDDLE or MAIN FACTS ^ PERORATION (= Conclusion), a structure which may be too general to be truly useful for preparing conference talks.

In Mears' view, the topical frame for the MIDDLE helps the speaker to hold on to the main points and not to get sidetracked. In addition to a good frame, the MIDDLE may need (i) some 'springs', i.e. smooth transitions from point to point in the subheadings or main headings, (ii) some 'padding', i.e. illustrations, examples, metaphors, (iii) some 'windows', i.e. which are in Mears' words described as 'the wise use of imagination" (Mears 1982: 43-6). In the development of the APPROACH and PERORATION the speaker's relationship with the audience is important and needs to be developed carefully. Yet, as we can see below, how the speech and its structure is developed and construed linguistically is not really the focus of Mears' instruction; rather, he merely suggests some general topics which may be included.

For developing the APPROACH, Mears (1982: 49-50) suggests the following general techniques, beginning with:

(1) Personal note (including the presentation of oneself)

(2) Introduction of audience (who are present)

(3) Focal point as theme note (what the talk is about)

(4) Topical note (e.g. something heard/seen/read on the topic in the media)

(5) Word spelling (inventing an acronym to stand for the most important ideas introduced in the speech)

(6) Local colour (relating the talk to the place where the talk is held)

(7) Historical background (giving historical reference to the topic)

(8) Humour

(9) Controversy (using opponent view as the starting point)

(10) Startling Opening (attempting to surprise the audience)[3]

Mears (1982: 46) considers the APPROACH easiest when one is speaking to one's colleagues: "If you are speaking on your own subject to those knowledgeable and keen, the right atmosphere exists already, and your task is easy, which explains why people can usually talk adequately on their own subject to those

---

[3] An example of this in practice: a previous colleague of mine, Andrew Chesterman, once started his conference talk from the back of the room and then slowly moved to the front of the room speaking all the time. The talk was about social conventions and his way of starting a conference paper certainly illustrated the effect of breaking social conventions and startled the audience and raised immediate interest to what he was going to say in his talk.

with similar interests." As we know, this assumption is, however, an illusion. Academic/scientific conference presenters also face the difficulty of building an interesting APPROACH, even though the field is shared.

Mears has relatively little to say about the successful construal of the PERORATION (Conclusion). He considers it important that the speaker summarises the points and appeals to the emotions of the audience. Appeals to emotions may be appropriate in public speeches, but are less likely to occur in conference presentations. An interesting device for the overall construction of the speech is the suggestion of holding on to certain parallelisms in the whole speech: e.g. if the speech has started with a question then an answer should be provided; if there is a beginning quotation from a famous author, then the speech could also conveniently end with a quotation from the same author (Mears 1982: 57).

The rest of Mears' book deals with the practical techniques for giving speeches; e.g. how to write numbered memory cards and how to deal with them while delivering the speech; how to file notes for your speeches; how to deal with nervousness; what you have to remember during the delivery (voice quality, posture, gestures).

2.4. Public Speaking in the 1990's.

The last example of 'Public Speaking' guides which novices may pick up for help with their presentations is Rigley's *Making Your Presentation Memorable* (1996). The intended target audience are business people. In its layout the book is a typical example of the 1990's textbook, where visual display, both pictures and layout, play an important role. The whole book is a hundred pages long and offers busy business readers a 'quick read in a plane, in a train ...' – another typical characteristic of 1990's instructional books on any topic.

Similarly to the instruction books reviewed earlier, Rigley (1996: 28-31) pays some attention to the overall global structures of presentations, and he does so in terms of generic differences. A presentation can, for example, be built around the PROBLEM ^ SOLUTION -pattern (SITUATION, PROBLEM, POSSIBILITIES, APPRAISAL, PROPOSAL), or the structure can be chronological, or descriptive. Here, however, Rigley does not suggest any global elements that form the overall structure as the ones given above; it seems that readers are supposed to know how to manipulate language to get their talk to function as a chronologically or descriptively organised presentation. A suggestion of the global structure for a scientifically oriented paper is: PROPOSITION, PROOF, CONCLUSION. Although his advice for global structuring may not be linguistically explicit, one suggestion that may be beneficial for novices is his advice to summarise and bridge points in different sections. The principle is made clear with Table 2:

Introduction	Point 1	Point 2	Point 3	Point 4
Opening	Intro to this section	Bridge from previous part	Bridge from previous part	Bridge from previous part
Establishing relevance of subject to this audience	Examples/ points	Intro to this section	Intro to this section	Intro to this section
	Summary of this section	Examples/ points	Examples/ points	Examples /points
		Summary of this section	Summary of this section	Summary of this section
		Summary of the presentation so far	Summary of the presentation so far	Summary of the presentation so far
				Conclusion

Table 2: Rigley's (1996: 31) representation of summarising and bridging points.

However, very little is said on how such summarising and bridging can be realised linguistically by speakers during presentations. At the beginning of the book, Rigley contrasts writing and speaking as media of communication. He advises his readers to think of organisational factors in speech as parallels with those in writing: introductions functioning as 'content pages' and overviews and summaries as 'section markers', while pauses in speech mark 'paragraphs' and 'punctuation' (Rigley 1996: 4-8). What is disappointing in both Rigley's and his predecessors' books is that language is not systematically related to building up the overall structure, summaries, and bridges. How else can the speaker realise these except in language? (Although, admittedly some other semiotic coding may partly take over the realisation.) In Rigley's book, too, language seems to be something that deserves an additional note. It is not the major means of realising global and local structure of talks, for example:

> ... successful communication means using language that gets into the minds of the listener. Plain English is best. Spoken English uses repetition and paraphrase, simple but dramatic and emphatic words, all to help the listener piece together the speaker's meaning (Rigley 1996: 8).

... the language of speech is more dramatic, more repetitious and in many ways more complex than written language. So don't use the language of writing when you are talking (Rigley 1996: 46).

It is true that the speaker/hearer is tied to the immediate communicative situation differently from the writer/reader – the speaker must continuously deal with the dynamic process of unfolding communication and the hearer cannot backtrack, as in reading, and check the meanings construed (unless by interrupting the speaker). Rigley brings some of these aspects into focus when discussing how the speaker can bring variation to his presentation delivery with the help of visuals (slides, transparencies, handouts, videos, etc.) and can maximise the flow of information with a multitude of media. Yet, as can be seen from his booklet, even the latest instruction books on 'Public Speaking' give very little advice to speakers on how to use language when speaking multimodally– how to actually linguistically manage the media difference (cf. Charles & Ventola, this volume). Advice to use Plain English, especially in the academic/scientific context, may not be appropriate. More helpful would be, for example, advice that guides speakers to use linguistic resources more cohesively in text creation. Conference speakers also need advice on how to unpack some of their densely packed written manuscripts when they prepare to give their presentations, e.g. by unpacking some of the complex grammatical metaphors and using grammatical intricacy instead (see Halliday 1985; Ventola 1996).

2.5. Evaluation of Public Speaking Instruction

This cursory historical overview of the instruction books within the field of 'Public Speaking' shows that academic conference presenters will get some useful general 'tips' and suggestions from these texts on how to improve their presentation skills. But largely, the whole genre and register of the conference is for them very much different from the 'public speakers' world'. Conference genres (plenaries, section papers, round table talks, poster presentations, etc.) are semiotically established in academic/scientific discourse communities. It is not the case that speakers are free to choose just any kind of overall organisation for their talks. As we shall see, *Genre* and the *Register* variables (*Field, Tenor, Mode*) restricts choice in the presentation situation. (These notions are from systemic-functional linguistics and will be explained below.) It is only rarely possible that we have someone talking about experimental physics in linguistic conferences and vice versa, unless there are established justifiable links. This is how the *Field* restricts. Most of the public speaking instruction books give guidance on how to pitch the talk according to the audience – the *Tenor*. It is obvious that expert scientists should not be addressed as if they were undergraduates just beginning their studies. Similarly, the instruction books pay some lip service to the *Mode*, noting that the spoken medium needs other linguistic realisations than the written medium. Although some attention has recently been paid to other modal possibilities, research into multimodal realisations of semiotics has just begun to interest linguists and media researchers (internet texts, videochatting through the internet, presentation software providing some examples; see also Goodman & Graddol 1996; Baldry 2000).

What is perhaps the most surprising aspect of the 'Public Speaking' instruction books, from a linguist's point of view, is how little these books actually deal with language itself – the linguistic realisation of speeches and talks. They seem to give minimal linguistic advice – which mostly deals with pronunciation, the choice of some words and phrases, and avoiding 'bad grammar'. The suggestions concerning smooth transition seem to imply the need of considering internal cohesion within and between the generic elements of presentation. Yet, in none of the instruction books reviewed is this aspect developed linguistically satisfactorily. Only the most recent books discuss the use of other semiotic modes (overhead slides, computer presentation programmes, etc.) and note how these modes work together with linguistic realisations to create coherent, effective messages in a given talk. Only a few of the books offer useful guidance to the presenters on how to combine talk and multimodal semiotics in presentations.

A further problem in finding advice in these kinds of 'Public Speaking' instruction books is that they are usually written for native speakers. Yet, the reality today is that conferences are multicultural, multilingual and multimodal events. They are perhaps not multilingual in terms of the 'language of the presentation', since English is so often today the only language used for presentations at international conferences. But the native languages of the members of the audience influences the construction of meaning-making and the delivery of the presentations, and the social talk at conferences is multilingual. Native speakers of English have to consider that all their listeners may not be able to understand the presentation as easily as the colleagues at their home universities. Non-native-speaker presenters have to struggle with not only the presentation problems indicated by the public speaking instruction books (pronunciation, gesture, posture, etc.), but also with the linguistic coding of the presentation in English, plus managing the discussion that follows the presentation. However well the non-native speaker of English has prepared his/her talk, the discussion is carried out impromptu, and it is difficult in advance to prepare what will be said in it. In Section 3, it will be argued that we need a more comprehensive and a more linguistically-oriented view on the problematics of academic/scientific conference presentations than the theories and instruction books on 'Public Speaking' have provided for us. Such a view will lead us to research conference language as a genre and register on its own right. The results of such an inquiry will eventually enable linguists to work together with practitioners of 'Public Speaking' in providing novice conference presenters (native and non-native) more useful instruction in the construal of meanings at conferences.

3. Conferences as social discourse events and the agnateness of conference genres

So far it has been suggested that academic conference presentations are worth studying in their own right. Yet, the tools offered typically by 'Public Speaking' are not linguistically very sophisticated. What we need is a more coherent view of conferences as social discourse events. We need to explore how different kinds of discourse types unfold in this event. The similarities and the differences enable us to sort out the agnateness of conference genres (plenaries, section papers, etc.). We are interested in seeing what kind of genres typically take place in conferences and how they are related to each other when they unfold as social processes. Further, we are keen to explore how these social processes are then further realised contextually appropriately in terms of register and further in terms of language and other meaning-making semiotics. The remaining sections in this paper will explore these matters.

Many scholars still seem to believe that writing a paper for publication and presenting a paper at a conference are one and the same thing, without considering that the two generic functions set totally different demands on the use of language. Conferences are multi-faceted speech events. When we look at conference situations, we discover that we are actually dealing with an array of related genres, *agnate genres*. The exact nature of these agnate genres is not yet fully researched. Thus Figure 2 captures only a fraction of such interrelatedness of the subgenres in question.

Linguistic problems are multiplied at international conferences, where participants come from different language and cultural backgrounds. Not only do the language skills cause problems, but so also do the differences in academic presentation traditions. But linguists have so far worked very little in this area (in contrast to that of written academic papers). Explicit knowledge about the nature of these agnate genres is still minimal. Further, we also need to find out in detail how the register variables are linguistically realised in these agnate conference genres. In other words, we need to know how the context of situation determines different stages of the discourse unfolding, how the *register* factors are realised: *Field* – what the topical orientation is, *Tenor* – what the interactant relations are, *Mode* – what the channels for the communication are. We need to consider the influence each of these register variables exercises on the linguistic choices in the unfolding of discourse. Without such explicit knowledge it will be more difficult to instruct novices in the appropriate linguistic realisation of the genre and register in question.

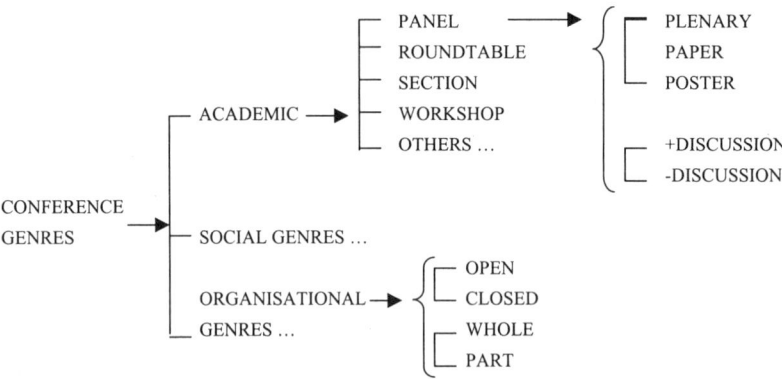

Figure 2:   A tentative synoptic view of conference genres: Agnate genres for conference discourse.

Due to lack of specific knowledge, preparatory courses for conference presentations are still relatively rarely offered in academic institutions, and where they are offered, it is after the manner of 'Public Speaking'. Graduate students are often instructed in how to write essays and theses, perhaps even research papers; but less so in how a section paper is construed and delivered at a conference, how the discussion afterwards can be managed, how a poster is designed, how questions that other conference participants might present are dealt with, how a workshop is run, and so on. Each of these agnate genres has its own characteristics, and each needs to be described in detail, if we are to advise novices in mastering them. Yet, very little work has been done in this area at all. Mostly we seem to leave young academics on their own with these genres. We expect that they somehow become socialised into these genres without explicit instruction. Properly trained linguistically with good presentation and discussion skills, they can draw the attention of the audience to their research and their academic careers could advance faster and more efficiently. Because precise linguistic knowledge of the problems encountered in conference situations is not that readily available, novices are forced to learn to manage these communicative situations by 'trial and error', and bad experiences may be very discouraging. The first step to getting applicable information about these genres is to look at the *synoptic* generic structures of conference discourses and then discuss with novices the different *dynamic* options for realisation of the staging.

Sections 4 and 5 will discuss these perspectives in one genre, namely a SECTION PAPER at a conference.

4. Synoptic view of the generic structure the Conference Section Paper and its Discussion

What is meant by a *synoptic view* in this context is the way discourse is seen to unfold situationally appropriately and in an expected way (linguistically and non-linguistically). We view genres synoptically when we consider social activity as typical within a certain context. The generic elements and the sequencing that is involved resemble the structures illustrated in 'Public Speaking', but are more genre-specific and more detailed, and eventually their register and linguistic (and other semiotic) characteristics will need to be elaborated by linguists. For example, in the unfolding of the generic structure of a Section, its Section Papers and their Discussion at a conference, the elements could synoptically be seen as in Figure 3.

```
SECTION AT A CONFERENCE
Chair          - Opening the Section

SECTION PAPER
Chair          - Introducing the Speaker
Speaker        - Thanking for Introduction
Speaker        - Contextualising the Paper
Speaker        - The Paper and its generic structure
               (e.g. Introduction, Materials & Methods, Results, Discussion, Conclusion)
Speaker        - Thanking the Audience
Audience       - Thanking the Speaker (non-verbal)
Chair          - Thanking the Speaker

ITS DISCUSSION
Chair          - Opening the Discussion
Discussant     - Question / Comment
Speaker        - Answer / Response
Chair          - Closing the Discussion

=> recycling the sequence: SECTION PAPER ^ DISCUSSION

Chair          - Closing the Section
```

Figure 3: A Generic Structure of a Section for individual papers at a conference.

The generic unfolding takes place stage by stage. When we take the novices' perspective and take them through this unfolding of the social activity in question, we must first present them with the generic structure and its realisations. A chart like the one in Figure 4 will probably better help novices to conceptualise the sequencing of events and their embeddedness and recursiveness in the conference section than the mere listing of the elements (Figure 3).

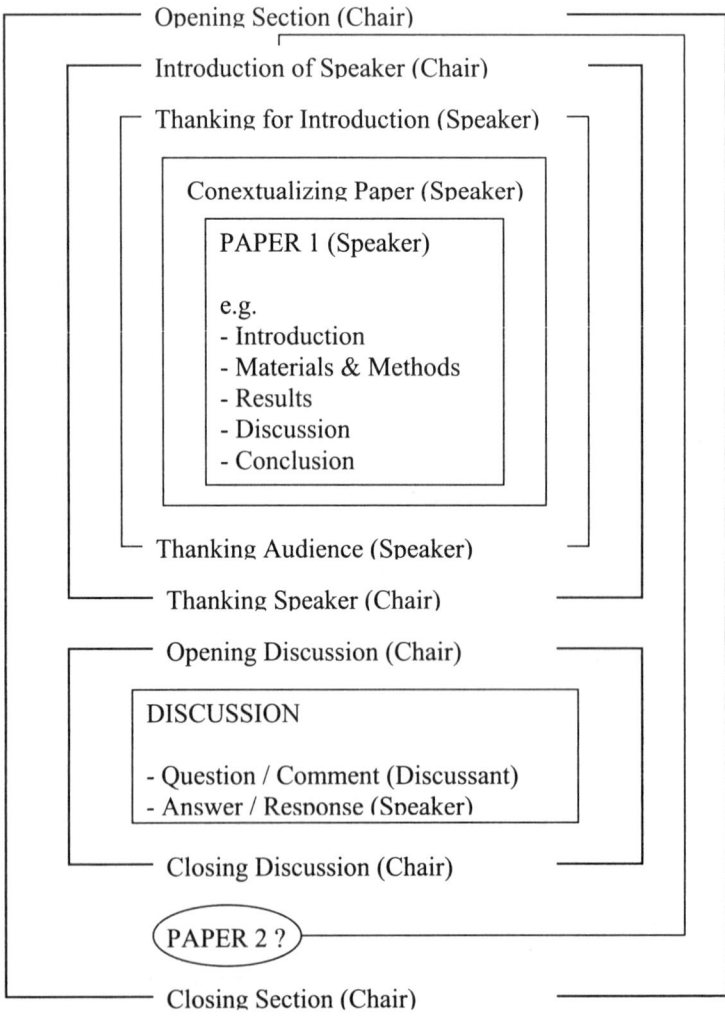

Figure 4: - Synoptic view: Generic Structure of a Section Paper and its Discussion.

Explaining the elements of the generic structure and showing novice presenters authentic examples of the expected linguistic behaviour will prepare them for the social practices that the audience expects. Finally, making them practise these steps and their typical realisations, and videotaping and analysing the novices' practice helps them feel more relaxed and more confident in the actual conference presentation situation.

Firstly, novice presenters need to understand, not just the typical sequential element realisations, but they have to be prepared for the *dynamic variation* in discourse unfolding as well. Secondly, they need to know the *register variation* possibilities in the realisation of the elements. Section 5 and Section 6 will briefly illustrate and discuss some of the issues that have emerged as focal from these perspectives. These matters and many more in conference language research will need further systematic exploration and description.

5. Dynamic generic structure variation in the realisation of the Conference Section Paper and its Discussion

What is meant by *dynamic generic structure variation in unfolding discourse* in this context? Both the Conference Section Paper and its Discussion may actually be realised *sequentially* somewhat differently than our synoptic views (Figures 3 and 4) suggests, especially in multilingual and multicultural situations. We have to account for this theoretically and also try to prepare our students and novices for these diversions in the unfolding of the generic structure. Of course, both the Paper and its Discussion are always realised dynamically as they unfold, but here dynamic unfolding refers also to the different ways conference papers may unfold. It is thus built as a resource for realising genres, and contrasts with our 'static' view of discourse. Some of the examples that will be used in the following sections will be in English, some in German (in which case a translation will be provided).

Let us first focus on dynamic variation in the sequencing of the proposed generic structure elements of the Section Paper. Looking at authentic data will indicate that the sequence that we perceive synoptically as culturally and situationally valid may, nevertheless, be somewhat modified in the actual situations. The examples below are simple, but illustrate the point.

In an 'on-line' realisation of generic structure elements, for example, speakers may not feel obliged to realise an element, e.g. they may not respond to INTRODUCING THE SPEAKER by thanking the chair for the introduction, or they may simply forget to do so, due to their inexperience or nervousness. In Example 1, we see the realisation of THANKING happening. It is performed by a

German speaker who has been introduced by the chair with a long, extensive turn, which makes it clear that both the chair and the presenter are 'academic pals'. In such situations, the speaker naturally feels more obliged to respond linguistically by THANKING FOR INTRODUCTION. Two other speakers, an American and a New Zealander, who were also videotaped at the same conference, do not seem to feel obliged to realise this element at all. (Their introductions were not as extensive, either, and did not indicate a personal 'pal'-relationship with the chair. Whether this kind of 'skipping' ('ø') of an element is instantially idiosyncratic or more systematic and why, is something that needs to be researched in the future.)

(1)

German (A) male	American (B) female	New Zealand (C) male
Vielen Dank für diese freundlich ermutigenden Worte. *Thank you for these friendly and encouraging words.*	- ø	- ø

In Example 2, we notice a further dynamic difference in the realisation of the generic elements in the videotapes of the same speakers as in (1). The synoptic Generic Structure presented earlier in Figures 3 and 4 did not include an element that could be glossed as SPEAKER GREETING THE AUDIENCE.

(2)

German (A) male	American (B) female	New Zealand (C) male
– ø	- Good morning.	- ø

Neither the German nor the New Zealand speaker realises this element. But the American speaker (B) chooses to realise it. The choice may be culturally influenced, the assumption being that American speakers are more audience-related or generally use more greetings in situations, or it may also partly be a gender-influenced choice, the assumption being that female speakers are more audience-related – this is something that future research also has to investigate. But whatever the case, we have to take into consideration this kind of possibility of dynamic variation in the unfolding of generic structures in conference presentations, and consequently build it in into our modelling.

Example 3 presents a further challenge to the presented synoptic view of generic structure (Figures 3 and 4).

(3)	**German** (A) male	**American** (B) female	**New Zealand** (C) male
	- ø (presentation in German)	At first I thought I would give my talk in a Polynesian language which might be more relevant for today. However I thought I'd be a bit more intelligible and do it in English.	I am going to speak in English and I hope that that does not cause a problem for too many people. Hope you can understand my somewhat convoluted New Zealand English. Um ... if there is a problem and when we come to a point where I shall go into German, for the benefit of my colleagues who do not speak so much German we'll make a summary

The same data from which the previous examples were drawn also include sections of discourse where speakers actually negotiate the language of the presentation, or rather they give an explanation of why their presentation will be given in English rather than in German. (See Ventola, Chapter 14 this volume.) The conference was an international conference that took place in Germany.[4] This element could be called NEGOTIATING LANGUAGE OF PRESENTATION. The German speaker gives his paper in German and makes no apologies to the non-German-speaking audience. The American speaker obviously feels embarrassed about not being able to deliver her paper in German in Germany; but she makes her audience aware that she is not monolingual and turns her inability to give a paper in German into a joke. The New Zealander makes an apology for his New Zealand accent and promises to switch over to German if necessary (and he was capable of doing it, since he had spent various research periods in Germany).

To summarise, discovering these additional phenomena of generic structures in the real data raises various questions about their status in the proposed synoptic view of the generic structure of conference presentations. Should they or should they not be considered as generic structure elements of conference presentations? How do we deal with them in theoretical description? Further, to what degree should we teach this kind of dynamic variation and what is the best way of teaching it to novices giving their first presentations? Detailed, systematic research in this area will surely enable us to establish the relevant generic structure elements in this genre and the notion of dynamic variation will

---

[4] Most of the papers were given in German and most of the audience were German speakers, but there were also some native English speakers and participants from other European countries present. Most of the audience understood both German and English, although they would not necessarily present papers or participate in the discussion in both languages. Some participants were codeswitching both in presentations and in discussions.

enable us to illustrate to novices to what extent they can vary the sequencing in the genre. A more flexible representation of generic structure is necessary to capture the extent of the dynamic variation witnessed in the real data. One possibility would be a flow chart representation (also because of its usability in the generative sense, cf. Ventola 1987). Figure 5 on the following page represents approximately the same information as Figure 4, but allows dynamic variation possibilities.

We could imagine this dynamic flowchart as being structured in secondary layers, so that, for example, if the speaker feels the need to greet the audience, the necessary element is activated 'from another layer'. This kind of activation is difficult to represent on paper, but in Figure 6 this 'popping up' of an element is represented by darker lines around the element. Thus, bringing in the possibility of GREETING into the flow chart as in Figure 6 is now presented as an option and the discourse can proceed to further elements.

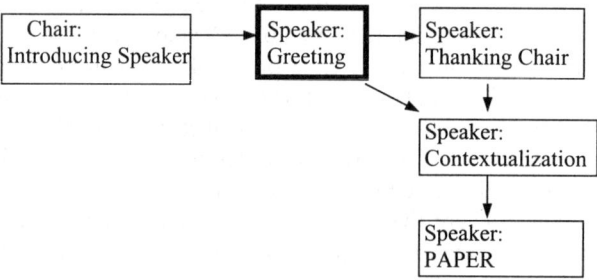

Figure 6. Incorporating the realisation of GREETING.

The elements and the process of realisation in the flowchart in Figure 5 would thus be subject to such changes activated by raising some needed elements from the secondary layer (or from some other genres, i.e. 'genre embeddings', see Ventola 1987). Developing such a flowchart that would display all the dynamic realisation resources for a Conference Section Paper will not be attempted here.[5]

---

[5] Some theoretical suggestive work has been done in Ventola (1987), in O'Donnell (1990) where contextual dynamic views into flowchart representations were discussed, and in Fawcett *et al.* (1988) where a combination of a network and flowchart were argued for.

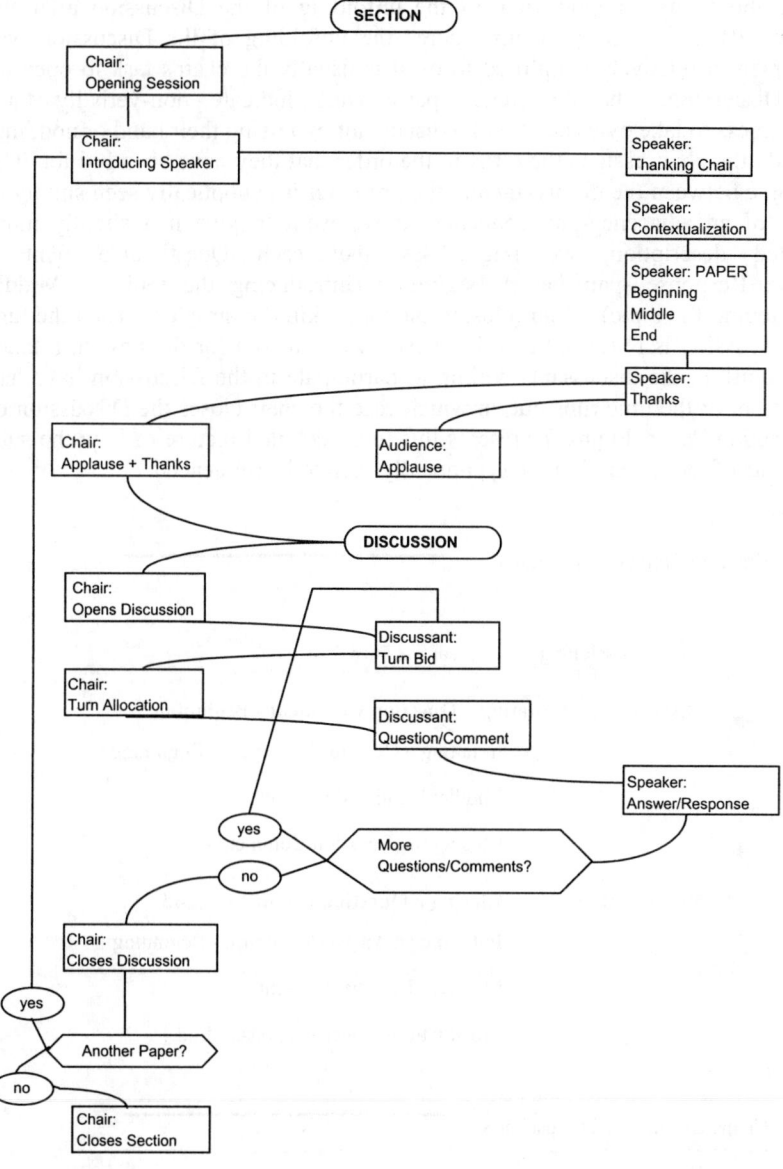

Figure 5: A tentative dynamic view of the flow of a Section Paper and its Discussion.

What about our synoptic view of the unfolding of the Discussion after the Section Paper? In the previous figures the unfolding of the Discussion was presented in relatively simplified form. It is usually the chair's task to open up the Discussion. The conference participants indicate non-verbally their willingness to take over the role of a discussant by raising their hand or nodding. Usually the chair assigns the turns in the order that they have been bid for. The dialogue between the discussant and the presenter is synoptically seen simply in terms of an adjacency-pair sequence. If we want to give it a slightly more detailed description, we might say that each Question/Comment – Answer/Response -pair has a Beginning (introducing the topic) – Middle (developing the topic) – End (closing the topic) kind of structure. Then the turn for Discussion is reiterated and the person who has bid for the next turn takes over, until all the discussants willing to participate in the Discussion have had their turn, or the time runs out, in which case the chair closes the Discussion of the Section Paper. Figure 7 presents this more detailed picture of how the sub-elements of the Discussion are synoptically seen to be sequenced.

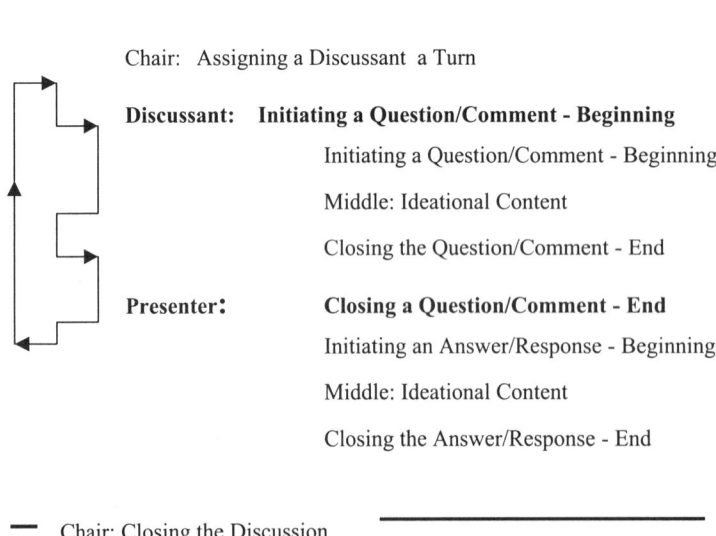

— Chair: Opening the Discussion

Chair: Assigning a Discussant a Turn

Discussant: Initiating a Question/Comment - Beginning

Initiating a Question/Comment - Beginning

Middle: Ideational Content

Closing the Question/Comment - End

Presenter: Closing a Question/Comment - End

Initiating an Answer/Response - Beginning

Middle: Ideational Content

Closing the Answer/Response - End

— Chair: Closing the Discussion

Figure 7: Sequencing of the sub-elements of the Discussion.

Yet, the realisation of the actual turns during the Discussion often proves to be more varied and dynamic. Example 4 illustrates this kind of 'off-the-synoptic-pattern', dynamic realisations.

(4)   *Discussant*: I'd like to ask a question. You can rather ignore it probably. Can people visit erm Göttingen the the collection the collection?
      Presenter: Pardon?
      Discussant: Can people visit the- these collections which are at Göttingen. I mean, if I- Is there- And everyone can go there?

In Example 4 the presenter has not heard the question properly and therefore asks for a repetition of the question. A further example of dynamic variation in the realisation of Discussion is of course the situation where the whole Discussion will not be realised. In spite of the fact that the chair opens the Discussion and invites participants to take a turn, no one does so, and the chair is forced to move onto the next speaker or close the section. Of course sometimes the speaker him/herself does not leave any time for a Discussion. Each of these instances mentioned raises further theoretical considerations in terms of reprentation in flowchart (or by other means) and they also raise applied issues for teaching novices about generic structure realisation after Section Papers. It is not, however, possible to elaborate on these issues here. The focus will next be on register variation in Section Papers and their Discussions.

6. Register variation in the realisation of the Conference Section Paper and its Discussion

We have so far established that conference discourses unfold generically in specific ways, but have not considered how the context of situation influences the linguistic (and non-linguistic) realisation of the genre in terms of register. What is meant by *register variation in unfolding discourse* in this context? Conference talks and their discussions are always about something, which we have already referred to as *Field*. Linguistic realisation of interpersonal *Tenor* relations between the presenter, the chair and the members of the audience as discussants are also observable as the social activity unfolds. Attention has already above been drawn to the written/spoken difference in academic/scientific genres. This difference we have seen as a difference in the realisation of *Mode*. We will find that this difference does not just apply to the genres (article vs. presentation), but that sections of the generic structure during presentations vary in their mode realisations when construed multimodally. Some elements are realised very much 'as spoken', almost as if they were casual conversations; while others are realised 'as written', as if they were parts of a published article; and others are realised with little or no accompanying language, e.g. when slides or pictures are shown. This kind of a variation view is adopted from systemic-functional linguistics and will be discussed below in more detail.

When we speak of register variation in Conference Section Paper presentations, variation in *Field* is perhaps the easiest aspect to understand. We understand that conference talks on medicine may be organised differently than, for example, talks on linguistics, sociology, or history. We also can accept the view that as the paper unfolds from element to element, there are also constant readjustments of *Field* – when we move from introducing the background of our study to discussing e.g. the medical patients we are studying, and so on. Here no example is considered necessary to illustrate this. *Tenor* variation is also ever-present in the conference talks: such interpersonal factors as gender, age, power, status, etc. influence the language realisation of conference presentations. In Example 1 (see above) a German male academic responded to the chair's, another German male scholar's, introduction of him as the 'next-speaker'. In Example 5, we see the chair's 'true laudatio' of his 'academic pal' (A) and his work. It is obvious from the language used that these two male scholars have known each other and each other's work well and have been in frequent contact.

(5)   ...will ich es recht kurz gestalten und gleich den ersten Referenten aufrufen. Erm FIRST + LAST NAME ich glaube es ist auch niemand hier im Hause, dem ich erm Herrn LAST NAME. vorstellen oder empfehlen muß. Er lehrt Literaturwissenschaft am F. College, University of M, in E, und erm ich denke erm jeder kennt erm das Buch über Einheit und Mannigfaltigkeit in Forsters Werk und die kritischen Lektüren, mit denen er über Jahre hinweg die Forsterforschung begleitet hat erm und ich möchte also statt erm einer bestimmten, nicht hinreichend gelingenden Zusammenfassung erm an ein Wort erinnern, das mir aufgefallen ist aus unseren Telefonaten im Vorfeld der Veranstaltung; da sagte Herr LAST NAME eines Tage zu mir: "Eigentlich bin ich ja nur ganz am Rande ein Forsterforscher." und das hat mich so verblüfft, daß ich erm eigentlich da gar nicht drauf reagieren konnte, und nach und nach dämmert mir, ob er vielleicht Recht hat und erm man in Forsterforscher nur am Rande sein kann und erm um so gespannter bin ich auf die Randgänge (laughing) zu Forster und erm möchte Sie ans Mikrophon bitten.

I am going to formulate it briefly and want to invite the first speaker. Erm FIRST + LAST NAME I believe there is no one here in this building to whom I have to introduce or recommend Mr LAST NAME He teacher literature at F. College , University of M. in E., and erm I think erm everyone knows erm the book about the Unity and Diversity in Forsters works and those critical articles with which he has lead the Forster research over the years erm and instead of a certain, not sufficiently successful summary I would therefore like to recount you of words that I noticed from our telephone conversation when preparing the conference; Mr. LAST NAME. said to me one day "Actually I am just in the periphery of research on Forster"and that baffled me so that I couldn't in fact react to that, and slowly it dawned to me that perhaps he was right and that one can only be in the periphery in Forster research and thus I am even more exicted about the boundaries of Forster's periphery and would like to ask you to the microphone.

When the same chair introduces the American female speaker (B), the *Tenor* is different, and consequently the chair's introduction of B is also linguistically very different. In Example 6 we just get what one could be call 'a minimalist Introduction' of the speaker. The chair has just tried to invite the audience to present more questions, and since there are none, he goes on with the next-speaker introduction.

(6)   Wenn nicht, würde ich vorschlagen, daß wir fortfahren er mit dem Vortrag von Frau LAST NAME der diesen Sektor der wissenschaftlichen Hinterlassenschaft in Form der Sammlungen ... der Biographie also eine ganz wichtige Sache behandelt.

If not, then I would suggest that we go on with Mrs. LAST NAME 's talk which deals with that part of the scientific legacy that has been left to us in the form of collections ... of the biograph, that is a very important subject matter.

When the female speaker is introduced, we get no reference to where she works, what her contribution to the field is, nor to what she might have written – and in fact she had published several articles and books in the field. One bibliography dealing with the topic lists 15 articles published by her, whereas the German speaker (A) who was so elaborately introduced to the audience had only three articles more than her. Further, most of his articles (10 out of 18) were published in the same journal, whereas hers were in different journals and edited books.

Introductions by chairs are important and socially valued as they highlight the importance of the speakers – the bigger the conference the more importance the Introduction of the speaker carries. Introductions of plenary speakers usually demand some preparation on the part of the chair. Introduction of speakers of smaller section papers demands linguistically less, as there generally is no time to give long introductions. In Examples 5 and 6 the Introductions were addressed to the whole of the audience – the speakers were thus in equal position in terms of the Introduction – yet, it is clear that the speaker in Example 5 is given greater attention, and his importance in the field is highlighted and construed interpersonally quite differently from the female speaker's. It is becoming apparent that we urgently need descriptions and explanations on how such *Tenor* relationships, gender, age, power, social and professional status, etc. influence the language realisation of conference discourse (see also Shalom in this volume).

Another example of differences in linguistic realisation is given in Example 7. It demonstrates how differently the speakers approach their task of realising elements linguistically. In this example, it is harder to explain why the three speakers realise the element CONTEXTUALISING THE PAPER so very differently. The German (A) and the American speaker (B) do it 'minimalistically', by merely stating the topics of their papers. The speaker from New Zealand (C) explains his motivations for the paper. This kind of variation may also be explained by *Tenor*, but is perhaps more difficult to systematise descriptively. The differences in realisation come from the speakers and their feelings about the audience they are confronting and what they think the audience needs to know for understanding the context. (But it may also be related to *semiotic spanning*, which will discussed in Section 7 below; i.e. it may be related to their reading other texts, attending other conferences, and giving other talks.)

(7)	**German** (U) male	**American** (K) female	**New Zealand** (H) male
	Ich spreche also über Georg Forsters Horizont. Die Weite seines Horizonts. *I thus speak about Georg Forsters Horizon. The extent of his horizon*	So I begin with Cook, the Forsters and Pacific Islanders: Three visions of Science, Curiosity and Art.	When I was first asked to give a paper at this conference, I really desperately wanted to talk more about biography rather than the history of science, because I think the story of the two Forster's biography is so central and vital to an understanding to what happened about the science. So I have to admit that I am going to be talking biographisch and also historically. On the 26th of November 1791, one year before he was to join ...

The *Mode* realisation differences in generic structures will be discussed in a later chapter (Charles & Ventola, this volume).

Registerial variation means continuous renegotiation of what is contextually appropriate as the discourse unfolds. We see 'the traces' of this registerial fine-tuning in the linguistic choices when we analyse the text from beginning to end. But what happens when the Discussion begins? Strictly speaking, at least in terms of *Field*, we should not have a lot of variation, as the audience is supposed to continue to show interest and ask questions about the *Field(s)* that the speaker has introduced. Yet there can be considerable registerial realisational differences in the Discussion. At this particular conference, there were various kinds of listeners among the audience. Many scholars were interested in the topic of the conference, although it was not their professional field. Sometimes, therefore, the 'other *Fields*' are tangible in the linguistic realisations. In Example 8 the discussant is a doctor and his *Field* of expertise is apparent in his comments to the presenter.

(8) *Chair:* {after a fairly long turn by the chair himself and then silence, he gives the turn to the discussant} ... (7 secs) Ja?
Discussant: Gestatten Sie mir einige Bemerkungen zu dem Besuch auf der Osterinsel ... erm die beiden Forsters wie de- wie der größte Teil der ganzen Besatzung waren sehr krank. Erlauben Sie mir, daß ich das sage. Ich bin nämlich Mediziner. Sie hatten alle Skorbut fast alle und der alte Forster beschreibt ja wie mühselig er gehen konnte. Das

lag an den dicken Beinen, die er hatte ... Ödeme, die sich da gebildet hatten in Folge dieser C-A A- Vitaminose, das war's übrigens nicht allein. Die Nahrung war qualitativ und quantitativ unzureichend. ... Deswegen ... ist ja auch Kapitän Cook so rasch wieder abgereist ... weil sie nicht genug zu essen bekommen haben ... und der ... jüngere Forster Georg ... der war ja damals noch gar nicht so alt noch. Der Junge war ja sehr jung ... erm der eine war ja erst 18 Jahre ... da ... erm der jüngere war so krank daß er also kaum sich an Land schleppen konnte. Vielleicht ist es doch nicht ganz uninteressant zu sagen wie diese Fülle von Materialien die die beiden schwerkranken Leute in zwei Tagen gesammelt haben. Das finde ich doch immerhin beachtlich.

Chair: {after a fairly long turn by the chair himself and thne silence, he gives the turn to the discussant} ... (7 secs) *Yes?*
Discussant: Allow me {to make} a few remarks concerning the visit to Easter Island ... erm both Forsters as well as the- as well as the main part of the whole crew were very sick. Allow me to say that. I am namely a doctor. They all suffered from scurvy, nearly all and the elder Forster describes how difficult it was for him to walk. That was due to the swollen legs he had ... oedema that had developed for all as a result of this C-A A-Vitamin deficiency, that wasn't by the way the only reason. The nutrition was qualitatively and quantitatively insufficient ... Therefore ... Captain Cook actually left so quickly again ... because they did not get enough to eat ... and the ... younger Forster, Georg ... who at that time was not that old yet. The boy was very young ... erm he was just 18 years ... when ... erm the younger was so sick that he could hardly drag himself on the shore. Perhaps it is not too uninteresting to mention what a wealth of material these both of these two seriously ill people collected in two days. That I still find all the same remarkable.

It is obvious that this comment comes from an expert in another *Field*. It is very often the case that in discussion discussants link up what they have just heard the presenter say to their own experiences of their professional field. Sometimes the whole Discussion sidetracks to another field: then, of course, it is the chair's duty to bring it back to the original field of the Section Paper. In Section 7, I shall refer to this kind of linking *semiotic spanning* (and cf. Ventola 1999).

Tenor choices are also traceable in the interpersonal realisations in the data, for example, in who dares to ask whom questions. The novice presenters must pluck up the courage to do so, whereas other experienced conference participants who know each other and each other's work feel more at ease asking questions. The use of certain address terms obviously gives an indication of what kind of *Tenor* relationship exists between the interactants, as the use of first name in Example 9 shows.

(9) *Discussant:* erm *Susan* do you think it is going to be possible in the next little while for us to do ...

Since the conference was held in Germany, the address terms follow German politeness rules of addressing colleagues - usually *Herr/Frau*, followed by the surname.

(10) **Chair***:* Zwei Wortmeldungen noch und dann müssen wir abschließen, damit Herr P. heute noch vortragen kann. Herr J. bitte.
Chair*: Two requests for a comment still and then we have to close, so that Herr P. can still deliver his talk today. Herr J. be so kind.*

Even the English-speaking presenters keep to this formality when referring to or addressing their German, as Examples (11) and (12) show.

(11) **Presenter***:* But I think it's erm I think it's something that we've got to come to terms with in force to research and I don't know if we haven't moved very far from where Professor A. left us 30 years ago

(12) **Chair***:* Ja, schließen wir jetzt. Herr S. sie wollten noch mal
Chair: *So, let's close now. Mr. S. you wanted a turn again.*
[Mr. S. has his turn to which the English-speaking presenter replies.]
Presenter*:* Danke, Professor.
Presenter*: Thank you Professor.*

As far as *Mode* realisations in Discussions are concerned, it is obvious that we are dealing with 'language as face-to-face interaction' rather than 'language as reflection', as is the case with 'read-out-loud' papers. Although some discussants take long monologic turns, especially when they are 'semiotically spanning' to their fields of expertise, there is also frequent turn-taking and checking whether messages have been correctly understood, as in Example 13. (Discussants are both native speakers; the presenter is German.)

(13) **Discussant 1***:* Maybe I missed it but ... did he not give any plants to Banks at all?
Presenter*:*   Oh yes yes **ja doch (=oh yes yes yes indeed)*
Discussant 1*:* *Well eh- (trying to interrupt the presenter,
                    indicated with * + underlining)
Presenter*:*   This this was on the bottom
Discussant 1*:* Oh oh
Presenter*:*   Perhaps you couldn't see it
Discussant 2*:* That's true I couldn't see that part
Presenter*:*   Yes
Discussant 2*:* Okay *he did-
Presenter*:*   *Yes this was- well the first set he gave away I think to Linné some
                    and to to Banks

In terms of turn-taking and checking-up on the communication flow this example resembles any casual conversation. This example is interesting also because it actually deals with the *Mode* realisations during the presentation, all participants not having seen the visual material shown by the presenter.

To summarise then, we have seen that both the paper and the discussion are structured units, and that there are established conventions for how these *generic structures* unfold. Most of the initiated members of the academic/scientific community have this *synoptic* view of how things proceed at conferences, because they have been socialized into these genres. We are also socialized into adopting the right *register,* and thus contextually tuning our discourse accordingly as we progress. When looking at actual data, we still find much linguistic and semiotic variation which we can only understand if we also adopt a *dynamic* view of discourse development in conferencing. A further factor that brings variation into the discourse of conferencing is *semiotic spanning*, which will be discussed next.

7. Semiotic spanning

Usually we consider the paper and its discussion as being connected – whatever has been introduced in the paper can then be discussed in more detail during the discussion. Many of the connections that are made between the discussion and the paper can be explained in terms of linguistic cohesion and coherence. Yet, there are connections to other semiotics, too; for example, when the discussion concerns the transparencies or slides shown. We can call this kind of connection *semiotic spanning* and consider it to capture the relations which exist between the paper and its discussion (see Ventola 1999; *semiotic,* because all modes of meaning realisation may be involved: written/spoken texts, visuals, actions, etc.). But Example 8 above has shown us that semiotic links in discussions can extend beyond the discussion to other discourses. We have, in Example 8, seen how a different field is incorporated into the discussion through the discussant's own medical specialisation. He makes experiential links between the topic and his own readings in his field of expertise. Links of semiotic spanning are thus formed between the discourse that is at that moment dynamically unfolding and the discourses that the discussant has previously experienced within another field (textbooks, articles, newspaper texts, films, slides, etc.). Sometimes semiotic spanning is realised so extensively in discussions that the audience can no longer follow the links that the discussant is making, and may easily consider such discussants as eccentrics, who always want to put themselves in the lime light. To be a good discussant means that one should also follow the Gricean (1975) maxim of 'being relevant' and not extending one's semiotic spanning to such spheres that one is no longer understood by others.

Discussants create semiotic spans to their own discourse worlds while they are listening to the presenter or while the discussion is going on. Presenters do this extensively already before their presentation. Anyone who has prepared an academic/scientific paper for a conference can verify to having exercised semiotic spanning. Various kinds of actions may be necessary for preparation of the conference paper, such as collecting data (experiments, interviews, etc.), and analysing them (laboratory tests, classifications, etc.). Then, at all stages of research the researcher has to familiarise him/herself with relevant literature. Sometimes this kind of semiotic spanning goes back centuries, as for example in the case of the conference presentations from which examples in this paper have been drawn. The topic of the conference was Georg Forster, an 18th century scholar and explorer. Thus a considerable amount of semiotic spanning is made by the scholars attending the conference to the actual writings of Georg Forster and his father, Reinhold Forster, and to the artifacts that they collected on their voyages and journeys. Much of the semiotic spanning to the artifacts is realised by visual mode, showing slides of the original artifacts to the audience; whereas the semiotic spanning to the Forsters is made by quoting their original descriptions of their experiences or rephrasing them. Both of the Forsters published extensively. Note of course that the Forsters have already taken the 'first step' in semiotic spanning: by writing down what they experienced. Thus, as I have elsewhere (Ventola 1999: 102) described, semiotic spanning can be seen to be functioning

> between various instances of genres within the speech event – the different conference papers and discussions within one section or during the whole of the conference when the discussions are built upon previous papers and discussions. It is also part of the other kinds of genres at conferences; e.g., when papers become part of other conference genres – dinner-table talk, coffee-time chats – what we call *talking shop*. And of course semiotic spanning exists between the presented paper and its source materials as well as with the final written version of the paper ... between the forthcoming written and spoken texts after the presented talks and their discussions at a conference and the influence they in turn have on other papers written for presentations and publication in the future.

I am suggesting that the notion of 'semiotic spanning' allows us to view conferences as multimodal events which have links to the past and to the future. On the one hand, we as presenters build links with other discourses – for example, with the sources etc. of the papers that we find relevant for our purposes. The discussants, on the other hand, build links to their own experiences of discourses (or other realisations of their semiotic world). Conference presentations and their discussions seem to come about through "a complexity of phenomena: reading of other texts, viewing visuals, making experiments, questionnaires, films, taking pictures and slides, etc.", and through the realised semiotic spanning we get "a cumulative increase of perspectives of knowledge and understanding" at conferences (Ventola 1999: 121). Figure 8 tries to capture these relations in a simplified manner.

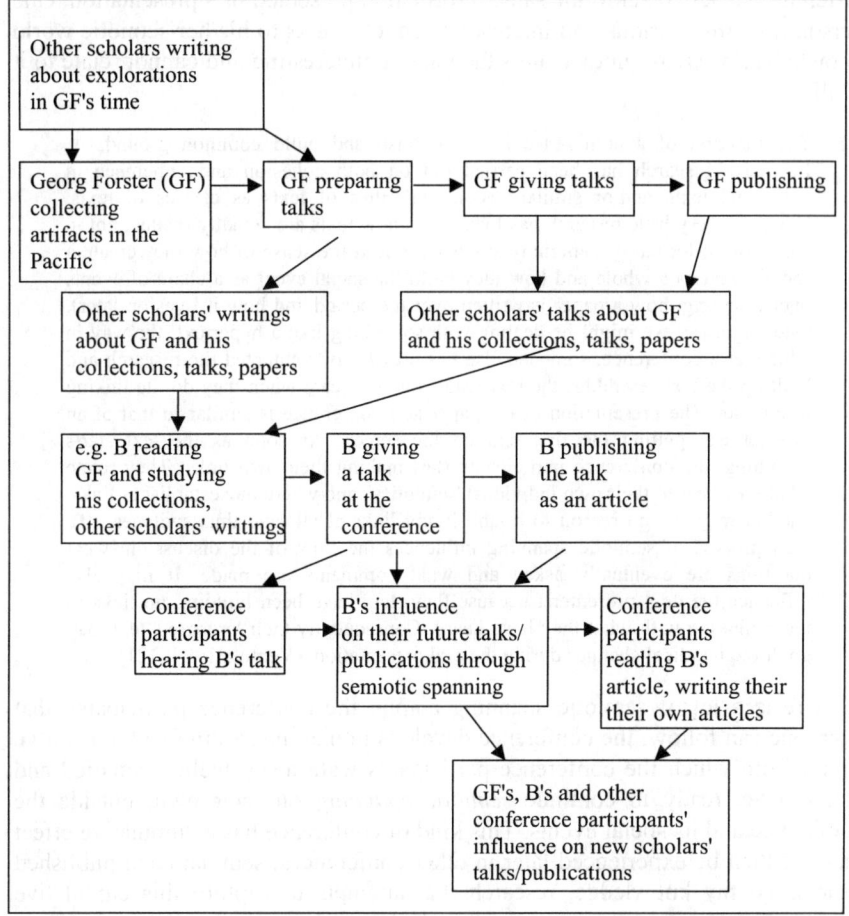

Figure 8: Semiotic spanning between the work of scholars.

Various scholars have written about 'intertextuality'. Mostly the term is used to refer to linking between written texts. This view seems too narrow for the study of conferencing. We need to take a more extensive view, where we do not only consider the relationship between the written and spoken mode in conferencing, and their division of labour. Furthermore, we also need to consider the other modes (e.g. visual) that play a role in conferencing. I have elsewhere (Ventola

1999: 121) suggested that what we need is an exploration of 'the life of a paper' after its instantiation, i.e. how it influences the other emerging texts, realised in different genres. So far, for example, we have very little knowledge of how different listeners react to the same information presented in a presentation. One person may find various and interesting semiotic links to his/her semiotic world knowledge, whereas another finds the paper uninteresting and cannot relate to it at all.

> The function of a conference is to establish and build common ground. ... Extensive research has been carried out on both cohesion and coherence in individual texts and/or similarities/dissimilarities of texts as classes of texts. However, very little research has focused on how texts are actually related, not in the sense of formal or generic relationship, but in the sense of how they create a social event as a whole and how they build the social event as a chain of events over time (e.g. how a paper is written over the period and how it lives on later). One might say we might be dealing with something like a hypertext: the way in which, at a conference, someone else has previously conducted the research and built up the text resembles the text readers/users create when they do the linking in internet. The presentation of the paper at a conference is similar to that of an internet-user getting the first text on the screen. As soon as the text starts unfolding, the conference participants start making their own links. They relate what they hear to their own individual 'semiotics', and where one establishes links, another may see no reason to establish any links at all (and thus switches off). This process of semiotic spanning influences the flow of the discussion: what questions are eventually asked and what comments are made. It may also influence the next presenters, because they, too, have been building up links in their thinking with what they have heard. Consequently their 'prepared' text may go through radical changes during the oral presentation. (Ventola 1999: 121)

If there is a lot of semiotic spanning among the conference participants that everyone can follow, the conference develops into an interesting and innovative event, from which the conference participants walk away feeling satisfied and enthusiastic, ready to continue *semiotic spanning* on their own, outside the conference and its social events. This kind of conference has a cumulative effect that can then be experienced later in other conferences, seminars and published papers. To my knowledge, research that attempts to capture this cumulative effect of building up on previous knowledge and enhancing it has not been carried out on conference data at all.

8. Conclusion

This first chapter in the volume has in many respects carved out a research niche for the study of conferencing and conference language. It has argued that conferencing differs semiotically and linguistically as a meaning-making social event from written academic/scientific papers. Conferencing and the language used in it deserves a focus in its own right. The chapter has shown that linguists interested in conference language and the rhetoricians of the Public Speaking tradition have some common interests. But the Public Speaking view will not enable us to develop a full semiotic and linguistic understanding of what is going on in conference talk.

The chapter has suggested that a suitable starting point for a linguistic view on conferencing and its language would be to use *generic* and *register variation* theory, as it has been outlined in various publications of systemic-functional linguistics. This framework will help us to explain how different kinds of conference events differ generically from one another (plenaries, section papers, round table discussions, etc.). It will also give us tools to study the realised register differences of *Field,Tenor* and *Mode*: for example, how medical experts' talk differs from social scientists', how interpersonal relations are expressed during talks, and how presenters can employ various modal realisations for their talks.

This chapter has further argued that our descriptions will have to extend beyond the study of instantiations – the conference papers and their discussions – to considering how the papers come about and what becomes of them after the presentation. The impact of a conference paper continues through other genres, as other papers in this volume also emphasise. It is as if conference papers start a life of their own in other researchers' talks and papers, thus contributing to the *cumulative momentum of increasing knowledge and understanding* of phenomena. This process is largely beyond the control of the presenter of the paper. It is not the case that only other published articles and presented papers have shaped our conference presentation, but rather a whole range of other genres are also coded in our talks: social activities ranging from laboratory work to cafe talks with colleagues or lectures to students. This has been called *semiotic spanning,* but it has only been possible here to touch upon the issues raised.

In a way, readers could also take this book as a representative example of semiotic spanning. Most of the writers of the chapters met at a small conference that was organised for the purpose of talking about conferencing. We all came together with our previous semiotic spanning to our own experiences and readings. During the conference we could link up with each others' talks during the official and coffee/dinner discussions. Then we went away and exercised more semiotic spanning between other different sources, as well as between ourselves by circulating draft versions of papers for reading and comments. Now we are handing the results of our semiotic spanning over to our readers, so that they can eventually continue the exploration in this exciting field of research and consequently build their own semiotic spanning links to this book on *Conference Language*.

References

Baldry, A. (ed.) 2000. *Multimodality and Multimediality in the Distance Learning Age.* Campobasso, Italy: Palladino editore.

Charles, C. & E. Ventola. This volume. "A multi-semiotic genre: The conference slide show".

Cox, E. W. 1867. *The Arts of Writing, Reading and Speaking in Letters to A Law Student.* Second Edition. London: Horace Cox.

Dudley-Evans, T. & W. Henderson 1990. "The organization of article introductions: Evidence of change in Economics writing". In T. Dudley-Evans & W. Henderson (eds). *The Language of Economics: The Analysis of Economics Discourse.* Hong Kong: Modern English Publications & The British Council, 67-78.

Eggington, W. G. 1987. "Written academic discourse in Korean: Implications for effective communication". In U. Connor and R. B. Kaplan (eds). *Writing Across Languages: Analysis of L2 Texts. Readin.* Mass.: Addison-Wesley, 153-168.

Eggins, S. & D. Slade 1997. *Analysing Casual Conversation.* London: Cassell.

Fawcett, R. P., A van der Mije & C. van Wissen 1988. Towards a systemic flowchart model for discourse structure. In R. P. Fawcett & D. Young (eds). *New Developments in Systemic Linguistic. Vol. 2. Theory and Application.* London: Pinter, 116-143.

Goodman, S. & D. Graddol 1996. *Redesigning English.* London-New York: Routledge.

Gregory, M. 1967. "Aspects of varieties differentiation", *Journal of Linguistics*, 3: 177-198.

Gregory, M. & S. Carroll 1978. *Language and Situation: Language Varieties and Their Social Context.* London - Henley - Boston: Routledge & Kegan Paul.

Grice, H. P. 1975. "Logic and conversation". In P. Cole & J. L. Morgan (eds*). Syntax and Semantics. Vol. 3: Speech Acts.* New York: Academic Press, 41-58.

Griffiths, F. J. 1935. *Speech Making.* London: Oxford University Press.

Halliday, M. A. K. 1985. *Spoken and Written Language.* Geelong, Vic.: Deakin University Press (Reprinted in 1989 by Oxford University Press.)

Halliday, M. A. K. & J. R. Martin 1993. *Writing Science.* London: Falmer Press.

Hinds, J. 1987. "Reader versus writer responsibility: a new typology". In U. Connor & R. B. Kaplan (eds). *Writing Across Languages: Analysis of L2 Texts.* Reading, Mass.: Addison-Wesley, 141-152.

Martin, J. R. 1992. *English Text. System and Structure.* Amsterdam / Philadelphia: Benjamins.

Martin, J. R. & R. Veel 1998. Reading Science. London: Routledge.

Mauranen, A. 1993. *Cultural Differences in Academic Rhetoric.* Frankfurt am Main: Peter Lang.

Mauranen, A. 1996. "Discourse competence - evidence from thematic development in native and non-native texts". In Ventola, E. & A. Mauranen (eds). *Academic Writing. Intercultural and Textual Issues.* Amsterdam / Philadelphia: Benjamins, 195-230.

McKinley, A. & J. Potter 1987. "Model discourse: Interpretative repertoires in scientists' conference talk*". Social Studies of Science,* 17: 443-483.

Mears, A.G. 1982. *The Right Way to Speak in Public.* Kingswood, Surrey: Paperfronts.

Murison, E. & C. Webb 1991. *Writing a Research Paper*. Sydney: Learning Assistance Centre, University of Sydney.

O'Donnell, Mick 1990. "Dynamic model of exchange". *Word*, 40, 3, 293-328.

Rigley, T. 1996. *Making Your Presentation Memorable*. Singapore / Kuala Lumpur / Hong Kong: Federal Publications.

Rowley-Jolivet, E. 1998. La Communication Scientifique Orale: Etude des Caractéristiques Linguistiques et Discursives d'un Genre. Unpublished Ph.D. Dissertation, Bordeaux: University of Bordeaux 2.

Räisänen, C. 1999. *The Conference Forum as a System of Genres: A Sociocultural Study of Academic Conference Practices in Automotive Engineering*. Gothenburg: Acta Universitatis Gothoburgensis.

Shalom, C. N. 1995. "The discourse management role of the chair in academic conference presentation sessions". *Interface. Tijdschrift voor Toegepaste Linguistiek - Journal of Applied Linguistics*. 10,1: 47-62.

Shalom, C. N. 2001. The Academic Conference: An Analysis of the Research Presentation Genres of Contrasting Academic Discourse Communities. Liverpool: Unpublished Ph.D. Dissertation. Liverpool: University of Liverpool.

Swales, J. 1990. *Genre Analysis: English in Academic and Research Settings*. Cambridge: Cambridge University Press.

Swales, J. 1996. "Occluded genres in the academy: The case of the submission letter". In Ventola, E. & A. Mauranen (eds). *Academic Writing.Intercultural and Textual Issues*. Amsterdam - Philadelphia: Benjamins, 45-58.

Swales, J. & C. B. Feak 1994. *Academic Writing for Graduate Students*. Ann Arbor, Michigan: The University of Michigan Press.

Thompson, S. E. 1997. Presenting Research: A Study of Interaction in Academic Monologue. Unpublished Ph.D. thesis. Liverpool: University of Liverpool.

Thompson, S. E. 1998. "Why ask questions in monologue? Language choice at work in scientific and linguistic talk". In S. Hunston (ed.). *Language at Work*. Clevedon, Avon: Multilingual Matters, 137-150.

Thompson, S. E. & H. Collins 1995. "Dealing with face threats in oral presentations". *Trabalhos em Lingüística Aplicada*, 26: 81-99.

van Dijk, T. A. (ed.) 1997a, *Discourse as Structure and Process*. London: Sage.

van Dijk, T. A. (ed.) 1997b, *Discourse as Social Interaction*. London: Sage.

Ventola, E. 1987. *The Structure of Social Interaction*. London: Pinter.

Ventola, E. 1992. "Writing scientific English: overcoming intercultural problems", *International Journal of Applied Linguistics*, 2, 2: 55-84.

Ventola, E. 1994a. "From syntax to text: problems in producing scientific abstracts in L2". In S. Cmejrková & F. Stícha (eds) 1994. *The Syntax of Sentence and Text*. Amsterdam/Philadelphia: Benjamins, 283-303.

Ventola, E. 1994b. "Finnish writers' academic English. Problems with reference and theme", *Functions of Language*, 1, 2: 1-33.

Ventola, E. 1995. "Englisch als lingua franca der schriftlichen Wissenschaftskommunikation in Finnland und in Deutschland". In H. L. Kretzenbacher, & H. Weinrich (eds). *Linguistik der Wissenschaftsprache*. New York / Berlin: Walter de Gruyter, 353-386.

Ventola, E. 1996. "Packing and unpacking of information in academic texts". In E. Ventola & A. Mauranen (eds). *Academic Writing.Intercultural and Textual Issues*. Amsterdam / Philadelphia: Benjamins, 153-194.

Ventola, E. 1999. "Semiotic spanning at conferences: Cohesion and coherence in and across conference papers and their discussions". In *Coherence in Spoken and Written Discourse* W. Bublitz, U. Lenk & E. Ventola (eds).. Amsterdam / Philadelphia: Benjamins, 101-123.

Ventola, E. and A. Mauranen 1991. "Non-native writing and native revising of scientific articles". In Ventola, E. (ed.). *Functional and Systemic Linguistics: Approaches and Uses.* Berlin/New York: Mouton de Gruyter, 457-492.

de Vito, J. A. 1978. *Communicology: An Introduction to The Study of Communication.* New York / Hagerstown / San Fransisco / London: Harper & Row.

THE ACADEMIC CONFERENCE :
A FORUM FOR ENACTING GENRE KNOWLEDGE

Celia Shalom

University of Liverpool, Liverpool, United Kingdom

Abstract - This chapter introduces readers to the linked concepts of genre, discourse community and genre knowledge, and claims their centrality to the study of the conference macrogenre and the language of conferencing. The academic discourse community has developed many conference genres, each with their particular linguistic (and non-linguistic) features, each advancing the knowledge pursuit and research aims of the specific community. While established members of an academic discourse community draw on their (often unconscious) genre knowledge during the conference process, novice academics are usually left to learn by example. However, as applied linguistics extends its understanding of this genre knowledge, and of how it relates to specific contexts of situation and contexts of culture, pedagogical practice can be better informed. In this way, novice academics can develop genre awareness and gain and extend their repertoires of situationally appropriate choices, thus enabling them to participate more effectively and confidently within the conference forum.

1. Introduction

English is today the lingua franca of academic conferences. This fact evidently puts non-native speaking academics, especially novice members of discourse communities (Swales 1990), at a disadvantage regarding full participation at conferences. The pedagogic motivation for this paper stems from the need to further our understanding of how academic discourse communities carry out their communicative purposes in the conference forum. Such genre studies inform our teaching and help both native and non-native speakers with liminal (i.e. novice) status in their discourse communities to participate more effectively in the social practices of their conferences.

Research into the nature of conference language is at a very early stage. The conference, as a social institution, was studied by teams of anthropologists in the 1950's and 60's (see e.g. Mead 1958 or Mead & Byers 1968), but (individual) linguists only started studying conference language in the 1980's. Notable for her pioneering studies of conference language is Dubois, who has investigated biomedical conference presentations (Dubois 1980a, b, 1981) and posters (Dubois 1985a, b).

Perhaps one reason for the reluctance of linguists to study the conference is the inherent diversity and complexity of the whole field. Conferences may be annual or biennial meetings of a professional association, with or without a general theme, or they may be specific - often interdisciplinary – symposiums which vary in size, prestige and location. While conferences may share common features relating to their structure, and to some extent their function, any one conference is a one-off real time event that will be experienced subjectively by the "conferees" (Lodge 1985).

This paper attempts to outline a 'way in' to looking at conference discourse using the concepts of genre, discourse community and genre knowledge. The first part of the paper discusses the conference as a macrogeneric event composed of research process genres such as the paper presentation session and the poster session as well as social genres. This event is held by a particular discourse community for the purposes of furthering the community's aims, research and publications. The second part of the paper suggests that our understanding of conference research process genres, and how they are enacted, may be informed by the notion of 'genre knowledge' (Berkenkotter & Huckin 1995).

2. The conference as a macrogeneric event

Genre is understood in a broad framework in the traditions of Swales (1990), Ventola (1987) and Bhatia (1993). Genres are abstract notions, classes of texts with particular communicative aims. They are "staged purposeful social processes through which a culture is realised in a language" (Martin & Rothery 1986: 243). In the academic context, each academic discourse community practises a particular academic culture; it has its own purposes, style and conventions. In this way, the relationship between genre and discourse community can be understood as mutually dependent, or symbiotic. Swales' seminal definition of genre has been cited on page 13 of this volume and is helpful in emphasising the dynamic relationships between communicative form (genre, its structure and its options), communicative purpose or purposes, and genre users (discourse community).

The conception of the conference presented here is that of a macrogeneric (or, possibly, an 'agnate') event. The conference event contains a number of interlinked *de facto genres* (Miller 1984) named by the user community itself and formally instituted on conference programmes. These genres may be divided into two types: the research process genres (Swales 1990) such as the paper presentation, the poster session, the plenary lecture and the book of abstracts, and the social genres such as coffee breaks, outings, lunch and the conference dinner.

Conference genres do not occur randomly on the programmes: conference organisers compile programmes whereby plenaries open and close the conference, thus denoting a progression through the conference, paper presentation sessions tend to run concurrently, the conference dinner traditionally takes place on the evening prior to the last day of the conference and so on. In this way, the enactment of the various genres during a conference contributes to the overall event.

The macrogeneric event is itself situated in a time chain. Genre activity is involved during three time phases: before the actual conference takes place, during the event itself, and after the event (see Table 1).

PRE-EVENT
call for papers -> submission of abstracts -> evaluation of abstracts -> drawing up of programme

THE CONFERENCE
opening plenary -> sessions and social programme -> closing plenary

POST EVENT
submission of papers -> evaluation of papers -> conference proceedings/publication

---

Table 1: The three time phases of a conference.

Before the conference, the call for papers goes out to which potential presenters respond by submitting abstracts for papers or posters. These abstracts are evaluated by the conference organising committee and accepted or rejected. Discourse communities differ in the status they give to the academic poster and the poster session. In our own community of applied linguists, for instance, the poster has lower status than the paper presentation. A paper abstract that is rejected may be accepted for the 'second best' option - that of the poster.

The conference itself serves as a forum for presentation and discussion through genre enactment. The conference programme, which will contain or refer to plenary, poster, presentation and panel abstracts, enables participants to make informed choices regarding their involvement at sessions. Further, the formalised and social genres, together with written artifacts such as the programme and book of abstracts, distribute information about the research process in the field. The publication that follows a conference usually takes one of two forms. Either there is a comprehensive conference proceedings that contains all abstracts and papers or there is a publication containing selected papers. In the latter case, a further stage of evaluation of papers etc. by the organising committee or editors will be added.

It has been seen that the academic conference event is situated in the middle of a time chain representing significant genre activity on the part of the members of a discourse community. The academic conference functions as a gatekeeper of research, a forum for presentation and discussion, and a distributor of information about research process.

The conference itself is typically held over several days and the event involves a complex interweaving of research-process and social genres. While the social genres of the conference are of some import to academic participation, it is the formalised research process genres that enable academics to establish themselves and their work. The status of these genres may also be indicated by the time and allocation of sessions on the conference programme or accompanying literature. For most of the research process genres (with the probable exception of the invited plenary lectures) academics will have submitted abstracts for consideration by the conference committee prior to the event itself. In these abstracts, the academics make promises about the presentation and sometimes about research findings. Many of the conference research process genres work not just to enable the research process of the community as a whole but to further individual research in that they may represent (and encourage) research in progress. The most typical research process genres found by the author at conferences in a range of subject areas is presented in Table 2 below.

The three time phases of pre, during and post conference illustrate the chains of research process genres that may take place. Abstracts of various types (paper, poster, panel, etc.) are written and submitted before the conference and are used as criteria for acceptance of a particular type of presentation. The book of abstracts, which may be distributed before or at the conference, is a colony text (Hoey 1986) that combines all the abstracts and employs a system of ordering. Together with the conference programme, the abstracts-book functions as a basis for choice of attendance by participants.

A book of papers is sometimes compiled and circulated before, during or after the conference. However, often papers are in embryo form and are not available to conferees at the conference stage but are used as the basis for different types of presentation. Relevant genre chains on the diagram indicate the process whereby presenters write up their papers, often incorporating comments by academics in the sessions, and submit them for evaluation. The conference proceedings will then represent a selection of the best papers published after the event.

PRE-EVENT		THE CONFERENCE	POST-EVENT	
	B			C
paper abstract =>	O	paper presentation session	=> paper =>	O
	O	{paper <-> presentation <->		N
	K	(discussion)}		F
				E
poster abstract =>	O	poster session	=> paper =>	R
	F	{poster <-> presentation <->		E
		(discussion)}		N
	A	poster session discussion		C
	B			E
panel abstract =>	S	panel/round table	=> paper =>	
	T	{paper/notes <-> presentation <->		P
	R	(discussion)}		R
	A			O
plenary abstract =>	C	plenary or keynote lecture	=> paper =>	C
	T	{paper/notes <-> presentation <->		E
	S	(discussion)}		E
				D
workshop abstract =>		workshop	=> paper =>	I
		{paper/notes <->presentation <->		N
		(discussion)}		G
				S

Table 2: Academic conference research process genres.[1]

The sessions at conference can be understood as complex genres in that they involve the linkage of more than one text type. The paper (or oral) presentation session, for instance, will consist of a number of papers (themselves normally texts comprising notes and visuals) which are presented and discussed, with a chairperson managing the discourse. It may be clearest for the presentation and discussion to be treated as two separate but linked genres that are phases of the same session. However, the discussion phase is subordinate to the presentation in that it must follow it and draw from it. This has been described as a hypotactic relation: paper being alpha, discussion beta. The discussion element is also optional as time may run out and, very occasionally, there may simply be no questions.

It has been noted that the paper is often not printed or fully written up but exists only as the basis for the oral presentation and as such is an artifact that stays in the hands of the presenter. The linkage between the written artifact and the presentation itself has been a preoccupation of ESP teachers who are aware of

---

[1] *Key:* ==> denotes genre chains; <-> denotes linked genres; ( ) denotes optionality.

the negative impact of 'manuscript delivery', whereby the presenter simply reads out a paper, on the effectiveness of the communication. A further important aspect of delivery is the incorporation of visual aids into the talk.

The case of the poster session is also complex. While formal poster presentations occasionally take place, the normal procedure is that poster authors are standing next to their posters, ready for discussion with other academics. In the sense that the poster is displayed for conferees to read, it is 'automatically' presented. Hence the poster + presentation + discussion become standard components in the session (although it is possible that there may actually be no discussion over a particular poster – certainly if the poster author is not present). Discussion is usually instigated by an interested conferee asking a question or making a comment, although some poster authors give a brief talk about the poster when academics gather round. Hence presentation and discussion take place concurrently during the poster session. (See Shalom 1996 for pedagogic suggestions for working with novices on the poster and poster session.)

The emphasis on the discussion element is also significant in the workshop discussion and the panel or round table discussion in that it is the presentation phase that is optional. However, if there is a presentation phase, it will occur before the discussion. The structure of such sessions could be represented as follows:

(Workshop presentation) ^ Workshop discussion

where brackets indicate optionality and ^ shows fixed order. Of course, the inclusion of recursion is typical in these sessions so the pattern can be generally represented as :

^{n}(Panel presentation) ^ Panel discussion

where inverted commas indicate repetition of the whole sequence.

The Tables 1 and 2 above represent a crude mapping out of the inter-relationships between the main conference research process genres in the macro-genre. At the level of individual sessions and of the macro-genre the conference is clearly an intertextual event par excellence. Initial research suggests that a high level of cohesion across the two linked genres of paper presentation and its discussion may lead to a greater perception of a successful session. Cohesion will also take place across sessions, including the social genres, and may also contribute to a conferee's sense of 'a good conference'. However, the interweaving of concepts and ideas seems to be of such linguistic complexity and works through a range of semiotic forms, that the concept of intertextuality may not be adequate to provide a satisfactory description of all the links made. As a result, the more inclusive notion of 'semiotic spanning' has been proposed (Ventola 1999, Chapter 1 of this volume).

In sum, the academic conference event is far more than simply an expression of the different genres that make it up. To quote Bateson:

> The aggregate is greater than the sum of its parts because the combining of the parts is not a simple adding but is the nature of a multiplication or a fractionation, or the creation of a logical product. (Bateson 1979: 86)

Since learning the genres of one's own culture is a necessary part of becoming a successful participant in that culture (Christie & Rothery 1989), a major concern of the ESP practitioner is to help the novice, faced with the complexities of a new discourse community and its ways, move towards effective participation, often in a foreign language, as quickly as possible. The focus will now move to that ability of established members of a discourse community to participate successfully in their culture, in other words their 'genre knowledge'.

3. Genre knowledge

A broad-sweep genre analysis of these academic conference research process genres across a variety of conferences and academic fields should enable us to identify a number of common generic patterns and purposes shared by discourse communities. However, the broad diversity and range inherent in academic conferences has already been noted. Such a recognition implies the need to take an approach to genre which is highly contextualised and which emphasises variation across discourse community. We must recognise that each community is likely to have different "beliefs about what can be known, how it can be known, in what form it can be expressed, and how it should be argued" (Bazerman 1988: 174).

Genre knowledge is the potential to participate successfully in genres. Berkenkotter & Huckin (1995: ix) define the term as follows:

> We use the term genre knowledge to refer to an individual's repertoire of situationally appropriate responses to recurrent situations - from immediate encounters to distanced communication through the medium of print, and more recently, the electronic media.

Of course, the notion of using language which is situationally appropriate is a familiar one to applied linguists and language teachers. Hallidayan linguistics uses the notion of language choices that are appropriate to situational variables as being an essential element in the ability to mean. Confusion may arise through Berkenkotter & Huckin's term 'response' since it is a label already used in dialogue description, so these will be relabelled 'situationally appropriate choices' for clarity's sake. What is of particular value in Berkenkotter & Huckin's work is their emphasis on the genre dimension, that of 'recurrent situations', that specifies particular contexts and communities.

Five theoretical principles constituting a framework for the notion of genre knowledge are outlined and developed by Berkenkotter & Huckin. These principles are: (1) dynamism, (2) situatedness, (3) form and content, (4) duality of structure, and (5) community ownership. The following section will relate these principles to the context of the academic conference.

3.1. Dynamism

Genres are not fixed, static entities but rather they evolve and change along with the communicative purposes they are used to fulfil. They are:

> dynamic rhetorical forms that are developed from actors' responses to recurrent situations and that serve to stabilise experience and give it coherence and meaning. (Berkenkotter & Huckin 1995: 4)

Dynamism is seen in the conference poster genre. There are speculations about its precise origins. Dubois considers that the poster entered the academic arena from trade fairs in which the poster is effectively used as a technical advertisement for a product or technique designed to attract and inform potential buyers (Dubois 1985a). It is also possible that the poster has been influenced by the academic article because of the IMRD[2] format that underlies the textual macrostructure of the scientific poster. The conference poster, then, shows certain communicative functions redolent of advertising but also provides a summary which gives enough information about pieces of research for academics to decide if they want to know more. Unlike the academic article which provides sufficient methodology for experiments to be repeated, the poster typically minimises the Introduction and Materials and Methods sections and focusses on the newsworthy information, i.e. the Results and Discussion.

However, it is clear that different discourse communities have their own 'house style' of poster. Further, some discourse communities, such as literature, mathematics and linguistics, are still working out their own particular uses and conventions for the poster and the poster session. Genres are continually

---

[2] I = INTRODUCTION, M = MATERIALS AND METHODS, R = RESULTS, D = DISCUSSION

evolving over time as new forms of expression are demanded, "in response to their users' sociocognitive needs" (Berkenkotter & Huckin 1995: 4).

Another example of dynamism may be found in connection with a genre known as the 'poster session discussion'. This is a formalised question and answer session that follows the poster session and takes place in a different venue. In this genre, a chairperson mediates questions and answers between conferees and specific poster authors and, optionally, a well-established member of the discourse community may summarise the notable content of the poster session previous to the discussion. Conferees at an interdisciplinary symposium were observed enacting the poster session discussion, which had been put on the programme by a member of the organising committee who came from biology. The majority of the conference, however, had had no experience of the genre and devoted a portion of the plenary discussion to reflecting on its application and utility (see Shalom 1993; and see also the principle of duality of structure in 3.4).

But genre is not only dynamic diachronically. Genre contains options that are realised dynamically by the actors involved and in this way the enactment of a genre is always open to potential change. It will be suggested later in this paper, for example, that appropriate linguistic selections by the paper presenter may include acts of positioning and apologising.

3.2. Situatedness

The second principle, that of 'situatedness', emphasises the crucial role of context in understanding (and enacting) genre. The intricate relationship between genre and context is an important source of genre knowledge:

> Our knowledge of genres is derived from and embedded in our participation in the communicative activities of daily and professional life. As such, genre knowledge is a form of 'situated cognition' that continues to develop as we participate in the activities of the ambient culture. (Berkenkotter & Huckin 1995: 4)

This knowledge about genre increases with exposure to and practice of participant roles such as presenter (of a paper or of a poster), discussant (who may question or comment on a presentation) and chair. These roles may be modelled and practised at conferences and, to some extent, at research seminars. So then, in the conference context, it is through enacting the particular genres of a discourse community, in the particular ways in which that community enacts them, that the novice academic learns about how to enact them.

3.3. Form and content

Genre knowledge will also involve knowledge of form and content. Textual forms may be understood as distinctive features and rhetorical frames or structures. The effective conference participants have a knowledge of the form and structure of the research process genres employed by their communities and of the particular conventions used. Surface scientists, for instance, typically integrate a large number of overhead transparencies in their oral communication, linguists may combine a smaller number of transparencies with handouts, while medics base their presentations on slides. The nature of the subject matter, and of the particular presentation type, will influence the form of the presentation. In this way, knowledge of content itself affects the form adopted.

Hence, genre knowledge will be situated knowledge of form and content in which the user has a keen sense of appropriacy to communicative purpose(s), situation and the specific moment in time in which it is enacted.

3.4. Duality of structure

Berkenkotter & Huckin (1995) take a social constructionist position influenced by Gidden's theory of structuration (Giddens 1984). They describe a duality of structure whereby the user of a genre simultaneously constitutes and reproduces the social structures involved. From this perspective, the human agent acts on genre to make meanings. Genre is not conceived of as a monolithic concept which curtails the user but as a scaffolding that may be exploited according to the user's communicative purposes.

Research on children's enactment of genres (e.g. Hon 1998) and on popular culture genres such as the personal advertisement (e.g. Shalom 1997) have noted the reflexivity of producers and receivers and how experimentation with and subversion of genres indicate implicit genre knowledge and agency in users. Conference participants also show such reflexivity and genre knowledge. For instance, participants at an interdisciplinary symposium on ecology were observed to discuss, in the plenary session, the effectiveness of one new genre (that of poster session discussion that took place in the main hall) timetabled at the symposium (Shalom 1993). Further examples of reflexivity can surely be found in most discourse communities. Among applied linguists, for instance, ongoing informal discussions about the form and status of the poster have taken place (e.g. at British Association for Applied Linguistics (BAAL) conferences). Furthermore, articles and letters critically commenting on the function of conferences and the appropriacy of specific genres may be found in the journals and newsletters of various discourse communities (e.g. Holden 1986 in *Modern English Teacher;* Stubbs 1997 in *BAAL Newsletter*).

3.5. Ownership

This principle of genre knowledge relates to the ownership of genres by a discourse community (Swales' fourth condition of a discourse community, Swales 1990: 26). Indeed, if discourse communities own genres and develop symbiotically with them, one may learn much about a discourse community through the instantiation of its genres:

> Genre conventions signal a discourse community's norms, epistemology, ideology, and social ontology. (Berkenkotter & Huckin 1995: 4)

While the examination of the relationship between genre and discourse community is full of complexity and in its infancy, applied linguists are beginning to carry out studies in this area. In a series of case studies, Berkenkotter, Huckin & Ackerman (1988, 1991) traced a graduate student's acculturation into a social science field of study and noted the relationship between his acquisition of discipline-specific text conventions and the particular research methodology of the field. Questionnaires administered to conferees at applied linguistics and virology conferences conferees showed up a correlation between (self-ascribed) status within the particular discourse community and familiarity with and use of genres (Shalom 2001).

Genre knowledge, then, is the complex situated knowledge that discourse community members need in order to communicate effectively and appropriately with each other. While Berkenkotter & Huckin focus on written genre knowledge, their five underlying principles also apply to spoken genres. These principles have been briefly illustrated in relation to the academic conference where knowledge of the spoken conference genres is equally important for access and contribution to community-based knowledge.

4. Situationally appropriate choices

Genre knowledge involves the discourse community member's ability to make situationally appropriate responses, or linguistic choices, and it is precisely this complex communicative ability that we, as ESP practioners, wish to foster in our students. Such choices are complex since genres are often "highly structured and conventionalised with constraints on allowable contributions in terms of their intent, positioning, form or functional value" (Bhatia 1993: 13). Indeed, the 'expert members' of the discourse community often exploit the constraints in order "to achieve private intentions within the framework of socially recognised purpose(s)" (Bhatia 1993: 13). It seems to me, then, that one of our aims is to investigate what these situationally appropriate choices might be for novice academics at academic conferences.

Comment has been made about variation across academic fields and discourse communities. One significant difference between the sciences and the humanities seems to be the relative reliance on the academic poster as against the oral paper as a form of presentation. Many of the sciences place great stress on the poster, and in these communities the novice presenter invariably gives a poster presentation but does not move to the oral presentation until he or she is more established in the field. In contrast, many of the humanities utilise the poster less - if at all. In applied linguistics conferences held by the British Association of Applied Linguistics, for instance, there will be one poster display consisting of less than a dozen posters. The relatively large number of paper presentations on the programme means that the academic has the opportunity (and the pressure) of presenting a paper far earlier in their career than in many science subjects. The communicative exigencies of this are of importance. The rest of this paper will focus on the paper presentation session and in particular on one dynamic aspect of the paper presentation of significance to the novice presenter.

It has already been noted that the paper presentation session involves one or more conference presentations and ensuing discussions. The paper presentation and its discussion have been characterised as interdependent, but separate, genres that set different linguistic demands on the participants (Ventola, Chapter 1 of this volume). Ventola's synoptic view of the generic structure of the paper presentation session is reproduced on page 27. Her diagram illustrates the embedded nature of the communicative event through use of frames. And it is the chair who is responsible for framing the session, by opening and closing it, and for marking the start and finish of both the presentation and the discussion phase (Shalom 1995). The key actor in the presentation phase is, of course, the presenter, while presenter and conferees engage in question-and-answer if the discussion phase takes place.

From this perspective, those stages of the session which are key **situationally appropriate choice areas** for the novice participant are those enacted by the presenter (or speaker), namely *Contextualising the paper* and *Presenting the paper* and by the presenter and delegate during the discussion phase, *Asking a question/making a comment* and *Giving an answer/response* by the presenter. (See the papers in this volume by Thompson on paper presentation and Webber on discussion of the paper).

Hence *Contextualising the paper* may be a crucial **situationally appropriate choice** point for the novice presenter. In order to illustrate this, a few examples of this move, taken from conferences in applied linguistics, will be given.

The first example is the first part of the introduction to the presentation given by a (native speaking) novice member of the discourse community of applied linguistics.

(1) 1. 'Yes I'm sorry um this is the last talk right before tea
     2. and I've given you a rather dense handout there with lots of numbers on it.
     3. I will try to keep you awake throughout the session in spite of that um
     4. I actually won't be going through every single one of those numbers much to everyone's relief but I thought you might be interested in having them.
     5. yeh I'm doing my PhD research with (ND) at (ID)
     6. um sorry to mention your name like that I take all the blame for everything okay
     7. in (TD) and the focus of the talk today is...'[3]

This presentation contains a long contextualising move which may be divided into listener-orientation (lines 1-6) and topic-orientation (line 7). The listener - oriented part makes use of downgraders or mitigators which act to get the audience on her side by softening the illocutionary force of the utterance. The elaborate apology stretching over several lines (1-4) includes the checking of channels regarding the handout with the understater *'rather' dense* (line 2) and the use of humour and forewarning to the audience (lines 2-4). The use of modals and negation serves as play-down. Listener-orientation is directed at the audience up until line 5 and then shifts to self-presentation (line 5) and involves another apology, directed at her supervisor who is in the audience (line 6).

Explicit self-positioning within the discourse community (line 5), specifying that she is doing a PhD, serves to effectively underline a role of modest knower, one with liminal status in the community. The specific naming of her supervisor and the institution is a complex speech act. Her supervisor is a well-established member of the discourse community who has published widely in the field. In this way, the novice presenter claims an explicit link with both a learned institution and with a person occupying a higher rank in the community. This link is potentially a protective one, since the student's work is now publicly connected to his name and is in some way an extension of him. (It might further be noted that she may in fact be better protected within the discourse community by having a male supervisor rather than an equally qualified female one.) Perhaps there is a boundary being laid here for the discussion phase: she has alerted the audience that her supervisor is present and direct criticism of her

---

[3] *Key:* ND = Name Deleted; ID = Institution Deleted; TD = Topic Deleted

work would result in his losing face. In other words, the presenter is using this move to align herself with her supervisor and prevent 'bashing' at the discussion phase (Ventola 1998).

We have seen that Example 1 contains a large amount of interpersonal work done by the novice. Such work, in the field of applied linguistics, does not seem to be atypical. Contextualising the paper may also involve emphasising the status of the research as 'research in progress') - and this strategy is not limited to novice members of the discourse community. The non-native novice may attempt to win over the audience by apologising for his/her English. I have observed a most successful presentation by a novice for whom English was not a first language that involved such an apology as well as an appeal to the audience for helpful suggestions in the discussion phase.

Contextualising moves may also involve impromptu utterances. Such an example is found at the beginning of Example 2, a presentation given by a fairly established member of the same discourse community.

(2)   1. 'Yes absolutely 'towards' is right
       2. I've already complained in various places following (ND) is you know hell so
          er how can you follow (ND) it's very nice in many ways you know to do that
          but er
       3. so the next thing is it's very much absolutely a work in progress workshop
          thing so
       4. and it's even more than it was when I actually arrived here because of course it
          was far too long so I spent a lot of time trying to shorten it and um
       5. so it'll be even more of a dog's breakfast than it was to start with so be
          understanding.
       6. I'm going to introduce my data in a minute
       7. you've got a handout you should all have a handout I hope
       8. it's an exploration of (TD) and I'm looking at (TD) and particularly....'[4]

The session has started very late as it followed an engaging plenary session that finished later than scheduled. The speaker is slightly flustered. Lines 1 and 2 seem to be impromptu - the orientation to the chair (line 1) refers back to her title and emphasises the theme of provisionality echoed at Line 3-4. Line 2, oriented to the audience, expresses slight annoyance about the organisation of the programme, refers indirectly to the late start and, in echoing the idea that 'it's a hard act to follow', clearly positions her as having lesser status within the

---

[4] *Key:* ND = Name Deleted; TD = Topic Deleted.

discourse community than the/a plenary speaker. In this way, the presenter humbles herself and gets the sympathy of the audience. The disclaimer involved in her evaluation of the status of the knowledge to be presented, *it's very much absolutely a work in progress workshop thing*, serves to lessen audience expectations and, possibly, to reduce potential criticism at the discussion stage. Statement of problem (*it was far too long*), response (line 4) and predicted result (*it'll be even more of a dog's breakfast than it was*) are followed by an explicit plea for support. The listener-orientation then moves to an audience-oriented check (Thompson 1997, 1998) of the communication channels. This is the first point at which the presenter claims ownership of the work (*my data*). Line 8 marks the beginning of the content orientation part of the move.

The last extract (Example 3), which also comes from the beginning of the presentation by a fairly established community member in applied linguistics, differs slightly in the way the contextualising move is enacted.

(3)   1. 'Yes, I realised far too late after I'd sent the abstract in that it was somewhat misleading because I'm not a little sceptical either it was just a nice example so.
        2. all I want to do in this paper is to present some a set of observations about some expressions as used in the spoken corpus from the (ND, ID).
        3. this corpus the spoken corpus comprises four million words and it includes data from various genres
        4. and it turned out because the genres are not distinguished within the corpus but it turned out that the genres of casual conversation and radio phone-in turn out to be particularly important to the expressions I'm looking at.
        5. and the particular expressions I'll be looking at are.....'

Line 1 shows impromptu listener-orientation to the chair, again relating to the title of the talk. The speaker does not have an audience-orientation as such but moves directly to content-orientation. There is, however, some mitigation involved in her first phrase *All I want to do* in that the effect may be to offset criticism and lower expectations. Interestingly, this speaker indirectly positions herself in the discourse community by mentioning the particular source of her data.

To summarize, examination of these examples suggests that, in applied linguistics at least, speakers need to develop a repertoire that encompasses some of these dynamic interpersonal meanings. It is probable that this is one of the key situationally appropriate choice areas for the novice presenter who needs to gain the support of the audience and position him/herself explicitly before the audience and within the discourse community.

The presence - and importance - of the contextualising move in presentations may be one of the key human aspects of the interaction between speaker and audience involved in the paper presentation session. Since this interaction is contextualised, both as an academic/professional event and within a particular discourse community, it may well be the case that the contextualising move is fuller and more important in some discourse communities than others. One could hypothesise that those discourse communities which rely more on the use of language in order to constitute knowledge (the humanities) place greater importance on such moves than do communities which use discourse in a more ancilliary way (the sciences). This is a useful area of future research.

5. Conclusion

This chapter has described the academic conference as a macrogeneric event which is held by a discourse community in order to extend its knowledge and further the community. Since the linkage across and between the research process genres and social genres that make up the conference event is so intrinsic to the nature of the conference, intertextuality and semiotic spanning are key areas of investigation.

It has been claimed that our understanding of conference research process genres and their enactment can be informed by exploring the notion of genre knowledge, the highly contextualised, culturally acquired knowledge that a well-established member of an academic discourse community has about genre. To have genre knowledge is to have 'communicative competence' (Hymes 1971) specific to a discourse community, to know what is possible, feasible, appropriate and 'done' in a particular culture for particular reasons. Hence, insights into not just what genres entail but also what **genre knowledge** entails for specific discourse communities will contribute to our overall understanding.

Huckin & Berkenkotter's (1995) five principles of genre knowledge: dynamism, situatedness, form-content, duality of structure and community ownership have been looked at in the context of the academic conference. It has also been claimed that, while all discourse community members are continually learning about genre and refining their situationally appropriate choices, such appropriacy of performance is particularly important for the liminal member. *Contextualising the paper* may be one such key point worthy of investigation across discourse communities.

There is a need to identify and research those key points in conference discourse where situationally appropriate choices are called for (and where the lack of such response or the inappropriacy of intervention will weaken the novice's

67

confidence and/or standing). The understandings gained through our research into conference discourse will directly inform our teaching and aid the novice's acquisition of a truly appropriate "repertoire of strategies for creating meaning" (Hopper 1988: 23). In this way, we can support the liminal member increase the pace of the natural disciplinary enculturation process.

References

Bateson, G. 1979. *Mind and Nature - A Necessary Unity*. London: Wildwood House.

Bazerman, C. 1988. *Shaping Written Knowledge: The Genre and Activity of the Experimental Article in Science*. Madison: University of Wisconsin Press.

Berkenkotter, C. & T. Huckin 1995. *Genre Knowledge in Disciplinary Communities*. Hillsdale, H.J.: Lawrence Erlbaum.

Berkenkotter, C., T. N. Huckin & J. Ackerman 1988. "Conventions, conversations, and the writer: case study of a student in a rhetoric Ph.D. program". *Research in the Teaching of English*, 22: 9-44.

Berkenkotter, C., T. N. Huckin & J. Ackerman 1991. "Social contexts and socially constructed texts: The initiation of a graduate student into a writing research community". In C. Bazerman & J. Paradis (eds). *Textual Dynamics of the Professions*. Madison: University of Wisconsin Press, 191-215.

Bhatia, V. K. 1993. *Analysing Genre: Language Use in Professional Settings*. London: Longman.

Christie, F. & J. Rothery 1989. "Genres and writing: A response to Michael Rosen". *English in Australia*, 90: 3-13.

Dubois, B. L. 1980a. "Genre and structure of biomedical speeches". *Forum Linguisticum*, 5 (2): 140-169.

Dubois, B. L. 1980b. "The use of slides in biomedical speeches". *The ESP Journal*, 1 (1): 45-50.

Dubois, B. L. 1981. "Nontechnical arguments in biomedical speeches". *Perspectives in Biology and Medicine*, 24 (3): 399-410.

Dubois, B. L. 1985a. "Popularisation at the highest level: Poster sessions at biochemical meetings". *International Journal of Social Language*, 56: 67-84.

Dubois, B. L. 1985b. "Poster sessions at biochemical meetings: Design and presentation". *The ESP Journal*, 4: 37-48.

Giddens, A. 1984. *The Constitution of Society: Outline of the Theory of Structuration*. Cambridge: Polity Press.

Hoey, M.P. 1986. "The discourse colony: A preliminary study of a neglected discourse type". In M. Coulthard (ed.). *Talking about Text*, Discourse Analysis Monograph 13. University of Birmingham: English Language Research, 1-26.

Holden, S. 1986. "Conferences, conferences and more conferences. Much ado about nothing?" *Modern English Teacher*, 13 (3): 40-45.

Hon, C. F. 1998. "Genre Awareness in Children". Liverpool: Unpublished PhD Dissertation. University of Liverpool.

Hopper, P. J. 1988. "Discourse analysis: Grammar and critical theory in the 1980s". *Profession*, 88: 18-24.

Hymes, D. H. 1971. "On communicative competence". In J. B. Pride & J. Holmes (eds). *Sociolinguistics: Selected Readings*. Harmondsworth: Penguin Books, 269-293.

Lodge, D. 1985 (1984). *Small World*. London: Penguin.

Martin, J. R. & J. Rothery 1986. "What a functional approach to the writing task can show teachers about 'good writing' ". In B. Couture (ed.). *Functional Approaches to Writing: Research Perspectives*. Norwood, N.J.: Ablex, 241-265.

Mead, M. 1958. "A meta conference: Eastbourne, 1956". *ETC*, 15: 148-151.

Mead, M. & P. Byers 1968. *The Small Conference*. Paris: Mouton and Co.

Miller, C. 1984. "Genre as social action". *Quarterly Journal of Speech*, 70: 151-167.

Shalom, C. N. 1993. "Established and evolving spoken research process genres: Plenary lecture and poster session discussions at academic conferences". *English for Specific Purposes*, 12: 37-50.

Shalom, C. N. 1995. "The discourse management role of the Chair in academic conference presentation sessions". *Interface: Journal of Applied Linguistics*, 10 (1): 47-62.

Shalom, C. N. 1996. "Using posters in the E.A.P. classroom". In M. Hewings & A. Dudley-Evans (eds). *New Directions in Language Teaching*. Phoenix ELT, 96-104.

Shalom, C. N. 1997. "That great supermarket of desire: Attributes of the desired other in personal advertisements". In K. Harvey & C. N. Shalom (eds). *Language and Desire: Encoding Sex, Romance and Intimacy*. London: Routledge, 186-203.

Shalom, C. N. 2001. The Academic Conference: An Analysis of the Research Presentation Genres of Contrasting Academic Discourse Communities. Liverpool: Unpublished PhD. Dissertation. University of Liverpool.

Stubbs, M. 1997. Letter. *BAAL Newsletter*, 55: 8-11.

Swales, J. 1990. *Genre Analysis: English in academic and research settings*. Cambridge: Cambridge University Press.

Thompson, S. E. 1997. "Presenting research: a study of interaction in monologue". Liverpool: Unpublished PhD Dissertation. University of Liverpool.

Thompson, S. E. 1998. "Why ask questions in monologue? Language choice at work in scientific and linguistic talk". In S. Hunston (ed.). *Language at Work: Selected Papers from the Annual Meeting of the British Association for Applied Linguistics.* Clevedon, Avon: BAAL/Multilingual Matters, 137-150.

Thompson, S. E. This volume. "'As the story unfolds': The uses of narrative in research presentations".

Ventola, E. 1987. *The Structure of Social Interaction: A Systemic Approach to the Semiotics of Service Encounters*. London: Pinter.

Ventola, E. 1988. Interpersonal choices in academic work. In A. Sanchez-Macarro & R. Carter (eds). *Linguistic Choice across Genres*. Amsterdam: John Benjamins, 117-136.

Ventola, E. 1999. "Semiotic spanning at conferences: Cohesion and coherence in and across conference papers and their discussions". In W. Bublitz, U. Lenk & E. Ventola (eds). *Coherence in Spoken and Written Discourse: How to Create it and How to Describe it.* Amsterdam: John Benjamins, 101-125.

Ventola, E. This volume. "Why and what kind of focus on conference presentations?"

THE CONFERENCE FORUM: A SYSTEM OF INTERRELATED GENRES AND DISCURSIVE PRACTICES

Christine Räisänen

Chalmers University of Technology, Göteborg, Sweden

Abstract - Conference practices vary widely from discipline to discipline which has implications for the role and status of conference genres in the production of disciplinary knowledge. This chapter examines the conference system of genres in a typical new, hybrid engineering discipline, automotive crash safety. Based on observations from conferences, interviews with conference participants, and analyses of all the genres deployed at these conferences, the paper looks at the interaction betweeen text and context. On the macro level, conferences are shown to be complex multifunctional fora that have evolved to fulfil the communicative needs of emerging academic communities. They comprise a system of interrelated and mutually dependent genres, which together contribute to construct meaning. As an example of this interdependence, the neglected call for abstracts is characterised.

1. Introduction

> I think my field [automotive crash safety] is no exception on the importance of conferences and the reason is you get to talk face-to-face with people in your field, find out what they are doing, who they are working with, what their current projects are. There's only so much you can get from a research article that you read. (Interview, ME, 1994)

Conferences are important "'rites of passage' along the road to professional advancement and promotion" (Swales 1984: 78). Apprentice researchers in most academic disciplines are socialised into their communities of practice (Lave & Wenger 1991) through attending and performing at academic conferences. However, the role and status of conferences in the construction of disciplinary knowledge vary widely from discipline to discipline. Although research on individual conference genres is growing, we still lack comprehensive studies of the conference as activity system, comprising a network of interrelated and mutually dependent genres.

Bijker (1995) in his study of sociotechnical change gives examples of two important functions of conferences in the construction of technological facts and artefacts. Conferences are sites for publicising research results and an open ground for confrontation, discussion and the ratification of meaning. Thus, today, in many engineering disciplines, refereed Conference Proceedings

Papers, CPPs, rather than journal Research Articles, RAs, are often researchers' first – and sometimes main – contributions to disciplinary knowledge. In these disciplines conference genres seem to have evolved to fulfil specific communicative needs of emerging communities to establish a viable forum where consensual knowledge claims are made and accredited.

In traditional academic disciplines in the pure sciences, humanities and social sciences, conferences are usually seen as an intermediary stage in the production and dissemination of knowledge claims (e.g. Dubois 1980 and Rowley-Jolivet, this volume). Conferences are therefore sites for publicising tentative claims, which may at a future date be accredited through publication in a research article. Conference papers, if published at all, may come out a year or so after the event, by which time they may not bear much resemblance to the original Conference Presentation, CP.

Despite these important disciplinary differences, there has been very little research into the socio-cultural aspects of conferences or into the relationship between context and texts. Performing at a conference does not only entail producing a spoken and/or written conference paper. There is a whole repertoire of generic exchanges leading up to the conference presentation, e.g. call for abstracts, conference abstracts, letters, peer-review comments, responses to comments, revised papers, discussant papers, conference-presentation manuscripts, and graphic material. All these genres are inextricably linked in a system of interrelated genres (Bazerman 1994), which *together* contribute to the production and consumption of a potentially successful conference paper.

The present chapter argues for a more context-sensitive approach to the analysis of conference genres, one that takes account of both the macro-level, the conference system, and the micro level, the role of each individual conference genre. Two questions have driven this study: How do we define "academic conference", and what role do conferences play in the construction of disciplinary knowledge? The chapter proposes an "extra-textual excursion" (Swales 1993: 690) into the conference practices of a "new" discipline, automotive crash safety. I characterise conferences on the macro-level and discuss their multiple functions in academia today. I argue that conference genres co-operate to construct meaning within systems of interrelated genres in which facts, artefacts, social relationships, personal identities and texts contribute. In order to acquire genre knowledge of one conference genre, it is necessary to view it in the context of the whole system of genres. As an example of the mutual interdependence of genres on the micro level, I focus on one particular and neglected conference genre, the Call for Abstracts. This genre serves to *regulate* conference events, *legitimise* participation and *instruct* submitters, and thus plays an important role both on the macro-level and the micro-level.

2. Method and corpus

To understand how genres work together to construct meaning, we need a better understanding of how different levels of context influence the production and interpretation of genres. Recently, Berkenkotter & Huckin (1995: 2) noted that:

> [t]o date, very little work on genre in rhetorical studies has been informed by actual case research with *insiders*. Instead, there has long been a tendency among genre scholars to reify genres, to see them as linguistic abstractions, and to understate their "changeable, flexible and plastic" (Bakhtin 1986: 80) nature.

To avoid such abstractions, the data for this study included on-site observations and interviews with most of the conference presenters and a large number of the attendees at four conferences: AAAM (Association of the Advancement of Automotive Medicine) 1994, IRCOBI (International Research Council On the Biomechanics of Impact) 1994; and IRCOBI 1996 and 1998. In addition, seven in-depth, one- to two-hour, recorded and transcribed, interviews with expert insiders were carried out. The interviewees had different backgrounds and approaches to crash safety, and represented typical areas of expertise, such as medicine, physics and biomechanical engineering. Four of the interviewees were members of conference committees. All had been or were active as referees or editors for the few scientific journals in the field. Several follow-up interviews were also carried out.

A corpus of 31 conference presentations from 1994 and 1996 (between 15 and 20 minutes) were audio-recorded and transcribed, and subsequently compared with their published conference proceedings paper counterparts (ca. 10 to 15 pages each). Twenty-five presentations from 1998 were video-recorded, but not transcribed. Twenty-five promissory conference abstracts and their published CPP-abstract counterparts were also compared (see Räisänen 1999: 19-24 for a more detailed description of the corpus). The CPPs are published in annual proceedings and are referred to here by Conference Association and year, e.g. AAAM 1994 and page. Furthermore, samples of all the genres relevant to the above-mentioned conferences were collected, e.g. call for abstracts, advice to authors, agendas of conference-committee meetings, reviewers' comments, and speakers' manuscripts.

To obtain a historical perspective and to gain insight into the epistemology of the crash-safety community, I collected primary material consisting of ca. 100 research articles and CPPs from 1965 to 1997, as well as secondary material consisting of scholarly and popular publications concerning the history of automotive safety.

3. Conferences in automotive crash safety: macro-level perspective

Automotive crash safety is a typical example of a 'new' multi- and interdisciplinary field of applied science, i.e. a hybrid discipline. Hybrid academic communities are becoming increasingly common as a means of coping with the growing complexity of modern society. They are shaped by their interfaces with the scientific community on the one hand, and by the exigencies of the professional sector, industry, government and the media on the other. The communicative needs of these new formations and their solutions to these needs differ from those in the traditional pure sciences. Crash safety can be seen as a rhetorical community, an agglomerate of a number of groups mutually dependent on the knowledge generated in each separate group. Information and new knowledge are disseminated by means of discursive forms created specifically to enable the smooth transfer of meaning between *all* the different groups of the rhetorical community. The conference has been one of the most viable discursive practices for carrying out communal business and consolidating community goals among the heterogeneous crash-safety groups. Over time conferences have evolved from being networks of informal communication to becoming established sites for making consensual claims public (Räisänen 1999: ch.3).

To gain situated knowledge of individual conference genres we need to explore the social character of the communities that created them and look at how and why these communities adopt, adapt and create discursive forms to suit their various activities and their intra- and inter-communicative needs. Much of this knowledge is not inscribed and therefore cannot be elicited from written texts. With this perspective in mind, it is useful to view the conference as an activity system, which according to Engeström's (1993: 67) definition

> Integrate[s] the subject, the object, and the instruments (material tools as well as signs and symbols) into a unified whole ... a human activity system always contains the subsystems of production, distribution, exchange, and consumption.

This definition focuses on context as the interrelationship between humans, non-human entities and texts. In these linked systems, texts "define possibilities for action and are defined by action" (Myers 1996: 9). Thus to understand the meanings encoded in the texts, we need to view them from the perspective of the activities of which they form a part.

The conference in crash safety is a historically generated activity system which has developed as a solution to social exigencies. It consists of a *conference event* including a sequence of social actions, i.e. genres which are in communication with each other within this circumscribed situation (see Fig.1). In addition, and more importantly, the genres and evolving genres of conference events are contextually, intertextually and dialogically linked in a wider system, the conference forum. Porter (1992: 96) defines *forum* as a local and temporarily constraining system "where several discourse communities intersect" but also interact, bound by a commonly established *ethos* and shared concerns.

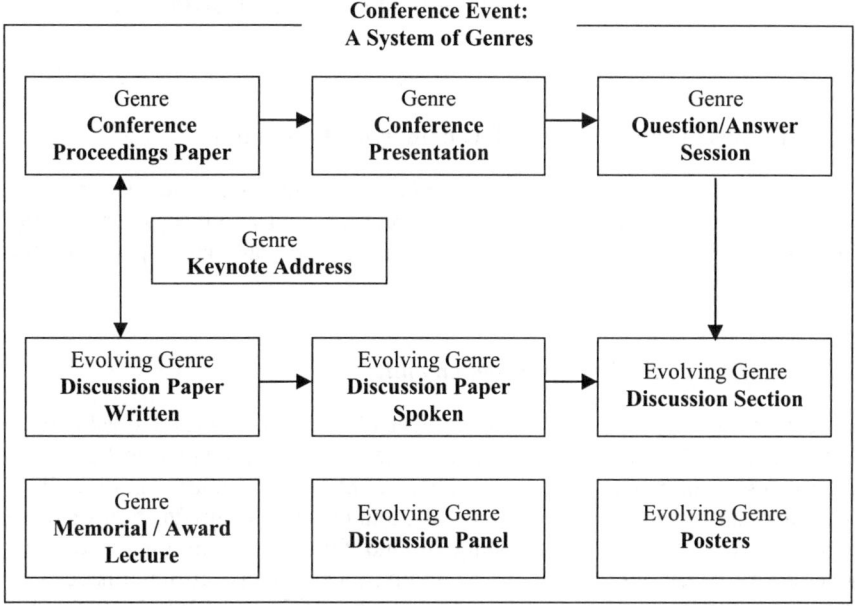

Figure 1: Genres and evolving genres at crash-safety conferences.

A strong reason for using this term is that the crash-safety community itself uses 'forum'[1] with similar connotations[2]. The forum includes the activities and genres of particular conference associations, their annual conference events, the published conference proceedings, and all the processes of production and distribution connected with these, *before, during and after* a specific conference

---

[1]   In the AAAM annual programmes for example.

[2]   According to Swales (1990), a discourse community's genre nomenclature may provide valuable insight about the genre or discourse practice, which further supports the use of the term in this connection.

event. It is the forum, not the conference event, which offers actors from a variety of communities of practice membership in a circumscribed community and a space in which to address common concerns and exchange information.

The crash-safety community today consists of a number of interdisciplinary academic conference fora, the principle ones being the STAPP Car Crash Conference, the AAAM, and the IRCOBI. These conferences are relatively small gatherings, on average about 300 participants, with a limited number of research topics, depending on the research orientation of the conference forum. As in all academic fields, the conference forum in new hybrid fields of technology serves a variety of functions, which strongly influence the communicative purposes and rhetorical structure of individual conference genres.

4. Functions of the conference forum in hybrid disciplines

Conferences in crash safety fulfil a number of disciplinary functions: they are fora for publicising knowledge claims, virtual as well as physical networking locales, fora for education, sites for bestowing rewards, and marketplaces for the purchase and exchange of expertise.

4.1. Conference forum as publication outlet

In academia today, there are two main types of conference fora, defined here as *before-print* and *after-print* fora[3]. The former model is prevalent in traditional disciplines in the humanities, social sciences and pure sciences, e.g. disciplines that have established a research journal tradition. The main function of these conferences is to serve as a testing ground for work-in-progress and peer-assessment of new ideas, methods or findings. The claims proffered have been defined as prefatory stages in the genesis of a scientific fact (Dubois 1980: 143) or as "proto-claims" halfway between informal communication and public knowledge (Rowley-Jolivet, this volume). The pivot of this conference type is the CP[4].

---

[3] To my knowledge there are no established terms to distinguish between these two conference types.

[4] It is becoming more usual for speakers to have a printed version of their talk or their graphs for distribution. It would be interesting to study what implications this has on citation practice. The whole issue of conference presentations and citation practice is controversial and there are no comparative studies of this phenomenon across disciplines.

However, new hybrid fields of technology lack the tradition of research journals and consequently the traditional knowledge-accreditation forum of a scientific discipline. The Research Article (RA) forum embodies a whole system of genres (Bazerman 1994), a process through which meanings have been negotiated and ratified in a joint venture involving the custodians of the new knowledge claims (authors), fellow experts (colleagues and advisors), sponsors of projects (financial supporters), and gatekeepers (referees and editors). The rules and conventions for this repertoire of texts have been developed over a long time to conform to the ethos of the scientific research community and, as Porter (1992: 109) puts it, "[t]he manuscript becomes part of an epistemological grid supporting the formation and the power relations that support the grid."

In new hybrid disciplines, conferences gradually evolved to include a peer-review process to provide such an epistemological grid. By the 1980s all the aforementioned academic crash-safety conference fora had established a gatekeeping system for CPPs. The pivot of *after-print* conference fora is thus the peer-reviewed CPP, published in a commercially available proceedings *prior* to the conference event. Moreover, it is the CPP rather than the conference abstract which forms the basis for an accepted paper, as described later on in this paper.

In crash safety, therefore the conference forum is often the first official publication site for apprentice researchers. A senior researcher describes the situation as follows:

> [I]t's conference proceedings because there's no, you know, single authority of journal that collects all the stuff. . . . It's IRCOBI proceedings for the last twenty years, Experimental Safety Vehicle conference proceedings, particularly for the sort of industrial hardware crash testing side. But then it's the American conferences, the STAPP conference. More specialised places like the *Journal of Biomechanics, Journal of Applied Biomechanics,* I mean there are journals that sort of come and go. (Interview, MA, 1994)

A survey of the references of the PhD theses (eight in all) produced at a department of crash safety in Sweden since 1991 showed that 60% of the references were to CPPs while only 18% were to RAs. The remaining references were to industrial reports, regulatory statutes or other. A similar survey at departments of production engineering and high-power electronics yielded similar results. Likewise, a survey of the two engineering-based conference proceedings, STAPP and IRCOBI, from 1965 to 1997 revealed that about two-thirds of the references were to CPPs. These results suggest that fields of engineering have developed their own research genre in which to publish consensual claims. Therefore, to gain insight into the epistemology, ideology and norms of these disciplines, we need to look at other genres than the RA. We also need to pay more attention to the contexts in which disciplinary genres are deployed.

4.2. Conference forum as communication bridge

One informant from industry described the conference as the meeting ground where academia and industry can negotiate meaning and disseminate their results, especially since research-and-development results in the automotive industry in Europe are not usually published in research articles[5].

Knowledge production in crash-safety research bears similarities to that in defence technology research as mapped by Van Nostrand (1997). His study concentrates on how knowledge is incrementally constructed through the marketing process, the negotiations between customers/users of the potential technology or artefacts and the potential vendors/producers.

> [C]ustomer and vendor both use one other instrument to contextualize their ideas: the formal conference paper, presented at joint meetings for specialists representing both customer and vendor within given fields of research ... The technical papers that are presented or circulated help to clarify a customer's interests or to inform customers of a vendor's capabilities. The papers tend to define the state of the art in any subdiscipline or where subdisciplines from different areas tend to merge. They emphasize needs and claims, depending on the author's perspective. And they engender follow-up discussions, both on and off the record (Van Nostrand 1997: 153).

This statement applies to crash-safety research as well, where the marketing genres and the meanings these negotiate in crash-safety research are inextricably linked to the academic genres in the discipline. The close interaction with industry also puts pressure on academics to publish their claims in the commonly established fora. This creates problems for academic researchers, as the following quote shows:

> Regarding my publications, I think that I have too many conference papers and not enough journal publications. My department chair recommends that I have 4 to 6 journal papers per year at this point in my career. This is a challenge. Our lab is growing quickly and I seem to have 10 to 15 conference papers per year in addition to the journal articles. Thus, there is a lot of publishing going on. *I would*

---

[5] Note that academic conferences are far from the only medium of exchange between these organisations. In the technological sciences there is extensive co-operation between academia, industry and government in the form of joint projects which are largely financed by industrial and governmental organisations. The main outlet for the results of these projects is the industrial report. For example the University of Michigan Transportation Research Institute produces on average 50 official reports a year. Most of this work is carried out under governmental contract.

like to publish more journal articles but our financial obligations necessitate the conference papers. (E-mail interview, CR, 1997, my emphasis)

It can also be noted here that the interaction with industrial organisations is manifest in the texts, especially in the acknowledgements section of the CPP, where sponsors and industrial partners, as a rule, are mentioned. This has implications for the way in which the content of the CPP is interpreted and evaluated. Sponsors are also crucial actors in the knowledge production process, being the first and often the most influential reviewers of a paper (Räisänen 1999: 197-99). This can lead to tension between the ideology of the objective academy and that of competitive economy-driven organisations.

Conference genres, therefore, more than other academic genres, function in a network made up of a multiple audience and serve to bridge differences by packaging and transferring information in such a way as to make it accessible and acceptable to all parties involved.

4.3. Conference forum as educational locale

One very important aspect of conference fora in crash safety is their didactic function. This is highlighted in all the programmes of the conference associations mentioned in this paper. In the AAAM programme, for example, the different types of activities of the conference event are advertised under the heading "Education Methods." Also, the AAAM attendees may receive accreditation for continuing education, which is sponsored by the Program for Continuing Education (PCE). Courses and workshops are often arranged in conjunction with conference events.

A senior researcher at the University of Michigan Transportation Research Institute emphasised the importance of extending education across disciplinary boundaries, which, he added, research journals cannot do since they address too narrow a group of experts:

> And you know there's a lot of education to be done not only in the doctor business but over on the engineering side. There's so many of these young engineers that are designing our new cars and they don't even know where the knee is. And that's what I would like to get more into is training at that young level, if you will, to get them stimulated and motivated. (Interview, HU, 1994)

In several of the CPs in 1994 and 1996, speakers appealed to the audience to increase education across expertise boundaries by spreading information about the research concerns in the respective sub-specialities. This is especially important today, when engineering research is increasingly factored into smaller and smaller sub-problems, increasing the risks that individual engineers lose track of the social and environmental causes and consequences of the research they are carrying out (Beder 1997).

Thus a function of conferences in crash safety is to "improve the dissemination of information in a very specific field." One way of doing this is "to stimulate the participation of young researchers in meetings" (IRCOBI 1982). The STAPP Foundation was established in 1995 "to promote and develop international scientific, engineering, and medical crash injury protection knowledge through the annual Stapp Car Crash Conference and the development of funds for education and scholarship" (STAPP programme 1996).

4.4. Conference forum as reward system and market place

Conferences are sites in which actors gain visibility and status. Keynote talks, award lectures, and discussion papers are privileged slots on the programme to pay homage to an individual's expertise. The association may also be connected to a foundation created to reward members for outstanding work. These are part of the reward system within the sciences (see e.g. Hagstrom 1965; Garvey 1979; Ravetz 1996) and strengthen the bonds between individuals operating not only in the same invisible college but also between those in different invisible colleges, thus widening the disciplinary network (Crane 1972). Both the STAPP and AAAM have an annual award for outstanding paper, and the STAPP has of late also established such an award for outstanding contributions by Ph.D. students. This can also be seen as part of the efforts to legitimise conferences by strengthening their ties to the scientific research community.

One more function of conference fora which must not be forgotten is that they are used as meeting- and marketplaces to settle other business related to the profession: recruiting young researchers to projects, procuring an external examiner for a viva, assessing possible project partners, and promoting and selling products such as crash-simulation programmes and crash dummies.

To conclude, conference fora and their annual conference events are information and knowledge-constructing systems, fulfilling important institutional and interpersonal functions. Each genre in this system has meaning and value for other genres in the system as well as for the system as a whole. Therefore, in my view, the analysis of one conference genre remains incomplete if its contexts of production and consumption are not taken into account. To exemplify, I now turn to the micro-level and look at the relationship obtaining between the individual genres in the conference system of genres.

5. Genres as interactive meaning-making systems

I want to argue here for the analytical value of viewing genres as linked in a dialogic chain of generic exchanges (Bazerman 1994: 9) within a system of genres. Genres are realisations of author intent and reader interpretation and they are responses and elicitation to other texts in the system, and between systems. Ventola (1999, this volume) proposes the term "semiotic spanning," which she defines as the linking up of a text with other texts or semiotic modalities as a means of creating contextual coherence and a new semiosis. In the conference forum, for example, conference abstracts and papers are elicited by a Call for Abstracts and quality-controlled by Reviewers' Comments, to which writers need to respond. In addition, the CPP and CP in these fora have a particular dialogic relationship to each other, since the oral presentation follows upon the CPP and not, as may be more common, the other way around.

Genres, according to Bakhtin (1986), are linked "in the chain of speech communication of a particular sphere." Each utterance or text:

> [R]efutes, affirms, supplements, and relies on the others, presupposes them to be known, and somehow takes them into account ... the utterance occupies a particular *definite* position in a given sphere of communication. It is impossible to determine its position without correlating it with other positions. Therefore, each utterance is filled with various kinds of responsive reactions to other utterances of the given sphere of speech communication (Bakhtin 1986: 91).

Bazerman (1994) developed Bakhtin's concept of dialogic generic exchanges in his notion of "systems of genres." The limited number of genres operating within such a system generally occur in a defined order and are mutually interdependent, or linked contextually. Although the systems of genres in the conference forum are more flexible, they nevertheless, as we shall see, follow a predetermined sequence and are mutually dependent.

Berkenkotter & Huckin (1995: 97-116) have shown how generic utterances are linked to each other to form *repertoires of rhetorical action* that function together to get things done. For a conference abstract to succeed, it must show alignment with community values and interests, "*as these are reflected in current conference theme statements*," or other clues in the Call for Abstracts[6] genre. The Call for Abstracts in this repertoire can be viewed as regulatory, signalling important cues about community norms, ideologies and current concerns at a particular point in time.

---

[6] The nomenclature of this genre (and its realisation) differs from discipline to discipline. In the above-mentioned study it is called a Call for Programme Proposals.

Bakhtin's notions of intertextuality and Bazerman's theory of mutually dependent genres in specific settings help explain the chain of actions that obtain in the conference system of genres. We will now explore this generic system and look more closely at types of links between certain texts within the system of genres, namely those of *genre set* and of *genre chain*.

5.1. Genre set

Devitt (1991) defines *genre set* as all the generic texts one person, e.g. a tax accountant, is likely to produce in his/her line of work. In this profession, the genre set is a limited number of texts many of which belong to the same overall genre, the letter, but whose communicative purposes and interpersonal relationships are distinct. All the texts in this genre set form the basis for the maintenance of a well-established institutional authority and are in turn based on the genre set of the general tax publications, which are the regulatory texts of the whole profession as an institution. All these texts, says Devitt, form complex webs:

> To discover such webs, however, we must examine the role of all texts and their interactions in a community – their genre systems and their rhetorical situations, their intertextual references and their epistemologies, their uses and community functions. (Devitt 1991: 154)

In the same way, we can say that there are well-established genre sets in academia, albeit they are much more varied. Undergraduate and Ph.D. students, and staff will have different, but overlapping, genre sets. In addition, the genres in one particular genre set will belong to different systems of genres within academia and they will also overlap with genres from other spheres, e.g. press releases for a head of department, job applications for all categories. Academic genre sets have common global features that fulfil common recurrent communicative needs in academic spheres, but they also have local differences depending on national proclivities, university conventions, disciplinary preferences and departmental idiosyncrasies.

The genre set in the context of conferences refers to all the texts produced by one party (person, group or institution) in this system, for example the gatekeepers of the forum, or the active participants in the conference event. These genre sets comprise spoken and written genres as well as the use of other semiotic systems, namely visual representations and demonstrations. Each genre in a genre set has its own combination of features from several systems: political, technological, legal, and/or financial.

5.2. Genre chain

In addition to system of genres and genre set, I would like to introduce the term *genre chain,* which refers to *a sequence of genres within a system of genres.* This sequence may involve two or more genre sets, which form a chain of utterances that follow upon each other in a determined sequence and contribute to the production of a particular genre in the system. For the conference system of genres, the CPP belongs to a genre chain comprising a Call for Abstracts, a submitted Conference Abstract (CA), a Review Process, an Invitation to Submit a Paper and so on, as illustrated in Figure 2.

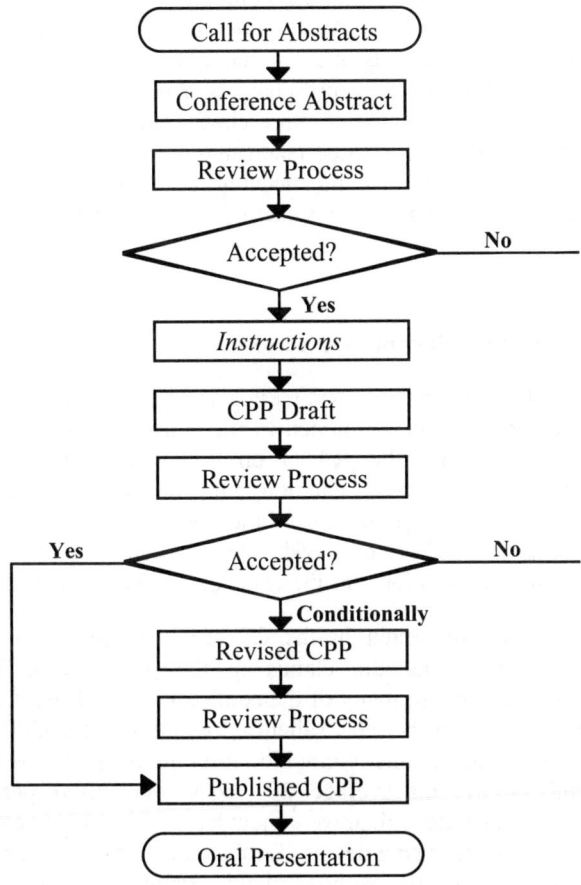

Figure 2: CPP genre chain.

Figure 2 is a flow chart of all the genres that interact and contribute to the production of the CPP and CP. Each genre follows upon the other in a predetermined sequence, the success of some of these genres being largely influenced by the way they respond to the genres to which they are most closely linked. Looking at texts from this perspective we may realise that some genres in academic and professional environments, which have tended to be dismissed as mere formalities, may in fact be influential in shaping community norms and structures. One such genre is the Call for Abstracts, discussed later on.

Thus, in this chain, transactions take place between the conference committee and potential participants. The former send out a needs document stipulating the conditions for the invited offers. A submitter then offers a tender, the CA, which, if found acceptable results in an invitation to offer yet another tender, a CPP. If the CA is rejected, the genre chain is aborted, ending in a letter of rejection. Each incremental text in a genre chain influences the way in which texts are constructed, and needs to be taken into account *before* the respective documents are produced. Likewise, the meanings conveyed in the documents are better understood in relation to the systems, chains and sets to which they belong.

6. CPs in an after-print forum: Some aspects

As can be seen in Figure 2, an accepted CPP is a prerequisite for giving a CP. In crash-safety, the CPP has been moulded to the constraints and rhetoric of the privileged scientific genre, the RA. From being a written chronicle or transcription of the conference presentation, published after the event, the CPP, as mentioned earlier, has become one of the main peer-reviewed publication outlets for a large number of crash-safety community members. This development has had implications for the value of the claims made in the CP.

Much of the material presented in the CP seems to serve the purpose of reinforcing and emphasising the claims in the published CPP. Thus to paraphrase a common view of many of the conference attendees: the purpose of a CP should be to highlight the most salient information in the CPP. One of the features used to reinforce claims is graphic representations. At the conferences observed in this study, on average 20 slides were used per 15-minute presentation, more illustrations than were included in the respective CPPs. Some of the slides served as organising devices for the audience, e.g. signposts such as "method", but most served the purpose of reinforcing the claims in the CPP. Some slides were also purely for entertainment, to provide some comic relief.

It is interesting to note that a majority of the conference presenters interviewed said that they used their graphic material as a means of structuring their CPs. A typical manuscript for a presentation, for example, consisted of copies of each slide accompanied by notes. Several speakers informed me that, rather than using a manuscript, they extemporised around their slides, which served as activators around which they built the context, on the hoof, so to speak. Video-films were also be used for the same purposes.

Thus the mix of discourses (formal and informal), and of semiotic systems (visual and aural), allowed by the CP, as opposed to a published paper, could be used by speakers as resources to influence the audience's interpretation of the CPP, as in the following:

> I would now like to show a video of ah some of the cadaver sled tests. OK. First I'm showing a 3-point-belt restraint cadaver sled test. [Pause to let audience watch] I would like you to notice how the shoulder belt is positioned in all these cadaver sled tests. [Pause] This is a 2-point-belt restraint knee-bolster. [Pause] You can see the knee impacting the knee-bolster. [Pause] This is another 2-point-belt knee-bolster test. OK, that's it. (Oral presentation, KU, AAAM/IRCOBI 1994)

While the CPP counterpart of this CP is a comparison between several studies (experiments and data-base analysis), the speaker chose to focus the presentation solely on specific experimental results, namely those that concern cadaver tests[7]. One reason for limiting the content of the presentation is of course time constraints. However, more interesting in this connection is what information speakers choose to highlight in the CP. A reason for the choice made here may be that cadaver tests are far less common than experiments with dummies (constructed human surrogates), and therefore have more news value for the given audience.

Another reason is that the immediate environment in which the actual discourse functions allows the audience to witness the results in the same form the researchers did. In other words, rather than to "virtually witness" the results through the mediation of words, graphic or schematic (re)presentations, as would be the case in the CPP (Shapin 1984), the audience is able to see the same slow-motion video sequence the researchers did. Thus the research results are given more persuasive force in the argument presented in the CP. Concluding the presentation, the speaker can support her claim by referring to what the audience has actually witnessed: "The film analysis of the cadaver sled tests *have shown* that the shoulder belt moves up the lower torso in occupants with 2-

---

[7] Cadaver is the term most commonly used in the field of crash safety.

point-belt restraints [and thus causes more damage]" (CP, KU, AAAM/IRCOBI 1994).

Moreover, the CP gives retrospective persuasive force to one of the concluding claims of the published paper, namely "The chest deformation gages in the Hybrid III dummy are unable to detect the lateral deformation of the lower torso that *was observed in sled tests* with cadavers in two point belt/knee bolster restraints" (AAAM/IRCOBI 1994: 46, my emphasis). The claim in this CP, as in many others, does not seem to be of the prefatory type that Dubois' (1980) corpus suggests, but rather its aim was to strengthen the claim in the published CPP.

This example suggests that oral and written conference genres *together* participate in an ongoing negotiation of meaning between author/speaker and reader/audience. This negotiation comprises both the ideational or content level of the text, as well as the personal identity and relationships established between interlocutors, the interpersonal aspects.

However, to get as far as to reinforce claims, a prospective speaker at a crash-safety conference must obtain legitimacy to perform. Senior members of the crash-safety community admitted that it was not easy for apprentices to gain entry to the crash-safety fora: one of the reasons for this may be that although apprentices may possess enough textual knowledge to make their texts *mean*, they lack the experience and knowledge to provide their texts with the appropriate force to make them *do*, i.e. to elicit the desired effect on the interlocutor. To gain some insight into the norms, ideology and epistemology of the forum, an aspiring candidate can find clues in the neglected conference genre called the Call for Abstracts.

7. Regulatory genres: Call for abstracts

This section describes the regulatory genre in the chain of genres leading up to the publication of the CPP. By *regulatory genre*, I mean genres or sets of genres whose main communicative aim is to define the needs of the conference forum as related to the elicited documents. These genres stipulate the form and content of consecutive texts within a circumscribed system of genres. In terms of type of utterance, they function as directives. "Instructions to Authors" and "Reviewers' Comments" in the conference system are regulatory genres since they prescribe form and content of the submitted papers. If authors fail to take these texts into account, if they fail to understand or interpret the illocutionary force of the generic exchange in the production of their own texts, the chances for the success of their texts are minimised, especially if they are new to the forum and lack have not established a community identity to back them up.

7.1. The Call for Abstracts signals the norms and ideologies of a forum

This genre, also called *Call for Papers* is the first textual link in the CPP genre chain, and in the conference system as a whole. It consists of a standardised text sent out about nine months in advance of the conference event, establishing the topical and temporal framework for the future conference event. The *Call for Abstracts* fulfils three main purposes: it invites, informs and regulates, as can be seen in the following:

> The Stapp Conference Advisory Committee invites information on prospective papers for consideration in the 42 Stapp Car Crash Conference. Papers are desired on biomedical, engineering, and medical trauma aspects of land vehicles crash injury and passenger protection, and correlations between test device performance and human dynamic responses. Paper offers should include:
>
> 1. A digest of 200 to 300 words that
>
>   - states the objectives of the study,
>
>   - outlines the problem the study attempts to solve and the methodology.
>
>   - states explicitly the type of data to be included, and
>
>   - summarizes the conclusions that will be in the paper.
>
> NOTE: The selection of papers is based upon the digest; therefore descriptive information is important.

The surface aim of this document is to act as a formal invitation to community members to submit a proposal for presentation in the upcoming conference event. Like most invitations, the Call for Abstracts informs potential conference contributors about the time and place of the event (not included in the example), the deadlines and criteria that apply should one decide to accept the *call*.

Linked to its informative purpose, is an underlying regulatory function. The Call for Abstracts sets the deadlines, both for authors and reviewers, and indicates the topic boundaries. The excerpt above is typical of the field. The IRCOBI, being European based with a majority of non-native English speakers, also stresses that abstracts, drafts, final manuscript and CP must be in English.

In the chain of utterances that precedes the conference event, the Call for Abstracts takes on different values for different members of the crash-safety community. For the Advisory Committee the document provides criteria for the decision to accept or reject a paper. This is a problem in many conference fora where neither authors nor reviewers are given any guidelines as to what is required of a Conference Abstract, CA, a CPP or CP.

For authors, the Call for Abstracts has different meanings depending on the person's familiarity with the forum. For expert members of the crash-safety community, the Call for Abstract is a familiar genre; the news value in each year's exemplar consists of the deadline dates and the geographical location of the conference. However, for those seeking entry into the field, this document takes on an entirely different force. It signals important ideological and rhetorical conventions. These signals can be very explicit, enforcing rigid constraints on all submitters, as in the case of the AAAM. These constraints can be seen as part of the process of academic professionalisation of the forum and the field.

The AAAM Call for Abstracts has further strengthened its regulatory role by constraining submitters to organise the content of their abstract according to a pre-printed form; (Fig. 4 below is a representation of the form for the 1996 conference). Prompts and typology are used as guidelines for the author. This form reflects the epistemology of the scientific community as a whole and follows the inductive structure of the scientific method, reflected in the organisation of the solicited CA. The template has been developed in response to changing communicative needs of the AAAM society, ensuring that content and form would be appropriate for the given audience.

Berkenkotter & Huckin (1995) argue convincingly that changed communicative needs have gradually reshaped the genre of the RA. To briefly summarise their results: items such as knowledge claims, findings and validation of research – the new information – have successively become foregrounded, whereas contextual details such as background orientation and methodology are being increasingly backgrounded. The actual realisation of these changes differs across disciplines, depending on how homogeneous a frame of reference the discipline has developed. For example in chemistry, physics and some fields of electronics, background information and methodology have been relegated to sections in smaller print at the end of the article[8]. In some fields, sections have been merged giving rise to a mixing of text types, for example *Summary and Introduction*, a new configuration seen in some journals of Optoelectronics (Räisänen 1995). What interests me here is how this match of form to function has generated changes in the Call for Abstracts, and as a result in the elicited CA.

---

[8] These are fairly new features only applying in certain fora. However, for the teaching of academic writing these changes cause problems since it is not just a question of reshuffling the content to fit the new form.

The AAAM prompts in Figure 3 not only force writers to focus on those details most relevant for the intended readers, but also to structure the information under given subheadings. Research on medical abstracts has shown that structured abstracts are more informative (Haynes 1993; McIntosh 1995) and reader-friendly. If space allocation is an indicator of importance, then the results and conclusions are the most significant details for readers in this context (Fig. 3, prompts 6-7). This conforms to our expectations of the most important news value for a research report, but may not be what we would have expected for a promissory conference abstract written almost a year before the actual event. However, as already mentioned, acceptance of a CA in this forum functions primarily as an invitation to submit a paper for peer review, and if the authors have no results by the time they submit their abstracts, they are not likely to have any about three months later at the due date for manuscript submission.

The IRCOBI and STAPP Call for Abstracts similarly require a specific statement of results. CAs that fail to describe the results of experimental research in some detail are generally refused on sight. Yet, although academic- and technical-writing textbooks signal the importance of a statement of results in RA abstracts, they characterise the CA as a "sales-job". As the AAAM form and the analysis of CAs (Räisänen 1999) show, such advice would need to be revised to fit the reality encountered by graduate students and professionals in engineering fields.

The source of the data (Fig. 3, prompt 5) is an important issue in this field, where the data used in crash-safety surveys and experimental studies have probably been collected for entirely different reasons (Evans 1991). For example, police reports are often used as data sources although unreliable and harshly criticised by some members of the community. Therefore, not only is the methodological procedure important for the replication and interpretation of results, but also the type of data used has implications on how the results are interpreted. It is interesting to note here that in the question/answer sessions (see Fig. 1), a large number of questions focused on the choice of data and how this could, or did, bias the interpretations of results.

1.

Request to Present Scientific Paper

(*As stated previously, DO NOT INCLUDE YOUR NAME OR
AFFILIATION ON THIS FORM)

2.

Proposed paper title:

3.

State the research question or hypothesis:

4.

Describe methodology used:

5.

What is the source of the data?

6.

Results:

7.

List the study's conclusion:

8.

What does the paper offer that is new to the field?

9.

Has the material been published previously? If yes, when and to what
extent?

10.

***NOTICE! ABSTRACTS WILL BE REJECTED IF COMPLETE
INFORMATION IS NOT PROVIDED IN RESPONSE TO ALL
QUESTIONS ABOVE. (*USE THIS FORM EXACTLY AS IT IS)
AND ATTACH ADDITIONAL SHEETS AS NECESSARY TO
PROVIDE COMPLETE AND DETAILED ANSWERS.**

Figure 3: 1996 AAAM Call for Abstracts form. Items have been numbered for ease of
reference. Text enclosed in parentheses has been added to the 1998 exemplar.

The weight that the committee will put on the results statements in the CAs is indicated in the following criteria given by the current Executive Director of the AAAM[9] for the rejection of an abstract:

- if the submitter did not provide all the information specifically asked for
- if the research had not yet begun at the time of abstract submission
- if there was no conclusion
- if the research method was judged to be inappropriate or flawed
- if the database as described was inadequate to support the conclusions
- and other such substantive deficiencies in the research.

It is also interesting to note in connection with the Call for Abstracts prompts that authors are asked to explicitly state the news value of their work twice (Fig. 3, prompts 8-9). This highlighting of the news value supports Berkenkotter & Huckin's (1995) conclusions that news value is becoming an increasingly important feature in scientific RAs and may be viewed as a generic feature of these texts. News value is also an effective generic feature for mapping the development of a genre and its power to accommodate social changes.

Another feature which does not tally with the literature on abstracts nor with our general sense of how a text should be structured is that there is no prompt that "functions to situate the reader in terms of a mutual frame of reference" (Nystrand 1989: 81). There is no prompt for background information or objectives of the study. The latter is a rhetorical move that is often considered obligatory in RA abstracts (Swales 1990; Bhatia 1993). Instead authors are required to state either their hypothesis or their research question (Fig. 3, prompt 3), implying that the expert readers will be able to fill in the context. What we can infer from these prompts is that we are dealing with a forum that has established a fairly stable common frame of reference.

It should be noted here that the lack of background information in the AAAM abstracts puts pressure on authors to be as informative as possible in the formulation of their titles, a rhetorical detail which they may not be aware of, but which may influence the readers' decisions to accept or reject their proposals.

In the humanities, Calls for Abstracts generally lack instructions as to what the abstract should contain. On the other hand, constraints as to format, length and thematic scope are common. Berkenkotter & Huckin, in one of the few studies of CAs, quote the following instruction to submitters:

---

[9] Personal communication.

Insofar as possible, the chair will try to include sessions that focus on current topics of interest and on critical issues in the profession. Proposals submitted will be chosen on the basis of their clarity, organisation, and potential interest to people attending the convention. (1995: 97-98)

What the conference chair considers to be current, critical and interesting issues would, however, require insider knowledge on the part of the submitter. The findings of the study revealed that accepted abstracts were those in which submitters had managed to demonstrate alignment with the theme statement of the programme committee and the current concerns of the research community (see also Kaplan *et al.* 1994). Thus here too the Call for Abstracts has a regulatory role, albeit not explicitly.

The AAAM abstract form is more than just a community's response to a communicative need in terms of immediate senders and receivers of messages. It is also a community's means of shaping an epistemology by wielding control over the genres produced in its various fora. The Call for Abstracts template is one method of responding to the social and political exigencies of academia to establish strong enough scientific credentials to compete with other fora in the field.

To summarise, the Call for Abstracts/Papers, and Advice to Authors, acts as a regulatory genre which submitters would do well to take seriously if they wish to gain entry to the conference forum. If the *ethos, pathos* and *logos* of the CAs conform to the established paradigm of the community gatekeepers, they have a better chance of being accepted. On the other hand, conference associations in all academic disciplines would benefit from a revision of their Call for Abstracts. Giving marginalised groups, such as non-native English-speaking groups or non-US based groups, proper guidelines as to the expected form and content-orientation of the CA may improve their chances of breaking their exclusion from many of these fora.

8. Conclusion

The purpose of this paper has been to advocate a more context-sensitive approach to the analysis of conference genres, one that accounts for the socio-cultural influences on the macro-level and the dialogic relationship between conference genres on the micro level.

To demonstrate how conference genres are dialogically and dialectically linked in a predetermined sequence encompassing genre sets and genre chains, I have drawn on Porter's (1992: 107) notion of forum as a "concrete local manifestation" of community practices and linked it to Bazerman's (1994) notion of interactive meaning-making systems of genres. All the genres within a conference system are spatially and temporally constrained by the *ethos* and shared concerns of the particular configuration of the community members that have shaped the forum. Focusing on a particular discipline and forum concretises the notion of forum and system of genres, enabling us to distinguish their distinctive characteristics.

Two main types of conference fora have been identified and characterised: *before-print* and *after-print* fora. This distinction is important for the understanding of the epistemology and norms of a discipline. The conference genres produced in the different situations, despite their common nomenclature, will, due to their different dialogic relationships to each other, have different communicative aims and rhetorical characteristics. In the after-print conference forum, the CPP is the pivotal genre, and the CP serves to reinforce the claims made in the CPP. For this purpose graphic material in the form of slides or video-recordings seem to be efficient tools enabling the audience to view the same evidence the claimants did. There is a need for further research into the multi-modal and interdiscursive nature of academic and professional genres.

This chapter has also shown that performing at conferences requires knowledge of more genres than the conference presentation. In crash safety, writers need to be attuned to the different practices CPP and CP production. Form and domain-content, although similar, are also subtly different. Moreover, regulatory genres such as the Call for Abstracts, for example, need to be paid more attention since they influence the texts they elicit. Knowledge of the social function of these texts – the constraints and possibilities that they signal – is important to gain entry to a conference forum.

Apprentices have usually not acquired sufficient situated knowledge of conference procedures to be able to recognise and use the rhetorical resources that genres offer. Moreover, they may also be handicapped in this respect by their education since genres are generally depicted as stable forms into which specific kinds of content should be fitted. Apprentice writers need to understand the whole process of production and interpretation of their texts to be able to make meaning of the discursive practices in their disciplines.

Furthermore, inexperienced writers trying to gain entry into a conference or journal forum are often unaware of the fact that their primary reader will be the editor and reviewers. These people's job is to scrutinise the text, be it a conference abstract or research paper, from the perspective of the particular norms and ideologies of the particular forum. An apprentice may not realise that the final fate of his/her manuscript will often depend on his/her ability to navigate through the rhetorical turns of a review process. Raising students' awareness of the intertextual relationships between the different texts in the systems of genres in which they commonly operate enables them to identify the local functions and communicative aims of the texts they are producing.

Since conference genres play a prominent role in the professional lives of academics, we need more contrastive research into disciplinary conference practices in order to develop academic-writing and presentation courses that more realistically reflect these disciplinary practices.

References

Bakhtin, M. M. 1986. *Speech Genres and Other Late Essays.* (Ed. C. Emerson & Holquist, trans. V W. McGee). Austin: University of Texas Press.

Bazerman, C. 1994. "System of genres and the enactment of social intention". In A. Freedman & P. Medway (Eds). *Genre and the New Rhetoric.* London: Taylor & Francis, 79–101.

Beder, S. 1997. "Beyond technicalities: Expanding engineering thinking". *Proceedings of the Second International Conference on Teaching Science for Technology at Tertiary Level.* Stockholm, 14-17 June. Stockholm: Royal Institute of Technology. (CD-ROM).

Berkenkotter, C. & T. N. Huckin. 1995. *Genre Knowledge in Disciplinary Communities: Cognition/Culture/Power.* Hillsdale: Lawrence Erlbaum Associates, Publ.

Bhatia, V. K. 1993. *Analysing Genre: Language Use in Professional Settings.* London: Longman.

Bijker, W. E. 1995. *Of Bicycles, Bakelites, and Bulbs: Toward a Theory of Sociotechnical Change.* Cambridge, Massachusetts: The MIT Press.

Crane, D. 1972. *Invisible Colleges: Diffusion of Knowledge in Scientific Communities.* Chicago: Chicago University Press.

Devitt, A. J. 1991. "Intertextuality in tax accounting". In C. Bazerman & J. Paradis (eds). *Textual Dynamics of the Professions.* Wisconsin: The University of Wisconsin Press, 336-357.

Dubois, B. L. 1980. "Genre and structure of biomedical speeches". *Forum Linguisticum,* 5, 2: 140-169.

Engeström, Y. 1993. "Developmental studies of work as a test bench of activity theory: The case of primary care medical practice". In S. Chaiklin & J. Lave (eds). *Understanding Practice: Perspective on Activity and Context.* Cambridge: Cambridge University Press, 64-103.

Evans, L. 1991. *Traffic Safety and the Driver.* New York: Van Nostrand Reinhold.

Garvey, W. D. 1979. *Communication: The Essence of Science.* Oxford: Pergamon Press.

Hagstrom, W. 1965. *The Scientific Community.* New York: Basic Books.

Haynes. R.B. 1993. "More informative abstracts: current status and evaluation". *Journal of Clinical Epidemiology,* 46, 7: 595-597.

Kaplan, R. B., Cantor, S., Hagstrom, C., Kamhi-Stein, L. d., Shiotani, Y. & Zimmerman, C. B. 1994. "On abstract writing". In *Text,* 14: 401-426.

Lave, J., & Wenger, E. 1991. *Situated Learning: Legitimate Peripheral Participation.* Cambridge: Cambridge University Press.

McIntosh, N. 1995. *Structured Abstracts and Information Transfer.* R & D report Report No. 6142. Boston Spa: British Library.

Myers, G. 1996. "Out of the laboratory and down to the bay". *Written Communication,* 13, 1: 5-43.

Nystrand, M. 1989. "A social-interactive model of writing". *Written Communication,* 6, 1: 66-85.

Porter, J. E. 1992. *Audience and Rhetoric: An Archaeological Composition of the Discourse Community.* Englewood Cliffs, New Jersey: Prentice-Hall.

Räisänen, C. 1995. "Academic writing in the technologies". In. B-L. Gunnarsson. & I. Bäcklund (eds). *Writing in Academic Contexts.* TEFA nr. 11. Uppsala: Uppsala Universitet, 84-101.

Räisänen, C. 1999. *The Conference Forum as a System of Genres: A Sociocultural Study of Academic Conference Practices in Automotive Engineering.* Gothenburg: Acta Universitatis Gothoburgensis.

Ravetz, J. R. 1996. *Scientific Knowledge and its Social Problems.* New Brunswick, USA & London: Transaction Publishers.

Rowley-Jolivet. This volume. "Science in the making: Scientific conference presentations and the construction of facts".

Shapin, S. 1984. Pump and circumstance: Robert Boyle's literary technology. *Social Studies of Science,* 14, 4: 481-520.

Swales, J. 1984. "Research into the structure of introductions to journal articles and its application to the teaching of academic writing". In R. Williams, J. Swales & J. Kirkman (eds). *Common Ground: Shared Interests in ESP and Communication Studies .* Oxford: The British Council and Pergamon Press, 77-86.

Swales, J. 1990. *Genre Analysis: English in Academic and Research Settings.* Cambridge University Press.

Swales, J. 1993. "Genre and Engagement". *Revue Belge de Philologie et d'Histoire,* 71: 687-698.

Van Nostrand, A. D. 1997. *Fundable Knowledge: The Marketing of Defense Technology.* Mahwah, New Jersey: Lawrence Erlbaum Associates.

Ventola, E. 1999. "Semiotic spanning at conferences: cohesion and coherence in and across conference papers and their discussions". In W. Bublitz, U. Lenk & E. Ventola (eds). *Coherence in Spoken and Written Discourse.* Amsterdam/Philadelphia: John Benjamin, 101-123.

Ventola, E. This volume. "Why and what kind of focus on conference presentations?"

SCIENCE IN THE MAKING: SCIENTIFIC CONFERENCE PRESENTATIONS AND THE CONSTRUCTION OF FACTS

Elizabeth Rowley-Jolivet

Université of Orléans, Orléans, France

Abstract – This chapter examines scientific conference presentations for the light they throw on the construction of knowledge claims. Previous research into this question has been based either on ethnographic studies of laboratory life or on the rhetoric of the research article and has not addressed the specific role played by the conference presentation genre in the process of knowledge construction. Based on a corpus of 90 research presentations from three fields (geology, medicine, and physics), the present study first positions conference presentation claims in the life of a fact and then focuses on the picture of scientific activity that emerges from conference presentations. The analysis shows that the genre is positioned at an early stage in the claim-making process, and that many traces of the contextual contingencies of research subsist in conference presentations, though with certain field-specific differences. It is argued that these results not only underline how highly conventionalised the rhetoric of the research article is, but also demonstrate that the construction of knowledge claims is a multi-staged process, in which various discourse genres have different, complementary roles to play: in this process, the conference presentation genre occupies a key position in the establishment of scientific facts by bridging the gap between the seemingly dichotomous worlds of laboratory life and refereed publication.

1. Constructivist studies of science: Bread and green apples?

Since the 1970s the sociology of science has considerably expanded its field of enquiry, moving from a Mertonian focus on the institutions of science (Merton 1973) to investigations into the contexts in which research is carried out and knowledge production is embedded (Sismondo 1993; Bazerman 1990). In doing so, it has addressed epistemological concerns and has come to occupy much of the territory, formerly the province of the history and philosophy of science. This shift of emphasis towards sociological analyses of the construction of scientific knowledge has not only opened up new directions for the sociology of science as a discipline, but has also painted a very different picture of knowledge production from that of neo-positivism: in the place of objective logic and ahistorical validity, scientific concepts are portrayed as being developed within specific, or local, socio-cognitive frameworks. Detailed ethnographic fieldwork on the realities of laboratory life (Knorr-Cetina 1981; Latour 1987; Latour & Woolgar 1986; Law 1985; Lynch 1984) have stressed the 'indexicality' of scientific research, a concept which has far-reaching consequences for it implies that contextual factors influence not only the process of knowledge production but also the cognitive content itself, of science.

These ethnographic investigations of laboratory life, when confronted with analyses of scientific research articles, have drawn two divergent, even irreconcilable, pictures of scientific activity and of the construction of scientific facts, with laboratory work characterised by an opportunistic logic and contextual contingencies, and the published article by an empirical stance unsullied by situational factors (Garfinkel *et al.* 1981; Knorr-Cetina 1981). Knorr-Cetina, after comparing what actually took place in the lab with the published version in the article, concluded in a total lack of correspondence between the two: events underwent a process of transformation, recontextualisation and conversion in their translation from lab work to the scientific paper. The inability to reconcile these two divergent versions of science led Gilbert & Mulkay (1984) to posit the existence of two dichotomous repertoires in scientists' discourse, the 'empiricist' and 'contingent' repertoires, and the lack of fit between reality and discourse has led to the research article being seen as a "phony story" (Berkenkotter & Huckin 1995: 54). Indeed, the Nobel laureate Peter Medawar answered his own question "Is the scientific paper a fraud?" in the affirmative, and concluded that the journal article does not reflect the human reality of the research process but is a rhetorical machine (Medawar 1990). These divergences have fuelled the debate about epistemological relativism, leading in extreme cases to "an extravagant ultra-relativism which relegates science to the status of mere belief" (Lévy-Leblond 1998: 37)[1], and its discourse to the rank of empty rhetoric, a pure production of ideology. Seen in this light, the contingency of scientific facts excludes the possibility of any correspondence between reality and science's discourse about reality. As Sokal in his spoof of such studies wrote, "... physical 'reality'... is at bottom a social and linguistic construct; ... scientific 'knowledge', far from being objective, reflects and encodes the dominant ideologies and power relations of the culture that produced it" (Sokal 1996: 217-218).

The question arises, however, as to whether these apparently irreconcilable divergences are not themselves to a large extent an artefact of the highly contrasted data used: by comparing on the one hand, the everyday, material activity in the laboratory or the private, informal conversations of scientists, with, on the other, the polished, public and written rhetoric of the research article, it may be, in the words of one of the physics speakers in our data that "... we're not comparing apples to pears but we're comparing maybe bread and green

---

[1] Translations by the author.

apples"[2]. If this is the case, it is hardly surprising that few points of convergence can be found between the context of production of scientific knowledge and the public face of its communication. A possible way out of this impasse, however, is to investigate how scientific activity and the construction of knowledge claims are presented in scientific conference papers, for as Dubois (1980: 143), in her pioneering work on biomedical presentations noted, this genre offers an intermediate stage between laboratory life and refereed publication:

> ... one sees the imperfect world of the laboratory reflected not only in the content of some of the speeches, but as well in their organisation (...) One glimpses research as it is actually conducted, before it is sanitized to present a picture of straightline progress toward public knowledge.

The conference presentation has, so to speak, a foot in both worlds: closely connected to laboratory life both by the oral nature of its discourse and by the fact that it is often the first public appearance of the research carried out there, a conference presentation is nevertheless a structured discourse genre delivered in a public forum and therefore also a close cousin of the research article in many respects. This particular position of conference presentations, situated midway between the informal, often highly speculative discussions that take place in the lab prior to any communication of results, and the rhetorically conventionalised, more assertive claims put forward in the research article, would therefore seem to be an ideal locus from which to reassess constructivist interpretations of the construction of scientific facts.

The present study therefore examines scientific conference presentations for the light they throw on the construction of knowledge claims, investigating firstly what specific role the conference presentation genre plays in the process of knowledge construction. It then focuses on the picture of scientific activity that emerges from conference presentations and inquires whether the socially contingent, indexical account given by constructivists is the whole story or not. Such accounts have stressed the following features, all of which are masked or simply omitted from the research article: the contextual contingencies and practical constraints impinging on research, the opportunistic or intuitive decision-making processes of the researchers, and the expression of personal rivalries and dissensus. These features are therefore given particular attention in this study.

---

[2] See Section 2 below for a description of the data used in the present study. The remark quoted here was made by the speaker when comparing very different designs for capacitors (paper P17).

2. The data

The data collected for this analysis comprise video recordings of 90 short (15-20 minute) presentations delivered at five international conferences which took place in 1993-94 in France. The language of communication was exclusively English. Three scientific fields were selected, covering a wide spectrum of disciplines in order not only to enable a genre-based study to be carried out but also to investigate areas of field-specific differences: one life science (medicine), and two hard sciences, one of which a historical science (geology) and the other an 'experimental-predictive' science (physics), to adopt Gould's distinction (Gould 1989). The specialities represented are: in geology, mainly mining geology with a few papers from sedimentary geology; in medicine, oncology, a field which enlists various sub-fields – radiotherapy, surgery, chemotherapy, molecular genetics ... – in its battle against cancer; in physics, electromagnetic environments. There is thus a bias towards the applied end of the pure-applied spectrum. In each field, 30 presentations were transcribed, equally distributed between native English speakers (15 per field) and non-native speakers (15 per field)[3]. A smaller number of papers (18 articles) were collected from the book of proceedings of the physics conference, in order to compare the spoken presentations and written papers with a set of parallel texts (same authors, topic and context).

3. The position of conference presentations in the life of a fact

The very fact that research communities have developed the distinct discourse genre of the conference presentation as one of their modes for formulating and communicating knowledge indicates that this genre does indeed have a specific role to play. In Bazerman's words (1988: 62): "A genre is a socially recognized, repeated strategy for achieving similar goals in situations socially perceived as being similar ... A genre is a social construct that regularizes communication, interaction, and relations". But as Fairclough (1992: 126) points out, genres should be seen and positioned in relation to one another, for "... a society, or a particular institution or domain within it, has a particular configuration of genres in particular relationships to each other, constituting a system". Conference presentations have not, to our knowledge, been precisely situated in relation to other forms of research discourse nor has their specific contribution to knowledge production been explicitly defined. This section addresses the issue of the role of conference presentations in the construction of facts.

---

[3] Due to technical constraints, the geology corpus comprises only 10 native speakers' (NS) presentations, and 20 non-native speakers' (NNS) presentations.

3.1. Novelty: "Your hot-off-the-press data"

The data provide abundant evidence that conference presentations are often the first public appearance, outside the laboratory, of much of the research that goes on inside it. This appears first of all in the stress placed on the novelty of the research.

An awareness of novelty is important in academic disciplines (Berkenkotter & Huckin 1995; Bazerman 1988): "Fully invested disciplinary actors are (...) aware of the need to be at the cutting edge, to push for novelty and originality" (Berkenkotter & Huckin 1995: 25). The role of conferences in this respect is vital, as they allow very recent results to be presented, whereas the journal publication process can take several months, or even years. Conference presentations provide a fast track to information on the latest developments in the field, both in terms of hard data and trends or research areas which are opening up. The 'news value' of much of the information circulating at a conference is high, as illustrated by the following remarks:

(11) I don't think that you'll find anything more up to date than some of these data that I'd like to show you now. (M10-NS)[4]

(12) I think it's a very new field of action and we, we need more, more series and we need more evaluation of this but I think it's a new start. (Session chair's comment on the topic of M23-NNS)

The latest results are eagerly awaited by conference participants and several references are made to information circulating in preprint:

(13) Q: Would you say there is agreement with Fisher and Price?
      Speaker: Yes.
      Q: With which data?
      Speaker: They are not published, I think, but we have the results. (G29-NNS)

In physics several presentations stress the novelty of the research in the title itself: "*A novel scaling of the gyrotron/CARM equations of evolution*" (P12); "*Development and characterization of new peaking capacitor arms*" (P17). This aspect of keeping up with the research front is probably even more important in smaller, specialist meetings than in the medium-to-large international conferences studied here, as the opportunities that the former offer for insider exchange of information is much greater: as one of our specialist informants, an

---

[4] The 90 spoken presentations are referred to as follows: a letter indicating the field (G for geology, M for medicine, P for physics), plus the number of the presentations (from 1 to 30), followed by NS (for native English speakers) or NNS (for non-native speakers). The proceedings papers in physics are referred to by PROC, the number of the paper, followed by NS or NNS.

Emeritus professor in medicine, remarked: "For me, the value of a conference has always varied in inverse proportion to its size!".

3.2. Preliminary results: "This is just a beginning work"

The position occupied by conference presentations – immediately downstream from laboratory activity – means that much of the research presented at conferences is at an early stage of development. This is evidenced by the numerous comments made by speakers as to the preliminary, unfinished and ongoing nature of the research. Indeed, a major role of the conference presentation genre, compared to other discourse genres of scientific research such as the journal article, the review article, edited collections of articles, etc., is to provide researchers with the opportunity to present early results of work in progress that are either too slight, exploratory or theoretically underdeveloped to be acceptable for journal publication. Many presentations mention the incomplete or very recent nature of the research; a few typical excerpts are reproduced in (14) – (17) to illustrate this feature.

(14) This is just a beginning work. (G17-NNS)

(15) I suppose this is the key diagram in this talk, the full implications of which we probably haven't fully worked through ... we still need to model but if you like these are our empirical results. (G6-NS)

(16) What I would like to present now is preliminary results of a small mesozoic alkaline plutonic body within Morocco ... So that as a preliminary conclusion, we think that ... (G17-NNS, *Introduction + Conclusion*)

(17) We're a long way from Star Trek, there's no doubt about it in this! We're only, this is infinitesimal in terms of bringing the technology up to anything very practical ...we are very, very, at the beginning of this process I think. Any suggestions would certainly be accepted with open arms. (P8-NS, *Question time*)

3.3. Proto-Claims

What do these two features – the novelty and preliminary nature of the research presented at conferences – tell us about the role of conference presentations in the overall process of constructing scientific knowledge? A key metaphor in studies of the construction of scientific facts is the biological metaphor of the 'life' of a fact. The very title of Fleck's seminal work – *Genesis and Development of a Scientific Fact* ([1935] 1979) – draws on the evolutionary parallel between facts and organisms: both are born, mature and spread, and eventually die. Fleck shows the birth of the 'fact' in the inner core of the esoteric circle of specialist researchers, and its centrifugal spread, through progressively less specialised discourse genres – journals, handbooks for specialists (vademecum), textbooks and finally the popular press – out towards the peripheral exoteric circle[5]. This basic concept of the life of a fact has been subsequently taken up and reasserted by various analysts, who have stressed the agonistic struggle-for-life of knowledge claims in the competitive world of modern science (Bazerman 1988; Latour 1987; Latour & Woolgar 1986). Survival of the original research claim is ensured only by its continued existence in the literature of the field. In Latour's (1987: 38) words: "To survive or to be turned into a fact, a statement needs the next generation of papers (...) Metaphorically speaking, statements (...) are much like genes that cannot survive if they do not manage to pass themselves on to later bodies".

Some refinements to Fleck's original scheme have been introduced: an important stage, prior to that of journal publication, and which impacts on the level of claim that is made, is the negotiation of the claim between the author(s) and the reviewers/editors in their role of gatekeepers (Myers 1990; Berkenkotter & Huckin 1995; Birch-Bécaas 1997); the specific role of review articles in (re)defining the field has been brought out (Myers 1991); and while a study by Winstanley in the 1970s, quoted by Myers (1992) found that the original claim about the structure of DNA did indeed follow the pattern of spread posited by Fleck, it is now increasingly the case in the faster-moving research fields that newsworthy discoveries "... are rushed, still steaming hot, directly from the laboratory to the popular press" (Lévy-Leblond 1996: 20; see also Berkenkotter & Huckin 1995) – although this promotional tactic, as several recent media 'scoops' have shown, does not guarantee that the claim will be accepted as a 'fact' by the scientific community.

Where does the spoken research genre of the conference presentation fit into this picture? It can be seen that none of the above approaches to the construction of scientific facts take conference presentations into consideration, despite the important functions that are fulfilled by conferences (Rowley-Jolivet 1999). While obviously citation analysis, which forms the basis of detailed studies on the life-cycle of facts, cannot be applied to oral conference presentations, since no traces of the speaker's original 'text' remain, this research genre clearly has a specific role to play in the construction and dissemination of scientific knowledge. Given the novelty and preliminary nature of the research presented

---

[5] Although the term of constructivism was to be widely used only many years later, Fleck (1979: 35) heralds its basic premise by the dynamic tension he sets up between active and passive constraints on knowledge making, in which the active elements are the stylized, socially constructed practices of thought collectives (such as the scientific community) which condition or direct what is 'perceivable' at a given historical moment – for "In science, just as in art or life, only that which is true to culture is true to nature" – while passive constraints are the empirical data which the 'directed perception' of scientific enquiry seeks to account for.

at conferences, indicative of their close relationship with laboratories, conference presentations can be situated in the life of a fact midway between oral laboratory discussions and different written forms of research (see Table 1).

	LONG LIFE[6]	SHORT LIFE
	genesis	genesis
1	laboratory discussions	laboratory discussions
2	**conference presentation**	**conference presentation**
3	proceedings paper	
4	negotiation author/reviewers	
5	journal publication	
6	citation in other articles	
7	citation in review article	
8	books for specialists	
9	lectures & student textbooks	
10	schoolbooks	
11	popular press	

Table 1: Conference presentations in the life of a fact.

Some conference presentations have a very short life: if no proceedings are produced, if the presentation is not selected for inclusion in the book of proceedings, or if the author does not publish the material elsewhere, then the presentation will in all likelihood remain a one-off event. Though it may have a passing impact on the audience present, any claims put forward in it can be said to die as they are unable to 'pass their genes on to other bodies'. If published in the proceedings, however, it can hope to be cited and enjoy a longer life, eventually becoming an accepted fact (cf. the notion of 'semiotic spanning' in Ventola (1999 and this volume). The vulnerability of the conference presentation claim is evident not only in its potentially short life-span, but also in the radical, sometimes aggressive questioning to which it may be submitted in the discussion phase following the presentation, as participants engage in hard bargaining with the speaker to negotiate a consensus on the level of claim that can be made (Shalom 1993; Rowley-Jolivet 1998; Webber this volume). Moreover, as we have seen, much of the research presented in scientific conference papers is still at a preliminary, 'immature' stage of development: the work is unfinished, still ongoing, and therefore the claim that can legitimately be made is necessarily tentative. To qualify the type of claim put forward in

---

[6] This is an idealised or simplified representation and does not imply a continuous timeline: some work goes into hibernation, so to speak, and is only taken up by the literature long after its original publication (examples are Bakhtin, Mendel, and Fleck himself).

conference papers, halfway between its embryonic stage in lab talk and its mature status in the research article, it is proposed to assign their knowledge claims the status of **proto-claim**. Clearly, this is a *generic* perspective, which attempts to capture the specific position of conference claims in the life of facts, and should not be taken as a valid description of all conference presentation claims. It does, however, fill a gap in our picture of the construction of scientific knowledge by defining an intermediate stage between laboratory life and the conventionalised rhetoric of the research article, and helps to explain various aspects of the picture of scientific activity that one gets from conference presentations, examined in the next section.

4. The contextual contingencies of research: "We were really getting killed by corona losses"

The close connection between laboratory life and conference presentations is evident not only in the preliminary stage of research presented in the latter, but also in the picture they give of scientific activity itself. Studies of laboratory life by sociologists and philosophers of science have stressed the numerous **contextual contingencies** which impinge on research, showing it to be driven not exclusively by abstract reasoning and theory, but also to be situated in time and place, subject to practical constraints and chance events. The salient features examined here, and which we confront with the picture of scientific activity found in conference presentations, are as follows: the *material* reality of scientific activity, in particular experimental expertise or practical know-how and the importance of observation as compared to theory (4.1.); *mental* activity, or the scientists' decision-making processes (4.2.); *interpersonal* relations, or 'bashing'[7] of other researchers (4.3.). If conference presentations do indeed, as it is argued here, bridge the gap between the laboratory and the research article, then one should find traces of these features of laboratory life, expunged in the RA, to be present in conference presentations.

4.1. Experimental expertise

Both Galison (1987, 1997) and Hacking (1983) suggest that we attend more seriously to the role of experiment in science, for not only do some experiments prepare the ground for theoretical breakthroughs – "Some great theories spring from pre-theoretical experiment" (Hacking 1983: 159) – but also

---

[7] The term is borrowed from Ventola's (1998) study of interpersonal choices in the discourse of linguists, where it is defined as a linguistic strategy of confrontation and opposed to the consensus strategy of Alignment.

"Experimentation has a life of its own" (ibid. 150): its goals, methods, successes, requisite skills and constraints are all different from those of theory, but equally essential to the advancement of science. Experimental expertise is therefore necessary because experiments are rarely straightforward – they do indeed 'have a life of their own'! The researcher has to contend with a variety of problems: the natural phenomena defy analysis, equipment is unreliable, certain batches of products may be sub-standard, materials break or induce unwanted and unforeseen side-effects, technical adjustments have to be made to the set-up in order to get it to run smoothly, theory is often but a poor guide as to what to do and to expect ... the list seems endless. Yet little or no mention is made of all these hurdles in the published article: as Galison (1987: 4) remarks, "significant features of the experimental conditions and procedures are omitted from the final articles". Indeed, the experimental or methodology sections in papers are increasingly downplayed, both in space and prominence (Berkenkotter & Huckin 1995: 37-8). In conference presentations, however, the problems and challenges posed by real-world experiments are frankly admitted, and the practical solutions that are found – what Knorr-Cetina (1981), following Jacob (1977) calls 'tinkering' – are discussed, as the quotations (18) – (22) illustrate[8].

i) Unexpected problems and constraints arise: some cannot be solved, while others result in modifications of the original experimental design.

(18)   A separation, a mechanical separation of the phosphates **resulted impossible**, so **we had to** go to a chemical separation. (G18-NNS)

(19)   It can be **quite fiendishly difficult** to get one's foot on the horizon. (G6-NS)

(20)   It's highly absorbent so **it is very difficult** to get a good analysis and it is cavernous and porous (...) Chris Stanley **tried very hard** to analyse for oxygen but he **didn't get** a good picture. (G24-NNS)

Conference Presentation	Proceedings Paper
(21) With antenna in air we have the diamond data points where **we were really getting killed** by corona losses (...) I'll call your attention to this little gas bag at the feed section. Actually **this turned out to be** too small, we **had to** put a gas bag all the way up to about this area to protect the feed section which has very high electric fields from corona losses. (P2-NS)	When very high voltage is applied to the antenna, losses to corona loading can be surprisingly severe. ... One means of reducing corona losses is to enclose the high field portions of the antenna in an insulating gas. (PROC2-NS)

---

[8]   Where available, the passage in the proceedings paper corresponding to the extract from the conference presentation is given, to highlight the difference between the spoken and written papers (in physics only).

Conference Presentation	Proceedings Paper
(22) At first we had measured this curve here, and **we were confused as to why** our peak measured power was decreasing as a function of the input beam current. Well, **it turns out that we realised** that we were having an air breakdown at the outside of the horn antenna and if you were to put an SF6 gas bag around the horn antenna, you suppress the air breakdown and you have this increase in power. (P14-NS)	At beam currents above 4kA air breakdown near the output window was observed. In order to suppress the air breakdown, a gas bag filled with SF6 was placed in front of the horn antenna. The amplitude and pulse duration from the crystal diode detector were observed to increase when the gas bag was used. (PROC14-NS)

The researchers have to submit, willy-nilly, to considerable constraints, as indicated by the structures printed in bold type above: *we had to ...*, the passive (*we were getting killed by ...*), and expressions of impossibility (*resulted impossible, fiendishly difficult*). They appear on occasion to be at a loss as they struggle to overcome these setbacks (*we were confused ...*) and are often forced to abandon their original line of investigation when they come up against experimental problems. It is also interesting to note the frequent occurrence of the verb "*it turned out that ...*", indicative of the serendipitous nature of much scientific discovery in the lab. A comparison between the oral and written versions of P14 above shows a revealing omission in the Proceedings paper: the researchers initial 'confusion' as to why the peak measured power decreased – their inability, in other words, to explain the experimental result – is openly admitted in the conference presentation but is not mentioned in the Proceedings, where the explanation for this phenomenon ('air breakdown') is presented as an unproblematical, self-evident 'observation'.

ii) Tinkering: the experimenter needs to be practically-minded and to adopt a hands-on approach to the problems. Again, these practical details are omitted in the written paper.

Conference Presentation	Proceedings Paper
(23) **I had to** build some small and fast Faraday cups to measure the emission off of the surface of these cathodes ... and **I fashioned my own Faraday cup** this way. **It turns out** that it has a frequency of at least 2 ½ Ghz ... along the wall of the diode there is less electron flow so **I had to build a bigger Faraday cup,** and I again built a machine, a little pin connected to fit inside. (P13-NS)	Local measurements of electron flux are made across the cathode surface with an array of Faraday cups that are fabricated from female SMA connectors. These small Faraday cups enable measurements of fast current-density variation ... .(PROC13-NS)

iii) Materials: the choice of material can make or break an experiment:

(24) ... so what we're saying here is that one must look at the materials. You can do some nasty things to your satellite [if the wrong materials are chosen] ... Surface materials are important – we covered one with copper and found no more interactions, no more arcing. (P8-NS)

(25) Well of course experimentalists can't behave like God [*unlike physicists doing computer simulations*] and say 'Let there be emissions on the anode', but they can do something which is closely equivalent, they can change the material in their experiment. (P11-NS)

iv) Theory may provide only general guidelines as to what to expect, or may even be misleading:

(26) The propagation equations are well understood [*=theory*]. There's some limits on what we need to do and how the parameters are to be adjusted but that comes with the real world experimentation. (P8-NS)

(27) We find in practice that this doesn't seem to present too much of a problem for some reason, I don't know why but if you terminate the line with a resistive load which is slightly more than the characteristic impedance of the line in the unstressed state then the problem with reflections is a lot less than you would expect from the theory – I don't know why that is. (P4-NS)

v) Being observant: Hacking has interesting remarks to make on the importance of observation, in the sense of "being observant", in the experimental process:

The good experimenter is often the observant one who sees the instructive quirks or unexpected outcomes of this or that bit of the equipment. You will not get the apparatus working unless you are observant. Sometimes persistent attention to an oddity that would have been dismissed by a lesser experimenter is precisely what leads to new knowledge (Hacking 1983: 167).

In the data studied here, it is in geology that the need to be observant appears the most clearly. All the visual aspects of the natural phenomena are closely observed, whether it be shape, size, orientation, colour, or texture, as they provide valuable information in this discipline. Observation can lead to unexpected or surprising findings but one must always be on one's guard to distinguish instrumental artefacts from physical phenomena.

(28) OK, well, **what we expected to find** from the results of the traverses across the quarry were sulphide and PGE band dunites followed by chromitites followed by sulphide-bearing PGE-enriched dunites. And **the first surprise was** that sulphides occur throughout each of the boreholes. (G1-NS)

(29) **A very strange animal.** This is generally palladium oxide but **under the probe my attention was drawn** to some peak. This was serium, caesium. (G24-NNS)

(30) and **when we were looking** at these we also discovered this particular mineral here. I was labouring up the peaks [i.e. examining the peaks on a chromatogram] and there was one here and **it turned out to be** a carbon peak. Now the samples are carbon-coated but the carbon coating peak is a very small one – you can see it here and here – and so there is a platinum-oxygen-carbon mineral which just might be a platinum carbonate, and **that's sort of unusual.** (G2-NS)

vi) Drudgery: as the verb choice of the previously quoted speaker shows (*I was labouring up the peaks*, G2, Example 20) another aspect of the somewhat unidealised picture of experimental research which emerges from conference presentations concerns the frequently repetitive and mundane nature of scientists' daily activities. Boring routine tasks, hard physical labour during fieldwork, and the need for innumerable counts and measurements, form a less inspiring but very real side to scientific research which is judged unworthy of mention in the published article but which is freely admitted by conference speakers.

(31) It's a drudgery for the radiotherapist because we must count about between 40 and 70 slices in view of measuring the volume of critical organs. (M26 -NNS)

(32) In order to find the drill targets, especially in the areas of no exposure, we did traverses, sampling the rock-soil interface using a pionjar, which is a hand-held drill which cored down to the base of the soil and collected the sample, and here you can see it's actually very hard work. (G2-NS)

4.2. Decision-making processes

As the preceding section has made clear, many decisions are forced upon the researchers by the constraints they encounter or are induced by unexpected observations. This type of decision is not related in the research article, where "scientists typically omit to describe the difficulties which were overcome and the wrong turns they took" (Gilbert 1976: 285). The impression of scientific activity given by the article is that "what *has been done* is all that *could be done*" (Knorr-Cetina 1981: 42, her italics), in other words, that the decision-making process obeys an implacable logic, governed by high-level theoretical considerations, when in fact, Knorr-Cetina argues, many of the decisions made in the lab are opportunistic. Yet again, the close link between the laboratory and conference presentations surfaces in the image which the latter convey of decision-making. One finds not abstract rationality but a complex, rather messier – and no doubt truer-to-life – mixture of pragmatic considerations, hunches, opportunism, and cultural factors, alongside solid theory and logic. The following excerpts illustrate the complexity and frequently opportunistic nature of decisions.

i) The choice of research subject itself may on occasion be contingent:

Conference Presentation	Proceedings Paper
(33) As **I was playing with** the different cathodes, I found it's sometimes very difficult to turn on with just 100kV a nice beam, so I **launched off into a little study** of the variety of cathodes that are available for such low-voltage systems. (P13-NS)	An experiment is under way to study the usefulness of several cathode materials as field-emission cathodes for low voltage ($\leq$100kV), repetitive (<1kHz) electron accelerators. (PROC13-NS)

(34)　We were looking at mutations of p53 and of K-ras, looking for prognostic implications and we used this as an opportunity to look at a different question, as **sort of a piggyback project** on the prognostic implication. (M1-NS)

ii) Financial constraints can have an impact: access to expensive equipment is limited, and cost-effectiveness is an element in decisions which conference speakers frankly admit:

(35)　The numbers are a bit truncated and it was simply a function of the budgetary con-straints, we were allowed to do so many MS [mass spectrometry] determinations and we obviously wanted to spread that budget to the areas which were really important. (G6-NS)

(36) To reduce the schedule, that is to say the cost of the experimentation, we limited the number of measurements and we combined data processing. (P29-NNS)

iii) Culture-specific factors can condition the approach that is chosen:

(37) I should say that the metasomatic hypothesis still remains popular in our country at least [i.e. in Russia]. (G14-NNS)

(38) It's very strange, *we* [i.e. French surgeons] are all in favour of tumorectomy, perhaps too limited just to the tumour and we may now be moving towards quadrantectomy, while *you* [i.e. Italian surgeons] started doing quadrantectomy and you'd now like to reduce it to tumorectomy. It's amusing to see how ideas evolve depending on one's habits. (M28, Question Time, our translation)

iv) In certain cases, the important thing, as Knorr-Cetina (1981) noted about laboratory work, is simply that "it works". When one finds a method that works, other possibilities – avenues of research, methods ... – are simply dropped:

(39) We have linked up with the oil generation kinetics to this type of maceral or whatever it is, I don't know what it is, I called it vitrinite, **but anyway, the point is that it works**. (G27-NNS)

(40) Now the gyrotron and megatron, the problem with both of them is that they're too successful, they, they work too easily. **The problem is, when you have a device that works like that is you don't necessarily do too much theory** in understanding how to make it work well and understanding the physics of it. (P12-NS)

(41) [*in answer to a question as to why he decided on that particular method*] This one turned out to be so perfect for this application that we just discarded all the other techniques. (P8-NS)

v) The pragmatic nature of some decisions comes out in the following remarks:

(42) This kind of work is very difficult to get accurate numbers out there (...) so **we're basically stuck** with our, with the glycolated values I show you here. (G9-NS)

(43) One can improve this approach by [using a more sophisticated method] but **it turns out this approach is not, for our problem, is not bad at all**. (P22-NNS)

(44) [*in answer to an objection that his explanation seems a bit paradoxical*] Yes, but I, I pre-cise that it's not the good, it's, **we used only as descriptive**, but we must change later the cumulus stage, perhaps by accumulation process. (G20-NNS)

(45) There's been no specific protocol. It's just been **by gosh and by golly** a little bit. (M6-NS)

As the above quotation from G9 (Example 32) makes clear, researchers sometimes have to make do with less-than-ideal data (*we're stuck with ...*) or need to resort to a heuristic approach (G20, Example 34: *we used only as descriptive*) in order to continue with their research.

One final point concerning the manner in which decisions are presented in conference presentations is the language in which they are couched. The overwhelmingly dominant form is the grammatically congruent one of sensor + mental process verb in the active (*we decided ..., we chose ...*) rather than the impersonal constructions and passives of the research article. The decision process is presented as a chronological narrative, as a puzzle-solving activity, often beset by failures along the road (see Thompson, this volume, for the role of narratives in conference presentations, in particular their role in relating failures).

(46)   ... so given those kinds of thoughts [i.e. how to minimize jamming and damage to satel-
       lites from RF energy], we were thinking, well maybe we could put a plasma together
       that would protect us against RF. ... So what we decided to do was to try to generate a
       glow-discharge plasma ... So what we did was build a small – and I mean this is really
       small – an 8-cm diameter satellite, 10 cm in length and we began to attempt to generate
       our plasma. So what we did initially was to generate a plasma by use of a hollow cath-
       ode source of electrons. That proves to be unacceptable in this case because one of the
       critical issues is symmetry and we were having difficulty in generating a symmetric
       plasma ... So what we tried [was] a planar magnetron concept ... (P8-NS)

As this extract shows, the authorial presence is strong in conference presentations (see Vassileva, this volume, for a detailed analysis of the *I-we-you* perspectives in conference presentations). This is but one among many indicators of the human element, a characteristic feature of the contingent repertoire of laboratory interaction and discourse, and which surfaces in conference presentations. For a brief illustration of this feature, we will focus on the expression of criticism of other researchers by conference speakers. The larger issue of criticism of the speaker him/herself by members of the audience during question time is also discussed in Webber (this volume) and Rowley-Jolivet (1998).

4.3. 'Bashing' other researchers

In the research article, "direct criticism is almost inadmissible" (Myers 1989: 30), and a variety of politeness strategies have been developed by scientific rhetoric in order to avoid face-threatening acts or FTAs (Brown & Levinson

1987)[9]. Outside the polite confines of the research article, in the informal atmosphere of the lab, however, as Gilbert & Mulkay (1984) have shown, there is no such ban on *ad hominem* attacks. It therefore seemed interesting to investigate whether, on this point also, the tone of conference presentations resembles that of 'shop talk', with which they have in common the oral nature of the discourse, and whether one finds manifestations of confrontation in conference discourse.

The answer to the question seems to be ... yes and no. While some examples of direct criticism are found in conference presentations, it is far from being the general rule. This can probably be explained by the simultaneous operation of two opposing contextual factors. On the one hand, because the discourse is produced in real time, it is often difficult or even impossible for the speaker to hedge his statements as carefully as s/he would do when writing; moreover, as the conference presentation is ephemeral and cannot be cited, speakers tend to express themselves more openly and frankly than they would do in writing. On the other hand, however, the conference presentation, unlike the privacy of lab discussions, is delivered in public; in addition, the presence of a live audience which can fight back in the discussion phase, asking questions and criticising, enjoins prudence on the speaker. The attitude adopted by the speaker in the conference context appears, from the data at our disposal, to be governed largely by the personality of the speaker him/herself: some revel in the opportunity to be more outspoken than the conventions of the article permit, while others – the majority – remain more reserved[10].

Criticism, when voiced, can concern either named individuals, a whole sub-field, or the quality of published research in general.

(47) Now **this particular study here with a 40% ulcer rate** [i.e. an abnormally high rate] **was done by Dr. X** when he was at [name of hospital], (...) and consequently you can see there's a very high ulcer rate. (...) Now then came a few studies that reported negative results and **I'm going to demonstrate to you how you can do studies and put them in the literature, they get published and yet they're bad studies. This is one of them. This is from** [name of institution]. (...) **This is the section that was included in the methods section that nobody reads** ... 47% [of patients] were not adequately treated and yet the conclusion of this study was, this type of treatment doesn't work. (M13-NS)

---

[9] As Montgomery (1996: 15) points out, insiders – the readers in the esoteric circle – have no difficulty in decoding these conventional strategies: "Those on the inside of such debates know the code: a few calm words can connote paragraphs of near-invective. But the public surface, the professional face of science, never ruffles ...".

[10] Cultural factors also impact on the degree of politeness or aggressiveness adopted both by speakers and members of the audience. According to our specialist informants in physics, conferences in their field can be placed along a cline from a high to a low degree of aggressiveness and direct criticism as follows: North America - Europe - Japan, respectively.

(48) X and X [names of 2 geologists] prepared the only serious report in the mineralogy, geology and ore geology of the Shinkolobwe, and there is one line saying "We have seen a black copper palladium oxide". **I never believed that. I thought they were very bad analysts.** (...) By the way, we have **a Brazilian colleague who is making a career** demonstrating that palladium oxide does not exist. **He has probably not had good samples.** (G24-NNS)

(49) The radiotherapy community must confess that some techniques during the last decades were a little bit drastics [sic] ... **people dead because of misuse of the Ellis formula.** (M26-NNS)

(50) The first results were obtained with **very debatable** techniques ... this technique is **very dangerous.** (M21-NNS)

On occasion, the tacit understanding that speakers are allowed to be more outspoken in a conference presentation than in the research article results in a discussant trying to lead the speaker on to express overt criticism of a colleague:

(51) *Discussant*: I would like to know the opinion of Mr X [the speaker] about the trial by Mr. Y [a fellow-surgeon], which is very similar to yours but in which he has a lot more recurrences than you have. I would like to know what your opinion is, in public, but then we're among friends here, you can say what you really think! (M28, Question time)

The speaker, an experienced researcher and authority in the field, while employing many of the face-saving strategies detailed by Myers (1989), is nevertheless drawn into admitting that his colleague's approach was *somewhat, er, risky*, which constitutes a serious criticism in oncology.

5. Field-specific differences

The previous two sections have examined the recurrent features across the board and have shown, first, that conference presentations do fulfil a specific role in the construction of facts and claim-making (called 'proto-claims' in this study), and second, that many traces of the contextual contingencies – material, mental, and interpersonal – surrounding research subsist in conference presentations. There are, however, significant differences between the three fields studied, related to their different research methods and deontologies, which result in a somewhat different 'positioning' of each field in relation to these aspects.

5.1. Novelty and the preliminary stage of the research

It is in geology that the status of conference presentation statements as proto-claims appears most clearly, with practically every presentation referring to the incomplete or very recent nature of the research: out of the total of 30 presentations, in nine the work is still in progress; in five others the data are too incomplete to allow general or definitive conclusions to be drawn; one paper presents raw data which have not yet been modelled or fully explained; a further six present the early or preliminary data from a research program, and a final four present recent results, or results that are confirmed by unpublished data circulating in preprint. A recognised, and specific, function of conference presentations in geology therefore appears to be that of presenting the stage of research attained on the D-day of the conference. As the work is, in the vast majority of cases, incomplete, the conclusions that can be drawn are of necessity tentative. Indeed, one of the roles of the discussion phase following the talk, analysed elsewhere (Rowley-Jolivet 1998), is to provide participants in geology with the opportunity to explore interesting but often speculative avenues by exchanging comments and hypotheses about these preliminary results.

References are also made in the physics presentations to the unfinished nature of the research which is presented albeit to a lesser extent than in geology. This may be due in part to the type of presentations filmed, one third of which were in applied areas of Research and Development. In such presentations, references to work in progress takes the form of the conventional move, in the conclusion, concerning future prospects and perspectives from which further improvements can be expected. The body of these presentations, however, which often have a commercial objective of 'salesmanship' for the laboratory's products, stresses the achievements and demonstrated results already obtained. The less tentative nature of the claims made in physics, compared to geology, even when the research is still in progress, can also be attributed to the different methods available in the two fields: in geology, the primary data are 'given' by nature; due to the operation of long historical processes, the samples are frequently scant, in poor condition (because of weathering, erosion, etc.), and have been subjected to various geological processes which can only be speculated about, not ascertained. In contrast in physics, an experimental-predictive science, the data are fabricated in the laboratory by setting up experiments in which all the variables can be controlled. In addition, in fields where laboratory-scale experiments are impractical, physics can have recourse to mathematical formalism and computer simulation in order to investigate a problem and predict behaviour with a high degree of certainty.

The situation in medicine is very different, as the 'material' in this field is human beings (the patients) and therefore cannot, for reasons of deontology, be experimentally manipulated. Consequently, in oncology, the only conclusions that can be asserted with an acceptable degree of certainty are those based on large randomised trials with a lengthy follow-up (five years on average in cancer research, to enable the significant survival factors to be determined). The medical community is distrustful of media scoops in which incomplete results with insufficient follow-up are published in the popular press, as practitioners are well aware of the impact that such revelations will have on the general public. As a result, relatively few speakers in medicine, compared to geology and physics, present recent or incomplete results. Several presentations (M3, M5, M9, M24, M27) are retrospective statistical analyses covering long periods (with data from 1960 to the present in M9, from 1971 in M28, from the early 1980s in M3 and M24), and half of the presentations contain no references to ongoing or preliminary research. A certain number, after having presented their main data with a 5-year follow-up, do, however, allude in the conclusion to trials still in progress and mention results which are too recent to allow reliable statistics to be drawn up. When it comes to the discussion phase, however, speakers and participants feel much freer to refer to studies still in progress and show great interest, as noted above, in the latest news. It should be pointed out that such constraints on follow-up do not hold for the six papers in experimental medicine in the corpus (three in molecular genetics, one each in nuclear medicine, biochemistry and mathematical modelling), as the material used here is not patients but genes, antibodies, cytokines, etc. As a result, one finds in all these presentations the same emphasis as in geology and physics on scant, preliminary or recent data.

5.2. Field-specific differences in contextual contingencies

The types of problems encountered during research are, naturally, closely linked to the methods and practices of each field. Unsurprisingly, it is in physics that experimental hitches, problems with materials, and the need for tinkering crop up most frequently, while, as previously noted (4.1.(v) above), geology attaches the most importance to the need to be observant. In medicine, unexpected problems are frequent and are often unpleasant surprises, requiring the surgeon to change tack on the spot. Events can take over and the physician loses control of the situation. Some unexpected results are fortunately of a more positive nature, however:

(52) ... **if something unpleasant is found** at the time of surgery ... (M12-NS)

(53) It may be **touch and go** as to whether you can remove it surgically via the operating proctoscope and you might want to go directly into an abdominal operation. (M7-NS)

(54) Complications though. We had one perforation which we had to convert to a low anterior resection, **we just couldn't control** the small bowel, it came in through the wall. (M7-NS)

(55) We increased our toxicity which was biliary toxicity, and therefore abandoned the study, **and then we noticed** that none of these patients were dying. (M13-NS)

(56) This is a very interesting man because (...) by all parameters he should have been dead in four months. This man went on to live six years. (M13-NNS)

5.3. Field-specific differences in decision-making

In geology, sampling is a source of difficult decision-making, as one can never totally ascertain the representativity of the sample. Though a major part of the decision on where or how much to sample can be made on objective criteria, a strong element of indeterminacy still remains, to judge by conference speakers' words. On one occasion (G24), sheer good luck (a chance encounter) also had a part to play:

(57) The choice of site was fairly critical ... we were able to convince ourselves that this scruffy little outcrop in fact is the main sulphide zone ... We went through the usual agonising about the size of the sample and to what extent we should sieve down and so on. (G6-NS)

(58) The situation was there when **I met a private collector**, a Belgian, who was poaching the diggings from the Union Minière, and very keen for any new mineral and he told me that he has seen a sample from Ruwe at the Maredsous Abbaye, and I went there and **I got the sample from the Padre** who gave me also his blessing and unfortunately died not long ago. (G24-NNS)

Decision-making in medicine presents particular problems, which have little in common with those of experimental sciences. Medicine is not an exact science, not only because of the diversity of human organisms[11], but also because a vast range of variables, many of which are not quantifiable, have to be taken into account in any medical decision: ethical problems, cosmetic aspects (for example in conservative surgery), patient quality of life, experience of the surgeon or physician, the freedom of choice of the patient him/herself, costs, misleading symptoms, the time factor (many decisions have to be taken in a medical emergency), unreliable diagnosis, ... It is hardly surprising, therefore, that, as Prince *et al.* (1982) have shown, physician-physician discourse in the hospital environment exhibits an extremely high degree of uncertainty, doubt and hedging (one hedge every 15 seconds in their data), not only on ethical issues but also more surprisingly when dealing with medical-technical matters.

---

[11] The difference here between medicine and, for example, physics was clearly stated by one of the speakers, a biophysicist, when examining whether electromagnetic fields – such as those generated by cellphones – can cause bioeffects or not: "... there's no question there's a bioeffect here, but there's enormous variability in biologic samples. And as a physicist, this is a very uncomfortable thing, it's like making measurements of solid-state materials and never knowing what the impurity levels are. ... Now physicists, you like to turn a knob, you like to be able to increase the noise slowly or over some period of time and see the effect disappear." (plenary lecture not included in the data analysed here).

Indeed, it is interesting to note that a significant proportion of discourse analysis studies of medicine have focused on hedging, which reflects, it would seem, not only a rhetorical strategy but also a fundamental epistemological dilemma of the practice of medicine. Certainty, not only as to the best decision to take, but even as to what exactly the problem is, is remarkably hard to attain.

As the previously mentioned studies of hedging show, many of these uncertainties feature in the medical research article. What appears, however, to be specific to the way decisions are presented in the conference presentation genre is, first, the very high frequency with which decision-making problems are brought up by speakers (and also, of course, in discussion time), and second, the frank admissions of past mistakes, fear of making the wrong decision, and divergences of opinion between physicians – in other words, a difference both in degree and in kind between the journal article and the conference presentation. Just as in geology and physics presentations where, as we have seen, decisions clearly appear to be complex configurations of theoretical knowledge, pragmatism, and opportunism and to reflect the type of discussions that go on in the laboratory, similarly in medicine, the picture of decision-making that emerges in the conference presentation is one of a highly complex process, akin to the exchanges which take place between physicians in the hospital environment rather than to the 'sanitized' discourse of the research article. Indeed, the major role of discussion time in medicine is to exchange opinions and experience as to the optimal decision to take in a given case. Some representative examples are given below.

i) Wrong decisions, and their sometimes fatal consequences, are frankly admitted:

(59) I've become over time fairly good at deciding which patients, by trial and error, having made some mistakes, finding out where that upper edge is (...) Some of them circumferential – bad mistake, one of the first few I did, were circumferential, that was a real chore. (M7-NS)

(60) ... a group that did very bad, and we know now not to operate in these patients, are those who ... We would now no longer do those. (M8-NS)

(61) We thought we were being very smart in doing this. However, we ruined our study in a sense because we have what we call crossover. (M13-NS)

ii) Consequently, fear of making the wrong decision is very high:

(62) It's not without some fear that one does a very low anterior resection. (M7-NS)

(63) We had to go through this learning curve with the surgeons ... the doctors that don't follow the liver function test, and don't do the flow scans and don't do all these things, you get horrible toxicities and then they back off, you know, they do a few, they see the

terrible toxicities and then they get scared ... Our surgeons were very frightened ...
Surgeons would say "Oh gee, I just don't like the idea of having done the resection and
then doing something to the hepatic artery, because, you know, I'm going to have more
complications and what if I thrombose?" (M13-NS)

(64) In 1974 or 75 X came to see me and said "Y, look, the results of our trial are very bad.
It's a disaster. I suggest that you stop your trial". And everybody around myself said
"Stop the trial, Y, you are into trouble. If you have too many recurrences you may be in
trouble, not only for your career but for your safety, they may put you in jail",
something like that, so I had a very bad time at that period. (M28-NNS)

(65) It's been a psychological help to me, so I sleep better at night. (M4-NS)

iii) Opinions diverge about the best decision to take, involving much discussion.
This is frequently reported in dialogue form in the conference paper as the
speaker reproduces snatches of dialogue that occurred with colleagues.

(66) Now we did this ERCP and we saw this narrow area here, and I was told by my radiolo-
gist that this is tumor wrapped around the bile duct, and said to them, "Well, you know,
her CEA is normal", I said, "let's just wait and see what happens", and sure enough, it
disappeared ... First we argued over whether ... (M13-NS)

(67) In '87, it was the beginning of the ultrasound in Lyon, and the specialist say "I see a
small nodes". I say "Okay" and I tried to find it with my finger, I felt nothing, and I say
"Well, it's a new technique, they don't know exactly what they are saying" and I didn't
believe that this thing was a node ... and 3 years later I could feel a node and the
ultrasound showed that node. (M25-NNS)

6. Discussion

Analysis of the role of the conference presentation in the construction of
knowledge claims – the functional slot that it fills – has shown that it does have
a unique function, unfulfilled by other discourse genres of science. The novelty
and preliminary nature of the results presented play important social and
cognitive roles both for audiences and for speakers at conferences: by creating a
discourse space for the public presentation of preliminary, ongoing or very
recent research, the conference presentation enables audiences to keep abreast of
the latest developments – a professional necessity in the faster-moving research
fields – without having to wait for journal publication in order to be informed; it
also enables conference presenters to 'stake their claim' to a patch of the research
territory without having to wait for the final results of their work (lab
experiments, exploration surveys, randomised trials ..., some of which can take
years) to be made available. The conference presentation can therefore play the
strategic role of upstaging potential competitors, in the agôn of modern science.

The novel and often preliminary results reported in conference presentations clearly show that this genre is positioned at a relatively early stage in the research process. The status of 'proto-claim' assigned in this study to the knowledge claims made during conference presentations can be justified on several grounds. Firstly, as Ochs & Jacoby (1997) have shown in their study of the 'countdown' to a conference presentation in a physics laboratory, the scientific content of a presentation is frequently not a definitive, fully developed research claim, but a compromise solution agreed upon by the authors[12] as the conference deadline draws near, and may be subsequently modified:

> The working consensus reached for a conference presentation may ... be temporary; final consensus closure among the co-authors may not be fully worked out until the last revision of a paper for publication (...). Thus is a working consensus forged as theorists and experimentalists come down to the wire of deadlines and time limits for public reports. For the moment, that is. In the aftermath of the conference, freed from the task of constructing a presentation rhetoric, the co-authors reopened their ongoing discussion on the meaning of measurements and the grounding of theory in their spin glass research (Ochs & Jacoby 1997: 483, 500).

Such an interim proto-claim would not of course be presentable in print, but it is allowable in the ephemeral, oral discourse genre of a conference presentation – and indeed, one could add, the pressure of the conference deadline may in fact act as a catalyst in accelerating scientific collaboration and consensus.

A second reason for considering conference presentation claims as 'proto-claims' has to do with the presence of question time immediately after the presentation. As various authors have shown (Shalom 1993; Rowley-Jolivet 1998; Webber this volume), the speaker's claims can be questioned or even nipped in the bud by members of the audience during the discussion phase. Unlike research articles, where the negotiation of claims takes place between author(s) and reviewers *prior to* publication, the conference presentation is subjected to minimal prior vetting (acceptance or refusal, by the scientific committee of the conference, of an Abstract), but it can be heavily flakked, *after* the claims have been made, by the audience. The claim presented by the speaker is, therefore, like a prototype machine, tested – and quite often found to be defective and sent back to the laboratory for further development. Conference speakers are aware of this test function of conference papers, and sometimes welcome the opportunity it offers to benefit from the insights and suggestions of other researchers in the audience to improve their cognitive 'product'. Clearly,

---

[12] The majority of scientific presentations and papers are multi-authored, often by researchers of different nationalities.

however, this signifies that the assertive weight of many conference presentation claims will be lighter than those of refereed publication.

Positioning conference presentation claims in the process of knowledge construction can also contribute to our understanding of the role that conferences play in the wider social framework of organised science. Sociological analyses of the complex sociotechnical networks created to turn claims into facts (Callon 1989; Callon *et al.* 1986; Latour 1987) have argued that scientific knowledge is constructed through the mobilisation of various allies in 'actant-networks', or hybrid alliances of human and inanimate actors bound together by a closely-woven mesh of links to ensure the consolidation and dissemination of scientific knowledge. At the hub of the technoscientific network, in this approach, lies the laboratory, which acts as a centre of production, synergistically converting inputs of various kinds – funding, scientific instruments, the literature, research expertise ... – into outputs, by perfecting new instruments and methods, producing articles and proposals, and exporting the laboratory's scientific know-how to other research centres. This in turn enables the laboratory to recruit fresh funding and expertise, and extend its network even further.

A neglected area in the actor-network model, however, is the role of scientific conferences in establishing and maintaining networks. This study, by situating conference claims immediately downstream from lab discussions, and by showing the numerous traces of lab activity that subsist in the conference presentation, highlights the close, symbiotic relationship between laboratories and conferences and indicates that the latter fulfil a dual function in extending the network. Indeed, as discussed elsewhere (Rowley-Jolivet 1999), conferences provide, first, a forum for much of the **output** of the laboratory: documentary output in the form of presentations and posters, cognitive output through the participation of members of the lab at various levels in conferences, and instrumental output in the devices and instruments 'marketed' via conference exhibits. Conferences also constitute a major source of **input** for laboratories: proceedings papers and presentations form much of the documentary input to the lab, markedly so in fields where technological progress is rapid, and "research front referencing" (Price 1986) or a high "immediacy index" (Meadows 1967) is the rule (quoted in Miller & Halloran 1993); the contacts made at conferences can also be an important source of financial input in more applied fields where funding agencies (government, the military, industry ...) play an active role in scientific conferences; exhibitions at conferences are evidence of the close network alliance between manufacturers of scientific instruments and the material life of the modern laboratory; most importantly, perhaps, conferences offer seasoned researchers an unparalleled opportunity for 'networking' and building international alliances for collaborative research projects. The social microcosm of a conference not only acts as a 'forum', or a concrete, local manifestation of the operation of a discourse community (Porter 1992), which reinforces discourse community cohesion, but also furthers the dissemination of research expertise.

An important finding that emerges from this study is that the two 'worlds' of concrete scientific research activity (in the lab, the field, or the hospital environment) and the rhetorical discourse of the research article, are not dichotomous worlds but rather two positions on a cline or two steps in a continuous, multi-staged process. In between them lies the conference presentation, which partakes of both worlds. Similarities with lab life surface in features such as: the oral nature of the discourse; an informal lexis – at least in the native-speaker presentations – and congruent grammatical forms; the importance of dialogue and discussion, either direct, as in question time, or reported, in the snatches of dialogue included by speakers, and in their use of interrogative forms; the evocation of problems, dead ends, failures, serendipitous discoveries and pragmatic decisions that make up their daily experience of research and show science as a human activity anchored in a local context; the tentative and speculative nature of many of the claims made. Yet at the same time the conference presentation can be seen to be moving towards the research article, of which it adumbrates many characteristic features: it is a prepared, structured monologue, limited in time, often couched in a more formal language than that used in the lab; the researcher has a claim to defend – s/he is not speculating off the top of his/her head – and supports it with visual material very similar to that found in the research article. The conference presentation, by partaking of these two worlds, creates a synthesis – a different genre – and bridges the gap between them.

It may be objected, however, that the analysis presented here of the contextual contingencies of research, the pragmatic side to decision-making, and 'bashing' of other researchers, confirms rather than invalidates constructivists' contention of the inescapable indexicality of science, and therefore the hollowness of science's claims to general truth validity. On observing the disparity between what happens in the lab and what is reported in the research article, constructivists have concluded that since no correspondence between the two is possible, all scientific facts are therefore contingent and that what passes for 'fact' is in reality a post hoc 'fabrication' accomplished by the discourse constructivists' rhetoric. While this present study certainly confirms their findings as to the existence of local, material and human constraints on the production of scientific knowledge – constraints that are freely admitted and taken as a matter of course by scientists themselves – it does not necessarily follow that scientific 'facts' can be defined and explained solely in social terms. An illuminating distinction on this issue is that made by Duhem ([1914] 1997) between "concrete facts" and "theoretical facts". In scientific experimentation, he argues, the scientist is constantly striving to relate two different orders of factuality: that of the concrete data observed, and that of the abstract, symbolic representations of theory, which enable the concrete phenomena to be interpreted. The two stand in a dialectical relation, in that there can never be total correspondence between the two, not least because in order to make concrete facts communicable, the scientist has to have recourse to symbolic (linguistic) expression. This dialectic is a source of flexibility, or, in his well-known phrase, of the "underdetermination of theory by experiment". Scientists are therefore constantly engaged in a cognitive process of turning the concrete narrative into an abstract judgement.

What is particularly interesting is that in conference presentations we see this cognitive process taking place in real time, so to speak – we see science in the making. In the narratives of failures (analysed by Thompson, this volume, and of which several examples are also given in this study), we find the concrete facts which never managed to become theoretical facts, as the disparity between the two orders of factuality turned out to be too wide to straddle; we also find in conference presentations, however, solid theorising and logic as the speakers seek to extract, from the frequently muddled and frustrating world of experimentation, the abstractions that have a general significance. The conference presentation, by reporting both the concrete and theoretical facts, fleshes out our understanding of the process of scientific reasoning. The research article, in contrast, selects only those facts which can be given theoretical significance. Should one therefore conclude that the research article is, after all, a 'phony story'? Not necessarily. One argument is provided by Montgomery (1996: 18):

> [It] is less an issue of scientific discourse being "fraudulent" than of it being a form of authorship. Leaving out many aspects of the unsuccessful or the unexpected, eliminating the messiness, the trial-and-error qualities of the rough draft, rearranging and rewriting the whole into a coherent story, upholding, in other words, an image of the writer as eminently rational and in control – this is all simply, yet profoundly, an integral part of composition itself. All writing ... seeks to idealize its author in this way.

A second is that the communicative purposes of the two genres, presentation and article, are different and they therefore stress different aspects of scientific activity. Taken as a whole, science clearly has social, cultural, interpersonal and cognitive dimensions; while the research article focuses exclusively on communicating the cognitive value of research (which requires ignoring many particularities in order to make generally valid statements), the conference presentation also reflects other, less abstract dimensions.

This highlights the importance of the mode (oral or written) and the genre (presentation or article) in the picture we get of the construction of scientific facts. It is noteworthy that speakers display considerable genre knowledge as to what can be said, and how research can be reported, in the conference presentation compared to the research article, even though the 'rules of the game' for conference presentations are tacit ones (unlike the detailed instructions to authors provided by journals). They have no qualms about admitting the loose ends and the dead ends of their research. Thompson (this volume) shows how the details of experimental problems, by revealing the human side to research, "draw the audience into the research process with all its attendant difficulties and problems". In addition to the interactional role highlighted by Thompson, the frank admission of problems can also be interpreted as an insider strategy, as evidence of the shared culture of conference participants – as a sort of "of course, we all know what really goes on in the lab, don't we?". Yet these very same researchers, in their written production, will conform to the conventions of the journal article. In itself, this genre awareness by the scientists themselves not only points up how highly conventionalised the rhetoric of the research article is, but also underlines the interest of studying a wide range of different discourse genres in any study of the construction of scientific knowledge.

7. Conclusion

This paper has attempted to fill in some gaps in our understanding of how scientific knowledge claims are constructed and disseminated by investigating the role of a neglected genre, the conference presentation, in this process. The novelty and preliminary nature of much of the research reported in conference presentations clearly show that the genre is positioned at an early stage in the life of scientific facts, midway between the embryonic, speculative claims made in the informal privacy of the lab, and the mature assertion of claims in the public rhetoric of the research article. This has led us to assign the status of proto-claim to the knowledge claims put forward in conference presentations. It has also highlighted the wider social role played by conferences in sociotechnical networks: due to the symbiotic relationship that conferences have with laboratories, for which they constitute a major form of input and output, they make an important contribution towards consolidating and extending scientific networks. Further evidence of the close link between conference presentations and laboratory life has been found in the numerous traces of the contextual contingencies of research, such as the importance of experimental expertise and observation, the complex, pragmatic or opportunistic nature of many decisions, and in the occasional 'bashing' of fellow-researchers. The presence of these contingent factors can be considered to be a generic feature of the conference presentation, as they are found across the board, though with certain field-specific differences depending on the methods, deontology or epistemology of the field. The fact that these traces of the indexicality of research subsist in the conference presentation but are expunged from the research article not only underlines the highly conventional nature of the research article itself, in which a radical selection of the elements judged worthy of publication can be observed, but also shows that the construction of knowledge claims is a gradual, multi-staged process, in which various discourse genres have different roles to play (cf. 'semiotic spanning', Ventola 1999, this volume). In this process, the conference presentation genre occupies a key position in the establishment of scientific facts by bridging the gap between the seemingly dichotomous worlds of laboratory life and refereed publication. As Bazerman remarks when discussing Halliday & Martin's (1993) approach to scientific discourse, by focusing solely on the image of science conveyed by the research article, we have but a partial picture, for in such an approach, "science is much as it presents itself in its texts", leading him to argue that "we have to find out how to read these difficult texts, and perhaps recover some of the concrete narrative that has been pressed out of the abstraction" (Bazerman 1998: 23). Conference presentations provide one means of recovering this concrete narrative.

References

Bazerman, C. 1988. *Shaping Written Knowledge*. Madison: University of Wisconsin Press.
Bazerman, C. 1990. "Discourse analysis and social construction". *Annual Review of Applied Linguistics,* 11: 77-83.
Bazerman, C. 1998. "Emerging perspectives on the many dimensions of scientific discourse". In J. R. Martin & R. Veel (eds). *Reading Science: Critical and Functional Perspectives on Discourses of Science*. London: Routledge, 15-28.
Berkenkotter, C. & T. Huckin 1995. *Genre Knowledge in Disciplinary Communication*. Hillsdale, N.J.: Lawrence Erlbaum.
Birch-Bécaas, S. 1997. "From author to reviewer to editor: Negotiating the claim in a scientific article. A study of French researchers publishing in English". *Anglais de Spécialité - Revue du GERAS (Groupe d'Etude et de Recherche en Anglais de Spécialité),* 15/18: 397-409.
Brown, P. & S. Levinson. 1987. *Politeness: Some Universals in Language Usage*. Cambridge: Cambridge University Press.
Callon, M. (ed.) 1989. *La Science et ses Réseaux*. Paris: Editions la Découverte.
Callon, M., J. Law & A. Rip (eds) 1986. *Mapping the Dynamics of Science and Technology*. London: Macmillan.
Dubois, B. L. 1980. "Genre and structure of biomedical speeches". *Forum Linguisticum,* 5 (2): 140-168.
Duhem, P. [1914] 1997. *La théorie physique – son objet, sa structure*. Paris: Vrin.
Fairclough, N. 1992. *Discourse and Social Change*. London: Polity.

124

Fleck, L. [1935] 1979. *Genesis and Development of a Scientific Fact*. Chicago: University of Chicago Press.

Galison, P. 1987. *How Experiments End*. Chicago: University of Chicago Press.

Galison, P. 1997. *Image and Logic: A Material Culture of Microphysics*. Chicago: University of Chicago Press.

Garfinkel, H., M. Lynch & E. Livingstone 1981. "The work of a discovering science construed with materials from the optically discovered pulsar". *Philosophy of Social Sciences*, 11: 131-158.

Gilbert, G. N. 1976. "The Transformation of research findings into scientific knowledge". *Social Studies of Science*, 6: 281-306.

Gilbert, G. N. & M. Mulkay 1984. *Opening Pandora's Box: A Sociological Analysis of Scientists' Discourse*. London: Cambridge University Press.

Gould, S. J. 1989. *Wonderful Life: The Burgess Shale and the Nature of History*. New York: W. W. Norton.

Hacking, I. 1983. *Representing and Intervening*. Cambridge: Cambridge University Press.

Halliday, M. A. K. & J. R. Martin 1993. *Writing Science. Lieracy and Discursive Power.* London: Falmer Press.

Jacob, F. 1977. "Evolution and tinkering", *Science*, 196: 1161-1166.

Knorr-Cetina, K. D. 1981. *The Manufacture of Knowledge: An Essay on the Constructivist and Contextual Nature of Science*. Oxford: Pergamon.

Latour, B. 1987. *Science in Action*. Cambridge, Mass.: Harvard University Press.

Latour, B. & S. Woolgar 1986. *Laboratory Life: The Social Construction of Scientific Facts*. Princeton, N.J.: Princeton University Press.

Law, J. 1985. "Les textes et leurs alliés". *Culture technique*, 14: 59-69.

Lévy-Leblond, J.-M. 1996. *Aux Contraires*. Paris: Gallimard.

Lévy-Leblond, J.-M. 1998. "La méprise et le mépris", *Alliage*, 35/36: 27-42. Special issue – Impostures scientifiques: les malentendus de l'affaire Sokal.

Lynch, M. 1984. *Art and Artefact in Laboratory Science: A Study of Shop Work and Shop Talk in a Research Laboratory*. London: Routledge & Kegan Paul.

Meadows, A. J. 1967. "The citation characteristics of astronomical research literature", *Journal of Documentation*, 23: 28-33.

Medawar, P. B. 1990. "Is the scientific paper a fraud?". In D. Pyke (ed.). *The Threat and the Glory*. New York: Harper Collins, 228-233.

Merton, R. K. 1973. *The Sociology of Science: Theoretical and Empirical Investigations*. Chicago: University of Chicago Press.

Miller, C. R. & S. M. Halloran 1993. "Reading Darwin, reading nature; on the ethos of historical science". In J. Selzer (ed.). *Understanding Scientific Prose*. Madison: University of Wisconsin Press, 106-126.

Montgomery, S. L. 1996. *The Scientific Voice*. New York: The Guilford Press.

Myers, G. 1989. "The pragmatics of politeness in scientific articles". *Applied Linguistics*, 10 (1): 1-35.

Myers, G. 1990. *Writing Biology: Texts in the Social Construction of Scientific Knowledge*. Madison: University of Wisconsin Press.

Myers, G. 1991. "Stories and styles in two molecular biology review articles". In C. Bazerman & J. Paradis (eds). *Textual Dynamics of the Professions*. Madison: University of Wisconsin Press, 45-75.

Myers, G. 1992. "Textbooks and the sociology of scientific knowledge". *English for Specific Purposes*, 11: 3-15.

Ochs, E. & S. Jacoby 1997. "Down to the wire: The cultural clock of physicists and the discourse of consensus". *Language in Society,* 26: 479-505.

Porter, J. E. 1992. *Audience and Rhetoric: An Archaeological Composition of the Discourse Community.* Englewood Cliffs, N. J.: Prentice-Hall.

Price, D. J. de Solla 1965. "Networks of scientific papers". *Science,* 149, 510-515.

Price, D. J. de Solla 1986. "Citation measures of hard science, soft science, technology and nonscience". In *Little Science, Big Science... and Beyond.* New York: Columbia Press, 155-179.

Prince, E. F., J. Frader & C. Bosk 1982. "On hedging in physician-physician discourse". In R. J. Di Pietro (ed). *Linguistics and the Professions.* Hillsdale, N.J.: Ablex, 83-97.

Rowley-Jolivet, E. 1998. *La Communication scientifique orale: Etude des caractéristiques linguistiques et discursives d'un genre.* Unpublished Ph.D. Dissertation. Bordeaux: University of Bordeaux 2.

Rowley-Jolivet, E. 1999. "The pivotal role of conference papers in the network of scientific communication". *Anglais de Spécialité - Revue du GERAS (Groupe d'Etude et de Recherche en Anglais de Spécialité),* 23/27: 179-196.

Shalom, C. 1993. "Established and evolving spoken research process genres: Plenary lecture and poster session discussions at academic conferences". *English for Specific Purposes,* 12: 37-50.

Sismondo, S. 1993. "Some social constructions". *Social Studies of Science,* 23: 515-553.

Sokal, A. D. 1996. "Transgressing the Boundaries: Toward a transformative hermeneutics of quantum gravity". *Social Text,* 46/47, Vol. 14: 217-252.

Thompson, S. This volume. "'As the story unfolds': The uses of narrative in research presentations".

Vassileva, I. This volume. "Speaker-audience interaction: The case of Bulgarians presenting in English".

Ventola, E. 1998. "Interpersonal Choices in Academic Work". In A. Sanchez-Macarro & R. Carter (eds). *Linguistic Choices across Genres.* Amsterdam/Philadelphia: John Benjamins, 117-136.

Ventola, E. 1999. "Semiotic spanning at conferences: Cohesion and coherence in and across conference papers and their discussions." In W. Bublitz, U. Lenk & E. Ventola (eds). *Coherence in Spoken and Written Discourse.* Amsterdam/Philadelphia: Benjamins, 101-125.

Ventola, E. This volume. "Why and what kind of focus on conference presentations?"

Webber, P. This volume. "The paper is now open for discussion".

METADISCOURSE IN ACADEMIC CONFERENCE PRESENTATIONS

Anni Heino, Eija Tervonen & Jorma Tommola

University of Turku, Turku, Finland

Abstract – 'Metadiscourse' refers to linguistic elements which lie outside the propositional core of a spoken or written message and deal chiefly with the discourse itself, the producer's confidence about the propositions expressed, or the relations between the producer and receivers. Metadiscourse fulfils various rhetorical and pragmatic goals. We describe the use of this device in spoken academic conference English by native speakers. Occurrences of metadiscourse in a selection of conference monologues were classified into structure-oriented, validity-oriented, interaction-oriented and context-oriented types. In terms of a word count, metadiscourse accounted for a third of the content of the presentations. In terms of the average number of instances of metadiscourse, structural signals were less frequent than validity-oriented markers associated with academic cautiousness and face-saving. We conclude by stating a principle which, while obvious, is often overlooked by conference presenters: spoken discourse is evanescent and must be processed by the listener in a single pass. The listener will therefore benefit from signals that guide the construction of a rich semantic representation of content and the speaker's attitudes. Metadiscourse is a key source for such signals, although its abundant use for pragmatic purposes may also reduce comprehensibility.

1. Introduction: Conference presentations and the concept of metadiscourse

Public speaking is always a challenging task, but an academic conference presentation – a highly specialised form of public speaking – is particularly demanding. Conference presenters, unlike most instructors, for example, must perform in front of peers, and often in front of listeners with expertise greater than their own. They must attempt to present their research questions, methods, findings and conclusions to a knowledgeable and sometimes critical audience in such a way that their contribution brings them new or continued acceptance within the scientific community. Conference speakers need justification from their audience.They express their ideas in the hope that the information they impart will be accepted as a relevant addition to knowledge and as a sign of their personal credibility.

So, when the speaker steps in front of the audience at an academic conference, he or she is conscious of *rhetorical* and *pragmatic* goals. A central rhetorical goal is to convey information effectively and to facilitate the listener's efforts to construct an internal representation of the content. To achieve this goal, the speaker must organise the presentation adequately, convey this organisation to the listeners, and express the content information clearly. The speaker's pragmatic goal is to establish or preserve his or her position in the discourse community while, at the same time, showing respect towards the listeners and the community as a whole, and not imposing his or her authority on the audience. This goal is connected with the concept of *face* (Brown & Levinson 1978): it is necessary for the speaker not to violate his or her own positive face or the negative and positive face of the audience.

An important tool for conference speakers in the effort to achieve these goals is metadiscourse – linguistic elements that lie outside the actual propositional content of the primary discourse. Typically, metadiscourse is used to comment on the structure of the primary discourse, to explicate the speaker's attitudes towards the primary discourse or the audience, to fulfil various interactional functions, and to refer to the situational and discourse context.

Metadiscourse in written text has been a frequent object of linguistic study since the early 1980's (e.g. Williams 1981). Recent classifications of written meta-discourse include, for example, Luukka 1992; Mauranen 1993; and Hyland 1998a, 1999. A number of studies have also dealt with spoken metadiscourse under various terms such as 'discourse markers' (e.g. Chaudron & Richards 1986; Fraser 1990), 'structural markers' (Bäcklund 1988, 1990) and 'conversational elements' (Weissberg 1993). Structure-signalling and inter-actional devices in spoken research presentations are also extensively discussed by Thompson (1997).

In this paper we examine the types of metadiscourse in spoken academic conference presentations, and illustrate the proportion of metadiscourse in relation to the primary discourse in a small corpus. Our classification of metadiscoursal elements in spoken conference English is broadly based on the concepts of organisational and evaluative bracketing introduced by Schiffrin (1980); on Crismore's (1984, 1989) notions of informational and attitudinal metadiscourse; on Vande Kopple's notions of textual and interpersonal metadiscourse (1985), and on the contextual functions of metadiscourse described by Luukka (1992).

2. Material

The material for this study comes from a set of almost one hundred videotaped English-language presentations at the 4th Conference of the European Association for Research on Learning and Instruction (EARLI)[1]. We selected three native-English-speaker presentations that were characterised by a high degree of spontaneity. The presentations were all approximately 20 minutes in length, and were given by a male British speaker (P1), a male American speaker (P2), and a female American speaker (P3). The total number of words, not counting voiced hesitations or incomplete words, was approximately 8700. The monologues were transcribed, their metadiscoursal elements were identified and categorised, and the frequencies of occurrence of types of metadiscourse were computed.

3. Metadiscourse in spoken conference presentations

Table 1 (following page) summarises the types of metadiscourse identified in the material. In the sections that follow (3.1 – 3.4) we discuss each of the categories, and then offer some quantitative observations and concluding remarks in sections 4 and 5.

3.1. Structure-oriented metadiscourse

Structure-oriented metadiscourse consists of items that indicate how the presentation is organised. Based on the familiar notions of van Dijk (1980) and van Dijk & Kintsch (1983), this class is here further divided into two subclasses, (1) superstructure markers – signals of formal, rhetorical organisation of the discourse – and (2) macrostructure markers – signals of the organisation of semantic content within the rhetorical sections.

(1) Superstructure markers signal the conventional rhetorical organisation of the research presentation. Four sub-categories (i-iv) were identified in this set of materials.

(i) Opening and closing signals often have a distinct interactive flavour. However, they are also stereotypical parts of the formal structure of oral presentations, and consist of general items of metadiscourse that relate to the entire act of presentation and precede or round up whatever other formally

---

[1] The analyses were completed in 1993 as a joint thesis by the first two authors within a project coordinated by the third author, who has edited the material into its present form.

distinguishable sections the speaker includes in the talk. An opening signal is typically a greeting or a statement of the title:

(1)   Right. Well, erm ... Hello everyone.

(2)   The study I want to speak about today is a study investigating the impact of attribution retraining delivered by a computer-assisted instructional program.

Closing signals alert the listeners to the approaching end of the presentation so that the final propositions do not come unexpectedly:

(3)   Just in concluding I would like to say that (...) thank you.

STRUCTURE-ORIENTED METADISCOURSE (3.1)	
(1) Superstructure markers	i opening and closing signals ii superstructure announcers iii section shifts iv reminders
(2) Macrostructure markers	i subtopic transition indicators ii subtopic organisers
VALIDITY-ORIENTED METADISCOURSE (3.2)	
(1) Validity of expression	i approximators ii definition hedges
(2) Validity of content	i hedges ii emphatics
INTERACTION-ORIENTED METADISCOURSE (3.3)	
(1) Attitudes towards content	i evaluative markers ii saliency markers
(2) Attitudes towards self and others	i self-oriented items ii audience-oriented items iii community-oriented items
CONTEXT-ORIENTED METADISCOURSE (3.4)	
(1) Reference to situation	
(2) Reference to material	

Table 1: Categories of metadiscourse.

While the familiar, smooth thank-you to the audience closed two of the presentations, the third speech (and a substantial number of the other talks not analysed here) ended with an abrupt announcement, often prompted by the chairperson, that the presentation now had to come to an end:

(4)   ... but I think that the, umm, the kinds of partnerships that we discussed earlier on today, erm, maybe need to be built upfront, erm, to avoid that kind of cart before the horse or

horse before the cart sort of problem that I think, erm, traditionally the research and practice has has been involved in, *I will stop at that.*

(ii) Superstructure announcers, in line with Swales' (1990) CARS model and the standard IMRD pattern typical of written research presentations, are moves with which the speaker explicitly identifies the rhetorical sections into which the actual substance of the presentation has been divided. Such announcements of standard reporting structure presumably allow listeners to activate an organisational frame that makes it easier to follow the presentation. Our expectation was that the fairly complex accounts of empirical research we analysed would extensively utilise this device to signal to the listeners which section was being dealt with. Some sort of general opening and closing items (section 'i' above) were invariably present, but none of the monologues we studied in detail explicitly and consistently provided superstructural cues as the talk went on, and the same applied to a large number of the almost one hundred other talks that were video-taped from the conference. The following was the single attempt to use this metadiscoursal device in our material:

(5)   that's sort of the background for the study, I'd like then to tell you about the method and the procedures.

The finding is in line with the observation that spoken research presentations are not necessarily organised in terms of the structure of the written research article – probably because the work was still unfinished at the time, or because the presentation had been inadequately prepared, or because a rigorous super-structural organisation was not considered necessary for a 'casual' spoken presentation – or because, in a spoken discourse situation, the research process is in general more naturally handled as a narrative (cf. Thompson 1997). It is of course possible, although we feel not probable, that speakers addressing an experienced audience also take it for granted that the listeners are fully aware of the canonical composition of research reports, and therefore want to save time by ignoring the explicit signals of superstructure.

(iii) Section shifts, the third type of superstructure marker identified in this material, are similar to superstructure announcers proper, but we established this category to distinguish between the explicit expression of rhetorical structure and more vague signals that mark the beginning or end of (implicit) rhetorical sections. Syntactically, these can be realised, for example, as initial clauses of purpose, as in

(6)   *now in order to explore this* I did a questionnaire survey

where the anaphorical reference provides a cue concerning a superstructural borderline. Contrary to our expectations, these less explicit signals, too, were virtually non-existent in the presentations studied.

(iv) Reminders, the fourth and last subcategory of superstructure markers, include phrases such as *We hypothesised remember...* which are used by the speaker to initialise a set of propositions which already came up in a previous rhetorical section and are now re-expressed with a metadiscoursal pointer to that section. In spite of the considerable cohesive potential which reminders possess, the three speakers we studied made infrequent use of these markers.

(2) Macrostructure markers. The macrostructure of a presentation refers to the organisation of content propositions in terms of topics and subtopics within the general rhetorical (formal) sections of the presentation. The signals of content structure are here divided into two subclasses, (i) subtopic transition indicators and (ii) subtopic organisers.

(i) Subtopic transition indicators consist of subtopic openers and subtopic concluders. These markers of topic boundaries occurred frequently in the presentations, but exhibited different degrees of explicitness. Occasionally, topic change was directly and explicitly announced:

(7)   let me move to macroadaptation erm for a moment.

Transitions between subtopics were also indicated by rhetorical questions immediately answered by the speaker, or direct requests asking the audience to focus their attention on the new subtopic:

(8)   so these were the attributions that we ... the program provided to students, *where do we get these from, why do we say these particular things to students*, we did a little pilot study

(9)   now ladies and gentlemen I want you to, to look at that list ... and ask yourself what on earth do they all have in common.

Topical transitions were also signalled by semantically empty 'new episode flags' or 'attention-getters' (e.g. Swales & Malczewski 1995) such as *well, now,* or *okay*. These openers were preferred by the speakers over the use of more explicit opening transitions. One reason might be that openers of this type tend to be habitual fillers used in instructional monologue. Additionally, because of their semantic emptiness, they can easily be used to tie together seemingly heterogeneous subtopics (cf. Schiffrin 1987), as in

(10)   so thanks very much indeed *now* in the united kingdom over the last ten years ... .

In topic conclusions, the most explicit device was a revision of the main points just presented:

(11) so we looked at academic performance, we looked at attributions, and we looked at persistence as the three dependent measures in the study.

An interesting and familiar detail of topic conclusion in one of the presentations was the speaker's frequent use (once in less than every three minutes) of *okay* with a rising intonation contour. This device was also fairly frequent in the rest of the materials recorded but not analysed here. Its function is ostensibly to check audience comprehension, and to give the listeners a chance to react interactively at topical transitions:

(12) ... which promote a high level of ownership and control, participation and involvement, and meaningful learning *okay*? now I don't think it has to involve all those three things at the same time, if it involves just one of those three, then you're into active learning *okay*?

The inherent danger in this mannerism, as all students and conference-goers will be aware, is that it easily makes the audience feel that their intellectual skills are being underestimated.

(ii) Subtopic organisers, the second main type of macrostructure marker, group together propositions within one topical section. Three types of subtopic organiser were identified. 'Sequencers' are typically list items which inform the audience that a particular marked item occupies a position in the internal list structure of the subtopic:

(13) and we had *three* hypotheses in the study, we ... we said that we believed that (...), *the second hypothesis* was that (...) and *the third hypothesis* was that (...).

'Section-internal reminders' point to propositions that already came up earlier within the same topical section, particularly when the section was lengthy:

(14) and they just basically worked through the set of programme in the sequential manner *that I described earlier.*

'Clarifiers' are typically appositional conjuncts such as *for example, that is*, which mark elaborations of preceding propositions,

(15) ... problem solving or investigational tasks from which pupils derive mathematical knowledge and understanding so *for example* instead of telling pupils that the three angles of a triangle add up to 180 degrees and ...

or conjuncts with a transitional role such as *incidentally* (cf. Quirk *et al.* 1972: 667*)*, which are used to direct the listeners' attention to supporting or justificatory comments:

(16)   there's a great deal of interest what so called learning styles ... now ... erm and *in fact* there are organisations ... like in the united states at any rate erm one organisation is the national association of secondary school principals ... .

The three speakers inserted clarifying, elaborative, or justificatory material into their talks with frequencies that reflect their individual presentation styles. A subtopic organiser of this type occurred on average once in every 45 seconds in P2 and once in 1.5 minutes in P1. Presentation 3 contained only three instances.

Macrostructure markers were considerably more frequent than superstructure markers in the presentations (12.7 vs. 2.4 per cent out of the word total).

3.2.   *Validity-oriented metadiscourse*

The term 'validity-oriented metadiscourse' is here used to refer to metadiscoursal items related to the speaker's perception of the validity of expression or the validity of content propositions. Speakers in academic contexts often express their concern about the adequacy of the linguistic formulation of their ideas or the terms they use. In addition, presenters are naturally cautious about the authoritativeness of their statements. Validity-oriented metadiscourse thus (1) signals the speaker's attitudes towards the forms of expression used, and (2) also indicates how assured or modalising the speaker is about the actual content.

Within metadiscourse concerning **(1) validity of expression** we identified two subcategories: (i) approximators and (ii) definition hedges.

(i) Approximators are lexical items and phrases such as *sort of, more or less* and *something like that*, which indicate the speaker's reservations about the precision of words or phrases used (cf. Prince *et al.* 1980, Aijmer 1986). Some of these come close to functioning as empty fillers that reflect a mannerism of speech possibly arising from insecurity, cautiousness, or face-saving needs, rather than actual deliberate use of metadiscourse:

(17)   that was *sort of* the first attribution

(18)   or whether this ratio of traditional teaching being dominant but some active learning occurring from time to time, remains a a stable *type of* balance.

(ii) Definition hedges consist of phrases which mitigate a definition by indicating that it is only preliminary:

(19) at one level it basically is a reaction to *what you might call* expository teaching or didactic teaching a very traditional approach to teaching.

As Myers (1989) has pointed out, definitions and terms which are not yet accepted by the community need to be attenuated so that the speaker does not pose a threat to the negative face of the audience. In general, the conference situation seems to create in the speaker the need to be cautious in front of an expert audience. The use of downtoning devices such as approximators and definition hedges is probably also related to the (at least semi-spontaneous) speech situation and the presenter's search for the right expression during oral discourse production.

(2) Validity of content. Our second type of validity-oriented metadiscourse is connected with epistemic modality. This type conveys the speaker's commitment about the truth value of what is being said (cf., for example, Coates 1987). We identified two types in our material.

(i) Hedges are here restricted to denoting linguistic elements which downgrade the speaker's subjective commitment to the truth value of statements (for written texts, cf. also Crompton 1997 and Hyland 1998b). The category includes, among other things, lexical verbs such as *think* or *guess*, adverbs such as *really* or *actually*, various time adjuncts, e.g. *often*, or attitudinal disjuncts such as *perhaps,* and the use of modal auxiliaries:

(20) *I think* it really increases the power of the computer as an instructional tool

(21) *to some extent* students, there is a trend for students to be more willing to attribute success to effort

(22) so it *on surface it seems like it perhaps would be* a good tool for delivering attributional retraining.

The distinction between hedges and definition hedges (cf. above) is that when the speaker suggests a tentative definition or a term, uncertainty about the propositional content of the statement is not necessarily present; rather, the speaker seems to be concerned about not violating the negative face of the audience.

(ii) Emphatics form the second subcategory within content-validity-oriented metadiscourse. They include lexical items such as *really, indeed,* and the auxiliary *do,* or comment clauses which intensify the speaker's subjective commitment to the truth value of the propositional content, thus boosting the illocutionary force of the utterance:

(23) they need to have positive expectations for future success if they *do indeed* invest effort in learning something

(24) *there's no question* about that individuals *do* differ, in in learning style, erm, *there's no question* about what is to ... possible to assess differences in learning style.

Our general impression concerning validity-oriented metadiscourse in this material probably again corresponds to the experience of conference-goers: hedges and approximators are a prominent feature, and abundant use of these devices often makes the speaker appear more hesitant than there would be reason for. Yet, hedges are effective politeness devices when the speaker does not wish to make over-authoritative statements. Cultural differences as well as the substance field of the work being reported will obviously influence the nature and number of validity-oriented metadiscoursal devices, as Ventola's (e.g. 1997) studies on written academic discourse suggest.

3.3. *Interaction-oriented metadiscourse*

Interaction-oriented metadiscourse includes linguistic elements that convey the subjective feelings of the speaker, and, interactively even if implicitly, guide the listener's evaluations of the content. This class of metadiscourse also includes items which reflect the speaker's direct interaction with the other participants of the conference situation or with the wider academic community. Thus the main subcategories are (1) metadiscourse indicating the speaker's attitudes towards content, and (2) metadiscourse indicating the speaker's attitudes towards self and others.

(1) Attitudes towards content are expressed with items that share certain features with metadiscoursal elements dealing with the validity of content and epistemic modality. However, the main point here is the speaker's personal view about the obviousness, interestingness, or surprise value of the content; i.e. the presenter's affective comment or value judgement on the content propositions. These are expressed in order that they may interact with the listeners' perceptions and direct the audience to evaluate the propositional material affectively and to respond to it. We divide this category of metadiscourse further into two types, (i) evaluative markers and (ii) saliency markers.

(i) Evaluative markers deal with the speaker's personal feelings towards and evaluation of the propositional content. They correspond to 'affect expressions' (Biber & Finegan 1989), and seem to be particularly frequent in the discussion and conclusion sections of the presentations. Speakers convey their subjective opinions about the significance and value of the results of their study, thereby wishing to make the audience feel the same way about their work. Evaluative markers include affect verbs, e.g. *dislike*; adjectives, e.g. *fortunate, interesting*; and adverbs such as *remarkably, regrettably:*

(25) I think that that it's particularly *discouraging* that we didn't get the changes we expected in the attribution ... in the attributions themselves.

(ii) Saliency markers, the second subtype, include adverbials such as *basically* or *exactly*. The speaker uses them to direct the listeners' attention to what are to him or her the central aspects of the presentation – although these items may also function as habitual and semantically empty fillers:

(26) the hope is that you can find out *exactly* why these over-all regressions come out the way they do.

(2) Attitudes towards self and others. Our second type of interaction-oriented metadiscourse reflects speaker-audience relations. In order to establish rapport with the audience, the speaker may emphasise his or her own role or that of the audience, or refer to fellow researchers or to the academic community in general. We identified (i) self-oriented, (ii) audience-oriented, and (iii) community-oriented expressions.

(i) Self-oriented metadiscourse is used by the speaker to draw attention to himself or herself by giving the listeners an account of personal experiences related to the research. The purpose is to establish rapport and an equal footing with the audience, and the speaker usually assumes a position that is open to judgement and criticism by the addressees:

(27) that's where my difficulties have arisen and in some ways I really wish that I'd never gone down this road.

However, the speaker might also opt for an opposite 'self-oriented' strategy and emphasise his or her own authority and professional expertise. One of the speakers in our material shared her professional background with the audience. Although this is obviously a sign of considerateness, it may also be a signal that the speaker wants to give of a certain degree of authority on the subject matter:

(28) I'm a special educator, I, I teach special education at the (...) and I've also been a special education teacher in my erm previous career.

(ii) Audience-oriented items of metadiscourse, on the other hand, make use of shared values and terminology as well as common beliefs. The speaker is here involved in an implicit dialogue with the audience by addressing them with the pronouns *you* or *we*:

(29) there's *as you are probably aware* there's quite a large body of literature about attributions.

The speaker may also use imperatives to ask the listeners to do something – for example to go back to certain points that have already appeared in the presentation. Furthermore, the speaker may refer to shared concepts and terminology, and attempt to involve the audience in common assumptions concerning background information, beliefs, or expected outcomes of research. This is typically done by adverbs such as *obviously, naturally* and *of course*, as in the following example where the speaker uses the word *obviously* and the immediately following interjections to invite the audience to share a feeling of disappointment about the outcome of the study:

(30)   *obviously* we had hoped – *ha! ha!* – that the ... this intervention would have a positive effect on students' attributions.

(iii) Community-oriented metadiscourse, our third subtype in this category, comprises references that the speaker makes to the general academic and discourse community of the discipline by citing the work of other researchers. The speaker may also use more implicit terms such as *people, researchers, evidence* and *literature*. Self-oriented and audience-oriented approaches tend to create togetherness and solidarity, whereas the community-oriented approach is generally more distant and impersonal:

(31)   but it *what evidence there is* would argue that students really don't know what's good for them.

Interestingly, the three speakers we studied in detail all chose different inter-active strategies in relation to the audience. One concentrated on self-oriented metadiscourse, allowing the audience to witness the problems and difficulties that were encountered during the research process. Another showed a marked preference for audience-oriented metadiscourse, frequently addressing the audience explicitly. The third presentation included a lengthy section on the present state of research in the field, which made use of the neutral community-oriented strategy at the expense of the more solidarity-oriented approaches typical of the other two presentations.

3.4. Context-oriented metadiscourse

Context-oriented metadiscourse is the fourth main type of metadiscourse in our classification. It corresponds to Luukka's (1992) contextual metadiscourse. Its purpose is to control the communicative situation. Two subcategories were identified.

(1) Reference to situation includes comments about the ongoing presentation or the entire conference. For example, speakers typically attempt to create a degree of 'intertextuality' in their presentations by referring to ideas that have come up in previous presentations. Often these allusions and explicit references – expressions that roughly correspond to Ventola's (1999) notion of 'semiotic spanning' – also have a clear interpersonal and audience-oriented flavour:

(32) two three or four groups of pupils involve in some type of group discussion about some mathematical idea, *the example that we heard about in the last paper.*

(2) Reference to material includes comments with which the speaker clarifies or explains the transparencies or handouts being used:

(33) has everyone got their copy of this paper you'll need it ... there's a table in the paper that people need to refer to.

Context-oriented metadiscourse was the least frequent main type of meta-discourse established in this study. Nevertheless, it is an integral part of conference language. Explanatory comments on the materials at hand in particular seem to be an effective means of clarifying the presentation and stimulating the audience. Visual material can also effectively contribute to the audience's perception of superstructure, although visuals were not used for this purpose in the talks analysed for this paper.

4. Quantitative observations

Metadiscourse accounted for almost one third (29.7 per cent) of the stripped word total in our material (total number of words minus incomplete words and filled hesitations). A considerable proportion of what is communicated in a spoken research presentation in native English is thus taken up by material outside the primary propositional content.

Figure 1 (following page) illustrates the proportions of each of the four main types of metadiscourse out of the total number of words. In terms of percentages based on the stripped word total, structure-oriented metadiscourse is the predominant type.

However, a comparison of the total number of *instances* of metadiscoursal items in Figure 2 (following page) reveals that validity-oriented metadiscourse was the most frequent type, followed by interaction-oriented, structure-oriented and context-oriented types. The reason for this is that validity-oriented items often consist of one or two words; cf., for example, the emphatic device in:

(34) the microadaptive instructional treatment really *does* seem to be best for everybody.

Structure-oriented elements, by contrast, are often complete sentences:

140

(35)   Iwould like to suggest the following definition of active learning.

and the same applies to a large number of instances of interaction-oriented metadiscourse, as in the following self-oriented item:

(36)   erm... I've got a problem that I want to share with you which is.

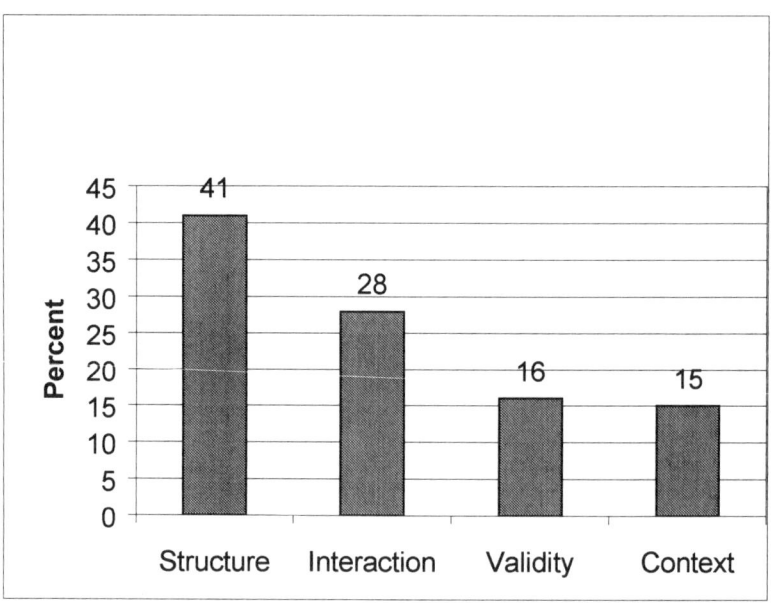

Figure 1: Proportions of metadiscoursal types out of total word count.

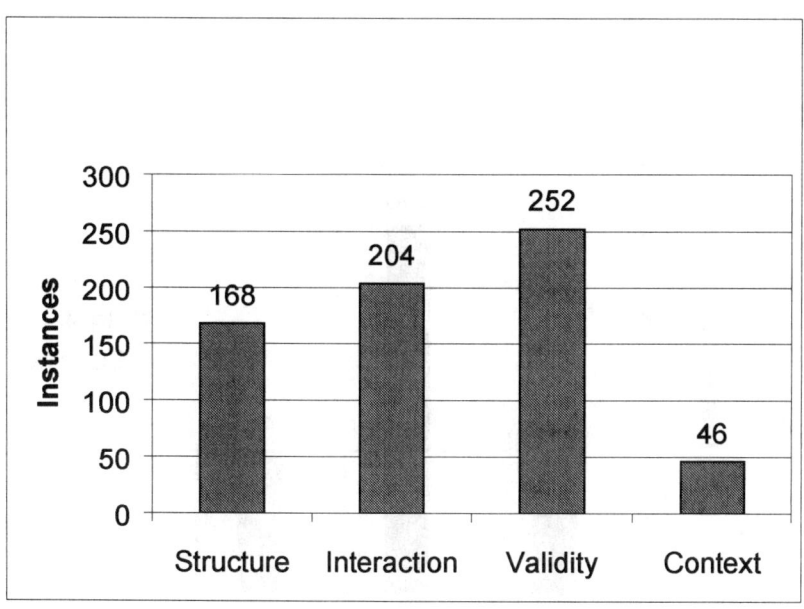

Figure 2: Instances of metadiscoursal types.

Figure 3 illustrates the degree of certainty with which the three native English presentations (P1, P2, P3) were given. The two columns per presentation correspond to the number of signals of hesitation and of certainty. Hesitation markers include approximators, definition hedges and hedges, and certainty markers group together emphatics, evaluative markers and saliency markers.

Figure 3 shows that hesitancy and certainty markers were relatively well balanced in P1 and P3, but signals of hesitation were the dominant feature in P2. The large number of these signals may, of course, be the result of various factors. It might indicate that the speaker was talking about a new research area, and hence needed to be considerate and wary, which led to the frequent use of hedging devices. The propositional content of P2 also revealed that the speaker actually made rather strong claims throughout the presentation, and it was probably necessary to soften them in the conference situation with hesitancy signals. Thirdly, it is also possible that the topic in P2 was more abstract and complex in relation to those of P1 and P3. This would also be likely to bring about a larger number of such signals.

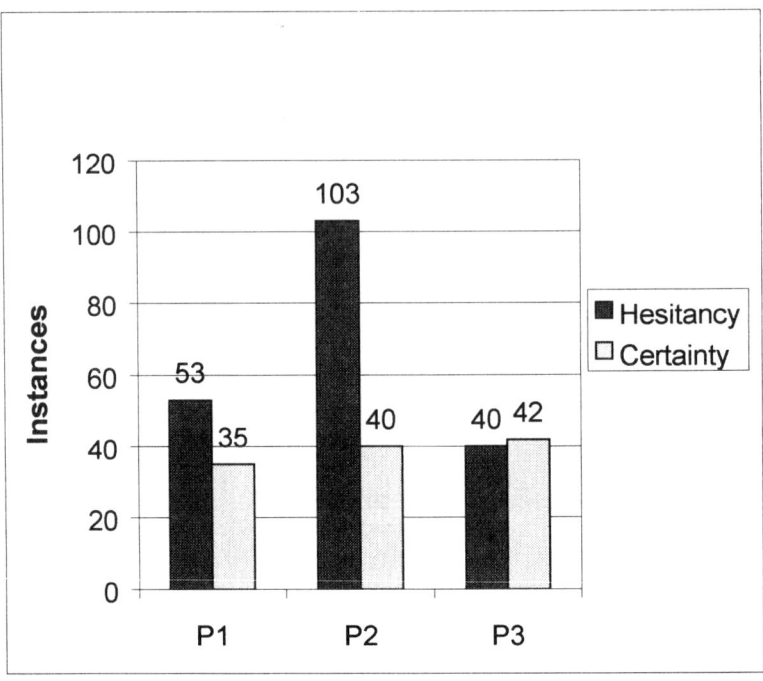

Figure 3: Speakers' degree of certainty.

Whatever the case, the presentations analysed here, together with the rest of the materials collected in our project, illustrate the point made by Thompson (1997): the conference presenter's role is not without its problems. One must appear confident and competent, yet avoid projecting an 'inflated ego'. The speaker must play the role of a 'modest or even self-deprecating expert' (Thompson 1997: 333), but must also strike an effective balance between these pragmatic and interactional needs and the rhetorical information-transmission goals of the presentation. Within the latter, an additional and central problem for novice and expert presenters alike is limiting the amount of information to proportions manageable by both the speaker and the listeners, given the floor time available.

5. Concluding remarks

We have described spoken-language metadiscourse in an academic conference setting. Our four-class model bears resemblance to Crismore (1984, 1989), Vande Kopple (1985) and Luukka (1992), but differs from these in certain respects, notably in dividing the single class of attitudinal (Crismore) or interpersonal (Vande Kopple, Luukka) metadiscourse into two, i.e. validity-oriented and interaction-oriented types. The reason is that our material consisted only of spoken discourse, in which the presence of validity-oriented material, for example hedging and approximators, was particularly clearly identifiable. Our 'structure-oriented' metadiscourse corresponds to some extent with 'textual' or 'informational' metadiscourse of previous classifications, but also highlights the potential for expressions of rhetorical structure typical of empirical work.

The categorisation of linguistic items is never unambiguous, and this applies to our material as well. Furthermore, metadiscoursal items often do not carry one function only. Almost nine per cent of the devices identified in this study had over-lapping functions, and were placed in more than one main category.

On the basis of the present material, it is not possible to draw conclusions on the general proportion of metadiscourse or on the types that predominate in spoken academic conference presentations. Extensive individual variation is likely to occur between speakers, particularly in the use of validity- and interaction-oriented devices. The presentations we analysed were given by educationalists, and the results are not necessarily applicable to oral discourse within other academic fields. The linguistic and cultural background of the speaker will also have a decisive influence on how oral research presentations are prepared, organised, formulated, and expressed.

Our material leaves us with a number of conclusions concerning the processing consequences of the use or non-use of metadiscourse in academic conference presentations. One is related to the frequency of devices which either introduce clarifying, supporting or justificatory material, or express pragmatically- and interactionally-motivated hesitation and uncertainty. Presentations with a sub-stantial number of these devices, particularly hesitancy markers – such as one of the speeches we analysed – tend to give the listener a subjective feeling of increased processing load. It is as if the listener were faced with two slightly separate but parallel comprehension tasks: grasping the essential information content and, in addition, following the superimposed discourse of hedging, modalisation, cautiousness, and explanation. Coaching given to prospective conference presenters might benefit from research that relates the time and content space taken up by this 'secondary' discourse and its markers to listeners' perceptions of presenter comprehensibility and effectiveness.

Another conclusion of some interest for studies of conference language, academic or more general types, and for intercultural communication, is that the significance of metadiscoursal devices will probably be highlighted in situations where the speaker has to cooperate with an interpreter. Whether working in the consecutive or the simultaneous mode, the interpreter must generate a full semantic representation of the source discourse, and an adequate mental model of the topic domain being handled. This distinguishes the interpreter from the 'normal' listener, who can get by with far less precise goals and attentional strategies. Interpreting is possible only through in-depth understanding where all the central aspects of discourse comprehension described by Graesser & Britton (1996: 350) are present: the construction of a multilevel representation involving the discourse itself, the context, and inferences – all within the constraints imposed by a dynamic but limited-capacity working memory. The interpreter is thus an exceptional listener to a conference presentation, and the processing by an interpreter is a test of the clarity, comprehensibility and organisation of the speaker's ideas. One prediction, which to our knowledge has not been subjected to serious empirical testing, is that efficient use of metadiscourse is likely to facilitate the comprehension processes and output produced by the consecutive and simultaneous interpreter alike.

Yet another conclusion our material suggests is that some types of meta-discourse – if used with moderation – will be a powerful tool for speakers of conference language when they organise their presentations for the benefit of the listeners. In particular, superstructure announcers, explicit indicators of macro-structural topic change, and reminders would seem to be effective ways of giving the audience a chance to orientate themselves towards the presentation and help them create an organised set of rhetorical, content-structural or situation-model 'pegs' on which to hang the emerging items of content (cf. however, Dunkel & Davis 1994 for non-facilitatory effects of lengthy advance organisers – and Flowerdew & Tauroza 1995 for a demonstration of facilitatory effects of certain discourse markers). The simple reason for the assumption of meta-discoursal facilitation is that spoken messages are ephemeral. Listeners are engaged in a process where regressions to previous material are not possible in the same sense as in reading. Successful understanding depends on whether their working memory can construct an organised representation of the input material during this single pass, and whether that representation can be transferred into the more permanent memory structures. The more complex the propositional content, the more important it may be that the speaker organises the presentation clearly and signals this organisation with explicit metadiscoursal tools.

References

Aijmer, K. 1986. "Discourse variation and hedging." In J. Aarts & W. Meijs (eds). *Corpus Linguistics II: New Studies in the Analysis and Exploitation of Computer Corpora.* Amsterdam: Editions Rodopi B.V., 1-18.

145

Biber, J. & E. Finegan 1989. "Styles of stance in English: Lexical and grammatical marking of evidentiality and affect." *Text,* 9: 93-124.

Brown, P. & S. Levinson 1978. "Universals in language usage: Politeness phenomena" In E. Goody (ed). *Questions and Politeness: Strategies in Social Interaction.* Cambridge: Cambridge University Press, 56-289.

Bäcklund, I. 1988. "To begin with, this is the problem, for example. On some reader-oriented structural markers in English expository texts." *Studia Linguistica,* 42: 60-68.

Bäcklund, I. 1990. "Cues to audience. On some structural markers in English monologue." In B. Odenstedt & G. Persson (eds). *Instead of Flowers: Papers in Honour of Mats Rydén.* Acta Universitatis Umenis. Stockholm: Almqvist & Wiksell International, 29-39.

Chaudron, C. & J. C. Richards 1986. "The effect of discourse markers on the comprehension of lectures." *Applied Linguistics,* 7: 113-127.

Coates, J. 1987. "Epistemic modality and spoken discourse." *Transactions of the Philological Society,* 110-131.

Crismore, A. 1984. "The rhetoric of textbooks: Metadiscourse." *Curriculum Studies,* 16: 279-296.

Crismore, A. 1989. *Talking with readers: Metadiscourse as a Rhetorical Act.* New York: Peter Lang Publishing.

Crompton, P. 1997. "Hedging in academic writing: Some theoretical problems." *English for Specific Purposes,* 16: 271-287.

van Dijk, T. A. 1980. *Macrostructures. An Interdiscplinary Study of Global Structures in Discourse.* New Jersey: Lawrence Erlbaum Associates.

van Dijk, T. A. & W. Kintsch 1983. *Strategies of Discourse Comprehension.* London: Academic Press.

Dunkel, P.A. & J. N. Davis 1994. "The effects of rhetorical signaling cues on the recall of English lecture information by speakers of English as a native or second language." In J. Flowerdew (ed). *Academic Listening: Research Perspectives.* Cambridge: Cambridge University Press, 55-74.

Flowerdew, J. & S. Tauroza 1995. "The effect of discourse markers on second language lecture comprehension." *Studies in Second Language Acquisition,* 17: 435-458.

Fraser, B. 1990. "An approach to discourse markers." *Journal of Pragmatics,* 14: 383-395.

Graesser, A. C. & B. K. Britton 1996. "Five metaphors for text understanding." In B. K. Britton & A. C. Graesser (eds). *Models of Understanding Text.* Mahwah, N.J.: Lawrence Erlbaum, 341-351.

Hyland, K. 1998a. "Persuasion and context: The pragmatics of academic metadiscourse." *Journal of Pragmatics,* 30: 437-455.

Hyland, K. 1998b. "Boosting, hedging and the negotiation of academic knowledge." *Text,* 18: 349-382.

Hyland, K. 1999. "Talking to students: Metadiscourse in introductory coursebooks." *English for Specific Purposes,* 18: 3-26.

Luukka, M.-R. 1992. *Akateemista metadiskurssia. Tieteellisten tekstien tekstuaalisia, interpersonaalisia ja kontekstuaalisia piirteitä.* Jyväskylä: Korkeakoulujen kielikeskus.

Mauranen, A. 1993. "Contrastive ESP rhetoric: Metatext in Finnish-English economics texts." *English for Specific Purposes,* 12: 3-22.

Myers, G. 1989. "The pragmatics of politeness in scientific articles." *Applied Linguistics,* 10: 1-35.

Prince, E. F., J. Frader & C. Bosk 1980. *On hedging in physician-physician discourse.* In R. J. Di Pietro (ed). *Linguistics and the Professions.* Hillsdale, NJ: Ablex, 83-97.

Quirk, R., S. Greenbaum, G. Leech & J. Svartvik 1972. *A Grammar of Contemporary English.* London: Longman.

Schiffrin, D. 1980. "Meta-talk: Organizational and evaluative brackets in discourse." *Sociological Enquiry: Language and Social Interaction,* 50: 199-236.

Schiffrin, D. 1987. *Discourse Markers.* Cambridge: Cambridge University Press.

Swales, J. 1990. *Genre analysis: English in Academic and Research Settings.* Cambridge: Cambridge University Press.

Swales, J. & Malczewski, B. 1995. "Attention-getters and New Episode Flags in MICASE. NASCLLT Abstracts." http://www.lsa.umich.edu/eli/micase/abstracthtml. 7.2.1995, retrieved March 1999.

Thompson, S. E. 1997. "Presenting Research: A Study of Interaction in Academic Monologue." Unpublished PhD dissertation. Liverpool: University of Liverpool.

Vande Kopple, W. J. 1985. "Some exploratory discourse on metadiscourse." *College Composition and Communication,* 36: 82-93.

Ventola, E. 1997. "Modalisation: Probability – an exploration into its role in academic writing." In A. Duszak (ed). *Culture and Styles of Academic Discourse.* Berlin: Mouton de Gruyter, 157-179.

Ventola, E. 1999. "Semiotic spanning at conferences: Cohesion and coherence in and across conference papers and their discussions." In W. Bublitz, U. Lenk & E. Ventola (eds). *Coherence in Spoken and Written Discourse.* Amsterdam: Benjamins, 101-125.

Weissberg, B. 1993. "The graduate seminar: Another research process genre." *English for Specific Purposes,* 12: 23-35.

Williams, J. M. 1981. *Style: Ten Lessons in Clarity and Grace.* Illinois: Scott, Foresman.

'AS THE STORY UNFOLDS': THE USES OF NARRATIVE IN RESEARCH PRESENTATIONS

Susan Thompson

University of Liverpool, Liverpool, United Kingdom

Abstract – This chapter examines how research presenters talk about the process of researching when they speak at public events such as academic conferences and research seminars. The paper focuses on the functions of storytelling in research talks delivered by native English-speaking academics in the fields of applied linguistics and science. Previous research into the language of scientific research articles has shown that research articles promote a view of the research process as objective and impersonal, focusing on concepts and techniques. The main question addressed by this chapter is, how far do conference presenters model their papers on the research article? By comparing the telling of the research 'story' in research presentations and their related research articles, this chapter demonstrates that the presentation differs in important ways from the research article in this respect. The analysis indicates the complex nature of the conference paper as a genre which, as a face-to-face event, highlights human aspects of the interaction between speaker and audience, but which, as an academic/professional event played out before a discriminating audience, must promote the research reported as valid, significant and 'scientific'. The chapter discusses the difficult task which faces the research presenter in attempting to satisfy the interpersonal demands of the presentation genre, and briefly considers the implications of the study for the development of academic presentation skills courses for novice researchers.

1. Introduction

The process of academic research can be characterised as the performance, interpretation and reworking of research events to enable the construction of a research story to present to the outside world (cf. Gilbert & Mulkay 1984; Knorr-Cetina 1981; Bazerman 1983; Latour & Woolgar 1986). The research process is a complex "interweaving of talking, working and writing" (Shalom 1993: 37). Within this process, the conference research presentation plays a number of crucial roles. It may provide a report of work in progress or a preliminary airing of new ideas; it may form the basis of a future research article, or it may be a candidate for publication in the conference proceedings (Swales 1990: 178).

A research presentation is, of course, not just a matter of transmitting neutral, factual information from researcher to audience (cf. Goffman 1981). Instead, the presenter creates a selective representation of the research world and research activity which is tailored to the specific needs and interests of the audience at a particular conference, research seminar or other kind of research meeting. The presentation is a rhetorical construct whose principal aims are to present the researcher's view of his or her research experiences, and to persuade the audience of the status, relevance and value of the research (Hunston 1993). In this, the presentation shares features of the research article; but the two are clearly distinct, if related, genres. Not least, as a face-to-face oral genre, the presentation invites the use of linguistic behaviour typically associated with spoken interaction. Presenters might decide to employ what Tannen (1989) calls 'involvement strategies', techniques such as storytelling, metaphor and constructed dialogue which "reflect and simultaneously create interpersonal involvement" (1989: 1) between speaker and listener. These techniques are perhaps more readily associated with casual conversation and informal oral personal narratives than with academic discourse. However, Tannen (1989: 194) argues that skilled public speakers can use such strategies to persuade an audience to accept their ideas and indeed to accept the speakers themselves.

Research presenters themselves may in fact refer to their own presentations as a piece of storytelling, as in Example 1:

(1)   I won't dwell too long on the techniques of the structure of magnetic measuring because this should come out *as the story unfolds*.

The present study examines whether, and to what degree, research presenters use narrative to talk about the research process, and, if so, what purposes these techniques serve. Studies of narrative in non-academic genres suggest possible reasons for the use of narrative in academic texts. Narrative in news reporting can be used to make an article more enticing to the reader. Cortazzi & Jin (2000: 119) discuss the role of personal narratives in the creation of coherence and identity in the lives of individuals and their associate groups. Eggins & Slade (1997: 229) focus on the interpersonal function of storytelling in conversations, where personal narratives offer a "resource for assessing and confirming affiliations with others". What all these different perspectives share is a view that storytelling functions to engage the reader/listener and draw her/him into a shared world with the writer/speaker.

2. The structure and functions of narrative

2.1. Narrative models

A considerable body of research on the nature of narrative text now exists (e.g. Labov & Waletsky 1967; de Beaugrande & Dressler 1981; Longacre 1983). From this research have come various templates of narrative structure and descriptions of typical lexico-grammatical features. Probably the most widely influential of these has been that of Labov & Waletsky (1967). It offers a structural model of a typical personal oral narrative which includes the following stages: an optional ABSTRACT which summarises what the story will be about, an ORIENTATION which sets the scene and introduces the characters, the COMPLICATING ACTION which creates the story, a RESOLUTION which resolves the story, and an optional CODA which links the story back to the present time of telling. The obligatory sequence of narrative clauses is accompanied by what Labov & Waletsky call 'free clauses', which may occur at any point in the narrative. Free clauses are essentially evaluative in nature, and are used to establish for the listener(s) "the contextual significance and tellability" of the story (Toolan 1988: 156).

While Labov & Waletsky's model has proved to be both influential and illuminating in a number of different fields of enquiry, alternative models of narrative have emerged over the past thirty years. One area of research of particular interest to the present study is that which attempts to sub-categorise different kinds of stories according to functional type. As Martin (1992: 559) comments, Labov's "unidimensional modelling" of the oral personal narrative fails to take into account the fact that, since stories may be told for different purposes, this will be reflected in variations in their generic structure. Plum (1988) proposes four different types of storytelling genres: the NARRATIVE, the ANECDOTE, the EXEMPLUM and the RECOUNT. The NARRATIVE loosely resembles the model proposed by Labov & Waletsky (1967), but the ANECDOTE, whilst similar to NARRATIVE in its focus on a crisis or problem, does not have a RESOLUTION to the crisis. Instead closure comes with a reaction to the crisis, such as laughter or an expression of feelings towards the crisis. The EXEMPLUM retells an incident, but crucially the emphasis is on "an explicit message on how the world should or should not be" (Eggins & Slade 1997: 237); the story is told to make a point. Finally, the RECOUNT consists of a straightforward 'record of events' and the speaker's view of these events; there is no highlighted event or problem. These sub-categorisations prove helpful in examining more closely the possible functions of stories in research presentations[1].

2.2. Narrative in academic genres

Relatively little research has been performed on the use of narrative in academic genres (although see Grimes (1975) for a comparison of scientific writing and fairy tales). Myers (e.g. 1990, 1994) compares the representation of the research process in popular scientific articles and research articles. In the popular articles, the researchers are presented as 'actors' and the research claim is presented as a 'discovery event' (Myers 1994: 183). The sequencing of information is temporal: we are taken through the steps which the researchers took to obtain their final results. There are strong similarities with the narrative model proposed by Labov & Waletsky (1967), and Myers terms this kind of development the 'narrative of nature'. In contrast, Myers finds that the scientific research article focuses on scientific concepts and techniques: research events happen without any apparent human involvement. The sequencing of results is non-chronological and the articles "follow the argument of the scientist" (Myers 1990: 142) rather than the chronological retelling of events. Myers terms this kind of development the 'narrative of science'. Myers' distinction is highly illuminating for the present study, in that it links the use or avoidance of narrative techniques to the purposes and audiences of each particular genre.

When we turn to the use of storytelling in the research presentation, Dubois (1980) finds that biomedical conference presentations normally include a narrative component relating to experimental procedure, and that some presentations are almost completely narrative (see also Swales 1990). However, views differ over the status of narrative in research presentations. Dubois herself (1980: 143) states that some biomedical conference speakers use an expository style to present their data as "scientific INFORMATION", apparently "derived in a cool, objective, orderly, unhurried procedure", while other more "prefatory" presentations fail to rise above the level of a "narrative of experiments, with all their real life incident". Weissberg (1993), in a genre analysis of the graduate seminar presentation, also finds some variation in the use of narrative by graduate student presenters, but with a bias towards the borrowing of the

---

1 In the field of narrative studies there is some considerable variation in the use of terminology by different researchers. In this article, the term *story* and *narrative* are used interchangeably as umbrella terms to cover all kinds of texts which are characterised by the retelling of a series of past events using cause-effect and temporal shifts and a focus on the actions of characters. The term NARRATIVE (upper case) is used to refer to that sub-category of Plum's (1988) model of storytelling genres. Wherever researchers have used the term *narrative* with a specific other meaning, single quote marks ('narrative') are used to indicate this.

research article's IMRD (Introduction ^ Methods ^ Results ^ Discussion) development and the non-narrative style of the research article. The graduate research presenters in Weissberg's (1993: 32) study did not usually "convey the 'personal' aspect of scientific enquiry, of what really went on in the laboratory or field". In contrast with Dubois (1980), however, Weissberg is critical of presenters who avoided using the more personal "narrative of experiments" approach, an argument which is supported by experienced academic informants interviewed in his study who valued the personal orientation of the research presentation. It should be noted that the fundamental differences in the types of presentations studied by Dubois and Weissberg (conference papers versus departmental postgraduate student presentations) are likely to have influenced each researcher's perceptions of what comprises appropriate generic behaviour.

Earlier research has, then, clearly shown that research presenters face a choice between representing their research activities using a narrative or a non-narrative type of development. Given this choice, the present study of research presentations in the fields of sciences and linguistics investigates what might motivate a presenter to choose one or other type of development to reconstruct the research process for an audience. In particular, the present study focuses on the movement within each presentation between the two types, and attempts to identify the purposes which motivate these shifts. It will be argued that the primary motivation for these choices is pragmatic, that is, choices are primarily determined by the image which the presenters wish to promote of certain aspects of the research process and of the researchers themselves.

3. The study

The study investigates the use of narrative in a small corpus of spoken and written academic texts. The data consist of a sub-corpus of ten research presentations recorded[2] at various conferences and public research seminars, comprising 67,825 words in total. These are paired with a sub-corpus of ten related research articles. The corpus was chosen to allow for direct comparative analysis between the pairs of presentations and articles. It was assumed that, by controlling the variables of text producer and topic, any differences between the articles and presentations could be attributed to the effect of genre choices. However, it was found that there was not always a one-to-one relationship between presentation and article: some presenters created more than one written

---

2 All the presentations were recorded in their natural environments, and it was therefore decided to minimise the degree of disturbance to speakers and their audiences by not video-recording the presentations. Audio-recordings were carried out as unobtrusively as possible (with the speakers' permission), using a small tape-recorder placed close to the presenter.

version of a presentation, or used material from different presentations to create a written article (cf. Swales 1990: 178). In such cases, it was decided to choose one of the researcher's articles which most closely resembled the information covered by the presentation[3].

Half of the presentations and articles were taken from scientific and applied scientific fields (e.g. physics, surface science), while the other half were taken from linguistics and applied linguistics (e.g. discourse analysis, TESOL). This allows for comparison of narrative choices across two different fields of enquiry, a factor which, to my knowledge, has not so far been considered by earlier researchers. All the presentations were delivered by experienced British and American academics at large-scale conferences or smaller-scale public research seminars in various European countries between 1990 and 1995. These presentations were all relatively informal events (at least as judged within the constraints on informality imposed by the conference or seminar event), delivered using notes or apparently spontaneously with the aid of visuals, rather than formal 'read-aloud' papers such as keynote speeches. Audiences varied in size between 20 and 100. The five linguistic and five scientific presentations were similar in size, with a total of 32,713 words in the linguistics texts and 35,112 in the scientific texts.

The presentations were first transcribed orthographically[4]. The presentation transcriptions and research articles were manually searched for all sections dealing with the reporting of the presenter's research activities i.e. data/materials, methods, and results/analysis. These sections were selected for analysis on the basis that they parallel the stages through which the research process develops, and therefore reflect the stages of the research 'story'. The relevant sections were analysed to ascertain whether or not they obeyed narrative conventions as outlined above. Both narrative and non-narrative sections were then analysed to identify how the presenters/writers described their data/materials and methods and reported the results of analysis or experiment. In particular, the analysis investigated whether presenters/writers

---

3   It should be borne in mind that, as is typical in the field of science, all the scientific articles were co-authored with other researchers, so that other 'voices' are also involved in these research articles.

4   The following transcription conventions were used. Unclear speech is marked by {...}. To preserve anonymity as far as possible, names of people and institutions were tactically deleted: deleted names of people are indicated by {NTD} and of institutions by {ITD}. The transcriptions were segmented into clause complexes (Halliday 1994), the unit consisting of a main clause plus any dependent clauses. However, given the fact that the presentations were spontaneously-delivered oral texts, it did not always prove possible to segment the text so neatly. On the other hand, the fact that the speakers had (apparently) prepared their talks carefully encouraged a higher degree of fluency in delivery and less 'fragmenting' of clausal units than one would expect in casual conversation (Crookes 1986; Ventola 1987).

focused on the researchers as actors or on research-related concepts and techniques (cf. Myers 1994).

4. Storytelling in presentations and articles

Analysis of the presentation corpus supports the findings of earlier studies that storytelling is a feature of research presentations, since each presentation contained at least one narrative passage. Overall, a total of 44 passages of story-telling were identified in the corpus of presentations, an average of 4.4 per individual presentation. Some of these were quite brief, while others, such as Example 2 below, were considerably lengthier. In Example 2, the presenter tells the story of how over a period of several years he and his research team were puzzled by a result in their earlier research work. In 1986, they were performing experiments using a mass spectrometer to observe photon-stimulated desorption on silicon surfaces, and found that, at a particular level of photon energy (36eV), they obtained excellent results. However, at that point they had no idea why this should happen. Only in a later experiment did the researcher discover the significance of the 36eV level:

(2) (i) when we first did this work I'll leave this up for a minute in 1986 we didn't really know what was going on
(ii) we knew we could make the F centres
(iii) we happened to be using 36eV because at 36eV clean silicon has a resonance in its surface states
(iv) so in trying to tell if your silicon surface substrate is clean this is a nice photon energy to use to tell that it's clean that the surface states are good
(v) so our spectrometer happened to be on 36eV
(vi) and we wanted to get a nice picture of the calcium chloride valence band
(vii) and we were watching the spectrometer scan
(viii) and started noticing something coming up here
(ix) and we found out at the time 36eV was wonderful
(x) we couldn't really produce reproduce it with other photon energies
(xi) and we published this
(xii) and then we tried using other photon energies
(xiii) and it never really worked
(xiv) and we never really understood why 36eV
(xv) but back then we left it
(xvi) and then I was working doing photon-stimulated desorption later on in my life
(xvii) and I decided to go back to calcium chloride and say OK let's look at the F+ ion yield versus photon energy OK
(xviii) and that's the red curve here
(xix) and it turns out to be fortuitous that if you look at the F+ ion yield as you make the photon energy move you see there's a very sharp energy peak here
(xx) 35 36 eV gives you F+ ions

(xxi) if you're a little lower than that or a little higher than that you get very few
       F+ ions
(xxii) and so that tells me that this is what's going on
(xxiii) this is why at 36eV we're able to make F centres so readily OK.

For most of this extract, the researchers are the actors and the focus is on the discovery events – what the researchers did, what they found out, and what they deduced from their results. Transitivity choices are primarily material and mental processes (Halliday 1994). The story follows a straightforward narrative development; the sequencing of information is basically temporal (*when we first did this work, and then, and then ... later on in my life*) and apparently matches the real-life sequence of events, and the predominant tense choice is simple past. The speaker takes us right through the research process from beginning to end using a story structure which is far closer to the Labov & Waletsky (1967) model than the IMRD model: units i-vi resemble an Orientation, units vii-xv the Complicating Events, units xvi-xxiii the Resolution. Like the oral narratives in Labov & Waletsky's study, this narrative also contains a number of free evaluative clauses in the present tense (iv, xviii-xxiii). These take us out of the narrative sequence to make explicit evaluative comments about the experimental procedure. In unit iv, the presenter justifies their use of a particular experimental procedure, while in xviii-xxiii he presents the Resolution in terms of the generalisable implications of what was found in the experiments.

Example 3 comes from an applied linguistics conference presentation on forensic linguistics, discussing the use of discourse analysis techniques to identify whether or not the police have falsified a witness' statement:

(3) (i) in fact there's a case I'm involved in where the police chief inspector is about to be prosecuted for falsifying the evidence
     (ii) and I've submitted a report
     (iii) and a member of the police investigation branch phoned me
     (iv) and said I've got to come and see you tomorrow to take a statement from you
     (v) and when he arrived he said I arrived early he said
     (vi) so I've been sitting in the car and I've written down your statement he said
     (vii) can I read it to you
     (viii) and will you sign it (*audience laughter*)
     (ix) interesting
     (x) but it didn't matter because he was basically wanting to put in his form what I would have said nothing more.

The story follows the ANECDOTE pattern (Plum 1988), consisting of an Orientation (i-ii), a Remarkable Event (iii-viii), and a Reaction to that event (viii-x). Unlike the NARRATIVE in Example 2, this ANECDOTE does not relate directly to the research process itself. Rather, it comes as an amusing little aside about the strange world of police investigations, interpolated into a longer introduction to the types of verbal evidence which can be presented in British courts of law.

A very clear finding is that there are no examples of storytelling whatsoever in any of the paired research articles in either the applied linguistic or scientific fields, supporting previous findings on the language of research articles (e.g. Brett 1994; Thompson 1993), and indicating a clear generic difference. The following extract from a surface science research article offers a typically detailed past tense account of the instruments and procedures used:

(4)   The experiments were carried out in two different UHV instruments equipped with LEED and either STM (Omicron) or single reflection Fourier transform infrared spectroscopy (FTIR) (Mattson Galaxy), described elsewhere. The Cu(110) crystals were cut and polished mechanically, and for STM experiments electrochemically, to a mirror finish before insertion into UHV where they were cleaned by standard Ar+ bombardment (typically, 500eV, 8mA/cm^{-2}) and annealing (850K) procedures until a clean surface was obtained, characterised by sharp (1x1) LEED patterns in FTIR and large flat terraces in STM *(a further 10 sentences on methods are omitted)*.

While the methods are presented using the past tense, this is not a true narrative. The use of passive voice and processes involving inanimate entities ostensibly removes human actors from the text. The reader can infer that there is a real-world temporal shift between at least some of the research events, but this is rarely signalled in the text itself. There is little sense that one part of the text motivates or is motivated by other parts of the text. The reader must turn to a completely different section of the text, the Results section, to find out 'what happened next'.

Research presenters may mix narrative and non-narrative modes, typically talking about the data/materials and methods in the past tense, using the RECOUNT method of storytelling (Plum 1988) which simply retells the events and offers the speaker's view of these events. This rather matter-of-fact recounting of research methods is particularly typical of the science presentations, as in Example 5:

(5)   (i)   so we did this one with the ethylene on it easily
      (ii)   and had a look
      (iii) because this was done in the omicron microscope we could not heat the sample in situ
      (iv)   so we had to take it out of the microscope
      (v)   heat it till we saw some ethylene coming off in the mass spectrometer
      (vi)   and then have another look.

In the case of these mixed-format research reports, presenters then change to the present tense as they talk the audience through the results (normally supported by visual materials such as graphs or slides) and interpret them. The same presenter as in Example 5 continues:

(6) (vii) and this is what we saw
     (viii) and particularly if you look at the empty states image here you can see now a low coverage of ethylene molecules sitting there and looking for all the world just like the ethylene molecules that were in the initial low coverage
     (ix)   plainly this seems to fit in well with the observations of the mass spectrometer that the ethylene that comes off just comes off as complete ethylene molecules
     (x)   and what stays behind is left behind as complete ethylene molecules.

However, although examples of narrative passages were found in the research presentations, it is clear that in both the applied linguistic and science presentations the *non*-narrative method of talking about the research process is by far the more dominant. This can be exemplified with an extract from an applied linguistics presentation on the washback effect of TOEFL classes:

(7) (i)   what I tried to do was to measure the atmosphere of the classes because typically people say in interviews and so on they say TOEFL classes are dull they're terribly boring to teach boring to see for other teachers
     (ii)   so I don't know
     (iii) how do you measure atmosphere
     (iv)   well how would you measure atmosphere
     (v)   well I measured it that way the number of incidents of laughter (*laughter, interruption and interchange*)
     (vi)   what you find is that in M's classes there's a lot more laughter than there are in B's classes particularly with respect to TOEFL OK
     (vii) the figures on the table this is the quantifier or quantification of atmosphere
     (viii) the atmosphere's better in M's TOEFL classes than in B's
     (ix)   B's TOEFL classes aren't very funny
     (x)   or they don't bring about laughter (*omission*)
     (xi)   again if you average these out what you find is that people laugh more in M's class than they do in B's OK
     (xii) and they laugh far more in non-TOEFL classes than they do in TOEFL classes
     (xiii) but this it looks as if you look at these data as if it's clearly the case that atmosphere as identified by laughter favours non-TOEFL classes on the grounds that it's more pleasant to be in a class with everyone laughing
     (xiv) so you could argue TOEFL classes are not good
     (xv)   TOEFL doesn't have a good effect on classes because students don't laugh very much OK
     (xvi) that isn't the case.

In this extract, we are first given the methods (i-v), followed by the results (vi-xii), and an interpretation of the results (xiii-xvi). The only uses of past tense during the whole extract come in units (i) and (v), where the presenter explains his aim and the method used to achieve it. Otherwise, the whole passage is non-narrative. The presenter justifies his choice of this method by what his subjects 'typically' say during interviews (i). He then asks the audience to consider what method they would choose in this situation (iii-iv). The results of his analysis are presented using the present tense (vi-xii), supported by a table on an overhead transparency. Finally, the presenter sets up a hypothetical argument (xiii-xiv) based on the results before going on to demolish the argument.

Rather than temporal shifts, indicated by temporal connectors, the major development in this extract is through matching relations (Winter 1977; Hoey 1983) of contrast (*what would you do* vs. *this is what I did*, *what M's class is like* vs. *what B's class is like*) and hypothetical-real (*what you might argue* vs. *what is really the case*), signalled by logical connectors such as *but* and *so*. To this extent, the extract more closely resembles Myers' (1994) 'narrative of science' than the 'narrative of nature' mode. However, there is a fundamental and crucial difference. Rather than focusing on the entities themselves, the speaker highlights the human involvement in performing actions in relation to these entities. The presentation displays a typical use of active voice plus the interactive pronoun *you* (e.g. *you measure atmosphere*, *if you average these out*, *you could argue*). Moreover, the presenter introduces a more explicitly interactive mode by asking the audience questions (which appear to invite audience participation and the setting up of a dialogic mode). We return to these important interpersonal features of research presentations in Section 5. These findings reveal a situation where research presentations seem to share features of both types of 'narrative' identified by Myers (1990, 1994), that of nature and that of science, but also display their own particular features: both implicit and overt interaction with the audience.

It is important to stress that no single method of development exists in the presentation corpus: presenters may report the sequence of materials/methods and results entirely in narrative mode, using past tense, or entirely in expository mode, using the present tense, or using a mix of both. The findings cast light on the apparently contradictory findings of Dubois (1980) and Weissberg (1993), that some presenters choose the narrative mode while others choose a non-narrative mode, and that the same presenter may choose one or the other within the same presentation. Clearly, the key question is what motivates one choice rather than the other in any particular situation; the following section focuses on possible factors.

5. Pragmatic uses of narrative and non-narrative modes

The analysis has found that, although the choice of past tense to talk about the research process actually reflects the real-world past-time occurrence of these events, the dominant tense choice for reporting research in the presentation corpus is in fact the simple present. One possible interpretation of this is that the use of present or past tense in the presentation corpus is associated with the *status* accorded by the presenter to the information being transmitted. Using past tense narrative makes a claim about something which happened in the past, distant from the present time. Claims for the generalisability or relevance of past events may of course come through the use of evaluative free clauses and/or an Abstract or Coda to link past events to the present time. Nevertheless, by telling a story the presenter distances the events from the present moment and the present audience. In contrast, by choosing to report results in the present tense, the presenter gives them the status of a general truth rather than simply events which took place in the past (cf. Dubois' (1980: 143) characterisation of past-tense narrative use as indicating a focus on the experimental process itself rather than on "what is universally true"). Thomas (1991: 94) makes a similar connection in research articles, finding that the use of the present simple tense to report previous research projects the information as "a general truth or an established fact" and "carries a very strong, though implicit, commitment on the part of the writer".

If, as appears to be the case, the choice of present tense allows a strong though implicit claim to be made for the generalisability and truth value of the results reported, the obvious question then arises as to why presenters would choose to use past tense narrative consistently throughout a complete sequence of Methods and Results. It will be noticed that the narrative in Example 2 given above tells the story of research work which had in some sense failed. In the research presentation corpus, the primary function of narrative passages appears to be to talk about research failures. To explore this function further, it proves illuminating to compare accounts of failed experiments in paired research presentations and research articles (although it is actually difficult to find such accounts in articles, since authors understandably appear reluctant to record their failures in print). The following example is one of only a handful of occurrences of an account appearing in both the presentation and paired article. The research presentation tells the story very explicitly:

(8) (i)   and we had a problem of measuring absorbing in adhesives
    (ii) and you guessed it
    (iii) what we tried to do was to cast an ingot in epoxy resin
    (iv) a nice homogeneous piece of plastic material was what we hoped we'd end up with
    (v)   but because resin curing is an exothermic reaction we ended up with a mushroom
    (vi) and if you cut a mushroom in half and take a look inside it you can see that it doesn't tell us about adhesive
    (vii) so we had to think of another way of measuring ultrasonic reactions with adhesive.

Because this is an account of failure, the story cannot make the transition from a past-tense narrative about past events to a significant generalisable fact in the present. It is interesting to compare the presentation in Example 8 of a failed experimental procedure with the associated research article, where it is referred to in one sentence in the 'Discussion and Conclusion' section. This section focuses on the importance and usefulness of the method eventually successfully developed by the research team to measure ultrasonic reactions with adhesive, and gives a number of advantages of this method over alternatives, including the following:

(9)   Also it may not always be possible to cast an ingot due to exothermic cure.

Another presentation/article comparison shows a similar contrast. The following presenter offers a fascinating insight into the story of the research process:

(10) (i)   so we thought we had a nice picture of this molecule
      (ii)   we were quite happy that the molecules that were forming this structure this orientation that they were forming a well-defined surface until we did some STM work with {NTD}
      (iii) and then our whole world fell apart for a while
      (iv)   but in rebuilding it it's turned out to be a much more complex world than we previously thought.

However, the only hint of such a dramatic upheaval in the progress of their research work comes in a mild evaluation of the structure in the Results section of the article, given here in Example 11:

(11) The α structure is relatively complex.

The problems and failures which are so cheerfully admitted in the research presentation are heavily disguised in the related articles. In telling stories against themselves, the presenters typically display equanimity or even self-deprecating humour, rather than any giving sense of frustration or embarrassment. To enliven the stories, they pepper them with direct speech, colloquialisms and idiomatic expressions, all of which are, of course, screened out of the research articles (see also Frobert-Adamo's article in this volume). What appears to be happening in these examples is that the failures and changes in direction which are so typical of the research process, and which may be openly admitted during the research presentation, are being muted in, or sometimes completely omitted from, the related research articles. Interestingly, the presenter in Example 8 (who was of professorial rank and at the time of recording the head of a British university Physics department) commented after his presentation that he could be "more honest" about his research in the presentation, despite speaking to a largely unknown audience, than in the published article, where what he called "political" considerations constrained what he could write.

However, the question arises as to why a presenter should bother to tell his or her audience about errors and failures. It appears likely that such stories of failed experiments or failed analyses actually play a crucial role in presenting research. These stories often highlight the important role of serendipity in the research process: the clear point of these stories is that failures can lead to new and more exciting avenues for the researcher, and may even provide the basis for later research successes. Research presenters, then, appear to use past-tense narrative to talk about their failed experiments and move to present tense to talk about experiments which are successful. Storytelling allows presenters to focus on the twists and turns of the research process, to present the 'human interest' side of their story, to introduce into the presentation an indication of how they felt and reacted to research challenges and problems. The distancing effect of past-tense narrative, however, may signal to the audience that this stage of the presentation is offering them background or even peripheral information. Movement to present tense mode alerts the audience to the central points of the reporting and interpretation of results.

The pragmatic purposes of narrative are again demonstrated by another, though minor, use of past tense narrative in presentations, which is to tell stories that do not directly relate to the research process itself but add what we might term a 'human angle' to the presentation. In Example 12, the presenter is talking about the types of instrumentation (or 'sources') used to form x-ray probes:

(12) (i)   this is in fact a source which was developed at {ITD} some years ago
     (ii) and about I think five or six years ago the funding got pulled out from {ITD}
     (iii) and we managed to buy this source for £249.99p because if we paid £250.00 or more we'd have to pay VAT
     (iv) so they sold us the whole thing including a computer vacuum pumps and everything for that.

Although such practical research-related information may be helpful to less experienced members of the discourse community, nothing would have been lost from the description of the source itself if the presenter had omitted this story. Such little stories of peripheral incidents may, for example, introduce a note of gentle humour or irony, as in the case of the police witness story in Example 3. The fact, however, that they are both short and relatively rare in the data suggests that this kind of story is not a key generic feature of the research presentation.

From the evidence of the data, then, it seems that the use of stories in research presentations marks these phases as a recounting of personal experience as opposed to generalisable research 'facts'. Stories relate to background information about past research events, or even to peripheral information which does not directly affect the main argumentation of the presentation. This is certainly not to argue that these stories are pointless or unnecessary (cf. Strodt-Lopez 1991 on the important role of asides in humanities lectures). The main point of these stories appears to be their interpersonal and persuasive appeal. The stories allow glimpses of the 'real' person beneath the persona of the research presenter (cf. Dubois 1980), a person who experiences emotions and disappointments, has a sense of humour, is modest about his or her achievements, and who knows a thing or two about the research world. These stories also appeal to the audience to share the presenter's world-view. A story "entertains and amuses, but more significantly ... gives the participants the opportunity to share experiences and to display agreement and shared perceptions" (Eggins & Slade 1997: 229). Research stories play their part in establishing and maintaining a good relationship between presenters and audiences, and minimising the danger that the presenter may seem arrogant, self-regarding or distant from the audience.

Moreover, the use of *present* tense to report research in research presentations is frequently marked by the employment of involvement strategies; one of the most obvious of these is the use of present tense along with a number of other features such as the choice of *you* and non-exclusive *we* as participants in the processes (Collins & Thompson 1996; Vassileva this volume). Such strategies are used to recreate the research events in the here-and-now, to take the audience through the research process rather than simply retelling the story to them as a completed past event, as can be seen in Example 13, in which the presenter has been presenting the results of experiments attempting to build molecules atom by atom:

(13) (i)   so what does this what can we infer from this four angstrom separation
      (ii) well if we look at the ionic radii of caesium and iodine and add them together we get four angstroms
      (iii) so OK maybe it's ionic
      (iv) let's look at covalent radii
      (vi) take the radius from a metal the radius covalent radius of iodine
      (vii) add those together
      (viii) oops four angstroms again.

We see a number of involvement strategies here: use of questioning, an attempt to include (however vicariously) the audience in the research activities through the use of *we* and imperatives, and the use of the informal lexical items *OK* and *oops*. We can draw a clear distinction between the strong tendency in the presentation to use audience-oriented interactive choices like these (cf.

Thompson 1997) to report research and the very strong preference in research articles to avoid such choices.

The research presentation, then, displays its own characteristic generically-related systematic choice of past or present tense to report research. This system appears to be motivated by pragmatic concerns, marking out for the audience how they should interpret the significance of the information in relation to the presenter's current state of understanding and evaluation of the status, value and relevance of his or her research. Both narrative and non-narrative modes can be associated with audience-related concerns in the research presentation. As has already been mentioned, past tense narrative in the research presentations is often associated with stories which appear to present the 'human interest' side of the research process, enlivening the presentation and perhaps introducing a note of mild humour. On the other hand, the use of present tense to describe key research procedures and results together with features such as interactive personal pronoun choices indicate the immediacy and relevance of the results for the audience, who hear (and often see by way of visual aids) the results in the here-and-now of the presentation event. While both the research article and the research presentation appear to use present tense to indicate that the writer is interpreting findings and seeking to show their generalisability (cf. Malcolm 1987), the research presentation also seems to use present tense for interactive purposes, to involve the audience more directly in the presentation. This focus on audience-involvement is clear in the strong emphasis in the presentations on the *human* aspects of the research process. Many research presentations (and certainly those represented in the present corpus) are associated with a published article. The research article must persuade its readership of the solid worth of the research on which it is based, in part by the quite detailed presentation of materials, methods and results. In contrast, the research presenter clearly prioritises interaction and involvement with the audience over the minutiae of research methods and results.

There are signs of field differences between the applied linguistics and science presentations in their use of storytelling. Essentially, the science presenters make greater use of stories about the research process (28 occurrences) than do the applied linguistic presenters (16 occurrences). It might be argued that this matches the real-world situation in which science researchers perform a series of experiments while applied linguistics researchers do not. However, all of the applied linguistics presentations are based on either experimental research or analysis of data, and so could equally well present research events in a narrative mode. A more important factor seems to be that the science presenters tell more stories about their failed experiments and about the events of the research process in general than do the language presenters. This difference of focus is underlined by other differences between the two fields. For example, the applied linguistic presentations display a much greater use of questions, dialogic phases and interruptions than do the scientific presentations (Thompson 1998: 147). On the other hand, the scientific presenters appear to rely more heavily on strategies to engage the audience such as a greater use of audience-oriented personal pronoun choices to involve the audience vicariously in reported research activities. The overall effect of such choices is to offer a different audience role in the two different disciplines, the applied linguistic audience being invited to participate in the real-world events of the presentation itself, while the scientific audience is invited to become involved in the hypothetical events of the research world. If this distinction is valid, then the higher occurrence of stories in the scientific presentations has a possible motivation: the storytelling may contribute to the interpersonal and persuasive power of the presentation by drawing the audience into the research process itself, with all its attendant difficulties and problems. Further research into such possible discipline-related differences is required, however, to show how far the findings of the present study can be generalised.

6. Conclusions

Analysis of narrative features in the science presentations has not borne out earlier views of the research presentation as being straightforwardly narrative (cf. Swales 1990). Nevertheless, the research presentation displays a number of features associated with narrative: the emphasis on human actions, a focus on the researcher's thoughts, problems and feelings, and temporal and cause-effect shifts. The representation of research in the presentation is much closer to the actual process of research than is the more distanced, 'objective' research article. Schiffrin's (1994: 307) definition of a story as "a reconstruction of an experience, told at a specific time, in a specific place, to a specific audience for whom the storyteller seeks to demonstrate the validity of a general claim (e.g. about oneself, one's experience, or the world)" indicates the importance of crafting a story for the specific needs and interests of a particular audience. Research presenters face the challenge of persuading an audience that claims about themselves, their research experiences and the research world are valid and worth hearing. In doing so, they can draw on a number of narrative techniques which enliven the representation of research, and which do not occur in the articles. The apparently quite deliberate use in presentations of informal lexis, idioms, questions and direct speech recalls the types of evaluative techniques identified by Labov & Waletsky (1967) in oral personal narratives. These techniques form the "pre-eminent constituent by means of which the narrator's personal involvement in the story is conveyed" (Toolan 1988: 156). Equally, such strategies work to draw the audience into the story by offering them "an enhancement of experience and heightened awareness and interest" (Cortazzi 1993: 139).

It has so far been argued that the 'humanisation' of the research process in the presentation is primarily a result of the presenter's desire to respond to the interests of the audience present. However, Myers (1994: 183) comments that the 'narrative of science' in a research article "results from the assembling of a number of different results to close off possible objections that could arise (*and that probably had arisen in conference presentations of the results before publication*)" (my italics). Given that the research presentation may well be delivered at an earlier stage in the research process where a presenter tries out his or her results on a live audience and hears their comments and criticisms, it is understandable that there is also a greater emphasis on humanising the research process for the audience in part as a defence against just the kinds of objections which might be raised by the audience during the 'question and answer'-section of the presentation (see Webber this volume).

Since the research article is the final, highly-polished product of a long process of research, it is not surprising to find that authors depend on a dense, abstract and technical style at least in part as a defensive barrier against peer criticism (Latour 1987). The "guesswork and groping that go into the formation of a scientific idea" are completely omitted from "the crisp hypothesis, results, and conclusions of the formal paper" (Bazerman 1983: 158). We can see the research presentation as a kind of 'half-way house' between the guesswork and groping involved in the development of research and the crisp conclusions of the research article. The presentation retains an interest in the twists and turns of the research process as well as reflecting the researcher's concerns with promoting his or her piece of research as a candidate for public knowledge (Dubois 1980). This explains in part why the presentation gives considerable emphasis to the problems and errors which dog the progress of any piece of research. The picture which emerges from the analysis is a complex one, in which we can discern a number of interrelating influences on how the presenter chooses to represent the research process. These include, on the one hand, the as yet uncertain status of the research results, and perhaps even the research procedures followed, and, on the other hand, the need to satisfy the interpersonal demands of the audience who appear to value the presentation as an opportunity to see the human face of the research process.

This study has underlined the fact that, although the research presentation is a crucial genre for novice researchers to acquire, the skills involved in preparing and delivering a generically appropriate talk are far from straightforward. Not least among these skills are the ability to tailor the presentation to fit the pragmatic demands of the genre, and the ability to involve the audience in the

165

presentation by arousing their interest and sympathy (cf. Thompson & Collins 1995, Frobert-Adamo this volume). It is clear that the novice presenter cannot simply rely on the research article as a model for creating a successful research presentation. Nor can s/he rely on telling a simple story of the research events. Instead s/he must acquire and put into use the specific practices, organisational patterns and linguistic repertoires of the research presentation. These generic features may also be tempered by discipline-related factors which can significantly affect what is considered by the specific academic community to be an appropriate representation of the research process. For those of us involved in the design and teaching of academic presentation skills courses (see, for example, Boyle 1996, Slepovitch this volume), the task of understanding what it is that we are actually trying to teach our students to do appears to be far from complete. It is hoped that this study will play its part in adding to our understanding of the interpersonal factors involved in the presentation of a convincing account of the research process.

References

Bazerman, C. 1983. "Scientific writing as a social act: A review of the literature of the sociology of science". In P. V. Anderson, R. J. Brockman, & C. R. Millert (eds). *New Essays in Technical and Scientific Communication: Research, Theory, Practice*. Fermingdale, N.Y.: Baywood, 156-184.
de Beaugrande, R. & W. U. Dressler 1981. *Introduction to Text Linguistics*. London: Longman.
Boyle, R. 1996. "Modelling oral presentations." *ELT Journal*, 50 (2): 115-126.
Brett, P. 1994. "A genre analysis of the results section of sociology articles". *English for Specific Purposes*, 13 (1): 47-59.
Collins, H. & S. E. Thompson 1996. "Grammatical aspects of roles in culturally diverse oral presentations". *D.E.L.T.A.*, 12 (2): 281-306.
Cortazzi, M. 1993. *Narrative Analysis*. London: The Falmer Press.
Cortazzi, M. & L. Jin 2000. "Evaluating evaluation in narrative". In S. Hunston & G. Thompson (eds). *Evaluation in Text: Authorial Stance and the Construction of Discourse*. Oxford: Oxford University Press, 102-120.
Crookes, G. 1986. "The utterance, and other basic units for second language discourse analysis". *Applied Linguistics*, 11 (2): 183-199.
Dubois, B. L. 1980. "Genre and structure of biomedical speeches". *Forum Linguisticum*, 5: 140-169.
Eggins, S. & D. Slade 1997. *Analysing Casual Conversation*. London: Cassell.
Frobert-Adamo, M. This volume. "Humour in oral presentations: What's the joke?".
Gilbert, G. & M. Mulkay 1984. *Opening Pandora's Box: A Sociological Analysis of Scientists' Discourse*. Cambridge: Cambridge University Press.
Goffman, E. 1981. *Forms of Talk*. Oxford: Oxford University Press.
Grimes, J. E. 1975. *The Thread of Discourse*. The Hague: Mouton.

Halliday, M. A. K. 1994. *An Introduction to Functional Grammar* (2nd edition). London: Edward Arnold.

Hoey, M. P. 1983. *On the Surface of Discourse*. London: George Allen & Unwin.

Hunston, S. 1993. "Evaluation and ideology in scientific writing". In M. Ghadessy (ed). *Register Analysis: Theory and Practice*. London: Pinter, 57-73.

Knorr-Cetina, K. D. 1981. *The Manufacture of Knowledge*. Oxford: Pergamon Press.

Labov, W. & J. Waletsky 1967. "Narrative analysis: Oral versions of personal experience". In J. Helm (ed). *Essays on the Verbal and Visual Arts*. Seattle: American Ethnological Society, 12-44.

Latour, B. 1987. *Science in Action: How to Follow Scientists and Engineers through Society*. Milton Keynes: Open University Press.

Latour, B. & S. Woolgar 1986. *Laboratory Life: The Social Construction of Scientific Facts* (2nd edition). Princeton, N.J.: Princeton University Press.

Longacre, R. 1983. *The Grammar of Discourse*. New York: Plenum.

Malcolm, L. 1987. "What rules govern tense usage in scientific articles?". *English for Specific Purposes*, 6: 31-44.

Martin, J. R. 1992. *English Text: System and Structure*. Amsterdam: John Benjamins.

Myers, G. 1990. *Writing Biology: Texts in the Social Construction of Scientific Knowledge*. Madison: University of Wisconsin Press.

Myers, G. 1994. "Narratives of science and nature in popularizing molecular genetics". In M. Coulthard (ed). *Advances in Written Text Analysis*. London: Routledge, 179-190.

Plum, G. A. (1988). "Text and contextual conditioning in spoken English: A genre-based approach". Unpublished PhD thesis. Sydney: University of Sydney.

Schiffrin, D. 1994. *Approaches to Discourse*. Oxford: Basil Blackwell.

Shalom, C. N. 1993. "Established and evolving spoken research process genres: Plenary lecture and poster session discussions at academic conferences". *English for Specific Purposes*, 12: 37-50.

Slepovitch, V. This volume. "English as a conference language for students of business in Belarus: Problems, solutions and prospects".

Strodt-Lopez, B. 1991. "Tying it all in: asides in university lectures". *Applied Linguistics*, 12 (2): 117-140.

Swales, J. M. 1990. *Genre Analysis: English in Academic and Research Settings*. Cambridge: Cambridge University Press.

Tannen, D. 1989. *Talking Voices: Repetition, Dialogue, and Imagery in Conversational Discourse*. Cambridge: Cambridge University Press.

Thomas, S. A. 1991. "A merging of voices: An investigation of the way discourse is reported in medical research articles". Unpublished PhD thesis. Birmingham: University of Birmingham.

Thompson, D. K. 1993. "Arguing for experimental 'facts' in science: A study of research article results sections in biochemistry". *Written Communication*, 10 (1): 103-127.

Thompson, S. E. 1997. "Presenting research: a study of interaction in academic monologue". Unpublished PhD thesis. Liverpool: University of Liverpool.

Thompson, S. E. 1998. "Why ask questions in monologue? Language choice at work in scientific and linguistic talk". In S. Hunston (ed). *Language at Work*. Clevedon, Avon: Multilingual Matters, 137-150.

Thompson, S. E. & H. Collins 1995. "Dealing with face threats in oral presentations". *Trabalhos em Lingüística Aplicada*, 26: 81-99.

Toolan, M. J. 1988. *Narrative: A Critical Linguistic Introduction*. London: Routledge.

167

Vassileva, I. This volume. "Speaker-audience interaction: The case of Bulgarians presenting in English".

Ventola, E. 1987. *The Structure of Social Interaction: A Systemic Approach to the Semiotics of Service Encounters.* London: Frances Pinter.

Webber, P. This volume. "The paper is now open for discussion".

Weissberg, B. 1993. "The graduate seminar: Another research-process genre". *English for Specific Purposes,* 12 (1): 23-35.

Winter, E. O. 1977. "A clause relational approach to English texts: A study of some predictive lexical items in written discourse". *Instructional Science,* 6 (1): 1-92.

A MULTI-SEMIOTIC GENRE:
THE CONFERENCE SLIDE SHOW

Cassily Charles and Eija Ventola
Paris-Lodron-Universität Salzburg, Austria

This chapter focuses on multi-semiotic conference presentations: that is, presentations drawing on language, as well as other semiotic codes (e.g. images, gestures, music, etc.) Despite the rise in multi-modality work, this is so far a relatively unexplored territory for linguistic research. As we know, preparing a paper for a conference involves a considerable amount of preparatory work: literature research, collecting and analysing the data, and preparing the presentation – written speaker notes, transparencies, hand-outs, electronic slide-shows, etc. All this work comes together when the paper is presented. The conference situation places a multitude of demands on presenters, who must be skilled in using different modes, codes and channels for getting the message across to the audience. There are hardly any functional studies on the various semiotic codes and modes that are actually put into use before and during conference presentations, or on what role language plays in their integration. The examples used for this chapter are from video recordings of an international conference. We draw on analyses of the switching of modes during the presentation, between speaking from a written text and commenting on a photographic slide-show. Our focus is on the demands such shifts set on the language used by the presenters, as discourse is unfolding in real time. In addition to giving us new theoretical perspectives on the application of discourse analysis to conference language, the study also has implications for English for Special Purposes training.

1. Introduction

This paper concerns itself with Slide Shows, as an example of multi-semiotic texts in conference presentations. While there has been some linguistic work on slides in academic presentations (e.g. Dubois 1980a & b; Räisänen 1999), there has been little or no work within the systemic-functional framework. The interaction and interdependence of semiotic codes in text (commonly called 'multi-modality') has recently become one of the major areas of innovative research in systemic-functional linguistics. Researchers in this field have focussed on the grammar of visualisation and how text and images construe meanings in various contexts. O'Toole (1994, 1995) extensively analyses the semiotics of various forms of art (paintings, sculptures, architecture). Kress & van Leeuwen (1996) offer us further analytical tools for analysing pictures and images in 'everyday' texts, such as advertisements. van Leeuwen (1996) discusses the analysis of films from a semiotic point of view. Ravelli (1996, 1998a, 1998b), Pang Kah Meng (2000) and Purser (2000) explore visualisation and texts in museum contexts, and Ravelli (2000) focusses on semiotic resources in application to the field of marketing. Articles in Baldry (2000) offer various examples of multi-modal analyses applied to the educational context of distance learning, and O'Halloran (1999a, 1999b, 2000) discusses the use of different semiotic codes in mathematics texts.

This chapter sets out to extend multi-modal attention to academic genres, focusing on the interactivity between semiotic codes in conference presentations. That is, we will investigate how one semiotic code in a multi-semiotic text (in our case, spoken English language) interacts with another (in our case, photographic slide projections). During a Slide Show, the register of the spoken part of a presentation must adapt to the presence or absence of visuals in the context. There is interactivity between the semiotic codes, even as both together form a single cohesive text, with the purposeful staging supplied by the Slide Show genre.

As has been discussed by Ventola in Chapter 1 of this volume, (and cf. Ventola 1999), all conference presenters draw on various experiences to produce a presentation (for example, the meanings made through reading, fieldwork, discussions with colleagues, interacting with the technology of text production, etc.) As meaning-making processes, these experiences are semiotic. Similarly, those sitting in the audience draw on their own diverse semiotic experiences, past and present, to interpret the presentation. In Chapter 1, these kinds of links between past meaning-making experiences and the instantiation of text were labelled as *semiotic spanning*. In this chapter, we elaborate the notion of semiotic spanning, to include not only the link between past and present semiosis, (e.g. between viewing original artefacts and telling an audience about them), but also between concurrent, co-textual semiotic codes, (i.e. between a photographic slide of an artefact, and the accompanying commentary about the image). Thus, the analysis of multi-modal (i.e. multi-semiotic) conference presentations offers at least two potentially fruitful perspectives on semiotic spanning. The first could be called a 'semiotic macro-focus', where semiotic links span different contexts in time and space; while the second, where the links between semiotic codes (language and pictures) create a single text, could be called a 'semiotic micro-focus.' Let us first consider the macro-focus.

1.1. Semiotic Macro-focus

The semiotic links or bridges which build a conference presentation may expand years back in the researcher's life and usually link up with other researchers' activities as well. Such links are here called *semiotic spans*. It is the configuration of shared semiotic spans within an academic discourse community that enables us to construe appropriate meanings in our conference presentations (and indeed in all our academic work). They form the basis on which researchers can claim that we are producing 'relevant knowledge' in our research, and on which we present it at conferences as valuable 'news' for the listeners. Once this 'news' has been transmitted in the conference, it begins a life of its own. It may be quoted in articles, in subsequent conference presentations, in university lectures, in café conversations, in newspaper reports, etc. Conference presentations, as culturally authoritative genres, give a special status to the semiotic spans which build them, and which then proceed from them. This is the process of knowledge production and transmission.

If we wish to understand, describe and train novices in the constraints and resources operating in our academic discourse communities, we need to move beyond teaching them academic text production in their instantiation in presentations and in academic articles. Taking a semiotic macro-focus means making a systematic investigation of which different kinds of experience can count as the basis for 'relevant knowledge', and how they are linked into texts. In the process of preparing a presentation this may, for example, mean visiting a museum, reading primary historical accounts, interacting with colleagues in an e-mail discussion or a coffee break. From this perspective, our task becomes not merely to explain how a text is produced, received and understood in the situation; but also to see how a text is a complex accretion of meaning-making, built by semiotic spans between numerous semiotic processes and experiences beyond the current situation. Semiotic spanning is suggested as a starting-point for beginning this investigation, and the analysis of multi-semiotic texts is suggested as a starting point for developing notions of semiotic spanning. When a text is multi-semiotic, this fact adds *visibly* to the sum of semiotic spans that must be built; i.e. between semiotic codes (e.g. language, visuals) in a text. This gives us an entry point into the complexity of semiotic spanning involved in producing and transmitting knowledge in academic communities and beyond.

1.2. Semiotic Micro-focus

In a semiotic micro-focus on multi-semiotic conference presentations, attention is directed to analysing the demands such texts set on individual presenters and their presentation skills. The analyses focus on what special cohesive resources are necessary in the case of multi-semiotic text, where different codes and modes (speaking, writing, non-verbal, images) need to be integrated into a unified whole. While a considerable amount of linguistic attention has been applied to teaching novices and non-native speakers to produce appropriate academic research papers and, to a lesser degree, presentations, (e.g. Swales 1990, papers in Ventola & Mauranen 1996 and others), there is very little literature on what additional competencies are necessary for producing multi-semiotic academic texts. What does it mean to integrate semiotic codes during a presentation? What linguistic and other semiotic skills are needed to achieve a coherent and cohesive multi-semiotic text?

This chapter begins with an exploration of the second focus, the micro-focus, in the hope that starting with the instantiation of multi-semiotic texts will be useful for developing analytical tools and theory for later venturing into the exploration of semiotic spanning at large. The analyses draw on a transcript from a videotaped presentation at an international conference held in Germany on Georg Forster, the 18th century explorer and scientist, who with his father, Reinhold Forster, took part in the second of Captain Cook's voyages around the world. During their travels, the Forsters collected a considerable quantity of artefacts, now spread out in various museums around the world. The conference presentation that has been studied in this paper was given by an ethnologist, whose native tongue is American English. The presenter reads mostly from a written text (manuscript delivery), but twice switches from reading to presenting slides of artefacts, illustrations, museums, and so on. These two Slide Shows are accompanied by unprepared spoken commentary (see Appendix B for a transcript of the Slide Shows). In Section 2, we draw on this data to propose a *synoptic* model of the functional structure of the Slide Show, showing the lexico-grammatical and discourse semantic realisations of its generic stages. (Here and elsewhere in this paper, we draw on theory and terminology from systemic-functional linguistics, following Halliday 1994 and Martin 1992.) In Section 3, we take a more *dynamic* view of the Slide Show, and investigate how the unfolding of this genre provides adaptive choices for integrating different codes into a cohesive multi-semiotic text. Section 4 will focus on semiotic spanning in the Slide Show which goes beyond integrating different codes, to invoking whole other contexts. The last section, Section 5, presents implications drawn from this study and suggests some issues for future research.

2. Synoptic structure of the embedded Slide Show genre

We have analysed the Slide Show as a genre in its own right, embedded within the larger conference presentation genre.[1] We follow the definition of genre as a purposeful, structured social event, built up of stages which each contribute their

---

[1] A full analysis of the parent genre, Conference Presentation, unfortunately cannot be given here for reasons of space. We have therefore not attempted to address here broader questions about the range of purposes multi-modal realisations can serve in conference presentations, or the range of possible ranks within the genre (e.g. embedded genre, simple generic stage, realisation within stages).

own specific function to the purpose of the whole (see e.g. Martin 1985, Ventola 1987). Here such a structure of stages is referred to as a *generic structure*. Therefore, each embedded Slide Show realises one functional part of the conference presentation as a whole. At the same time, the Slide Show has its own internal generic structure of functional stages, which together achieve its overall purpose.

Within the particular conference presentation we have analysed, two embedded Slide Shows each realise a functional stage in the parent genre (i.e. the conference presentation) which we might label ILLUSTRATION (cf. Dubois 1980b on transparencies in conference presentations). That is, as an embedded whole, each Slide Show serves to support points the presenter has made in the text of the preceding stage of the presentation. However, this support is not in the form of a convincing concrete example following a more abstract claim, as in the familiar pattern of EVIDENCE supporting ARGUMENT. Rather, the Slide Show simply adds a further semiotic realisation (visuals) to experience which has already been realised through language alone, earlier in the text. That is, the sole purpose of the Slide Show, in this presentation, is to thicken existing semiotic spans for the audience, by introducing the same material via an additional semiotic code.

In the presentation that we have taken for analysis, the generic structure for the Slide Show could be represented synoptically as in Figure 1^2:

CODE TRANSITION ^ (SLIDE ^ IDENTIFICATION ^ CONTEXTUALISATION) ^{n} ^ CODE RETURN

Figure 1. A linear, synoptic representation of the Slide Show genre.

So, in this model, the Slide Show genre must begin with a CODE TRANSITION, and end with a CODE RETURN. In between, there must be a SLIDE, followed by an IDENTIFICATION, followed by a CONTEXTUALISATION. The sequence SLIDE ^ IDENTIFICATION ^ CONTEXTUALISATION may be repeated any number of times. An explanation and discussion of these generic stages follows. As well as giving a summary of the function of each stage, we comment on each in terms of register, (field, tenor and mode), and the linguistic and non-linguistic realisations of this register. (See Appendix A for a sample break-up of the Slide Show into generic stages.)

---

[2] In this notation, the circumflex '^' represents the necessary order of elements; e.g. CONTEXTUALISATION must follow IDENTIFICATION in this genre. The superscripted ^{n} represents any number of optional repetitions. In this case, optional repetition applies to SLIDE, IDENTIFICATION & CONTEXTUALISATION together, represented by the parentheses '( )'.

2.1. Code Transition

The CODE TRANSITION is illustrated by example (1) from the data.

(1)   So I begin to show you some slides over the Pacific collections from the
       Forsters and erm especially the collection in the Pitt Rivers Museum. [The
       chair darkens the room for the Slide Show] Can you hear me if I stand
       over here?

The purpose of the CODE TRANSITION is to introduce the incorporation of the
new channel and semiotic code – in this case, the visuals of photographic slide
projections. The presenter needs to check that the audience can see the slides,
and hear her commentary as she changes position to show the slides. She also
makes appropriate links between the subject matter of her earlier talk and the
slides, and justifies the use of the new semiotic code. This stage can be
functionally specified by the register variables field, tenor and mode, which each
have a range of linguistic and (in some cases) non-linguistic realisations. Each
of the variables is discussed and exemplified in turn below.

Field: Consistent with the whole presentation, the field is ethnology, specifically
in relation to some artefacts collected by Georg and Reinhold Forster in Tonga
in the 18th century. In the CODE TRANSITION to the Slide Show, the field is
extended to include the visual representations of the subject matter and the
audience, the speaker and their physical surroundings. In linguistic realisation, it
is worthwhile to note that when the new referent *slides* is introduced, it is in an
extended nominal group which is qualified by Participants previously introduced
in the presentation text. This achieves the important first step in a semiotic span
between experiences previously constituted solely through language, (in the
foregoing stage of prepared speech read out by the presenter,) and those which
will be realised visually: *some slides **over the Pacific collections from the***
***Forsters** and erm especially **the collections in the Pitt Rivers Museum**.*
Additionally, the Processes of perception are made explicit: the audience and the
presenter are introduced as pronominal Participants around mental and
behavioural Processes associated with watching the Slide Show: *I begin to **show***
***you** some slides; I just want to **show you**; can **you hear me**.*

Tenor: The relationship between the presenter and the audience is slightly
adjusted for the Slide Show. As a result of the new code, the semiotic experience
moves closer to being a shared one, as the presenter and the audience together
view the slides; whereas in the earlier text the presenter is simply an authority
who creates the experience for the audience through her statements. In the first,
the audience is questioned in the interrogative Mood for the first time, as experts
on their own sensory perceptions – ***can you** hear me?* In the CODE TRANSITION

to the second Slide Show, by referring to herself as Subject of her own mental Process, and by using engagement/hedging at a discourse semantic level (*I just want to show you*), the presenter makes herself more approachable, accountable, and equal in the experience of viewing the slides. (This can be compared to her earlier presentation part, where the presenter refers to herself and her own mental processes infrequently. There, she more often uses the passive voice which is typical of academic genres, eliding the authority for evaluation: *it can still be concluded that the importance of these voyages... .*)

Mode: Mode is the register variable in which change would be expected to be most marked – since the introduction of the Slide Show means the addition of a new medium, which brings corresponding changes in how information flows and is structured. The presenter prepares and checks the channels of semiosis: both the new one (visual projection) and that which is adapting to it (spoken language). As well as linguistic realisations, there are important non-linguistic realisations of mode in the CODE TRANSITION. The room is darkened for the slides to be better visible. The projecting equipment is checked. During the period of adjusting the visual medium (10 seconds), neither the presenter nor the chair (who is assisting her) speak. Rather, a range of gaze, body posture, and gesture resources are used to express attention, uncertainty and impatience with the adjustments (e.g. partially extending the forearm, palm uppermost, and turning the wrist – 'what's going on?'). When the adjustment is complete, the presenter moves into another position from which to view the slides without obscuring them, and tests the volume of her voice away from the lectern. Linguistically, the mode becomes more 'spoken' than 'written.' There is more grammatical intricacy and lower lexical density[3]: *Can you hear me if I stand over here?* (This contrasts with the earlier text in her read-out-loud presentation: e.g. *There was no systematic publication of the botany, zoology, geology or anthropology by the Forsters or anyone else.*) Pronominal Participants are retrievable extra-linguistically, from the sensory environment, and signalled by an appropriate reference item: e.g. *over here.* The CODE TRANSITION stage is introduced with the internal conjunction *so* as textual Theme *(so I begin to show you some slides ...)*, overtly connecting the whole Slide Show with the previous text, and introducing it as a logical next step in the whole presentation.

2.2. Slide

Example (2) shows a SLIDE stage from our data.

(2)   [A photograph of a building interior appears on the screen behind the lectern.]

---

[3]   For grammatical intricacy and lexical density, see e.g. Halliday 1989.

The function of the SLIDE stage is to display the projected image to the audience. It is the brief, essential core stage of the genre, which is realised completely non-linguistically.

Field: Each SLIDE stage represents a specific artefact, illustration, museum building or a scene from contemporary Tonga, realised by its visual representation in photographic form.

Tenor: The tenor of each SLIDE is constant. The presenter shows the image to the audience without modality, as a visual statement of fact: a photographic 'truth.' The image is non-interactive and still, without overt addition or decoration. There is no trace of the producer of the image.

Mode: The mode of each SLIDE is also constant – purely visual, without other accompanying semiosis, e.g. music, language. (In practice, there is often overlap in time between the SLIDE stage and the IDENTIFICATION stage, realised by spoken commentary. However, in this synoptic model of the genre, and precisely because of that mode difference, the two stages are treated as separate. For further discussion of these issues, see Section 3 below on dynamic representation of the Slide Show.) In the visual medium, there is no marked framing of each slide, nor any visual realisation of information structure. The textual relationship between the images is simply one of temporal progression, as one image succeeds another.

2.3. Identification

An example from the data of the IDENTIFICATION stage follows.

(3)   This is the Pitt Rivers Museum.

The IDENTIFICATION stage in the Slide Show is the most important stage for semiotic spanning between the visual and language codes. The presenter brings the image into the realm of her presentation text, by identifying it with Participants and Processes which have been established previously through language alone.

Field: Crucially, the field of the IDENTIFICATION stage is the same as the field of the SLIDE stage; i.e. the specific artefact, illustration or Tongan scene depicted in the image. The function of this additional stage with the same field is precisely to conflate experiential semiosis from the visual code of the image with experiential semiosis realised in language. Linguistically, the adaptive work of building this span is realised experientially by relational identifying processes, with the image as Token, and previously mentioned Participants and

Processes as Value: ***this*** (Token) *is **the Easter Island hand that was collected*** (Value); ***this*** is ***the Pitt Rivers Museum.***

Tenor: In the IDENTIFICATION stage, the presenter has the role of authoritative knower, explaining to the audience. Just as the SLIDE stages are visually realised as unmodalised photographic 'truths', the IDENTIFICATION stage is linguistically realised only by statements in declarative Mood, without modality. The experiential content of the SLIDE is usually Subject: ***this*** *is* ... .

Mode: The image is visible during the IDENTIFICATION stage, so that this is necessarily the most multi-semiotic portion of the presentation. Referents in the image are retrievable into language through exophoric deictics: e.g. ***this*** *is the Easter Island hand that was collected*. Information is organised from the starting point of the image, which is always topical Theme. Meanwhile, Rhemes presume knowledge of Participants, (being either anaphorically retrievable from earlier text, or homophorically retrievable from shared knowledge.) These are realised by nominal groups, frequently extended, incorporating rank-shifting and/or grammatical metaphor, to tightly pack previously given information: e.g. *this is **the catalogue of curiosities that was written apparently by George Forster that accompanied the collection when it went erm to the Ashmolean Museum in the 18th century**.* There is usually no Thematic progression from one sequence of (SLIDE ^ IDENTIFICATION ^ CONTEXTUALISATION) to the next. Occasional textual Themes in the IDENTIFICATION stage are limited to the additive conjunction *and*. The Slide Show therefore has an extremely 'flat' texture, with respect to method of development: it proceeds with the succession of images. That is, information flows purely between the semiotic codes, in successive independent pulses. During the IDENTIFICATION stage, the presenter underlines the multi-channel organisation of communication non-linguistically, by turning to face the image as she identifies it. Visually, information flows from the SLIDE to presenter and audience equally. Linguistically, information flows only from the presenter to the audience.

2.4. Contextualisation

A sample CONTEXTUALISATION stage from the data is shown below.

(4)   which is um as you can see a rather old-fashioned museum which is arranged by artefact type rather than by area.

The function of the CONTEXTUALISATION stage is to build on the semiotic spans around the SLIDE, in the co-text of the whole presentation and the context of the particular academic situation and culture. Where the IDENTIFICATION stage builds the basic link between the visual semiosis of each SLIDE and the relevant linguistic semiosis of the preceding text, the CONTEXTUALISATION justifies that link with respect to the whole text, and the academic culture of which it makes part. In the presentation taken for analysis here, there is a noticeable difference between the first embedded Slide Show and the second, in terms of how the SLIDE + IDENTIFICATION are contextualised (e.g. with respect to what things in the world – museums versus times in history). This has to do with the ILLUSTRATION function of each Slide Show in the structure of the parent genre, (i.e. the whole conference presentation). That is, where the first Slide Show illustrates the importance, size and location of the Forster artefact collection, the second illustrates the ongoing relevance of Tongan artefacts to the Tongan people. Accordingly, the CONTEXTUALISATION stages in each Slide Show appeal to the respective functions of each show as a whole. An additional point of interest in the presentation we studied is that, of all the stages in the Slide Show genre, this one shows the greatest variety of contextual and linguistic realisations. The presenter variously makes evaluative assessments and justifies her own authority to show and comment on the image and/or elaborates on the content of the SLIDE, its connection to the topic, and/or to the textual organisation of the presentation.

Field: The field of each CONTEXTUALISATION incorporates and elaborates the field of the preceding IDENTIFICATION (i.e. the linguistic correlate of the artefact/scene from the SLIDE), locating it in the world as represented in the paper as a whole, and then out in the wider academic field of ethnology. Field-specific taxonomies are invoked: museums, periods in history, explorers, points of geography. Relational attributive Processes are a frequent realisation: e.g. *it* (Carrier) *is **a unique piece and now in the Pitt Rivers Museum*** (Attribute)*; it **was** still in quite good condition;* [they] **are** *very similar to the collections made in the 18th century.* Key Processes and Participants from the earlier presentation text are re-introduced: *and one of these unique pieces was **collected by the Forsters**; and these were the only two human images that were **collected** apparently **during the second voyage**.* Processes and Participants also appear which are not mentioned in the earlier text, but are familiar elements from the field of discourse for audience, as historians or ethnographers: e.g. ***Easter Island** hand; given by the Forsters to erm **the British Museum**; a rather old-fashioned museum which is **arranged** by **artefact type** rather than by **area**.*

The audience and presenter are also present as the pronominal Participants, 'you' and 'I'. The presenter is the Sayer of verbal processes and Senser of mental processes, making meta-commentary on the text: *as I said; what I wanted you to look at.* The audience is regularly the Senser and Behaver of mental and behavioural processes to do with perception, and occasionally cognition: e.g. ***you can see** that it is illustrated here...; **if you have examined** the illustrations* *in the official account...; you note at the lower right hand corner is the island of ...; look at erm the human images...; as you can see a rather old-fashioned museum...* . What is particularly interesting is that the Participants and Processes introduced in these clauses are not limited to those which are visible in details of the image, but also include some which are available elsewhere – for example in museums, or in Tonga or Germany. Processes of perception, particularly those to do with vision, are used to thicken semiotic spans with not only the immediately visible semiosis of the SLIDE, but also with other experiences in the pursuit of ethnographic research, actual or potential, elsewhere in time and space. What is more, the 'you' Senser of these processes is at times extended beyond the specific audience the presenter is addressing, to the generic 'you' – standing for perhaps 'any member of our professional community'. For example: *Some of the important objects can al- you can only figure out what they were used for by looking at illustrations. This is an illustration by Hodges.* This is a nice example of the spilling, prosodic nature of semiotic spanning: from between different semiotic codes in one text, to between different semiotic experiences in place, time and abstraction.

Tenor: It is particularly with respect to tenor that the CONTEXTUALISATION stage is clearly distinct from other stages. The presenter takes on the role of justifying both the value of the SLIDE and her own authority. This is realised in various linguistic ways. Contrasting with other sections of the presentation, the presenter uses attitudinal lexis and amplification in this stage – e.g. *a really excellent collection; still in quite good condition; a rather old-fashioned museum; this wonderful feathered head-dress; in exactly the same way as they were 200 years ago.* These are discourse semantic resources of Appraisal (Martin 2000) for introducing speaker evaluations and adjusting their intensity. They bring the presenter and audience closer together, sharing emotive responses. In monologic written academic genres, these are typically absent, or of a restrained intensity;[4] whereas in the CONTEXTUALISATION stage of the Slide Show, the intensity is often quite high, as shown above, and lexis is often more in line with informal conversation. The audience is addressed directly at times as 'you'. On several occasions, this is in cases where there is an issue of the different experience levels of the presenter and audience: e.g. *this is the country house in Wörlitz, if any of you have not been there; if you have examined the illustrations ... you will note.* At other times, this works as a resource of Engagement (White 1998) at the discourse level, inviting the audience to share the same response: e.g. *which is erm as you can see a rather old-fashioned museum; you can see that it is illustrated....* The presenter makes commands, congruently realised in the imperative mood, to draw the audience's

---

[4] For a discussion of how interpersonal resources such as Appraisal are used in academic texts for the purposes of "bashing" or "occupying territory", see Ventola 1998a & b.

attention to details of the image. This places the audience in a position of lower power, relative to the presenter, as expected provider of goods and services: e.g. *and **note** the little human images on the top;* ***look at** the erm human images.* That these commands are behavioural Processes, affiliated with cognition and perception, adds an experiential dimension to the tenor: the presenter is in a position to direct the audience's learning; i.e. she has the authority of someone who has already seen and understood. This authority is often more overt than covert: the presenter uses some explicitly subjective modality for her claims, e.g. ***I suspect** they- that the Forsters…*

Mode: In terms of mode, the CONTEXTUALISATION stage is closer to face-to-face informal communication than the other portions of the Slide Show. Examples of linguistic realisations include exophoric references to presenter, audience and SLIDEs, the Appraisal lexis in spoken register, and a variety of speech functions and Mood: e.g. *note the little human images on the top.* In this presentation, there are no non-linguistic realisations of pointing in the CONTEXTUALISATION; deixis is only realised linguistically. The realisations of this at the discourse semantic level are particularly interesting for us. As seen above, the CONTEXTUALISATION stage connects the experiential content of the (SLIDE + IDENTIFICATION) with the field of the presentation text preceding the Slide Show and with the broader field of discourse. Achieving this textually means that semiosis flows in more than one direction across time, place, and semiotic code. Presumed referents in the CONTEXTUALISATION stage may be retrievable anaphorically, from earlier text in the presentation, (e.g. *the Forsters*), or they may be retrievable homophorically, from the discourse knowledge shared by the presenter and audience, (e.g. *the British Museum*). They may also be retrievable exophorically, from the surrounding context, (e.g. *and look at the um human images).* This last example, of course, is a case of retrieval from another semiotic code: the visuals of the SLIDE.

2.5. Code Return

A realisation of the CODE RETURN stage in the data is shown in example (5).

(5) [Presenter turns to lectern and begins to read.] The collections and works of the Forsters are important elements for cooperative work between ethnographers, curators of collections and the indigenous Pacific peoples…

The function of the CODE RETURN stage is to notify the end of the Slide Show, and return to purely linguistic semiosis. The visual medium for the projections is ended and the language becomes more formal. As a transitional stage between the parent presentation genre and the embedded Slide Show genre, the CODE RETURN shares features with the opening stage, CODE TRANSITION (see 2.1).

Field: The field is returned to that of the earlier presentation. The individual artefacts/scenes represented in the slides no longer appear, but are indexed at the discourse level by higher order terms: e.g. *the collections and works of the Forsters.* (Compare with the CODE TRANSITION: *some slides over the Pacific collections from the Forsters.*) Similarly, the actual presenter and audience no longer appear as individual Participants. Rather, extended nominal groups stand for communities with which they may identify: *co-operative work between ethnographers, curators of collections and the indigenous Pacific peoples.*

Tenor: The relationship between the presenter and audience is adjusted in response to the return to a 'conference speaker' to 'audience' relationship. The presenter again becomes the sole authority, using only statements, congruently realised as declaratives, without modalisation. The audience is no longer addressed. There is an evaluative summary with positive Appraisal of the field of the Slide Show: *The collections and works of the Forsters **are important elements for co-operative work... .***

Mode: The presenter returns to monologic, purely verbal, written-to-be-read-aloud mode. An internal conjunction, *and finally*, at the last IDENTIFICATION flags the approaching stage change. The presenter returns to academic register; grammatical intricacy is reduced, lexical density is increased, with large groups packing material previously more congruently presented: e.g. *the collections and works of the Forsters are important elements for co-operative work... .* Information flows through, more than into, language. References are more often generic or endophoric (i.e. retrievable in language or text) than homophoric (i.e. retrievable from shared cultural knowledge,) and no longer exophoric (i.e. retrievable from the immediate environment.) There are of course also non-linguistic realisations of mode in the CODE RETURN: the presenter turns away from the slide screen and returns back to the podium and starts to read from her notes when the lights are turned up.

In summary, this kind of synoptic view of the Slide Show genre is useful for establishing the different generic elements and their realisations, their functional relationship to one another and to semiotic processes outside the Slide Show, and the purpose of the genre as a whole (i.e. in this case only discussed as a functional stage of ILLUSTRATION in the total conference presentation). The switch between mono- and multi-semiotic text processes, between the parent genre and the embedded Slide Show genre, is structurally flagged – shown above in the bounding stages of CODE TRANSITION and CODE RETURN. In between these bounding stages, in the core stages of the Slide Show, semiotic experience is 'imported' from one semiotic code to another – from the visual to the verbal (SLIDE stage + IDENTIFICATION stage). The semiotic span built in this process is then contextualised with anchoring ties, both with the experiential 'fact' of field and the interpersonal 'value' of tenor (CONTEXTUALISATION stage). Importantly, this CONTEXTUALISATION works with reference to semiosis outside the Slide Show – i.e. to earlier text in the rest of the conference paper, or by way of intertextuality and other semotic spans with shared professional or cultural experience. There is no other logic of progression between individual SLIDEs. At the end of the Slide Show, the contribution which has been made to the parent genre – i.e. the function of the Slide Show as a whole – is the illustrative thickening of semiotic spans via an additional semiotic code. Taking this kind of genre-based approach to the Slide Show allows us to see how this integration of semiotic codes is supported by the functional staging of a generic structure. This kind of analysis, however, can still be usefully supplemented with a more 'dynamic' understanding of the unfolding of the text, as will be discussed in the next section.

3. Dynamic approach to the Slide Show

While a synoptic view, such as we have taken above, provides useful insights into the function and realisation of genre in general and the Slide Show in particular, it is not enough on its own to complete some parts of the picture. In Section 2, Figure 1, the Slide Show was represented in a linear way, one element following another, with only one possibility of recursion of sequenced elements (SLIDE $^\wedge$ IDENTIFICATION $^\wedge$ CONTEXTUALISATION)^n. This kind of representation gives us a rather rigid picture of how the social process of showing slides may unfold in an actual situation. A complementary dynamic view reveals aspects of genres as social processes which are obscured by modelling genre as a static structure.

3.1. Dynamic versus synoptic approaches and models

Even though, as interactants in social situations, we have common expectations of how particular genres typically unfold, we often seem to realise them in a much more varied way than static models of social behaviour (i.e. genre) can account for. In real life communication, we frequently adjust the unfolding of genres to changes in the situational context. Indeed, the process of communication may actually change the context of situation, which then in turn influences the next stage of social meaning-making. For this reason, recent years have seen considerable work in systemic-functional linguistics on modelling the social process of genre as *dynamic*. (Extensive reviews of the developments on dynamics are to be found in Ventola 1989; O'Donnell 1999.) Debate about the necessity of dynamic perspectives began in response to early work on 'Generic Structure Potential' (Hasan 1977, Hasan in Halliday and Hasan 1985). In that framework, the context of communication is seen as relatively fixed for the whole interaction, so that there are only limited possibilities for varying the realisation of a genre. That is, obligatory stages are 'genre-defining', while there may be options for sequencing or for non-obligatory stages. This approach has provided the model for our synoptic perspective on the Slide Show above, and the representation in Figure 1. (However, see also Martin 1985 and 1992 for examples of a more exhaustive synoptic representation of genre, as a network of choices.) Subsequent to the development of Hasan's model, it has been argued that linguists need to study not only the *static* products of interaction in context, but also the *dynamic* processes; i.e. how texts actually unfold, in adaptive ways, in interaction (Ventola 1987: 66-69). To complement the synoptic representation of genres, graphically represented by linear 'Generic Structure Potentials' (Hasan 1977, in Halliday and Hasan 1985) or as 'networks' (Martin 1985, 1992); various dynamic, 'process' angles on genre have been developed. In these approaches, the unfolding of genre in context has been represented by 'flowcharts' (Ventola 1987), 'systemic flowcharts' (Fawcett et al. 1988), or 'dynamic transition networks' (O'Donnell 1990, 1999).

While this work has meant important steps forward in understanding human interaction in social contexts, issues of representation are still in debate. O'Donnell (1999: 90), for example, has criticised existing dynamic models as being too prescriptive, and for leaving important factors unaccounted for: e.g. subjectivity, the uncertainty of the consequences of our actions, and the possibility of intentionally "inappropriate" behaviour. Recognising the need for further development in the way dynamic processes of genre are represented, we have not here pursued an exhaustive representation of all the dynamic genre potential in the Slide Show. Rather, more modestly, we have adopted a dynamic *perspective* on our data. This enables a discussion of those parts of the Slide Show where the genre unfolds in ways which cannot be predicted or explained simply with reference to linear models like the one in Section 2. Taking a complementary dynamic view reveals adaptive potential in the genre, and allows discussion of some of the reasons and choices that presenters have for realising the Slide Show in different ways.

3.2. Dynamic unfolding in the Slide Show

In the unfolding of the Slide Show there is the potential for alternative realisations of generic elements. One way of looking at this kind of adaptation is in terms of *choice* (varying the realisation of generic stages, for global purposes of cohesion or coherence) versus *necessity* (when something unforeseen occurs and must be integrated). However, it can be seen that 'choice' and 'necessity' are more closely related than appears on the face of it. Each is a question of (re)negotiating the balance between the needs of different variables in the context of situation – including the interaction between semiotic codes. For that reason, the insights offered by a dynamic view of the Slide Show genre go to the heart of just what is involved in the on-line production of multi-semiotic text.

The Slide Show data shows alternative realisations for the functions of each generic stage, which move beyond the static structure presented so far – within important limits. An over-riding restriction on flexibility in the unfolding of the Slide Show is that all essential elements (represented by the ordered stages in the synoptic model in Section 2) be realised *in some way*. That is, there is flexibility in how elements are ordered or realised, on the condition that necessary functions are achieved. For the Slide Show, this requirement has structural implications for the alternatives available. Since the intrinsic function of each IDENTIFICATION and CONTEXTUALISATION stage, in conjunction with the SLIDE, is to import and anchor semiosis from the visual code into the verbal code, (and since the slides are organised with respect to the text before or outside the Slide Show, and not necessarily with respect to one another), these three elements – SLIDE, IDENTIFICATION and CONTEXTUALISATION – are closely bound together into a kind of unit, or macro-stage. It would clearly be incoherent, for example, if the speaker were to contextualise or identify *the Easter Island hand* several slides after the image of the hand had disappeared from the screen. In none of the data which we have analysed are these three functional stages separated from one another, (although the ordering and realisation does vary, as we shall see below). Further, there are additional particular restrictions on the ordering of the SLIDE and IDENTIFICATION functions. Together, these form the 'interface' between the visual and verbal semiotic codes. What is more, the semiotic spans these two elements build together proceed in only one direction: from image to word. For this reason, each IDENTIFICATION always occurs after its SLIDE – that is, after the appearance of the SLIDE, and while it is still visible on the screen.

The function of the CONTEXTUALISATION element, however, allows for much more flexibility in its realisations. In our data, CONTEXTUALISATION shows the most dynamic variation, both in terms of its ordering with respect to the SLIDE and IDENTIFICATION elements, and in terms of its linguistic realisation. In contrast to the relationship between SLIDE and IDENTIFICATION, semiotic spans built through the CONTEXTUALISATION element do not necessarily proceed in a single direction, from the visual code of the slide to the verbal code of language. Spans may be built from the verbal code to the visual code, (e.g. redirecting the audience's attention to a detail of the slide), from the language of the IDENTIFICATION back to the mono-semiotic text which precedes the Slide Show (e.g. referring to previously discussed collectors), or from the current text to shared discourse knowledge of museums, geography, explorers, dates and scales of value. For this reason, the CONTEXTUALISATION function may be realised before or after the appearance of the SLIDE, and before or after the IDENTIFICATION; indeed, it may be prosodically realised at intervals.[5] These alternatives for structural realisation are of course not random, but responsive to pressures exerted by variables in the context of situation, and textual requirements of coherence and cohesion, as discussion of the following examples will show.

3.3. Examples and discussion of dynamic realisations

As presented in Section 2 above, the canonical order of the core elements is SLIDE ^ IDENTIFICATION ^ CONTEXTUALISATION, as in the example below.

(6)	**SLIDE**	[An image of a stone/clay hand appears.]
	IDENTIFICATION	This is the Easter Island hand that was collected.
	CONTEXTUALISATION	It is a unique piece and now in the British Museum but was given by the Forsters to um the British Museum.

In our data, as example (7) shows below, one alternative realisation to this order of elements has the SLIDE element *spread through* the IDENTIFICATION element.

(7)	**SLIDE**	[Side view of two buildings appears.]
	IDENTIFICATION	and these are the little buildings
	SLIDE (continued)	[Front view of one building appears.]
	IDENTIFICATION (cont.)	in which the objects from um the Forsters, who have their own special little building
	SLIDE (continued)	[Front view of another building appears.]
	IDENTIFICATION (cont.)	for the objects made for them
	CONTEXTUALISATION	and it- as I said, it is a really excellent collection and when I visited it was still in quite good condition.

There is a single SLIDE element here of three parts – 3 separate projected images, with varying experiential content (i.e. realising slightly different parts of

---

[5] It is interesting that in this respect, and in its function of anchoring a generic purpose in contexts of situation and culture, CONTEXTUALISATION in the Slide Show seems to work similarly to EVALUATION in Narrative genres.

the field). That they form one functional element is made clear by their distribution across a single clause, which realises the IDENTIFICATION element.[6] In the IDENTIFICATION, information from the three images is imported from the visual code into language with an exophorically retrievable (i.e. outside the linguistic text) Token, *these*, and an endophorically retrievable (i.e. inside the linguistic text) Value, *the little buildings in which...* . The Participants *these* and *the little buildings* are formally plural, but each fills a single experiential function.

This variation of the order of SLIDE and IDENTIFICATION elements is an example of dynamic realisation, because it is a re-negotiation in response to pressures between different aspects of the context of situation: between register variables (field, mode, tenor) and thereby between their linguistic (experiential, textual and interpersonal) realisations. In example (7), above, there is a negotiation between the field and the mode, in that visual content is spread across more than one image, projected sequentially. Something which fills a single experiential and textual function in language (realised by *these*) must be mapped to multiple textual functions in the visual code (realised by three separate house images). Realising the SLIDE element in parts, all contained within the clause of the IDENTIFICATION, is a resolution of this pressure.

Example (7) is a case of dynamic realisation in the Slide Show as *text-planning*. That is, the pressures between situational and metafunctional requirements exist prior to the instantiation of text – the speaker knows she has three images for one thing – and staging of elements in the Slide Show can be re-negotiated ahead of time. Example (8), below, is similar in this respect. Here, components of the CONTEXTUALISATION element are realised both before and after the IDENTIFICATION.

(8)	**SLIDE**	[Image of a coloured drawing appears, depicting a scene of people in canoes.]
	CONTEXTUALISATION (i)	Some of the important objects can al- you can only figure out what they were used for by looking at illustrations.
	IDENTIFICATION	This is an illustration by Hodges
	CONTEXTUALISATION (ii)	and note the little human images on the top...

Here, alternation in the normal order of elements is a result of pressure exerted by the field, on both tenor and mode. The SLIDE here introduces a new kind of Participant. Rather than a photograph of an artefact, a museum or a Tongan

---

[6] To represent this in written mode above, the IDENTIFICATION element is also represented discontinuously, to show the 'intrusion' of the three image-parts of the SLIDE element. However in multi-semiotic 'real time', the IDENTIFICATION is one uninterrupted stream on the auditory channel.

scene, like the Participants represented in other slides, it is a reproduction of a drawing. To allow the audience to make sense of this shift in the field, and to give it its appropriate connection to the rest of the field, CONTEXTUALISATION is needed before the SLIDE can be identified. A hypernym is introduced, to fit the SLIDE into a discourse semantic taxonomy appropriate to the field; the drawing is a type of 'illustration'. The generic Participant, *illustrations*, then stands at the head of a Participant chain, linking it to *an illustration by Hodges*. There are textual and interpersonal renegotiations involved in this alternative realisation. Textually, there is a *generic* Participant (*illustrations*) in this part of the CONTEXTUALISATION, instead of one with homophoric, exophoric or endophoric reference. That is, the SLIDE here is not linked to a shared context of the culture of ethnography, nor to the context of the conference environment, nor to other parts of the text; but to a generalised type of Participant. In terms of tenor repercussions, the presenter moves into a role of justifying the inclusion of this new type of image. Key interpersonal realisations of this are the modulation for ability, *you **can** only figure out what they were used for...*, and the generic Subject, *you*. The case of dynamic realisation in example (8) shows how diverse the potential of the element is, for 'thickening' semiotic spans. We have represented the two sections of the CONTEXTUALISATION as parts (i) and (ii) to underline the different kinds of contextualising done by each. While part (i), above, prepares the context for the new semiotic span to be built in the IDENTIFICATION, there is always the possibility of further, and different kinds of, 'anchoring' in the context of culture or situation. In this case, part (ii) goes on with elaborating **situational** spans, by directing attention from language back to the image: *and note the little human images...* .

As the presenter continues from this point, there is an example of dynamic alternation in the genre which contrasts with the two cases discussed above. Variation in examples (7) and (8) above could be called a matter of 'choice' as *text planning*: adapting the unfolding of the genre for cohesion and coherence, where pressures in the context are known beforehand. In example (9), below, adaptation is a matter of 'necessity' as *on-line processing* – when there is an element of the unexpected.

(9)	**SLIDE**	[Image of a coloured drawing appears, depicting a scene of figures in canoes.]
	CONTEXTUALISATION (i)	Some of the important objects can al- you can only figure out what they were used for by looking at illustrations.
	IDENTIFICATION	This is an illustration by Hodges

CONTEXTUALISATION (ii)   and note the little human images on the top
[Photograph of a headdress appears.] of the um-
ah sorry [Tries to return to coloured drawing
slide.] the um- What I wanted you to look at was
the- the- um the man wearing this wonderful
feathered head-dress and one of these unique
pieces was collected by the Forsters and is now in
the Pitt Rivers Museum.

The IDENTIFICATION in example (9) builds the span from the visual code to language: from an image of a drawing to *this*, and *an illustration by Hodges*. The function of part (ii) of the CONTEXTUALISATION above, as it was begun, is to thicken that span in the context of situation, by directing the flow of information from language back to the visuals. This is realised linguistically by exophorically presuming reference, picking out elaborating details: *and note the little human images on the top of the...* . When the original image is no longer available to resolve this reference, because of the mistaken change of slides, an alternative is necessary so that the CONTEXTUALISATION function can be realised. This case of disruption in the channel is an example of one part of mode (the visual part) pushing unexpectedly on the context of situation: i.e. on field and tenor, as well as on the linguistic component of mode. A change in context means the presenter must dynamically adjust the realisation of the CONTEXTUALISATION.

The tenor change is apparent in the presenter's changed relationship with the audience: she takes responsibility for the problem and apologises – *ah sorry*. In addition to this interpersonal shift, there is an experiential shift, as the field is expanded to include the presenter and the audience. The presenter represents her own mental states, as Senser, in relation to the audience's projected behavioural Process: *what I wanted you to look at was...*. Textually, these shifts lead to a repackaging of information: the loaded nominal group, *what [[I wanted you to look at]]*, is then able to stand for the referent which was lost with the change of image.[7]

The next development is interesting, in that this nominal group is the Value, in an Identifying process, and the presenter searches for a Token: *what [[I wanted you to look at]]* (Value) *was* (Identifying process) *the- the- um...* (Token...). The presuming Deictic, *the*, directs attention to a known, retrievable Participant. This reference is then resolved exophorically, from the visual code, as it would have been originally, if the appropriate slide were still visible. However, in the dynamically 'repaired' unfolding of the genre, the reference is resolved not in the image which was expected, but by bridging to the image which has appeared in

---

[7] The double brackets here, "[[ ]]", indicate a clause embedded in a nominal group.

error, a photograph of a headdress: *the- the- um the man wearing **this** wonderful feathered headdress.*

In this way, the CONTEXTUALISATION of the Hodges illustration SLIDE is conflated with the IDENTIFICATION of the following headdress SLIDE, through another dynamic resource for adapting generic elements: rank-shifting and embedding. The IDENTIFICATION is textually repackaged. Instead of being realised as an identifying clause (e.g. **"This** is the feathered headdress") it is embedded in the Qualifier of the extended nominal group, *the man [[wearing **this** wonderful feathered headdress]].* It might also be argued that the interpersonal Appraisal function of *wonderful* realises a CONTEXTUALISATION function in the same group. (Compare this with the Appraisal used in more canonical realisations of CONTEXTUALISATION: e.g. *it is a **unique** piece.*)

It is perhaps fortunate for the presenter that the channel disruption occurred where there is this continuity of field between the two images, which she can draw on for textual cohesion (i.e. a man in the drawing wears a headdress, and the following slide is a photograph of a headdress). We imagine that the original intention was to point out a figure in the illustration wearing a headdress, and then to proceed with the headdress as Theme for the next SLIDE + IDENTIFICATION. This appears to be the case in the next two slides, where information flows between a CONTEXTUALISATION and the next IDENTIFICATION through reference:

(10) **SLIDE (1)**   [Another coloured drawing of a canoe scene appears on the screen.]

    IDENTIFICATION (1)   [Elided]
    CONTEXTUALISATION (1)   and look at the um human images on the front of the- um um the canoe

    SLIDE (2)   [An image of a human figure in wood appears.]
    IDENTIFICATION (2)   and here are the two that were collected by the Forsters
    SLIDE (2 continued)   [Another image of a wooden human figure appears.]
    CONTEXTUALISATION (2)   both of them given um to the Pitt Rivers Museum; and these were the only two human images that were collected apparently during the second voyage.

A reference chain between CONTEXTUALISATION (1) and IDENTIFICATION (2) is formed between *the um human images* and ***the two** that were collected by the Forsters.* As we have noted in Section 2 above, this kind of textual cohesion between slides is an optional, not a necessary, feature of the Slide Show as revealed in our data. In general, the (SLIDE + IDENTIFICATION + CONTEXTUALISATION) blocks are only organised with respect to text or context *outside* the Slide Show, without thematic progression, reference chains, etc. between them. We could draw from this a cautionary tale for novices, in the light of the presenter's fortunate headdress 'repair' in example (9). Although some cohesive resources may be optional or redundant in some genres, plenty of cohesive redundancy is, at the very least, good insurance against times when things go wrong. (See Section 5 for further discussion of ESP/pedagogic implications.)

We have not attempted to map out all the possibilities for dynamic adaptation in the unfolding of the Slide Show genre, or even to show all the examples from our data. However, the examples discussed above give an indication of the kinds and extent of dynamic variation there can be in the unfolding of such a text in an actual situation. Implicit in this discussion has been the claim that the realising of genre involves an integration of variables in the context of situation – field, tenor and mode. Where there are conflicting pressures, a re-negotiation of these factors has repercussions in the ordering of generic elements and their realisation in language – experiential, interpersonal and textual (cf. 'dynamics of context', O'Donnell 1999). When a genre is multi-semiotic, like the Slide Show, the intricacy of negotiating between such pressures is likely to be much greater, as the presenter must integrate variables from more than one semiotic code. In some cases, the need to take up alternative options in the genre can be foreseen, and make up part of text-planning. In other cases, things go wrong or unfold unexpectedly, and alternatives are dynamically negotiated on-line. In addition to managing the linguistic and contextual variables discussed so far, the Slide Show presenter also needs to allow for appropriate links with social experience *beyond* the current text and context. This process, semiotic spanning, will be the focus of the following section.

4. Semiotic spanning in the Slide Show

Ventola discusses the importance of semiotic spanning as a way of looking at how "a cumulative increase of perspectives of knowledge and understanding is achieved at conferences" (Ventola 1999: 121 and cf. Chapter 1 in this volume). In the unfolding of academic genres, complex processes build spans between the current text in its context and other semiotic experience. Semiotic spanning builds connections across time and space, which may link different activities and entities in the world (e.g. historical events, museums, artefacts, voyages, conferences, tourism); different interactants, (e.g. explorers, theorists, colleagues, future generations); and different forms of semiosis, (e.g. voyage journals, conversation, drawings, scholarly literature, photographs). The effectiveness of all academic texts has a great deal to do with successful semiotic spanning. In order to find out how this is achieved, we might ask ourselves the following questions: Which kinds of semiotic experience can appropriately be spanned in an academic genre, and whose? What linguistic resources do we use for doing this? How much contribution to semiotic spanning do receivers make, and how much is done by the text producer? The Slide Show we have taken for analysis provides rich ground for beginning to approach these questions in more detail.

4.1 Semiotic spans between things and texts

As Ventola (1999) points out, many of the semiotic spans built by texts in their context can be understood with respect to the concepts of cohesion and coherence, genre and intertextuality. *Cohesion* and *coherence* provide for spanning within a text, as the means of making it a unified whole; and for spanning between the text and its contexts of situation and culture, as a means of making a text a functional social activity. *Genre* and *intertextuality* are ways of examining how each text enters into complex relationships with many other texts. That is, each text is an instance of a particular text type, and is thus related to other texts of that type; each text belongs to a discourse community and is thus related to other texts in that discourse community; a text imports other texts and text types, through reporting, or referencing, or satire, or simply through using familiar collocations, idioms, proverbs, and so on. However, these models do not exhaust all there is to say about semiotic spanning. One of the key reasons for proposing a study of semiotic spanning, as an extension of existing approaches, is the need to describe relationships built in text which go beyond a static context of situation or culture, and beyond the relationships between texts as products.

Taking the Slide Show text as a departure point for making these issues more explicit, we might start by looking at the semiotic spans which link different representations of the world. Here, we need to go beyond the concept of 'field'; i.e. beyond the more or less stable alignments of things and activities in the context of situation. In the Slide Show, the field changes from one generic stage to another, but keeps to certain regular patterns. The entities in the world are, for example, the Forsters, artefacts, museums, Tonga, the 18th century, and sometimes the speaker and audience and their environment. The activities are things like collecting, exploring, donating, being (some kind of thing/ in good condition/ in a certain place), researching, and sometimes thinking, saying, hearing and showing. Importantly, these entities and activities are organised with respect to field-specific discourse taxonomies and expected activity sequences for historical ethnography. For example, the Forsters are an example of explorers, among other explorers; the headdress is a part of a collection, among other types of artefacts; the expected sequence is that an explorer collects an artefact, then an explorer classifies an artefact, then sells or donates the artefact, then a museum shows an artefact, etc. The need to take a semiotic spanning view arises when we become aware that the same entities and things make part of more than one kind of field organisation, in different times and places, different contexts of situation and culture for different generic purposes; and that these borders are bridged multi-semiotically in new meaning-making events.

For example, let us examine the semiotic spans which are built around *the headdress* in our Slide Show. The relevant stretch of text is reproduced here, with contextual notes.

(11)   [An image appears on the screen: a coloured drawing of figures in canoes.] Some of the important objects can al- you can only figure out what they were used for by looking at illustrations. This is an illustration by Hodges and note the little human images on the top... [Another image appears on the screen: a projected photographic slide of a feathered headdress on a stand.] of the um ah sorry...[Presenter presses slide control button and looks toward the projector. The image remains on the screen.] the er what I wanted you to look at was the the the um the man wearing this wonderful feathered headdress and one of these unique pieces was collected by the Forsters and is now in the Pitt Rivers Museum.

The field which is realised here includes the headdress as an artefact among other artefacts, which was collected by the Forsters, is in an illustration by Hodges, is now in a museum, was at one time used for something, and whose use someone is trying to figure out. This is all in line with the contexts of situation and culture for a Slide Show in an academic conference on ethnography in the 1990s. However, there are some salient semiotic experiences which are *not* part of the field of this text in the usual sense. To begin with, someone made the headdress as a form of semiosis, in or before the 18th century, in Tonga, in a particular situation in another culture. The field for that semiotic experience was quite different. The headdress was not an artefact among artefacts, but an artistic/economic/religious/utilitarian item among others in the culture. The expected action sequences for that field would have been quite different from those expected in ethnography. We could imagine it to be, for example: person dies + family collects feathers + artist makes headdress + artist presents headdress + family member wears headdress + family burns headdress during a burial ceremony. Finding out about these semiotic processes is precisely what ethnography tries to do, of course. When the Slide Show presenter says, *you can only figure out **what it was used for**,* this could be analysed as a case of grammatical metaphor which tightly packs the original field for the headdress-semiosis, in order to bring that context into language, and thus into the context of situation and culture of the presentation on ethnography. When this semiotic span is realised through language, it could be argued that one whole context becomes a Participant in a new context (realised by the nominal group, *what [[it was used for]]*).

However, in the Slide Show there is evidence of many other kinds of semiotic span which are not so straightforwardly realised. For example, complex spans between the headdress, the Hodges illustration, and the presenter's slide. Consider these semiotic processes, which all have their own differing contexts of situation and culture: Hodges drew a representation of Tongan activity (seeing and representing according to his own culture and his artistic training at that time), including the use of a headdress as one Participant in the visual semiotic field. The Forsters collected a similar headdress. The process of collecting was itself a semiotic activity, realising an 18th century system of classification. Today, in an "old-fashioned" museum, this headdress makes meaning as part of a semiosis of display, which shares similar field classifications to those of 18th century collection. Then the presenter shows *and* comments on slides of both the headdress and the illustration, bringing them into the field of modern ethnography, which has quite different expected taxonomies (e.g. artefacts are organised with respect to culture and geography, rather than type). It is in the multi-semiotic Slide Show – through the integration of the visual code of the slides with language – that we get a clue about how spanning to the earlier fields is needed to make sense of the current text in context. When the photograph of the headdress appears before the presenter has finished commenting on the Hodges illustration, she instead refers to the photograph: *what I wanted you to look at was the the um the man wearing **this wonderful feathered headdress** and one of these unique pieces was collected by the Forsters and is now in the Pitt Rivers Museum.* This exophoric reference in language means that the photographic slide of the headdress, as well as referring in visual code to the physical headdress itself, is construed as referring to the earlier illustration which includes a similar headdress *and* by extension, *the man* who was wearing it. To make sense of this reference, the audience needs to make a semiotic span to the field of Hodges' semiotic process of illustrating: in some other context, he was seeing and drawing Tongan people. Simultaneously, spans are activated between the headdress collected by the Forsters and the drawing by Hodges (so that they stand together as somehow the same), not to mention the museum visited by the presenter, and the photographic slide displayed on the screen. We cannot see all the traces of these semiotic spans in either language or image, within our current analytical framework, but must nonetheless assume it is formed by both audience and presenter – if we are to interpret this text as coherent.

4.2. Semiotic spanning between different interactants

As well as building links between different representations of the world and its parts, the Slide Show builds spans between different semiotic interactants: different semiosis producers and receivers, across the boundaries of the current context. In preparing her conference paper, the presenter read journal entries written by the Forsters and viewed illustrations by Hodges, as well as articles written by other scholars. However, she may also have spoken to curators of museums, to Tongan people, to colleagues and members of her family. In her travels around the world, the presenter has also seen visual and physical semiotic representations such as weddings, artwork, dances and tourism materials produced by Tongan people, as well as their representation by curators in various museums. Only some of these 'voices' appear in the final multi-semiotic text. Producing an academic text involves choices about who takes part in the semiosis, and what their roles are: e.g., which audience is addressed, how the 'receiver(s)' and 'producer(s)' are related, who or what are appropriate authorities for judgement, and which institutional loyalties and value systems apply. In addition to the interaction between the presenter/writer and audience/listener/reader, some easily recognisable spans to extra interactants in academic texts include referencing, quoting or reporting. However, there are other links between semiotic interactants which are not so easily recognised.

As Firth (1964: 91) notes, from childhood onwards we are linguistically socialised for the many different roles we need to play in our cultures:

> For each stage there is a relevant living space, a relevant culture, a relevant language. The biological individual gradually becomes a bundle of *personae*, a social personality with many ear languages, one or more eye and hand languages, and one or two tongue languages – a Babel in himself.

As social semiotic agents, we all incorporate a multitude of semiotic roles, potential and actual, linked to our own previous experience and observation of others: conference audience member, presenter or discussant, tourist or museum visitor, writer of articles, teacher, customer, colleague, etc. In context, we realise these roles in language or other semiotic codes: e.g. through either offering or demanding information, or goods and services; by adjusting our attitudes through modality and evaluative resources; and through hiding or showing subjective or objective sources of authority. In the Slide Show, while the tenor of the context shifts with each stage in the unfolding genre, it is maintained within a certain range. That is, in this context the presenter fills the role of an authoritative knower primarily responsible for semiosis 'production', and the audience members fill the role of respectful listeners and receivers. The linguistic realisations include mostly statements by the presenter, with a generally low level of modality, and no statements by the audience. However, to qualify as an appropriate academic presentation in context, some of the other roles for these interactants must be spanned, which go beyond the current context.

The semiotic event and genre 'Conference Presentation' realises social purposes of knowledge production and distribution. The 'distribution' component involves the creation and maintenance of discourse communities and networks, and is thus open-ended. That is, for the full realisation of the Slide Show's social semiotics, it is understood that these audience members will go on in other contexts to be presenters, writers, colleagues and teachers who may incorporate portions of the Slide Show into later semiosis in those other roles. For example, an audience member who simply receives information in the conference presentation may go on to exchange information in a more dialogic way in the discussion section of the presentation, or to talk about it casually in a café with the other conference participants, or to visit the Pitt Rivers Museum themselves. In an important sense, there are therefore semiotic spans to the *potential* of those other roles in other contexts, which are necessarily built to make the current Slide Show a functioning instance of its academic genre.

More work needs to be done to develop existing analytical tools, to make explicit how these spans are realised semiotically and multi-semiotically. Nonetheless, within our existing framework there are visible starting points. Take for instance the following example from the Slide Show:

(12)   [A photograph of a large house appears on the screen.] I start with Wörlitz. This is the country house in Wörlitz, if any of you have not been there. [A photograph of two smaller buildings, viewed obliquely.] And these are the little buildings [A frontal shot of one building appears.] in which the objects from um the Forsters who have their own special little building [A frontal shot of another building appears.] for the objects made for them and it- as I said it is a really excellent collection and when I visited it was still in quite good condition.

The relevant spans here are between the presenter in her current role, her earlier role as a witness (or receiver of information) at the Wörlitz museum, and a potential role for audience members as witnesses in Wörlitz. In the early clause complex, there is an internal conjunction: *This is the country house in Wörlitz, if any of you have not been there.* This is an internal conjunction because the *if* makes a relationship between the two clauses which is based not on experiential and logical functions, but on textual and interpersonal functions. That is, the discourse semantics here are not that **the image represents Wörlitz** because some of the audience may not have been there. Rather, **the presenter is identifying the image of Wörlitz** because some of the audience may not have been there. To make sense of this, other roles and authorities – i.e. semiotic interactants – are activated in the Slide Show, beyond the current text and context. Firstly, the audience members' potential past role as interactants in the Wörlitz museum semiosis. The authority of the presenter's (implicitly objective) identification is linked with the subjective authority of the audience members: i.e. if they had been there too, they would say the same. Secondly, the presenter's actual past role in the semiotic interaction at the Wörlitz museum. Later in example (12) above, in the CONTEXTUALISATION, the presenter becomes Subject, and enters into the experiential content as a visitor: *it is a really excellent collection and **when I visited** it was still in quite good condition.* There is interpersonal work being done here, as well as experiential. That is, the presenter does not only represent her visit as a **time-frame** for the collection's good condition; but also as an **authority** for judging the collection's good condition. Both this and the previous example are discussed by White (1998) as discourse semantic resources of Engagement: means of adjusting the responsibility and degree of commitment to semiotic roles, often by indexing other sources of authority. We would extend from the concept of Engagement, and say that the *whole* previous context and semiotic text of the presenter's visit to Wörlitz is bridged to the current text and context. This semiotic span is not limited to, but includes, a link from the presenter's current role to her previous role as museum visitor, the 'collector' of semiotic experience in another text and context. Moreover, this spanning across contexts is necessary for the full realisation of the tenor of the Slide Show.

4.3. Spanning between different channels, codes and modes of semiosis

While far and away the most important code for academic texts is language (and typically written mode in preference to spoken mode) semiotic spanning to other kinds of meaning-making are necessary for their complete realisation. The primary concern of academic texts in the humanities (and, arguably, the sciences as well) is to present and/or engage with (interpret/critique/analyse/ classify/apply) already existing social meaning of one form or another. The Slide Show, and indeed the whole conference presentation, is not only a multi-semiotic text in its own context, but also stands on the shoulders of many different kinds of semiosis in other contexts: physical artefacts and rituals in 18th century Tonga, classificatory collections, illustrations of Tongan scenes, written travel journals and catalogues, museum displays, photographs of all these things, etc. Semiotic spanning is needed not just to link the experience that these 'texts' represent, or the interactants who are/were/will be involved, but also different *ways* of meaning. As noted in the opening section of this chapter, the integration of multiple semiotic codes and modes in text, as in the Slide Show, is a very visible example of semiotic spanning. In all academic texts, spans are built to other texts and text-types, representations of the world, alignments to authority, voices and systems of value. In addition, as Kress & van Leeuwen (1996: 39) point out, all texts span to other *channels, codes and modes*:

> [L]anguage, whether in speech or writing, has always existed as just one mode in the totality of modes involved in the production of any text, spoken or written. A spoken text is not just verbal but also visual, combining with 'non-verbal' modes of communication such as facial expression, gesture, posture and other forms of self-presentation. A written text, similarly, involves more than language [...] The multi-modality of written texts has, by and large, been ignored, whether in educational contexts, in linguistic theorising or in popular common sense. Today, in the age of 'multimedia', it can suddenly be perceived again.

Just as quoting and reporting make spans to other voices and authorities explicit, the incorporation of other media, such as visual slides, makes the spans to other codes and modes more explicit. The interface between the SLIDE and IDENTIFICATION elements in the Slide Show is of course the peak example here. The constant Theme, Subject and Token in the IDENTIFICATION is the exophoric Deictic, *this*, retrievable from the projected image. Thus, to make sense of the Slide Show it is necessary to repeatedly switch between the visual channel and the auditory, from visual codes of drawing and photography to language; and to build semiotic bridges from one kind of meaning-making to another, in a way that allows meaning from both to work together in a unified text.

In the IDENTIFICATION element, semiotic spanning between the visuals and language is regular and would seem fairly unproblematic from the viewpoint of contemporary multi-modality approaches. Within a unified text in context, regular linguistic features realise a straightforward span which draws meaning from the visual channel and codes into the auditory channel and language. However, even in this case there are issues for spanning between types of semiosis (channels, codes and modes) which extend beyond a 'multi-modal text' perspective – i.e. because there are spans which extend beyond text-in-context boundaries (and so beyond our current models for multi-modality) but which are nonetheless crucial for the coherent unfolding of our text. Take, for example, the spans needed to interpret 'human images' in example (13) from the Slide Show, below:

(13) [A coloured drawing of a canoe scene is on the screen.] and look at **the um human images on the front of the- um um the canoe** [Photograph of a carved wooden

human figure against plain blue backdrop appears.] and here are **the two that were collected by the Forsters** [Photograph of second human figure with same blue backdrop appears.] **both of them** given um to the Pitt Rivers Museum and **these** were **the only two human images that were collected apparently during the second voyage**.

All the nominal groups shown in bold above take part in a lexical chain linked to 'human images' (this is done at the discourse semantic level through, variously, reference, substitution, ellipsis and co-hyponymy). That is, one way or another, each nominal group above is a realisation in language of the same (kind of) experiential thing. But note that the projected slides also realise, in visual code, the same (kind of) thing. Of particular interest for our discussion of semiotic spanning are the links between them.

The link between the slide of the canoe scene and the first mention in language is pushed by presuming (exophoric) reference. That is, by saying *look at the human images*, the presenter directs the audience to see a *known* Participant in their immediate environment, i.e. the visuals on the screen. Through resources in language (i.e. reference and phoricity), 'human images' are located as a meaning which is common to both the verbal and visual (illustration) codes, and transferrable between them. Semiotic spanning is apparently achieved fully in this instance within the text in context. Other links in this excerpt, however, depend on spans which go *beyond* text in context, and are not so clearly or completely construed through language.

The experiential content realised by the two photographs is identified in language as *the two that were collected by the Forsters*. (Here, 'human images' are understood and elided: *the two* [human images] *that were....*) This is again a presuming reference, but it cannot be resolved as the same Participant. It can be resolved as a co-hyponym of the *human images* on the canoe; i.e. another one of the same kind. But to make sense of this, the audience needs to have access to a hypernym; i.e. a general type of 'human image' of which these Participants are examples. There is none available in either the visual or verbal codes in this text or the context, so a semiotic span must be built to other texts in contexts outside this one. That is, the audience needs to bridge to semiosis in another context for the drawing (human images were present on a canoe in Tonga and someone drew them) and for the photograph (human images were present in Tonga and someone collected them and someone photographed them) and compare them (so, Tonga has/had a class of things, 'human images', some of which were illustrated, and some of which were photographed, and which are now being talked about). The semiotic span goes beyond what we can identify in language or in visual code, with the tools we have now. However, we can see the results of this semiotic span in the coherence of the interaction between codes. Put another way, for the interaction between codes to be coherent in this Slide Show, spans between ways of meaning in different contexts must be built somehow. This example highlights the role of the conference audience as active contributors to meaning-making. It is not only the presenter who 'draws on past experience' to produce a conference paper. The presentation in context only comes together coherently when the relevant semiotic experiences outside the here-and-now are spanned for or (perhaps more crucially) *by* the hearers.

As a final point for our discussion of spanning between semiotic codes and modes, let us look at what happens when the presenter becomes a writer, and the Conference Presentation, with its embedded multi-semiotic Slide Shows, is 'written up' as a published paper. Written academic genres carry a lot of prestige and potential for knowledge production and distribution. They are portable, reproduceable and referenceable, and also – due to their mode – more perfectable than spoken genres such as teaching or conference presentations. In the current publish-or-perish academic environment, published papers are also increasingly important to the professional lives of their writers. For these reasons, we might look on the written article as more likely to represent the important 'essentials' than the conference presentation.

In the written version of the Forsters paper (published in the conference proceedings in German), the images projected in the Slide Show are not reproduced. In field and tenor the written text is quite close to the prepared speech sections of the presentation: i.e. everything *except* the embedded Slide Shows. The Participants realised in the Slide Show by the SLIDE + IDENTIFICATION elements (i.e. the specific artefacts) are not mentioned in the body of the written text. However, there are extensive tables, in parallel German and English, which list the artefact *types* by their location of origin (Tonga, New Zealand, etc.) and the number of pieces of that artefact type in each museum. A small excerpt from these tables follows.[8] (Where English headings appear in square brackets, these are translations added by us. All other English translations appear in the original.)

The Participants in Table 1 below – museums, geographical locations, numbers and types of artefact – are typical of those found in the CONTEXTUALISATION elements in the Slide Show. In Section 2 above, we analysed the SLIDE + IDENTIFICATION as the generic elements forming the primary span between the visuals and language, and the CONTEXTUALISATION element as a secondary 'anchoring' through semiotic spans with the co-text (in the rest of the presentation), the context (of conference situation and academic culture) and

---

[8] To preserve the anonymity of the presenter, no reference is given for this excerpt. This is a reproduction of selected fragments from the published tables, keeping as closely as possible to the original formatting.

beyond. So it is interesting to note that these 'secondary' spans are those which continue in the written version of the paper, while the 'primary' ones do not. The Slide Shows we have analysed are embedded genres which realise a generic element in the Conference Paper which has an illustrative purpose (see Section 2). That is, the presenter does not build up an argument on the evidence of the slides, but uses the visual medium to add 'interest' – a supporting semiotic 'thickness'. The tables in the published article stand in the same illustrative relationship to the body of the written text. What is interesting for us is how, in both cases, there is a 'seeing is believing' effect produced by switching between semiotic codes: i.e. between spoken commentary and slides in the conference presentation, and between written text and graphic table in the published paper. The content which is shared by slides and table entries is that part which depends on building diffuse and diverse semiotic spans between the current text-in-context and semiotic processes involving other interactants, experiences and ways of meaning in contexts distant in time, space and culture.

Insel/Objekt [Island/Object]		Oxford	Göttingen	Wörlitz	Stockholm	Cambridge
Tonga [Tonga]						
Keulen	Clubs	10	9	2	2	2
Panflöten	Panpipes	1	2	1	1	
Kopfstützen	Headrests	2	1	1	1	1
Halsketten	Necklaces	9	1	2	4	
Lebensmittelstampfer	Food pounder	1	1	1		1
Neuseeland [New Zealand]						
Mäntel	Cloaks	6	1	1	1	
Mattengurt	Mat belt	1				
geschäftete Dechsel	Hafted adze	1			1	
Taiaha *(Waffe)*	... (weapon)	1	1			
Osterinsel [Easter Island]						
gefiederte Kopfbedeckung	Feathered headdress	1				
Knochen-Anhänger	Bone pendants	2				

Table 1. Reproduced table from the published paper, showing artefact types in different museums.

5. Summary and implications

It is important to note that the features of generic structure and realisation noted here are restricted to those attested in our data. Further research is needed to answers questions about the range of agnate genres which exist for Slide Shows, the variety of functions they may serve when embedded/mixed with Conference Presentation genres, how these are related to non-academic Slide Shows and other multi-semiotic verbal-plus-visual genres, and what the range of realisations are. For example, in our data the Slide Show is embedded as an ILLUSTRATION stage in the parent Conference Presentation genre at the ethnology conference. In other conference presentations, such as in the physical sciences, where slides might perform a function of EVIDENCE, we would expect significant differences in generic structure and linguistic realisation to those found here: e.g. more textual cohesion between stages, as argumentation is built up over the duration of the Slide Show.

Nonetheless, analysis and discussion of the Slide Show in this single conference presentation raises important issues for the study of multi-semiotic academic genres, and its application in the training of novices. We have taken complementary perspectives on genre here. Both synoptic and dynamic approaches provide useful ways of talking about the integration of purpose and structure in the realisation of diverse social meaning-making activities, including academic presentations. What is more, both approaches are able to accommodate multi-semiotic realisations, such as the Slide Show. While linear synoptic representations are important basic tools for teaching novices, analysis of the Slide Show has shown that a dynamic approach to genre is particularly necessary to equip novices with the skills for integrating codes in academic genres. For the successful production of a multi-semiotic genre such as the Slide Show, presenters need to: a) know which elements are essential in the genre, and what restrictions there are on their ordering and realisation; b) know that alternatives to the 'normal' realisation are possible; c) be able to recognise where pressures in the context of situation can be resolved by dynamic alternation; and d) have the linguistic skills for realising these alternative realisations, both in text planning, and 'on-line.'

In addition to all this, academics need awareness of the appropriate semiotic spans between the instantiation of their texts in their contexts and the world of semiotic experience beyond. When semiotic spanning is inadequate or inappropriate, academic texts may be coherent but nonetheless fail in the stakes of successful knowledge production and distribution. That is, they may be received as trivial, boring or obscure. They may take insufficient account of the other roles of their audience (teachers? students?) and so be unable to live on in connection with future meaning-making. Or they may be perceived as either overwhelming, unconvincing or 'behind the times' in terms of the range and kinds of codes, modes and channels they span. Our discussion of the Slide Show data in Section 4 has focussed on those instances where semiotic spanning extends beyond text-in-context, and so is beyond the reach of tools and vocabulary in existing theories of cohesion, coherence, genre and inter-textuality. If the aim, therefore, is to be able to give novices explicit accounts of semiotic spanning, in the same way as we can do for (other aspects of) genre, then questions arise which have broader implications for the boundaries of text linguistics. Accounting for successful semiotic spanning may require more awareness of cognitive processes in the study of text in context and/or increased focus on text *receivers* as more active contributors to cohesion and coherence than is commonly allowed for.

The issues and questions raised by this paper are not limited to multi-semiotic academic texts. However, as academic genres begin to catch up with those in other areas of social life, applied linguists will face more visible challenges when accounting for the integration of semiotic experience in text. In this light, the need for linguistic research into how semiotic spanning is achieved both in and beyond text becomes more pressing.

References

Baldry, A. (ed.) 2000. *Multi-modality and Multimediality in the Distance Learning Age*. Campobasso, Italy: Palladino Editore.

Dubois, B.L. 1980a. "The Use of Slides in Biomedical Speeches". *The ESP Journal*, 1,1: 45-50.

Dubois, B.L. 1980b. "Genre and Structure of Biomedical Speeches". *Forum Linguisticum*, 5,2: 140-68.

Fawcett, R. P., A. van der Mije & C. van Wissen. 1988. "Towards a systemic flowchart model for discourse structure". In R. P. Fawcett & D. Young (eds). *New Developments in Systemic Linguistics*, 2: 116-143.

Firth, J. R. 1964. *The Tongues of Men & Speech*. Oxford: Oxford University Press.

Halliday, M. A. K. 1989. *Spoken and Written Language*. Oxford: Oxford University Press.

Halliday, M. A. K. 1994. *Introduction to Functional Grammar*. London: Arnold.

Halliday, M. A. K. & R. Hasan. 1985. *Language, Context and Text*. Geelong., Vic.: Deakin University Press. [Reprinted 1989 by Oxford University Press]

Hasan, R. 1977. "Text in the systemic-functional model". In W. Dressler (ed.). *Current Trends in Textlinguistics*. Berlin/New York: de Gruyter.

Kress, G. & T. van Leeuwen. 1996. *Reading Images. The Grammar of Visual Design*. London-New York: Routledge.

van Leeuwen, T. 1996. "Visual English: The visual language of film". In S. Goodman & D. Graddol. *Redesigning English*. London-New York: Routledge, 81-106.

Martin, J. R. 1985. "Process and text: two aspects of human semiosis". In J. D. Benson & W. S. Greaves (eds). *Systemic Perspectives on Discourse*, Vol. 1. Norwood, N. J.: Ablex, 248-274.

Martin, J. R. 1992. *English Text. System and Structure*. Amsterdam/Philadelphia: Benjamins.

Martin, J. R. 2000. "Beyond Exchange: Appraisal systems in English". In S. Hunston and G. Thompson (eds). *Evaluation in Text*. Oxford: OUP, 142-175.

O'Donnell, M. 1990. "A dynamic model of exchange". *Word*, 41: 293-328.

O'Donnell, M. 1999. "Context in dynamic modelling". In M. Ghadessy (ed.). *Text and Context in Functional Linguistics*. Amsterdam/Philadelphia: Benjamins, 63-99.

O'Halloran, K. L. 1999a. "Interdependence, interaction and metaphor in multisemiotic texts". *Social Semiotics*, 9 (3): 317-354.

O'Halloran, K. L. 1999b. "Classroom discourse in mathematics: a multisemiotic analysis". *Linguistics and Education*, 10 (3): 359-388.

O'Halloran, K. L. 2000. "Towards a systemic functional analysis of multisemiotic mathematics texts". *Semiotica*, 124 (1-2): 1-29.

O'Toole, M. 1994. *The Language of Displayed Art*. London: Leicester University Press.

O'Toole, M. 1995. "A systemic functional semiotics of art". In P. Fries & M. Gregory (eds.). *Discourse in Society: Functional Perspectives*. Norwood, N.J.: Ablex Publishing House, 159-179.

Pang Kah Meng, A. 2000. *Designing Children in 'Changing World, Changing Hopes': A Multisemiotic Analysis of a Museum Exhibition*. Unpublished B.A. Honours thesis. Singapore: National University of Singapore.

Purser, E. 2000. "Telling stories: text analysis in a museum". In E. Ventola (ed.). *Discourse and Community: Doing Functional Linguistics*. Tübingen: Narr, 169-198.

Räisänen, C. 1999. *The Conference Forum as a System of Genres*. Göteborg, Sweden: Acta Universitatis Gothoburgensis.

Ravelli, L. 1996. "Making language accessible: successful text writing for museum visitors". *Linguistics and Education*, 8: 367-387.

Ravelli, L. 1998a. "The consequences of choice. Discursive positioning in an art institution". In A. Sánchez-Macarro & R. Carter (eds.). *Linguistic Choice Across Genres*. Amsterdam-Philadelphia: Benjamins, 137-153.

Ravelli, L. 1998b. "Making meaning: how, what and why?". In K. Vesk (ed.). *Museums making meaning – communication by design*. Sydney: Museums Australia Inc., 1-11.

Ravelli, L. 2000. "Beyond shopping: Constructing the Sydney Olympics in three-dimensional text". *Text*, 20 (4): 1-27.

Swales, J. 1990. *Genre Analysis: English in academic and research settings*. Cambridge : Cambridge University Press.

Ventola, E. 1987. *The Structure of Social Interaction*. London: Pinter.

Ventola, E. 1989. "Problems of modelling and applied issues within the framework of genre". *Word*, 40 (1-2): 129-161.

Ventola, E. & A. Mauranen (ed.) 1996. *Academic Writing. Intercultural and Textual Issues*. Amsterdam/Philadelphia: John Benjamins.

Ventola, E. 1999. "Semiotic spanning at conferences: Cohesion and coherence in and across conference papers and their discussions". In W. Bublitz, U. Lenk & E. Ventola (eds). *Coherence in Spoken and Written Discourse*. Amsterdam/Philadelphia: John Benjamins.

Ventola, E. This volume. "Why and what kind of focus on conference presentations?".

White, P. R. 1998. *Telling Media Tales: The news story as rhetoric.* Unpublished Ph.D thesis. Sydney: University of Sydney.

Appendix A. Sample generic break-up in the Slide Show

------------------------------------- *Prepared speech before the Slide Show* -----------------------------------

... When used together the Forsters' artefact collections, their writings about them and the illustrations form a treasure for ethno-historical research. For the islands visitor, the jewel within this treasure is the collection from Tonga. Tahiti and New Zealand were visited during the first voyage and base-line collections and information were collected and written about by Captain Cook and Joseph Banks and illustrated by Parkinson and others. The collections from the Marquesas, Easter Island, New Hebrides and New Caledonia are also extremely -portant important but contact was short and the collections small. From Tonga however the collections are large and varied. At least 150 pieces can be identified and contact was more extensive.

----------------------------------- *Embedded Slide Show begins* -----------------------------------

Generic Element	Realisation
CODE TRANSITION	So I begin to show you some slides over the Pacific collections from the Forsters and erm especially the collections in the Pitt Rivers Museum [Presenter fiddles with console in lectern. Chair comes over, and fiddles with console. House lights dim. White light comes up on projector. Both look to screen and direction of projector. Both indicate uncertainty/impatience with gaze, posture and gesture. Slide appears and Chair returns to seat. The presenter moves to the side of the lectern.] Can you hear me if I stand over here?
⌈ SLIDE ⎨ IDENTIFICATION ⌊ CONTEXTUALISATION	[A photographic image of a building is on the screen.] I start with Wörlitz. This is the country house in Wörlitz, if any of you have not been there.
⌈ SLIDE ⎨ IDENTIFICATION SLIDE IDENTIFICATION SLIDE ⎨ IDENTIFICATION ⌊ CONTEXTUALISATION	[A photograph of an oblique view of two buildings appears.] And these are the little buildings [A photograph of the front of one building appears.] in which the objects from erm the Forsters, who have their own special little building [A photograph of the front of a second building appears.] for the objects made for them. And it, as I said, it is a really excellent collection and when I visited it was still in quite good condition.
⌈ SLIDE ⎨ IDENTIFICATION ⌊ CONTEXTUALISATION	[A photograph of a hand in clay/stone appears.] This is the Easter Island hand that was collected. It is a unique piece and now in the British Museum but was given by the Forsters to erm the British Museum.
CODE TRANSITION	[The presenter is handed a microphone.] It's okay? Okay.

SLIDE	[A photograph of the interior of a building showing display cases and shelving appears.]
IDENTIFICATION	This is the Pitt Rivers Museum
CONTEXTUALISATION	which is erm, as you can see, a rather old-fashioned museum which is arranged by artefact type rather than by area.
SLIDE	[Photograph of a handwritten page appears.]
IDENTIFICATION	And this is the catalogue of curiosities
CONTEXTUALISATION	that was written apparently by George Forster that accompanied the collection when it went erm to the Ashmolean Museum in the 18th century.
SLIDE	[A coloured drawing of people in canoes appears.]
CONTEXTUALISATION	Some of the important objects can al- you can only figure out what they were used for by looking at illustrations.
IDENTIFICATION	This is an illustration by Hodges.
CONTEXTUALISATION	And note the little human images on the top
SLIDE	[A photograph of a feathered headdress on a stand appears.]
	of the erm- ah sorry- [The presenter attempts to go back: the image of the headdress disappears and reappears.] the um- what I wanted to look at was the- the- erm the man wearing
IDENTIFICATION	this wonderful feathered head-dress.
CONTEXTUALISATION	And one of these unique pieces was collected by the Forsters and is now in the Pitt Rivers Museum.
CODE TRANSITION	[The presenter turns to face the projector.] Now I can't move it forward.
SLIDE	[Another coloured illustration of a canoe scene appears.]
IDENTIFICATION	[Elided]
CONTEXTUALISATION	And look at the erm human images on the front of the- erm erm the canoe.
SLIDE	[A photograph of a carved wooden human figure appears.]
IDENTIFICATION	and here are the two that were collected by the Forsters
CONTEXTUALISATION	both of them given
SLIDE	[A photograph of a second carved wooden human figure appears.]
IDENTIFICATION	erm to the Pitt Rivers Museum.
CONTEXTUALISATION	And these were the only two human images that were collected apparently during the second voyage.
SLIDE	[A coloured drawing of a house and a person wearing a costume appears.]
CONTEXTUALISATION	The um people on the voyage, especially the Forsters and Hodges, were interested in the Tahitian mourning costumes
IDENTIFICATION	as you see at the left.

CONTEXTUALISATION	And apparently ten of these huge costumes were collected during the second voyage, two of them by the Forsters.
SLIDE	[A photograph of a building interior showing a display of artefacts, including a costume.]
IDENTIFICATION	This is the one in the Pitt Rivers.

CONTEXTUALISATION	[Elided]
SLIDE	[A photograph of a large costume appears.]
IDENTIFICATION	And this is the one in Göttingen.

| CODE TRANSITION | [The presenter turns to face the projector.] Won't move again. |

CONTEXTUALISTION	[Elided]
SLIDE	[A photograph of another large costume appears.]
IDENTIFICATION	Sorry. This is the one in Göttingen. The other one was in Pitt Rivers.

Appendix B.   Full transcript of the embedded Slide Shows

Note: Hash marks (#) in the text show where a new image appears on the screen.
Comments on non-verbal activity are enclosed in square brackets.

… When used together the Forsters' artefact collections, their writings about them and the illustrations form a treasure for ethno-historical research. For the islands visitor, the jewel within this treasure is the collection from Tonga. Tahiti and New Zealand were visited during the first voyage and base-line collections and information were collected and written about by Captain Cook and Joseph Banks and illustrated by Parkinson and others. The collections from the Marquesas, Easter Island, New Hebrides and New Caledonia are also extremely -portant important but contact was short and the collections small. From Tonga however the collections are large and varied. At least 150 pieces can be identified and contact was more extensive.

So I begin to show you some slides over the Pacific collections from the Forsters and erm especially the collections in the Pitt Rivers Museum. [Presenter fiddles with console in lectern. Chair comes over, and fiddles with console. House lights dim. White light comes up on projector. Both look to screen and direction of projector. Both indicate uncertainty/impatience with gaze, posture and gesture. Chair returns to seat when slide appears. The presenter moves to the side of the lectern.] # Can you hear me if I stand over here? I start with Wörlitz. This is the country house in Wörlitz, if any of you have not been there. # And these are the little buildings # in which the objects from erm the Forsters who have their own special little building # for the objects made for them. And it, as I said, it is a really excellent collection and when I visited it was still in quite good condition. # This is the Easter Island hand that was collected. It is a unique piece and now in the British Museum but was given by the Forsters to erm the British Museum. [Presenter is given a microphone.] It's okay? Okay. # This is the Pitt Rivers Museum which is erm, as you can see, a rather old-fashioned museum which is arranged by artefact type rather than by area. # And this is the catalogue of curiosities that was written apparently by George Forster that accompanied the collection when it went erm to the Ashmolean Museum in the 18th century. # Some of the important objects can al- you can only figure out what they were used for by looking at illustrations. This is an illustration by Hodges and note the little human images on the top # of the erm- I'm sorry- [Presenter attempts to go back. The headdress image disappears and reappears.] the um- What I wanted you to look at was the- the- erm the man wearing this wonderful feathered head-dress. And one of these unique pieces was collected by the Forsters and is now in the

Pitt Rivers Museum. [The presenter turns to face the projector.] Now I can't move it forward. # And look at the erm human images on the front of the- erm erm the canoe. # And here are the two that were collected by the Forsters both of them given # erm- to the Pitt Rivers Museum. And these were the only two human images that were collected apparently during the second voyage. # The um people on the voyage, especially the Forsters and Hodges, were interested in the Tahitian mourning costumes as you see at the left. And apparently ten of these huge costumes were collected during the second voyage two of them by the Forsters. # This is the one in the Pitt Rivers # and this is the one in Göttingen. [The presenter turns to face the projector.] Won't move again. # Sorry, this is the one in Göttingen the other one was in Pitt Rivers. # These are the objects collected in New Zealand and some of these if you have examined the illustrations in the erm official account you will note that the adze on the top, the *toki pou tangata*, and the scarifier on the bottom were both illustrated in the # official voyage account. This was an exhibition held at the Pitt Rivers showing the New Zealand and Marquesan objects all collected by the Forsters. And this is ah one of the encounters in the New Hebrides, not Tonga. # And the objects collected in erm New Caledonia and the New Hebrides. # And a piece collected also in the New Hebrides erm by Sparmann in the Sparmann coll- in the Sparmann collection in Stockholm. # Now the biggest collection as I said was made in Tonga. This is an a map from Cook's second voyage and you note at the lower right hand corner is the island of Tongatapu and it was the edge the lower edge of the island # that they visited. This is what it looks like from a plane today, this is the area. # They encountered canoes that were illustrated beautifully by Hodges. Unfortunately they could not collect a canoe or I suspect they- that the Forsters probably would have done so. Won't move again. Thank you. # And they illustrated houses. Again, they could not collect houses so the illustrations are very important as erm an example of the architecture of the time. # Now when they ar- arrived in erm one of the friendly islands, one of the Tongan islands, an interesting analysis was made of what they saw by the Forsters especially George. And he talks about erm this meeting but also he talks about the mourning - that is, crying, that kind of mourning - for the dead and the cutting # off of the fingers of the little finger. And you can see that it's illustrated here erm by Hodges or by the person who actually engraved this illustration. # And this was an important erm analysis that was done by the Forsters on one of the erm mourning ceremonies by cutting off the little finger and you can also see it here. This gentleman also has his little finger removed. # These are some of the objects collected erm in Tonga and as you can see there it's a very large collection. # Erm- and if you look at the illustration from the official account you will see that most of the pieces that are illustrated in the official account are Forster pieces. And erm and note the- # the eh bucket a wooden bucket covered with basketry that is illustrated there. # And then have a look at the one that is in the Forster collection in the Pitt Rivers. # Also the baskets, # of which they tried to collect one or more of each type. # These are all Tongan basket types and the largest eh collection of types here is in eh Oxford. # Also collected were these objects that were held that were hung from the top of the roof of a house to keep objects safe from rats, so that rats could not get to them. Baskets were hung on the hooks and then the disk above kept the rats from coming from the top. Now the disk here is original but the eh hook part is a replica # but the one collected by Sparman in Stockholm is the original. # This is another piece of it. # They collected neck rests of two types. # Flywhisks. # Wooden bowls. # Food pounders. # A rasp which is, a rasp, I guess that's what you'd call it. # And tools. The top tool here is made of a shark tooth hafted into a handle of wood and the lower one is a nail, a European nail, hafted in the same way. Now the Forsters collected it and according to the people they collected it from, it, the nail, came from Tasman's voyage. So that was thought to be a very important piece and used to make their wooden clubs. # This is a lure to catch octopus. # A Tongan fish hook. Stuck again. # The flutes played by the nose. # Panpipes. # Dance paddles. # And a very interesting neck piece, which was a huge piece made from a whale bone worn on the neck. There is one like this in Göttingen as well so they collected two of them but they are very rare. These are the only two known pieces from the 18th century. # And necklaces of various kinds, with little pieces of carved ivory, hung from the shells, # which they probably collected as much for the shells they were made from, as being a necklace. # This one is made from pieces of bird bone. # Combs for the hair. # Pieces of bark cloth. Stuck. # And the bark cloth is of various types and designs. # This is a mat with an in-woven design. # And another mat which has little tufts of hibiscus fibre. # As you can see these are all in very good condition. And all of the types of mats they collected. This one is pandanus. Stuck. # This one is made of hibiscus fibre. Stuck again. # And this is the one in Stockholm of the same type, made of hibiscus fibre. # A spear. # A bow and arrow. # And clubs. # # [Presenter leaves the last slide visible on the screen, returns to the lectern and resumes reading.]

In 1778, Reinhold Forster noted about the Tongans that their "utensils, manufactures, agriculture and music bespeak their inventive genius and elegant taste." So that we see that the Forsters were really quite taken with what they saw in Tonga and their descriptions are still excellent and use, useful for today. Now the more than 150 pieces illustrate his admiration and include many objects that are no longer made. But they are treasured by Tongans as their cultural heritage. Even so this large collection lacks many objects of every day and ceremonial life. So what can these objects tell us about Tonga in the 18th century? And are they of any importance today? I wont go into this in detail, but if you are interested, I refer you to a 1971 article which I wrote about how Tongan artefacts from the Cook collection have became very important and they are useful for understanding the 18th century social system of Tonga. Now the Forsters were scientists, but to Tonga- but to the Tongans today, science is irrelevant, and these objects are their cultural heritage. Now as ethnographers are responsible both to science and to the people they study, my research is aimed at using the Forsters science and collections in the services of ethnography and to Polynesian cultural identity. Ethnologists today combine traditional anthropological concerns with post structuralist concepts dealing with identity and the social and cultural construction of the self. The cultural politics that derive from colonisation and decolonisation are becoming ever more potent in a world concerned with national identity and the construction of modern traditions from the remains of traditional systems of knowledge. Many aspects of custom and identity are based on objects, manuscripts and illustrations now in museums. These and their curators are continually consulted by a wide range of people, from the descendants of their makers to interested laymen. Understanding the politics of culture and identity, how modern traditions are concer- are constructed through social and political change, and why it is imperative that such concepts are understood, in our explosive world, are ethnologists' concerns today and are met through research, publication, and exhibits as well as by assisting indigenous individuals and groups to carry out their researches on these subjects, especially where traditional cultural forms and systems of knowledge are becoming endangered. And the curators of these collections are responsible to not only science, but also to present day Polynesians. The modern Pacific Islander sits in the midst of many worlds. Many of the rituals and presentations still exist as part of the modern world, and traditional artefacts can be used to understand life in its present form. Although objects can no longer be exchanged for a person, and women who use taboo artefacts are not subject to death or sanction, many objects of similar type are still used in traditional ways, such as funerals, investitures of- investitures of titles, dance, and marriage.

And I just want to show you a few modern ceremonies that use these same kinds of objects as I just showed you from the 18th century. [Presenter moves to the side of the lectern. There is a slide still visible on the screen.] This is the funeral of Queen Salote in 1965 where they are wearing the same kinds of mats that were collected by the Forsters as mourning clothing. # This is a piece of bark cloth, again very similar to the collections made in the 18th century. This piece was used for the investiture of the title of the present king of Tonga in 1967. # Their dances are still performed in much the same way as they were in the 18th century. And pieces of bark cloth as you see being presented here are still presented in exactly the same way as they were 200 years ago. # And these are the traditional objects, the mats, baskets, clothing and et cetera that were used for the marriage of the present king's daughter in the late 1970s. The marriage couple is on the far left over here, wearing layers and layers of mats. # And finally, tourism is now very important in many of these areas. This is the Tongan visitors' bureau in Nuku'alofa, Tonga in which some of the images have been recarved at the top of the posts as the entry way to the Tonga visitors' bureau. #

[The presenter leaves the last slide visible on the screen, returns to the lectern and resumes reading.] The collections and works of the Forsters are important elements for cooperative work between ethnographers, curators of collections and the indigenous Pacific peoples who are now part of an international world but value their modern lifestyle combined with tradition and Christianity. And here we see a slide showing their traditional ways of living, but also a Christian church. [Presenter does not turn to the screen.]Now, everyone seems to believe that Polynesians have irrevocably changed, but this is really not the case. Just as we are interested in admiring the churches and clothing of 18th century England and Germany, and- but have no problems riding in cars and airplanes rather than carriages, so Pacific Islanders also no longer live in the 18th century, but are interested in their temples, tools, and clothing, of their 18th century, and have no problem riding in cars and airplanes rather than canoes. But in many ways, Pacific Islanders have changed less than we. Unlike us, their 18th century material culture is still important as in the slides I show you- showed you and used during life crises and important events. Having predicted the ruin of indigenous culture, George Forster would probably be happy to know that at least in this case he was wrong. Thank you.

HUMOUR IN ORAL PRESENTATIONS: WHAT'S THE JOKE?

Monique Frobert-Adamo

Université Claude-Bernard Lyon 1, Lyon, France

Abstract – The primary objective of this chapter is to focus on the handling of humour as one among the psycholinguistic parameters that merge to determine the linguistic choices of the conference presenter in Europe. How does the awareness of being an insider or an outsider to the culture modify one's comportment when involved in a professional exchange forum? To what extent does it influence our conception of conference language as a genre? Why and how is English used at conferences in Europe? It is a fact that English is the communication vector used by either native or non-native speakers to convey complex information to specific target audiences composed of native and non-native speakers. The former and the latter share common knowledge. Yet, what is expected of the presenters is to contribute to extending this knowledge by transferring it efficiently to their peers. It may be a truism to say that satisfactory communication skills are of outmost importance: is humour perceived as a major ingredient in the recipe, or simply as an additional flavouring? Although it can be quite challenging for the presenter, humour is a means for probing the intercultural community. The analysis of the mechanisms that make it function or disfunction should contribute to broadening perspectives on the cultural issues involved in conference language.

1. Introduction

Conference language as a speech act has all the characteristics of a social act: indeed, communicating in this context is not a solitary process. We can distinguish the observable utterance and the underlying intention or act of will. Both condition interpersonal concerns in relation, on the presenter's side, with the desire for achievement and on the audience's side, with the sense of intellectual satisfaction. Humour may therefore appear as a paradoxical twist to the audience's expectations.

The word *humour* itself is a word of many meanings. The root of the word is *umor* meaning liquid or fluid. In the Middle Ages, humour referred to an energy that was thought to relate to a body fluid or an emotional state. This energy was believed to determine health and disposition. In modern dictionaries, humour is defined as "the quality of being laughable or comical" or as "a state of mind, mood, spirit". Humour is then flowing, involving basic characteristics of the individual expressed in the body, emotions and spirit. Besides, the word *to heal* comes from the root word *haelen* which means *to make whole*. Bringing together the body, mind and spirit can be healing. The physiological implications of the linguistic use of humour should not be put aside, since oral presentations imply the actors physically.

How to legitimate the role of humour in the communication process that takes place during conference presentations? Speaking does not mean freedom of speech. Neither does it mean that speaking is cost-free, since the act of speaking has to be clearly targeted.

Paradoxically, conference presenters have an ambiguous status, which is both *didactic* – they are perceived as knowledge and know-how vectors, and *entertaining* – conference goers are not very different from theatre goers, who expect the show to be flawless, and will be all the more critical as they, conference goers, belong to the same professional community, and may therefore lack the necessary distance.

I therefore intend to raise three main points: first, taking into account the fact that, when interviewed about the subject, many conference presenters are almost unaware of why and how they introduce humour in their talks, is it acceptable to consider humour as a communication *skill*? Second, as seen from the listener's point of view, is humour perceived as a purely *linguistic tool*, or does it pertain to a *global rhetoric*, hence could be labelled as a *hedge*? Lastly, is it to be antici-pated that humour might interfere with the transference of complex professional scientific topics, or does it set up a global context of conviviality that brings a significant improvement to sometimes – not always – dry technical data?

This paper is divided into two main parts. The first part deals with the following subsections: is humour a communication skill? (Section 2), is humour perceived as a hedge or a linguistic tool? (Section 3), does humour interfere with the transfer of supposedly complex scientific topics, or does it pertain to a global context of conviviality? (Section 4). The final part of the paper provides an account of how humour should be approached in a systemic functional theoretical context, therefore considering the following points: can humour be tackled as a function of language? (Section 5), at what level of discourse is humour generated? (Section 6), metaphors of Mood vs. cohesion and coherence (Section 7). It should be noted here that the scope of this paper is not to provide definite answers to 5), 6) and 7): yet, raising these points should provide openings for further analysis. The concluding section highlights the specificity of humour as one of the dimensions of verbal meaning.

My original intention in this chapter was to dwell on a topic that I assumed not to have been tackled often, namely how humour used in oral presentations is perceived by the audience. It so happened that the implications of the investigations I carried out through e-mail (see Section 2) rapidly extended beyond the field of purely and strictly speaking linguistic parameters to involve psycholinguistics as well as cognitive sciences: therefore the approach, initially implying a systemic-functional analysis, occasionally comprises a number of perspectives whose objective is mainly to cast a complementary light on the rhetorical study. Analysing the impact of humour on the audience will lead to highlighting the result of the strategy as a communication device used either to improve the linguistic framework or to offset its possible deficiencies, whether it be in the case of native or non-native speakers.

2. Is humour a communication skill?

Communication skills are based on a range of parameters that govern the type of formal oral presentations I intend to focus upon in this chapter.

I shall specifically concentrate on *the deliberate strategies* involving humour. I think it relevant to leave aside the involuntary effects due to lack of linguistic competence, although a statistical analysis of blunders, slips of tongue and other mishaps might have opened up perspectives. The primary objectives of conference presentations traditionally are to inform and instruct, to share data, to persuade, to clarify: the *didactic function of discourse* appears as the most evident (to inform and instruct), the *exchange basis* is the necessary foundation (to share data), yet at some point *discussion* will become an unavoidable ingredient of the communicative process (to persuade) and *further explanations* may be required (to clarify). At first sight, there is no reason why humour should be excluded a priori from any of these objectives. The point that is to be highlighted here is the following: is it possible for conference presenters to keep humour *under control* at every step of their presentation? What I would call *humour containment* pertains to an (almost) perfect mastery of the linguistic tool.

As a CNRS researcher, I belong to the U.R.A. *Silex* (Syntaxe / Interpretation / Lexique) whose headquarters are located in Villeneuve d'Asq, near Lille, which gave me several opportunities to conduct informal interviews with co-researchers and colleagues on the role played by humour in their oral presentations. First and foremost, it appeared that *the handling of humour* was one among the typical difficulties or obstacles that they thought could inhibit the effectiveness of their oral presentations. Although rarely explicitly stated, the boldest respondents would identify *nervousness* as their main cause for concern. Their perception is that nervousness leads to *a mishandling of humour*, either through awkward attempts or through lack of adjustment to the audience. The fact that many professionals are afflicted with *presentation phobia* or *stage fright* may lead to paradoxical results: for some of them, this kind of pressure is a basic requirement for the presentation to function efficiently. Whereas *the awareness that humour is being mishandled* is rather negatively perceived both by audiences and presenters. Most interviewees agree on the fact that, in order to create humour, two sets of preliminary conditions have to be taken into account: firstly, the definition of *a target* is inherent to creating humour; it will be either the audience, the presentation contents, or the presenters themselves. Secondly, adequate linguistic tools are required to create humour: puns, exaggerations, riddles, anecdotes and so forth; humour represents a linguistic achievement for both native and non-native speakers.

You will find hereafter excerpts of some of the interviews conducted in the course of my investigations. A straightforward list of questions was dispatched through e-mail; they were intended to be manageable even in the midst of a heavily-loaded schedule and sufficiently flexible to leave space for personal reformulations.[1]

Questions [e-mailed to 20 targets]:

'I am currently compiling data on the use of humour in oral presentations. I would like to know how you feel about the following:
- How do you perceive humour in oral presentations?
- Is it an improvement or a hindrance?
- Is the lack of linguistic competence the only cause for the mishandling of humour?
- What are the mechanisms that make it function?
- Is humour a communication skill?'

You will find hereafter a sampling of the most representative answers. They were selected on cultural grounds as well as the degree of relevance.

Answer 1 (Northwestern University – Chicago / Anthropology):

'Nothing gets my attention like humour, especially in oral presentations. In my view, highlighting the key parts of a/n (evidently very good) presentation is the only way first to make sure that everyone keep a great memory of the speaker and the contents/key messages, second have the attendance take a breather (they WILL be grateful), third have everyone take a laid-back perspective to embrace the matter, which is the only good way to consider a topic and think it thru. Plus nothing looks as intelligent as GOOD humour in all the RIGHT places. But here precisely lies the challenge: although humour does improve formal presentations A LOT (be it the 'well-prepared' kind, or the spontaneous sort that you have to rely on for unexpected happenstances), very few people are able to handle it the right way. Nevertheless, mishandling does not go hand in hand with linguistic challenges (it would be all too simple, wouldn't it?). Except for cases where the

---
[1] Identifying data will be restricted to host institutions and research fields.

understanding / knowledge of idiomatic stuff is useful (I have to admit that these cases are not rare, alas ...), much of humour handling does not depend on linguistic competence at all, and it does cross cultures (at least Western ones) pretty easily. So my feeling would be that either you've got it (and that's just ingrained in your personality/attitude, and can be applied successfully in many different situations), or you do not (and then being extra good at any language will not change the deal). So, for the last two questions: what makes it function. The answer on top of my mind here is 'mismatch/surprise'. And finally: is humour a communication skill? Well, now, can I say anything else ... Yes, a major one – the sizzling part of speech.'

Answer 2 (Université Lyon 1 / Earth Sciences):

'My perception of humour in oral presentations all depends on the context. It can be completely misplaced as well as a real kick. The lack of linguistic competence is the only cause for the mishandling of humour. Imagination is the mechanism that makes humour function. I would say that humour is a communication skill.'

Answer 3 (Université Claude-Bernard / Mesozoic fossil woods laboratory):

'If humour does not remain too conventional, it will be a remarkable means, although often subjective, to transfer a message through sympathy and connivance. Unfortunately, many colleagues use it involuntarily or barely in order to be 'witty'. A wide range of cultural references are not necessary: body language and intonation may be enough. No mechanisms, since humour is pure magic! Yet, the point is to determine whether it is possible to control humour. It is a communication skill in so much as both verbal and non-verbal humour are controlled.'

Answer 4 (University of Minnesota Medical School / Psychiatry):

'Humour is highly desirable, but not essential. An empathetic and scholarly talk can get by without humour. It is particularly useful in establishing a link between the speaker and audience when they are strangers. It can be distracting if there is no substance. Humour allows the speaker to express certainty and doubt at the same time and refer to topics that are too painful to touch otherwise. The lack of linguistic competence is only occasionally the cause for the mishandling of humour. Mishandled humour is vulgar and exploitative. It obviously functions at someone else's expense. Effective humour stimulates the audience to listen since it represents the unexpected as soon as you know what I'm going to say you stop listening as intently. So humour maintains uncertainty, e.g. 'where is he going with that?'. The mechanisms that make it function or disfunction are respectively timing and lack of coercion. If humour is forced then its failure sets up a gap between speaker and audience. If the humour is ironic or satiric, failure does not derail the process. In other words the most effective humour does not require a response. If it gets one, great; if not, the comment still made sense and the monologue continues. I hate the notion of communication skills, as if relating to people was a form of commerce, which of course it is. Yes it is a skill. It is a way of being sensitive, of being humble, of being unpredictable, of being gentle.'

Brief analysis:

Answer 1 (A1) is a sample of American culture, although strongly Europeanised. The emphasis is both on presenter-audience connection and on the personal components that are inherent to the presenter's mindset. Humour is seen as providing a relief in a sometimes tense professional environment: therefore it is seen simultaneously as a vector for effectiveness. Humour is seen as a means to select and memorise data. Restrictions are expressed concerning the level of linguistic competence. *Humour is presented as an unexpected component of discourse*, which confirms that it is not inherent to conference presentations.

Answer 2 (A2), sent by a French biologist, is more clearly targeted on the lack of linguistic competence: humour *is* seen as a communication skill.

Answer 3 (A3), sent by a French paleogeologist, enhances the perceptive aspect and reveals a strong awareness of mismatch. Humour being *pure magic* either implies mysterious mechanisms or highlights the complexity of these mechanisms. Interestingly, non-verbal discourse markers are referred to, e.g. intonation and body language.

Answer 4 (A4) is a sample of American culture. This Professor of Psychiatry considers humour both as *a modality* whose objective is to express certainty and doubt and *a modulator* whose marked feature is to modify the communication process. As in A1, *humour is presented as an unexpected component of discourse.*

A number of reflections mentioned in these answers are echoed in Henri Bergson's philosophical essay *Le Rire* (1940: 2), in which he wrote about humour and its outward acknowledgement signal, laughter, as being "methodical" as well as "reasonable". According to Bergson, "humour provides data on the collective social imagination."

3. Is humour perceived as a hedge or a linguistic tool?

The analysis of these answers provides ground for a series of remarks.

The power of a joke would then consist in setting up a barrier between the presenter and the audience, which is confirmed by A2. The linguistic content of a joke fits *two different frames* at the same time: the first meaning should be 'transparent and innocent', while the second meaning could be 'reprehensible and disguised'. Non-native speakers present in the audience may recognise only the 'transparent and innocent' meaning, yet may not have access to the 'reprehensible and disguised' meaning. It arises from various experiences made when attending oral presentations that jokes rarely go beyond certain limits: I doubt whether Freud's discrepancies (1905: 34) could apply to conference presenters' discourse. As for the audience, the degree of enjoyment and awareness of humour, punctually exemplified by a joke, will depend on the two meanings being identifiable: once the first interpretation is firmly planted in the mind, a final turn of word or phrase suddenly replaces it with the other one.

Humour is a quality of perception that enables us to experience joy when faced with adversity: a new vision of immediate reality becomes therefore accessible. The kind of *adversity* one encounters when presenting a paper in a conference pertains to the widely-experienced *stress*. Using humour then has therapeutic consequences. Selye, a pioneer researcher in psychosomatic medicine in the thirties, defines stress as "the rate of wear and tear within the body" (1978: 109) as it adapts to change or threat. Humour is a specific response to stress: hence presenters use it as *a hedging strategy*. According to Swales (1990: 45), hedges are "rhetorical devices for projecting honesty, modesty, and *for diplomatically creating space*". Hence, humour would be a protective device deliberately hammered out by the presenter to play the role of a buffer between him/her and the audience. The perspective provided by Hyland (1998) in his book *Hedging in Scientific Research Articles* is both complementary to Swales' as well as diverging from it: "(…) any linguistic means used to indicate either a) a lack of complete commitment to the truth value of an accompanying proposition, or b) a desire not to express that commitment categorically". Complementary, since it highlights one of the goals of hedging, i.e. not to commit oneself openly: this becomes possible once the presenter has (skilfully) created space. Diverging, since it apparently leaves out the impact of *the lack of complete commitment* and/or *the desire not to express that commitment categorically*. Swales's analysis appears to be particularly relevant to the use of humour in oral presentations in so much as it puts forward the notion of *space*, which is the one condition for the existence of a buffer between the presenter and his/her audience. Moreover, space contributes to setting up the contextual environment for a joke to be operational. At the other end of the chain, laughter's only function from the listener's point of view is to provide *relief from tension*. There is actually no clear-cut, predictable response that would inform presenters whether they have succeeded in convincing their listeners; yet, when they are telling jokes, laughter serves as an experimental test that nonetheless functions in an ambiguous manner, since laughter may express agreement as well as lack of it.

Humour can also represent *a time loss*, if it splits the community into two groups: the persons who react positively are clearly those who understand and cooperate and those who do not react are either those who understand, but do not cooperate, or those who do not understand and therefore cannot cooperate, whether it be positively or negatively. This raises the issue of how presenters perceive the audience, if they have a clear vision of the effectiveness of their presentation. Through the process of integrating humour, presenters create a prism that influences their presentation.

When one writes out the formal text of one's oral presentation, humour does not emerge as a linguistic tool. Therefore, in a previously 'calibrated' and rehearsed oral discourse, humour may appear additional, even redundant, depending on how it is perceived by the audience. Following Banks in the results of his investigation on 'The French Scientist and English as a Conference Language' (this volume), it can be safely assumed that the majority of (French) presenters speak from notes, "though a quarter find it necessary to have the text of their paper written in advance." Since "the main feature (…) was the importance that presentations taking the form of a *commentary on transparencies or slides* have acquired," and although Banks' sampling follows rigorous rules, this type of presentation is more likely to leave space for humour. Hence it provides a useful complement to the conference presenter's portrait as a whole.

The objective now is to determine the incentives, i.e. the conditions that trigger the use of humour: *when, why* and *how* is humour used? The reader should check on the percentages compiled by Vassileva (this volume), in relation, among other parameters, to the percentage of *jokes* in oral presentations made by Bulgarian presenters in English: 1% in English, and 0.25% in Bulgarian English! Jokes are seen here as "a means of direct speaker-audience address."

Time constraints are inherent to conference presentations: as a counterpoint to previous remarks concerning *time loss*, the impact of humour can represent *a time gain, whenever based on shared knowledge*. It is then handled as a means to bridge the gap between the presenter and the target audience, or between the target audience and the topic. But, of course, this is not specific of humour: any shared-knowledge basis contributes to a better handling of the communication process.

4. Does humour interfere with the transfer of supposedly complex scientific topics, or does it pertain to a global context of conviviality?

The saying goes that to analyse humour is a task as delicate as analysing the composition of a perfume with its multiple ingredients, some of which are never consciously perceived while others, when sniffed in isolation, would make one wince. What seems to emerge, at this stage, is the counter-productivity of humour, if applied in isolation. Oral presentations in symposiums and conferences obey a strict code: the participants deliver formal, sometimes manuscript, speeches on some aspect of a central subject or theme. In such a context, humour could confuse the listener, as it introduces *ambiguity* at discourse level. Actually, humour has a twofold impact: *harmful humour* is insensitive, malicious, exclusive and sarcastic (see A4). It ridicules, slanders, belittles and puts down people: in the same sense, absurd results of reasoning must be tabooed as thoroughly as social mistakes and inanities. *Healing humour* (see A1/A4) creatively and invisibly connects the usual with the unusual for the purpose of personal support. Whether it relates to harmful humour or healing humour, the most readily visible, audible and accessible signals that presenters will send to their audience consists in hammering out *jokes*. Why do they have such peculiar psychological effects? Freud (1905: 64), in *Jokes and their Relation to the Unconscious*, explained that we form censors in our minds as barriers against forbidden thoughts. Most jokes, he said, are stories designed to fool the censors: humour in oral presentations alleviates pressure (see A1) and allows the audience to enter a new dimension of oral discourse (see A3).

5. Can humour be tackled as a function of language?

Humour in presentation discourse will be illustrated with examples of situations in which it is used to attain different objectives: humour is a *modal* means of communication. According to Halliday's (1994: 74) perspective on the Clause as Exchange, "the term *modal* is ambiguous, since it corresponds both to mood and modality". To what extent does this statement apply to the present study?

As we will see in the following examples, a humorous sentence refers to some structure already in the audience's minds: what we call *understanding* is a huge accumulation of signs. Verbal discourse used by conference presenters creates *three interdependent kinds of social and cultural meanings*:

– it constructs social relationships among participants and points-of-view;
– it creates verbal representations of activities;
– it construes relations of parts to wholes within its own text and between itself and its contexts.

Therefore, humour can be categorised as one among a wide range of parameters in the *anaphoric discourse pattern, because its impact extends beyond the utterance*. In the information unit, humour is the New element that pertains to the unexpected (see A1), which can only be justified by the Given element, which pertains to the global *context-dependent* presentation (see A2).

Example 1: The lifebuoy – Humour can be used as *a lifebuoy*, as was the case for a presentation about some text analysis software in Toronto in August 1997, when the computer system decided not to function. If a technical problem arises when everything in the presentation relies on hardware, humour is used as a shield for embarrassment. The audience – a very friendly one, I must say – could hear the unfortunate presenter make remarks like: 'One should not rely on high-tech ...', 'Nothing like pen and paper stuff ...', 'Any handouts? ...'.

In this context, the New element and the Given element are, as is always the case, interdependent. And, naturally, in that particular instance, humour did *not* function satisfactorily.

Example 2: Alma Mater – Humour is intended here to emulate *connivence*. In Orlando, in March 1997, when running short of handouts, the presenter, in an attempt to justify the scarcity of material, exclaimed: 'The Lady Alma Mater is not rich ...!' Among the ways and manners chosen by researchers and presenters to refer to restricted financial means, humour is certainly one of the most effective to highlight the fact that no one among the audience is unconcerned by this type of pragmatic constraint.

Rowley-Jolivet (this volume) in her chapter titled 'Science in the Making: A Constructivist Perspective on Scientific Conference Papers', puts forward the "role of scientific conferences in establishing and maintaining networks". Humour, in such circumstances as mentioned above, significantly contributes to reinforcing the sense of belonging to a community.

Example 3: Interrelations – By alluding to *a previous presentation*, which happens quite often either because the circle is restricted or because the reference to a prominent specialist validates one's presentation, conference presenters will probe *the intercultural community* so as to determine how sound the exchange basis will be. This is what could be heard in the process of a presentation in a 'Colloque' organised in Paris in the fall 1998 at the American University: 'I need X's [prominent specialist] help here ...', 'X [another prominent specialist, viewed from a different angle] expatiated on the issue this morning, I needn't revive painful (?) memories ...'.

When fitting humour into the pattern of their presentations, conference presenters shift from technical discourse to *a different register* and to a certain kind of *adjunct narrative discourse*: in Example 1, the presenter clearly asks for help; in Example 2, the message concerns both the presenter and the audience embarked in the same boat; in Example 3, both the presenter and the audience trace their shared knowledge back to previous presentations, about which some of them may have mixed feelings.

Metatextuality is thus being constructed: humour is the metaphenomenon created by projection.

6. At what level of discourse is humour generated?

Humour functions at every level of the clause structure. It will consequently be assumed that "the English clause is a composite affair, a combination of three different structures deriving from distinct functional components". (Halliday 1994: 123). Humour provides an additional meaning to the discourse substrate (see Figure 1). The structures present in the audience's minds are most likely to be formulated as follows:

– "How is he going to solve the problem?"
– "All of us are in the same boat, then!"
– "Indeed!", or "What's he talking about??"

The three situations generate implicit structures of various natures: investigating *the mental processes* that took place in the audience's minds at the moment of the utterance could be an extension to the present study. One of the flaws of humour is that, once 'launched', no one can fully control the mechanisms and the organisation of the implicit layers of discourse.

The metafunctions imply the following classification:

– textual [Clause as Message]: Transitivity structures
– interpersonal [Clause as Exchange]: Mood structures
– ideational [Clause as Representation]: Theme structures

The proposed examples express three largely independent sets of semiotic choices: Transitivity structures express representational meaning – what the Clause is about, typically some process, with associated participants; Mood structures express interactional meaning – what the Clause is doing, as a verbal exchange between speaker-writer and audience; Theme structures express the organisation of the message – how the Clause relates to the surrounding discourse, and the context of the situation in which it is being produced.

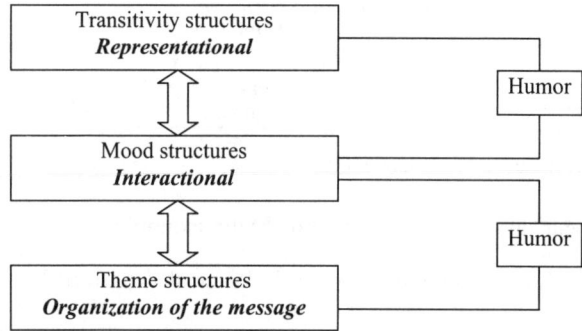

Figure 1: Role of humour in message construction.

As can be observed in Figure 1, the part played by humour is not restricted to one metafunction in particular. In effect, in addition to being a means to organise the implicit layers of discourse, humour is present in these three structures:

- once uttered, *jokes* – mentioned as such to exemplify a certain type of occurrence of humour – are shaped out in Transitivity structures that provide a representation for *a twofold reality*: the presenter's and the audience's.
- once uttered, jokes find their justification in the Mood structures that *transfer humour, successfully or not.*
- once uttered, jokes focus upon the Theme structures: whether they will be common ground or not for the presenter and the audience depends on *the extent of the joke's power.*

Humour does not have to be present in the Clause for it to be semantically and syntactically valid. As it interacts and weaves itself into the layers of meaning to reconstrue *the representation model* in a Chinese-box manner (see Figure 2), it introduces *ambiguity* at every level of discourse.

Among the parameters that were identified by the respondents, mismatch / surprise was one parameter that was assumed to make humour function (A1). Since 'humour maintains uncertainty' (A4), the Chinese Box could become Pandora's Box.

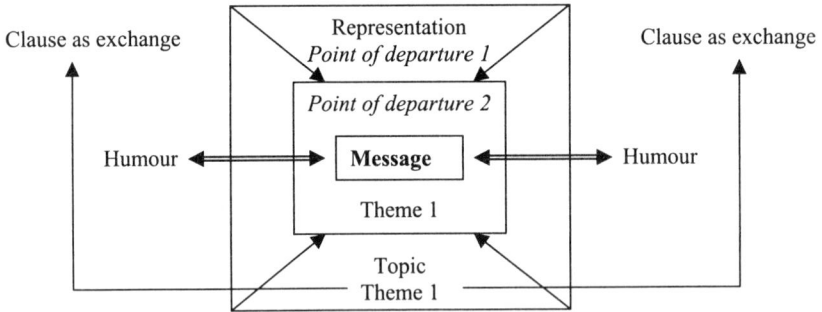

Figure 2: Humour and the Chinese Box.

Let us focus on Example 2, the Alma Mater example.

Theme 1: *Limited funding in our lab*: Point of departure 1 – Representation of the topic.

Theme 2: *Alma Mater/ not rich*: Point of departure 2 + Humour.

Both Theme 1 and Theme 2 merge to elicit *Clause as exchange*, on such an *implicit interrogative statement* as ('How about you?'). Either this implicit interrogative statement reaches its goal and triggers off the expected outward signals of connivence, e.g. laughs, or it does not reach its goal and triggers off indifference and/or misinterpretation.

The Theme within the Theme leads to a direct jump to Clause as an exchange. The element typically chosen as Theme depends on the choice of Mood. In the above diagrammatic representation of our model of experience, humour belongs to the world of consciousness and sensing. Humour is not a universal pattern, and in this respect it raises an issue that is beyond systemic grammars. Leaving the domain of material processes, we enter that of mental processes at the cross-roads of affection (liking) and cognition (understanding) (Halliday 1994: 118).

7. Metaphors of mood vs. cohesion and coherence

Humour plays the role of a metaphor, since what is non-metaphorical is 'literal': therefore we shall look here at the metaphor from 'above', "as variation in the meaning of a given expression" (Halliday 1994: 342).

It is also a fact that humour reflects a vast range of rhetorical modes, e.g. hedging, teasing, wordplay, doubletalk: each of these rhetorical modes would deserve an extensive study. Interpersonal rhetoric is at stake here: through effective transference, the audience *is* involved in the communication process. Handling humour involves a new responsibility represented by common-speech formulae that convey modulated commands. However, as humour pertains to the unexpected (see Example 3), *it seems to run counter to the notion of cohesion*, which goes beyond the boundaries of the individual text created.

The cohesive structure, or texture, contains chains of semantic relationships that may be scattered through the text. Cohesion chains have none of humour's properties and are built on a variety of chain-membership principles, all of which specify a particular kind of relation of meaning among the items. Humour disrupts the cohesion chains.

On the one hand, it is worth highlighting that complex texts like conference presentations require *sub-units within the text*, since they often change genre types as the presentation unfolds. And humour may well be considered as one of these units. Swales (1990: 61) remarks that "Jokes have temporal sequences, agent orientation and plot, but the resolution of the plot is specific: the moment of the resolution needs to be overtly signalled (the onset of the punch line) whilst the manner of resolution needs to be unpredictable". From this perspective, humour alleviates monotony, if need be, and relieves tension (see A1/ A2/ A4), whether it be physical, mental, perceptible on the presenter's side or the audience's.

Coherence, on the other hand, concerns the relationship that the text, or the production of humorous discourse and jokes, has to its situational context. It is widely acknowledged that humour thrives only in its native climate, embedded in its native logic (Hall 1976: 67): when one does not know what to expect, one cannot be cheated by one's expectations. The coherence of a humorous discourse pertains to two interactional levels:

– inward-bound coherence: finds its justification in *context-free discourse construction*. It is *utterer-oriented*: humour becomes a communication tool that plays a role at the expressive and declarative levels (see A1: 'the sizzling part of speech'). It is an illocutionary act endowed with the illocutionary force (see A3: 'Humour is pure magic') as understood within the framework of Speech Act Theory (Searle 1969: 34): dialogue acts, utterance units and dialogue units are generally an attempt to model communicative acts. When integrating humour in conference discourse, the presenters set up a strategy to fit humour into the communication model: Example 1 is based on *inward-bound humour*.
– outward-bound coherence: is endowed with a dynamic feature in so much as it is *listener-oriented*. This type of coherence is *context-dependent*. Humour as a speech act is well-accepted at international conferences, on the assumption that it takes the cultural community's parameters into account: Examples 2 and 3 are based on *outward-bound humour*.

8. Conclusion

This paper has been an attempt at determining the impact of humour on verbal discourse in conference presentations. The analysis of humour in such contexts raises issues that lie beyond the description of rhetorical patterns, as humour is a momentous phenomenon that reflects what presenters think and feel.

The question that still remains is to determine how appropriate the use of humour is in conference language. When the communication exchange is reshaped to be published as a written text, humorous episodes are edited out, since they have been fleeting, unexpected, and almost shapeless utterances. Can it therefore be safely assumed that they are perceived as useless parasites? Or

225

have they merely lost their targets? This view does actually illuminate the obviously discrepant status of written texts vs. spoken words.

References

Banks, D. This volume. "The French Scientist and English as a Conference Language".

Bergson, H. 1940. *Le Rire*. Paris: Presses Universitaires de France.

Freud, S. 1905. *Jokes and Their Relations to the Unconscious*. London: Methuen.

Hall, E. 1976. *Beyond Language*. New-York, Doubleday.

Halliday, M. A. K. 1994. *An Introduction to Functional Grammar*. London: Arnold.

Hyland, K. 1998. *Hedging in Scientific Research Articles*. Amsterdam: John Benjamins.

Rowley-Jolivet, E. This volume. "Science in the Making: Scientific conference presentations and the construction of facts".

Searle, J. 1969. *Speech Acts: An Essay in the Philosophy of Language*. Cambridge: Cambridge University Press.

Selye, H. 1978. *The Stress of Life*. New-York: McGraw-Hill.

Swales, J. 1990. *Genre Analysis: English in academic and research settings*. Cambridge: Cambridge University Press.

Vassileva, I. This volume. "Speaker-audience interaction: The Case of Bulgarians presenting in English".

THE PAPER IS NOW OPEN FOR DISCUSSION

Pauline Webber

Universita di Roma "La Sapienza", Rome, Italy

Abstract – This chapter will focus on the Discussion Phase which takes place at the end of most medical paper presentation sessions, when the paper is opened to the floor. This Question/Response session is an important part of the conference as it offers the opportunity to refine certain aspects of the research presented following the audience's reactions. The discourse is partly rule-governed, although many of the rules are unwritten or part of the accepted code of the specialist community, informed by the common purpose lying at the basis of all scientific argumentative discourse: that of arriving ultimately at a consensus. However, in reality speakers may be competing to impose their own claims and thus have conflicting goals. The Discussion Phase presents particular difficulties both for the Presenter and for the Discussant asking the questions, especially for the non-native speaker. This is clearly because the course of the interaction is unpredictable, but also because underlying disputes may be brought out into the open and flaws in the study be open to attack. The ensuing debate is in part jointly constructed and unrehearsed, so tends to share features of spontaneous conversation, albeit under the constraints of discourse which takes place in public and is moderated by the Chair. This chapter analyses the techniques used by academics to overcome these difficulties: the linguistic realisations of politeness and solidarity, on the one hand, and competition and dispute, on the other. It considers the different kinds of Question and Response found in a collection of recorded international medical conference discussions. The language of conferences, and of the Discussion Phase in particular, is very different from that of scientific textbooks or university lectures already extensively studied elsewhere, because in peer communication of this kind the functions of organisation of information and management of social relations are equally important. The genre of the Discussion thus presents distinctive characteristics and certainly merits closer investigation than it has been afforded in the past.

1. Introduction

The purpose of the present study is, firstly, to analyse the different question types and the participants' reactions both to the presentation and to the Questions and Responses which follow it, and, secondly, to compare the interactive features of the Discussion Phase with those of the presentation on the one hand and of casual conversation on the other. It is argued that the characteristics of this genre are dictated largely by the participants' desire to persuade other researchers of the validity of their claims in a difficult situation, that is, in face-to-face interaction in public.

In the course of this study it became clear that the analysis of the Questions and Responses is closely linked to the motivations scientific researchers themselves have for attending conferences. Therefore, science specialists who regularly attend conferences were interviewed to find out something about their motivations. The main reasons for conference attendance given by these specialist informants were: the desire to present research which is still in a preliminary stage so as to obtain feedback from the audience, to get stimulation from other people working in the same field and to pick up ideas. Other reasons given were: the opportunity to discuss one's work with others, to merge two or more groups doing the same work so as to obtain more funds or resources, and to find out if an experiment has already been done or if the claims seem convincing and therefore if it is worth going ahead with the research.

The overall impression was that Presenters want to tell other experts about work they are engaged in, but may not want to divulge too much, whereas listeners may want to know more than the Presenter is willing to tell. Thus, the purpose of the questions is often to probe, to ask for more information than was contained in the paper (for example, more details on the methods) and to compare what the Presenter is doing with the Discussant's own research. The discourse of the Discussion is thus influenced by these underlying intentions, which may be pulling in different directions.

In this paper, Section 2 will give a brief description of the data, and Section 3 will first address the problem of classifying the Questions and analyse a sample of Questions and then Responses. Section 4 will review the same examples, and add a few others, to focus on some of the interactive features found in the data. Section 5 concludes the paper. A complete transcription of some of the longer exchanges is found in the Appendix.

As this is goal-oriented interaction, Discourse Analysis techniques are used, in particular Applied Discourse Analysis, because of its concern with real life contexts and professional activities where discourse is an essential part of the interaction between persons. The study also draws on Conversation Analysis techniques, because they are useful for analysing dialogue (Ilie 1994; Eggins & Slade 1997), even though the Discussion is obviously far from casual.

2. Data

The material presented in this study is from a corpus of taped recordings of international medical conferences at which the author was present and which were held in English by speakers from various linguistic backgrounds. Most of the data are from two European Association for the Study of Diabetes annual

Conferences held in Stockholm and in Helsinki. All names of participants are fictitious.

A total of 130 questions from Discussions are analysed with their respective replies. The data are from what the conference organisers themselves term either workshop or symposium presentations of research, not from plenary lectures, because at the conferences concerned plenaries were not followed by questions from the floor. Workshop presentations were essentially the same as symposium presentations, except that they were shorter.

There are widely differing conventions and formats in the types of communication at conferences in different fields. Here there are just three roles: the speaker, whom we shall refer to as the Presenter, the Chair, usually assisted by a Co-Chairperson, and the audience members. The delegate who asks a question will be referred to as the Discussant, following Ventola (1993). Each exchange generally consists of two turns: a Question and a Response, but at times the Discussant may ask a further question and the Presenter will usually respond to this follow-up question, at which point the Chair allocates the next speaker. It is up to the Chair to see that as many people as possible get a fair chance to intervene, even though the time is very limited. In the conferences attended, each Presenter is allocated twenty minutes for the talk in a symposium and only ten minutes at a workshop, whereas about five minutes are allocated for the Discussion in each case, ranging from five to seven questions per session. Occasionally, the Chair may ask the first question to start the ball rolling, or even later on if there is a lull in the discussion, so as to keep the interaction running smoothly.

3. Questions

3.1. Some Problems of Classification

Shalom (1993) found a high number of challenging questions in her data. This difference may be due to the different genre investigated (*Poster Session Discussions* as opposed to *Workshop Discussions*) or to the classification criteria for challenging questions. In this corpus only 30% of the 130 questions were definitely critical of some aspect of the presentation; however, it must be noted that even a neutral request for clarification may be perceived as a challenge by the Presenter if it is difficult to answer. This, of course, also raises the issue of appreciating the pragmatic and argumentative value of the Question. In some cases a question might seem innocent to the non-scientist, whereas in fact it contains veiled criticism. Assertions cannot always be taken at face-value, but must sometimes be taken at a deeper level. For this reason, sometimes it was necessary to interview a field specialist informant. It must also be admitted that where an utterance is ambiguous to the analyst, it may also be so to the participants themselves. It is worth noting that the word *challenge* itself is used in different senses, reflecting the ambiguity of the term. These may be summarised as "something difficult which requires effort and determination", or "a questioning of the truth or value of an idea" or even "an invitation to someone to fight or compete with you in some way" (COBUILD: Sinclair 1995). In all these cases, the question may cause difficulties for the Presenter. It may not be the Discussant's intention to ask a challenging or difficult question, but the Presenter may nonetheless find it difficult to answer or alternatively may suspect that the question is meant to challenge his or her ideas or authority. Language is by its nature ambiguous and misunderstandings can arise. For the analyst, the way the question is formulated may at times give a reasonably clear indication of the intended meaning, whereas at other times it is only from the Response that it can be seen how the question is taken by the Presenter. In any case, the interpretation of this kind of data will remain problematic.

3.2. Question Types

Ilie (1994) distinguishes between information-eliciting and action-eliciting questions. It is the former that predominate in Discussions, while a request for action (such as speaking more loudly or repeating a question again) occurs only rarely. Here it seemed useful to classify the Questions first according to the Discussant's apparent purpose when intervening in the debate, but in some cases adjustments need to be made on the basis of the Presenter's Response.

According to this criterion of the questioner's purpose, Questions in this corpus appeared to fall into five categories and have therefore been classified into five types:

Q-Types:
    i. information eliciting questions - about a) facts, b) opinions (see 3.2.1)
    ii. criticism or attack (see 3.2.2)
    iii. suggestions (see 3.2.3)
    iv. comment (see 3.2.4)
    v. mixed – comment plus information eliciting (see 3.2.4)[1]

---

[1]   It must be noted that these are just convenient labels, because, although some Q-Type-ii items are blatantly critical; others are not so easy to categorise and could be allocated to one of the other types.

Henceforth these will be referred to as Questions or as Q-Type i-v according to the five types listed above. Some samples of each type will be presented in this section, together with a possible analysis, because the classification of the questions automatically entails an interpretation, however tentative. Percentages of the different Question Types are shown in Table 1 below. The Discussion Phase is seen as made up of sequences of interdependent discursive acts constituting an argumentative debate, rather than the rule-governed forms of behaviour using mainly invented examples investigated by early speech act theorists. The Questions will be expected by the participants to refer to the preceding paper presentation stage, or possibly to the content of the abstract in the book of abstracts distributed to participants on registration, in which case, some Discussants could have already had a Question in mind before hearing the presentation. Hence, as noted by both Ventola and Shalom in this volume, the phases of *Conference Abstract – Paper Presentation – Discussion* are interdependent. It is interesting to note how the questions are taken up and acknowledged – or not acknowledged – by the Presenter. The examples given in the following section may give some idea of the kind of Questions posed and how participants attempt to meet the challenge of providing an answer. The Questions are presented starting from the most frequent type rather than in order of occurrence.

i.	Information-eliciting questions		
	a: about facts	32%	
	b: about opinions	17%	49%
ii.	Criticism or attack		30%
iii.	Suggestions		9%
iv.	Comments		3%
v.	Mixed comment + Q-Type i		9%
	TOTAL:		**100%**

Table 1. Question Types.

2.2.1. Information-eliciting Questions

About half the questions were judged to be of the first type, and of these, three fifths were of Q-Type i-a. Q-Type i-a are often realised as yes/no interrogatives, whereas Q-Type i-b use expressions such as: *could you comment?* or *what is your opinion?*.

It is notable that information-eliciting Questions often appeared to seek answers on some topic not included in the talk at all, but on some aspect outside the scope of the paper. The answer sought may be about facts, as in Example 1.

(1)   Q: Have you done any experiments to show whether the x cross-reacts with y or vice versa?
     R: *It does not cross-react with y.*
     F: Thank you.[2]

It may be seen from the response in Example 1 that Presenters are sometimes reluctant to be led away from the main subject of their paper. This might in Example 1 account for the rather brusque reply to the Discussant in this brief exchange, with no mood adjunct of denial or other lead-in to soften the response, *It does not cross-react with y*. The speaker may find the question beside the point and want to get it out of the way as soon as possible. From the intonation, it would seem the speaker is not necessarily irritated by the question but rather he does not wish to waste any of his limited time on irrelevant topics. Again, we cannot always be sure of the correct interpretation, but I would like to advance a possible explanation for these off-the-topic questions. As pointed out by Myers (1989) and confirmed by my specialist informants, the audience may be either from the inner circle of specialists in the field or they may be 'outsiders' from a wider audience. At a large international congress such as the one considered here, where anyone can attend for the price of a registration fee, the audience will be mixed (even though individual workshops are divided according to very specific and narrow fields of research), and so all kinds of questions may crop up. The questions after the second presentation in the 'Hypertension' workshop, for example, came from academics from countries as far afield as Bangladesh, Finland, Australia and the UK (see Appendix). They may represent different groups (not only geographically) and presumably, many of these academics are involved in their own research. Participants tend to relate the content of the talk to their own experience, a tendency which forms part of what Ventola has termed "semiotic spanning" (Ventola 1999, Ventola Chapter 1, this volume). Moreover, participants' motivations play a role here, as Discussants will often take the opportunity to ask for information not only for research purposes but also for practical help in clinical decision making for their patients.

The Presenter's motives for avoiding answering may also vary. On the one hand, the Presenter may not find the question interesting. The notion of 'interestingness' lies at the heart of the conference paper (Berkenkotter & Huckin 1995; Swales 1996). Certain issues attract attention for a time and are then

---

[2]   *A note on transcription*: All names are fictitious. The text is transcribed as faithfully as possible, with punctuation added to ease comprehension. For reasons of space, the complete transcript of longer exchanges cannot be included here, and so some more technical passages, and particularly drug names, have been substituted by x or y. An untimed pause is represented by (.) and ellipsis by ... , unclear passages by ?? Abbreviations: Q = Question, R = Response, F = Follow-up, P = Presenter.

superseded by others. On the other hand, the Presenter may not feel in a position to give an adequate answer, as in one case, where the Presenter asks the Chair to answer in his place (see Section 4 below).

Q-Type I-b is about opinions, as in Example 2.

(2)   Q: You have not mentioned the role of x ... Could you make a comment a little bit on that?
      R: Yes, erm. I vaguely alluded to it at the end of my topic (.) er talk, but I decided to keep to my target (renal protection and hypertension), but I agree with you that the potential vascular protection not only of x but even of some y ... may act to reduce heart failure or recurrent myocardial infarction. I think this is where we are going to find the power of these agents. I would be surprised if we don't see that these changes in renal protection are also seen with respect to cardiovascular protection.

In the case of Example 2, it is necessary to see how the question is taken up by the Presenter to appreciate what is going on at this point in the debate. Far from being irritated by this off-the-topic question, the Presenter seems only too glad of the invitation to say more about it, as can be seen from the response.

At this point, we may also note that the question is posed by the co-chair, and questions from the platform, in this corpus, are usually 'friendly'. The aim of the Chair in general is to try to make the session a success, that is to foster interest in the discussion and encourage members of the audience to ask questions.

When the question is on the topic, this can also be seen from the Presenter's response, as in Example 3.

(3)   Q: Do you think there is also a possibility you can start from insulin resistance and go on to obesity and diabetes proper?
      R: Absolutely ...

3.2.2. Criticism or attack

Some questions are friendly in tone, but others are less so and may be assigned to the type implying criticism or attack, (the latter is more direct and threatening than the former). Both of these are of the 'bashing' variety described by Ventola (1998). Shalom (1993) found that a successful challenge could force speakers to defend their basic aims and assumptions. In the small corpus under study here, however, it appears that attacks challenging other aspects of the study (apart from aims and assumptions) may be equally damaging. An academic who wishes to challenge or attack the Presenter will look out for weak points in the study, wherever they may be. Critics often challenge the choice of population studied, the inclusion criteria, the number of subjects, and so on. Questions of Q-Type ii, displaying criticism or attack, may thus refer to the content of any of the six moves in the presentation corresponding to the well-known IMRD format[3] of written articles.

The examples given in this section may serve to illustrate some of the strategies used in Q-Type ii questions and some of the difficulties inherent in classifying Questions. The challenges are based partly on classical principles of argumentation theory (van Eemeren *et al.* 1992, 1997; Jacobs & Jackson 1982) such as: sufficiency and validity of evidence, establishment of premises and justification of conclusions. This is apparent where speakers are anxious to avoid fallacies such as the post hoc propter hoc fallacy, as is evident in the following excerpt from a response.

(4)   R: I would be very hesitant in proposing that x may be owing to y.

Problems of cause-effect are crucial in medical research, and not always easy to pin down as may be seen in Example 5.

(5)   Chair: We'll open your paper for discussion. We've got about five minutes for questions. Gunther?
Q: David, the beneficial effect of ACE inhibition on the progression of x is of considerable interest. Was this positive effect totally related to a decrease in diastolic BP, or could (.) be other factors (.) also be involved ...?

The Discussant's question could be classed as an information eliciting question (Q-Type i), but could also be insidious. In other words, do the results really prove what the Presenter claims they do, or are there too many variables? We shall later (Section 3.3) see how the Presenter dealt with this question. However, Example 6 is definitely of the bashing type.

(6)   Q: You know how much I like your work, Giorgio, but I just can't understand – you take 23 patients and you say you found GMT-1 antibodies are expressed at the onset of type 1 diabetes and are significantly correlated with the presence of GAD antibodies. First of all, what do you mean by 'express'? ... This was predictable because they were older.

The Discussant here finds fault with the quantity of evidence (*23 patients*) which is made to seem statistically insufficient, and even implies that the Presenter's finding is unsurprising (*this was predictable*). In fact, challenges and defences are based not only on logic and argumentation strategies, but also on modern principles of statistics and evidence-based medicine. Furthermore, it is a

---

[3]   Written Research Articles in medicine have to have the format: introduction-methods-results and discussion. The content of the oral presentation has elsewhere (Webber 1997b) been divided as follows:
DISCOURSE STRUCTURE MOVES: Introduction – to rouse interest and prepare audience - Creation of a Research Space - Objectives of The Study - Design of The Study - Presentation of Results with Detailed Explanation.

common tactic in arguments to pick on a word used by one's interlocutor (such as *express*) and ask for a more precise definition, thus creating difficulties for the addressee.

In some cases, as in Example 7, questions raise doubts about the procedures used.

(7)   Q: I just wanted to know the concentration used in the ELISA. Where did it stop short? The reason I ask is that we have experienced problems with antibody binding.

Note here the justification provided for the observation, which perhaps mitigates any intended criticism.

Then again, as in Example 8, the rationale behind the study may be called into question, although this is less common:

(8)   Q: John, you seem convinced about the usefulness of micro (.) er reduction in microalbuminuria as a proxy marker for renal protection. Firstly, are you that convinced? Secondly, if you are, how do you explain that when you stop ACE inhibitors in the few studies that you have done, the proteinuria goes back to greater than pre-treatment levels – I think in some cases – and, given that, how do you think ACE inhibitors are actually doing their job? ...

Here we find some typical instances of the language of argument and logical reasoning – *firstly, secondly, if so ... then, given that ... how*, and so on.

Some of the Discussions are about the interpretation of data, as in Example 9, which again raises issues of cause and effect.

(9)   Q: Your point is well put, but I think you have misunderstood the evidence. It's not a matter of x causing hypoglycaemia. It is a question of patient awareness..

When the basic aims and assumptions are challenged, of course, this will create even greater difficulties for the Presenter:

(10)   Q: Are we sure that these substances work the way we think they do. What do we know about the mechanisms of x in lowering cholesterol levels?[4]

Besides interpretation of data, the Discussion may be on facts, and particularly, figures, as in Example 11.

(11)   Q: David, what's the evidence base for the blood (David, I'm in the middle) – what's the evidence for the blood pressure levels that have been taken by JNCV and the ADA and so forth of 130 over 85 – what hard evidence is there that these targets should be

---

[4]   This, after a long discussion on details of administering and dosages of a cholesterol lowering drug, is addressed to a speaker who is clearly in favour of these drugs. Note, however, the use of the inclusive *we* as a mark of positive politeness and solidarity with the scientific community.

achieved, leaving aside the problem of getting there in the first place?
R: Well, I think not really very much … P. will no doubt tell us this afternoon that there
are good reasons for getting BP down even lower than that …

In the rather non-committal reply to the question in Example 11, the Presenter
has recourse to the appeal to a recognised authority on this topic. In fact, several
speakers during the symposium refer to the keynote speech to be held by the
eminent researcher P. in the afternoon – another example of the sense of
alignment, or belonging to a school or group, but also of the appeal to authority
recognised by Argumentation Theory.

3.2.3. Suggestions

A more neutral type of question in this discourse is the suggestion, such as *Have
you tried doing x ...?*. Many presentations described some problem which had
not yet been solved, and questions which implied a suggestion of some course of
action on the part of the Presenter to solve these problems were included in the
Q-Type iii category. As with the other Question Types, there is no strict
correlation between form and function, but Questions formulated following the
Why don't you? or *Couldn't you?* kind of pattern were considered to fit into this
category. Examples 12 and 13 may be considered to belong to Q-Type iii:

(12) Q: Do you think analogue would be more useful for decreasing aggregation of
    molecules…?
    R: Yes, I suppose (.) it could be, it could be. It's an interesting point whether insulin
    delivery is slowed down (.) or not. I'm not sure.

(13) Q: Did you look at the waist/hip ratio…?
    R: We didn't look at that, but we can.
    Q: Good!

Suggestions may be looked on as contributions to the debate and therefore
positive questions, as the purpose of the whole event is, ostensibly at least, to
arrive at a consensus leading ultimately to the advancement of science.
However, to suggest someone ought to do something might also imply criticism,
as the Discussant may have suggested a solution the Presenter had not thought
of. On the other hand, the Presenter may consider the suggestion a poor one and
reject it, thus gaining a position of superiority.

3.2.4. Comments

The last two types of question listed above (Q-Types iv and v) will be
considered together. Q-Type iv is not really a question in grammatical or formal

terms but in the sense defined by Schegloff *et al.* (1973, cited in Schegloff & Sacks 1984), Weber (1993) and others, that is, part of an adjacency pair which is felt to be incomplete if there is no response. Hence, Presenters feel they are expected to respond to the comment in some way. There are only four instances of pure comments not followed by a question, whereas Q-Type v – comments used as a lead-in or preface to the question – are more common (9%). Comments generally offer some explanation for unexplained phenomena described in the presentation or make a comparison with the Discussant's own experience, but without suggesting any course of action as Suggestions do.

Participants themselves are aware of making comments, as may be seen in Examples 14 and 15 below.

(14)   Q: This is more a comment than a question.

(15)   Q: Can I just comment on the age of onset of x in the patients. In the series we have studied ... actually the prevalence is about ... it ranges from 4 to 40 years.
R: –

Comments may also be followed by a request for information as in the following mixed Q-Type v in Example 16.

(16)   Q: It is Walter ... David, in – David, I'm over here – in your intervention study there was a clear treatment effect ... and that raises the whole issue of redefining the entity of microalbuminuria, because in non diabetic individuals a much lower threshold is predictive ..., as we are presenting in Poster 1748 ... *How would you like to comment on that?*

There are two aspects of Example 16 which are intriguing. Firstly, the formulation of the question (italics in the citation), which has an almost provocative ring about it (compare the other four question forms in the Discussion at the end of the first paper in the "Hypertension" workshop (see Appendix): 1. *Was this positive effect totally related ...?*, 2. *Would you agree ...?*, 3. *What's the evidence base ...?*, 4. *Can you suggest some cut-off limit ...?*). The same request for a comment is expressed much more tentatively and modestly in Example 2 above (*Could you make a comment a little bit on that?*). We might consider re-classifying this question as Q-Type ii. From the intonation and the prominent stress on the word "that", we have the impression that this could be a second turn rather than the opening question in the exchange. In fact, it turned out on listening to the tape again, that this was a second question posed by the same person who had asked the previous one (given as Example 11 above), and who was awarded a second turn. It was not immediately clear that this was the same speaker because the floor was in relative darkness. Therefore, Example 11, previously discussed among the Q-Type ii questions challenging issues of facts and figures, may now be better regarded as a lead-in to the even more confrontational Example 16. The Discussant is obviously committed to the position put forward in his own poster – and this time there is an instance of the exclusive *we* referring to his team. This is a clear example of how difficult it is to analyse utterances taken in isolation. The analyst's interpretation must also take account of the continuation of the dialogue and may need to adjust the allocation of the item to one of the Question Types in the classification above, which must be considered a working rule rather than a definite categorisation. It is also difficult to judge how far the apparent provocativeness of a question may be simply part of what may be termed 'international English'. It is difficult to establish the native language of some of the participants. For example, in the 'Hypertension' workshop given in the Appendix, the co-chair appears to have a German accent, whereas the Discussant we have called *Klaus* has a German name but a British accent.

Secondly, a basic assumption is questioned here: the definition of microalbuminuria. As often happens in medical discourse, even the use of an apparently objective technical term may imply things such as personal stance or the theoretical basis of the speaker's work. At what point is a subject to be termed microalbuminuric or hypertensive or diabetic? This usually implies some form of measurement or threshold – such as a certain blood sugar level, above which the subject is classified as diabetic and an appropriate course of action is taken. These norms are often established during conferences of this kind by a group of the association's members or by recognised national health committees or WHO. They are then published in official position papers or guidelines. A decision of this sort taken by a working group set up to decide on a specific issue and reported in the course of a conference may have widespread consequences, and hence decision-making in medicine involves high stakes and can lead to disputes between opposing groups. The results of numerous research efforts may eventually lead to decisions taken at top level. However, these official criteria are not stable, but are subject to change, and so may be considered a 'working consensus', to borrow a term from Goffman (1959).

3.3. Responses

Here we shall consider some further examples of Responses, because it is particularly interesting to see how Presenters react to the Questions. Reactions may be expected to range from direct confrontation to convergence or submission. Listeners may choose from a wide range of responses, but in any Discussion which takes place in public (whether at a law court or a scientific debate such as that considered here) most public speakers will try to respond in some way, as the Question builds up expectations. In this respect, the Discussion is no exception, as the Presenter generally attempts to respond, even when this is not easy. Cases where there is no response, as in Example 15 above, are very rare (this is the only instance in this corpus). Any reaction, including silence, will be looked on as significant by the audience, and will here be referred to as a Response. The conventional term 'Question/Answer' session is not very appropriate here, also because it is clear that not every reply may be considered an answer. There have been several studies on the problem of answerhood in conversation. Grice (1975) bases his analysis on the principles formulated in the framework of conversational logic, Levinson (1983) stresses the importance of conditional relevance as opposed to strict adjacency criteria, whereas Stenström (1984) considers the answer more from the point of view of the addressees and their intentional reactions. Other criteria adopted are: appropriateness (Lakoff 1971), directness and sufficiency (Lakoff 1973) and informativity (Grewendorf 1981).

The Discussant generally expects an answer to the point raised in the question, and this is particularly true in the kind of institutional setting involved here, and so relevance is particularly important. In the brief time slot of the Discussion, it is difficult to appreciate whether Discussants find the Responses adequate and sufficiently informative. Presumably they may at times be dissatisfied with the answer, but in this corpus there were no instances of Discussants complaining or directly accusing the Presenter of *not answering*, as often happens in political debates. However, there are claims of misunderstandings. The Presenter is in a dominant position compared with the audience, as he or she is given more speaking time and is free to judge whether a question is relevant or not.

Obviously, some questions are entirely predictable for experienced Presenters, as may be seen in Example 17, the response to the question previously discussed as Example 5.

end of (5): Q: ... Was this positive effect totally related to a decrease in diastolic blood pressure or could (.) be could other factors (.) also be involved ...?

(17) R: Yes, this is the question we always get asked. In the analysis, which you can go and see in poster 1966 (you remember?)... you'll see all the details of the analysis there... We have statistically sort of tried to adjust this for differences in blood pressure which occurred quite early on in the trial, but some people were not happy with the way we have done that and we could probably look for other ways of analysing the data ... .

It is clear the Presenter in Example 17 is expecting this objection, but how successful is his answer? From the last sentence it seems there may be a flaw in the study, and the research team involved have still not found a satisfactory solution to the problem.

The Response may also be very straightforward, as in Example 1 above (*It does not cross-react with y*). However, you do not always get a straight answer to a simple question. How do Presenters react when in difficulties? There may be a plea of ignorance – 18 times out of 100 the answer was *I don't know*, and twice *This question is still open*. At times the Presenter does not want to be led astray from the main subject of the talk, as in Examples 18 and 19.

(18) Q: What about hypertension in diabetes?
     R: I didn't go into this at all. It was not one of the aims of the study.

(19) Q: You mentioned that oxidative metabolism. Does that mean that you...?
     R: We did not test brain cells.

The answer in Example 19 is again rather abrupt, as in Example 1 above. It is as if an outsider wanted to take the opportunity of asking the expert speaker for some extra information on a pet subject which the Presenter does not want to address. These attempts are swiftly brushed aside.

The fact that questions may create difficulties for the Presenter is shown when the speaker flounders and searches for a suitable reply, pausing at length before committing himself, Examples 20-21 or declines to answer, Example 22.

(20) R: (long pause) er the issue is er let me think about this for a moment (.) for sure I would treat them like this ... .

(21) R: Thank you, these are very interesting observations. I will have to think about that er because of the complexity (.) er. I would like to see those data and I'd like to take the opportunity to think about it.

(22) Q: I'm Dr. K. from India. These ACE inhibitors are supposed to be nephrotoxic beyond certain levels of creatinine. Can you suggest some cut-off limit beyond which we should not use them ...?
     R: I wouldn't care I wouldn't even attempt to answer that question ...

Presenters may choose to be evasive, but here they must exercise caution, because to be successful, speakers must construct their utterances in such a way that they can be recognised as responses even if they do not constitute answers. As Weber (1993: 28) says: "a relevant answer is a matter of social accomplishment." Occasionally, there are problems of understanding and making meaning, as in the answer to the question in Example 8, given here as Example 23, and also in Example 24.

(23) R: First of all, Klaus, I would have thought that my - (.) obviously - I'm (.) I obviously have been misinterpreted, but it's probably my fault. I *don't* assume that reduction in urinary excretion reflects improvement in renal function ... I'm sorry if I didn't make that clear ... a small study from another group ... showed (.) prevention of membrane thickening was obtained in rodents, and I think probably there is an effect of these

agents on renal structure (.) and you're more of an expert than I am, but I would believe that preserving renal structure must be a good thing. What do you think, Klaus?

In Example 23, the Presenter avoids answering the question directly, and eventually asks the Discussant for his opinion, a move which is quite unusual. This example is similar to Example 24.

(24) R: There must be a misunderstanding; the rise is always between 2 and 4 a.m.

In both these instances, Examples 23 and 24, the Presenter uses forms without an explicit agent by choosing either the passive or an impersonal form in referring to the misinterpretation and thus avoids any direct accusation such as *you don't understand* – although this is the congruent meaning here.

The Presenter may also reject the Discussant's view, as in Example 25.

(25) Q: From what you said, and what the international literature says, it would seem logical to initiate therapy with x in every diabetic patient, even if their blood pressure is low ... R: I don't (.) I don't think there is evidence to introduce ace-inhibitors in all patients. I think if one looks at the 8-year data it seems – and I'm sure Dr P. will discuss this in more detail later – the point I'm making is you might believe that you want to prevent a rise and prevent overt renal disease, actually it may not be too late to treat them when they have microalbuminuria, so you might be treating some unnecessarily ...

In other cases, there may be convergence, as we have already seen in Example 3 in 3.2.1 above. The full response is reproduced here as Example 26:

(26) R: Absolutely. There are several patterns of insulin resistance, so very definitely we have people ... who perhaps convert and others who don't.

To conclude this section, it seems clear from the analysis of the Discussants' Questions and the Presenters' Responses that, although only about a third of the Questions are directly critical, many of the other types may also present difficulties for the Presenter, because of misunderstandings, differences in speakers' agendas, points of view or alignment with different schools of thought.

4. Interactive features

From the Questions and Responses it may be seen that the negotiation of social relations between speaker and audience is important in these debates. Participants generally attempt to show solidarity with the other researchers present, even though they may belong to competing schools. Interactive features may therefore be expected to play an important role in the debate, and the following section will review some of the items presented so far and present a few other items to illustrate some interactive discourse aspects such as exchange structure (see 4.1.), choice of discourse markers (see 4.2.), politeness devices and interpersonal distance (see 4.3.).

4.1. Exchange structure

Sacks *et al.* (1974) mentioned that the chaired meeting falls between the two extremes of conversation on the one hand and formal debates on the other. We may expect the Discussion Phase therefore to share some features of these two genre types. The Discussion is considered here as a *sub-genre* of the paper presentation session, whereas Swales (1991) considers casual conversation a *pre-genre*.

In comparing these exchanges with casual conversation, we must consider that, whereas in conversation participants have to recognise what is a question and thus be ready to respond to it adequately according to the local management of turns described by Sacks *et al.* (1974), in the conference Discussion there is a special slot provided when questions are invited from the floor by the Chair and the Questions alternate with Responses from the current speaker, whatever form these questions may have. Bids are therefore sanctioned by the Chair within a formal framework and any intervention from the floor is expected to evoke a response from the Presenter, whether it is in the form of a question or not. It is the task of the Discussant to formulate a question in such a way as to be understood by the Presenter, and, for the latter, to provide an adequate reply. This is not always simple, because people have different points of view and there may be a mismatch in their approach to an issue. It may be necessary to adapt to one's interlocutor's standpoint to some extent. In such a situation, de Beaugrande & Dressler (1981: 178) recommend the following tactics: a) reject the opposite viewpoint, b) question it, c) ignore it, d) replace it with one's own view, and in any case attempt to put the situation in a new light rather than attack the opposing position. There are traces of these tactics in this corpus, but participants' commitments are not always clearcut. Certainly, the choice of the various linguistic realisations of Questions and Responses is motivated by pragmatic purposes as well as exchange of information.

While the Conference Discussion differs from conversation, we may note that it is also different from the presentation it is based on. It represents a freer exchange phase than the paper, which is entirely pre-allocated and summarised in the programme of abstracts, so that the audience know in advance what the paper will be about. In the Discussion, on the other hand, it is not surprising to find some elements which are typical of spontaneous conversation.

When the exchange consists of several turns or when a third delegate joins in (which occurs three times in this corpus out of a total of 130 exchanges), it may resemble a private conversation, but in fact the speakers are using microphones and the interaction is taking place in public, with the audience listening in. Moreover, the Chair has the right to cut short the exchange, which hardly ever goes beyond two questions per Discussant, and to allocate the next speaker. So, as noted by Ventola (1996), this is mediated negotiation. Nonetheless, the exchanges may occasionally be very dialogic, as in Examples 11 and 16 above (Section 3.2.3 and 3.2.4), where the same Discussant asks a follow-up question.

As we have seen in Example 23 above, there is a departure from the norm, as the Presenter himself asks the Discussant a question in his turn and so sends the ball back into his court. The response is given here as Example 27.

end of (23) R: What do you think, Klaus?

(27) Klaus: Well, I agree, but I think the jury is still out to show that they do.

In Example 28, the response to Example 22 (Section 3.3), the question is re-routed and so another speaker, in this case the Chair, joins in the Discussion.

(28) R: I wouldn't even attempt to answer that question, not being a person dealing with patients with renal failure, but Marco may have more experience ...
Chair: You want me to answer the question?
Presenter: I – yeah (.) yeah ...
Chair: Well, the risk of precipitating acute renal failure ... .

We get the impression of an action which really is jointly constructed here. These more dialogic exchanges, however, never go very far, because they are very quickly cut off by the Chair. In fact, such variations in the turn-taking system are rare, because of the time constraints, unless there are no questions immediately forthcoming. The rigid turn-taking system of the chaired meeting in a way inhibits any true conversation, which is more likely to take place outside the conference hall. In the case of the presentation which Example 27 was taken from, the Presenter, in order to support his claim, includes in his long turn references to various studies, some of which very recent and not yet published at that time. He seems therefore quite capable of defending his position, yet he appeals to the Discussant and it appears at the end of the exchange that neither of the two speakers can provide a definite answer. This is just one of the many unresolved issues in medical research.

At other times the Presenter reverts to monologue, and the response may be quite long. In some cases, a brief summing up of the response will be given, when it is long and complex, to make sure the audience understand (Examples 29-31).

(29) To conclude, we were not able to show x, but we were left with the hope that ...

(30) So there is some evidence that ... but these new trials may give us a better idea of whether there is a lower threshold for treatment benefit ...

(31) So what I am saying is ... .

4.2. Discourse markers

Schiffrin (1987) refers to discourse markers as contextual coordinates of talk which contribute to local discourse coherence in conversation. They include items such as *oh, well, I mean, you know* and some uses of *because, now* and *then*. These occur frequently in conference discourse (Webber 1997a) and there are some instances of them in this corpus, such as the use of *well* in Examples 32 and 33.

(32) R: Well, I think not really very much ...

(33) Chair: Well, the risk of precipitating acute renal failure ...

If we look at the question in Example 34, we see a use of *because* which occurs often in conversational argument, not as a causal conjunction but as a discourse marker of motive and support for the argument presented by the speaker.

(34) Q: What was the control population that you used for GAD, because one of the explanations might be that your threshold is too low.

Here *because* corresponds to *the reason I am saying this is*, which, together with the caution expressed in the words *one of the explanations* and the epistemic modal *might* give an impression of tentativeness and a wish not to impose. It may be partly for this reason that the question appears helpful rather than threatening and can be looked on as a suggestion.

Example 6, here reproduced as Example 35, is more aggressive and contains the expression *I just can't understand*, which also resembles casual conversation mode rather than formal academic argument.[5]

(35) Q: You know how much I like your work, Giorgio, but I just can't understand – you take 23 patients and you say you found GMT-1 antibodies are expressed at the onset of type 1 diabetes and are significantly correlated with the presence of GAD antibodies ... .

The aggressiveness is downtoned by the conciliatory *Yes/But* preface: *You know how much I like your work, Giorgio, but.* Such tokens of appreciation followed

---

[5] This is reminiscent of Tannen's title (1990) for a study of casual conversation *You just don't understand: Women and men in conversation.*

by a challenge are also often found in conversation and are probably face-saving devices, which are particularly important when an argument takes place in public.

4.3. Politeness devices and interpersonal distance

Many of the utterances display features of dispreferred parts described by Levinson (1983), such as delays, prefaces and accounts. The spontaneity of these dialogues makes them seem closer to the more informal end of the formal/informal cline than other academic genres. However, as they take place in public, there is great attention to politeness and so even the expression of conflicting opinions rarely degenerates into open hostility. There is caution in the lead-in to the question and in the use of hedging devices, both shields and approximators, and of discourse markers generally, expressing modesty and uncertainty: *I wonder if I may ask ..., Can I ask you, er if ..., I was just wondering if perhaps ...* . This form of subjective modalisation and the higher incidence of personal reference are more typical of the conference than the written paper (Thompson 1997; Webber 1997a, 1997b). These form part of the negative politeness pragmatics of scientific discourse.

Myers (1989) includes personal attribution and hedging among politeness strategies used in written texts on molecular genetics. As regards hedging, we must distinguish between the hedging system normally used in written reports as described in Salager-Meyer (1994) and that which is more reminiscent of conversational modes. Items such as *associated with* and *related to* (see Example 5 above) or *suggest* are common in written medical texts as well as in conference language (Webber 1996: 32-34, Skelton 1997). These serve to dissociate the writer from any too strong commitment to a proposition. In unrehearsed spoken interaction, the problem of commitment is even more acute and we find expressions which are more typical of conversation than academic prose, such as *actually, I don't think, my own belief is, I would believe, I can't help you there*, and *I am sure you're right*. As Halliday says (1994: 89), when we say we are *certain*, this is an expression of modalisation which usually indicates we are not certain of something.

Other features which may be considered among the expressions of solidarity and which place the Discussion Phase more in the realm of informal, unedited language are the use of address forms and banter or repartee.

Regarding the former, we note the frequent use of first names, for those present and also in referring to researchers who are not present but evidently well known to some of the participants. First-name familiarity is probably considered more appropriate in this context in some cultures rather than others. It may have two effects: of bonding and cameraderie on the one hand and a feeling of exclusion in those delegates who may not know the other participants in the Discussion so well and will feel outside the special club or inner circle of regular members of these debates. Those who know each other well probably communicate regularly even if they live in different countries. When speakers address the Presenter by name, this may be considered a redundant vocative (one used when there is already sufficient contextual information available for the nominated person to be the assumed next speaker), described by Eggins & Slade (1997: 145) in casual conversation as indicating an attempt to establish a closer relationship. In the Discussion it has the effect of lessening the distance between participants. These expressions of solidarity also belong to the positive politeness strategies of this genre.

Apart from numerous second person references as in Example 36, we may note a reference to a third person who is not present at the proceedings, in Example 37.

(36) R: ...Thank you, yes (.) there's a question there (.) Walter

(37) R: I've discussed this with Sally and can offer no good explanation for her findings.

As noted in Frobert-Adamo (this volume), there is also a certain amount of banter or joking, particularly at the beginning of an exchange or in the procedurals, which form part of the subsidiary discourse in Montgomery's terms (Coulthard & Montgomery 1981). Humour is an invitation to establish a closer relationship and may serve here to introduce a more relaxed atmosphere into a context which is potentially face-threatening or tense. It also gives participants a sense of belonging to a group. In fact, we find an instance of this in the Chair's move in Example 38 and in 39 (the response to Example 17).

(38) Chair: I think there is another question (.) I think it is Walter ... I can't quite see you ... must be old age.
      Q: It is Walter. No, you're not used to seeing me wearing a tie, that's probably why.

(39) R: In the analysis which you can go and see in Poster 1966 (you remember?) (you're not German, you're Austrian, aren't you?) (.) you'll see all the details are there – we have statistically sort of tried to adjust this for differences.

This refers back to a joke made in the body of the talk about Germany winning the World Cup in 1966. This last example shows how the Discussion section is linked to the presentation by a form of 'semiotic spanning' (Ventola 1999) and how shared knowledge can be built up even in the short space of a talk and ensuing discussion (generally not more than 25-30 minutes all together).

The expression *sort of* in this last example is another feature reminiscent of conversation - the deliberate use of vague language (Dubois 1987, Channell 1994, Bertuccelli Papi 1995). Eggins & Slade (1997) include these expressions among the mitigators or general resources for grading used widely in conversation. Two further examples illustrate this.

(40) R: I think (.) I'm sure you're right, but as far as I recall, in the K study the use of x in rat models has had some renal protective effect, but ...

(41) R: ... something around 40% positive ...

The use of vague language in spoken science gives the utterances an air of unassuming modesty, of not wanting to appear too dogmatic or sure of oneself.

5. Conclusion

The purpose of the Workshop Discussion Phase is to allow an exchange of ideas among experts in a smaller group interested in a special subject. According to the conventions of the genre, participants use informal language, politeness devices, address forms and other resources which lower interpersonal distance, but in spite of this there may be tension and conflict in the interaction. Although there are more direct speaker-audience features in the Discussion than in the pre-planned phase of the presentation, this is certainly not just a chat among friends, however friendly it may appear at certain moments. Co-presence involves risk. In spite of the first-name familiarity, the jokes and the apparent modesty in the choice of language found here, speakers are on their guard and prepared to face criticism. This may stem from conflicting ideologies and interests or loyalties to some school or group, but also from the fact that a great deal is at stake in the decision-making process. Exposure is necessary but is particularly risky in the conference situation, where Presenters may prefer to be reticent about certain aspects of their research until it is ready for publication.

It is difficult for participants to arrive at a consensus in this kind of large international conference, where the Question/Response exchange tends to be rather fragmentary because of the time constraints and frequent change of Discussant. Whereas in conversation, turns are linked to some previous utterance in the exchange, participants here have to wait to intervene at the invitation of the Chair. As a result, the Discussion tends to skip from one topic to another, so that it is rare to find an in-depth discussion on one point leading to some kind of overall conclusion. Meetings which arrive at a consensus are usually specially convened for that purpose at the end of a period of investigation into a particular topic. Hence, this might occur in smaller, more targeted meetings, but at workshops participants rarely arrive at a consensus, because there are constantly new advances in science and research is in a continuous state of flux as new theories are put forward and old ones are discarded. However, as one of the delegates in this conference corpus says, "controversy should be welcomed, since it is only through controversy that science advances."

One of the limitations of this corpus is that it is small, but even in a larger corpus it may not be easy to find patterns revealing definite correlations between function and form. However, by looking at reactions to questions in context, we can find clues for an appropriate interpretation. For example, as noted by Antaki (1994), whether an exchange develops into an argument depends not only on how an utterance is taken up by the addressee, but also how the first speaker confirms the disputability of the initial utterance, and so arguments often have a three-part structure. Conference Discussions often have no third part, but where the analyst is not sure of the Presenter's intentions, the continuation of the exchange may at least shed light on how it is interpreted by the audience. This may not always be the correct or only interpretation, because misunderstandings can arise, but it is evidently one possible interpretation.

The kind of argumentative discourse in medical conferences is different from that described in legal proceedings and political debates by Ilie (1994) and others, where speakers support the prosecution or the defence in court or their party line in politics. The parties in a legal or a political dispute are committed to one point of view, whereas at times the impression here is that participants are groping for solutions to the problems put forward. They often refer to known facts, but there is a great deal of talk about phenomena which are as yet unknown or unclear. Hence, after the confrontational question in Example 6, both speakers in the end recognise that clear evidence of the truth is lacking. Participants in scientific inquiry strive to distinguish what is not yet known or only partially understood from what is considered known, in a continual search for solutions to problems. It is often said that each scientific study makes only a small contribution to the advance of science. At the conference presentation stage, the claims seem to be even more tentative, because they are not yet ready for publication, and this affects the kind of language behaviour of the participants. From the analysis of the Questions and Responses presented here, it is clear that participation in the Discussion represents a challenge and therefore creates difficulties for all but the most accomplished conference speaker, and the interpersonal features found in the corpus are a part of speakers' natural attempts to create a rapport with the other academics and so overcome some of these difficulties.

References

Antaki, C. 1994. *Explaining and Arguing*. London: Sage.

de Beaugrande, R. & W. Dressler 1981. *Introduction to Text Linguistics*. London: Longman.

Berkenkotter, C. & T. Huckin 1995. *Genre Knowledge in Disciplinary Communities*. Hillsdale NJ.: Lawrence Erlbaum.

Bertuccelli Papi, M. 1995. "Semantic vagueness and degree-of-precision adverbs". *Textus, VIII:*313-332.

Channell, J. 1994. *Vague Language*. Oxford: Oxford University Press.

Coulthard, M. & M. Montgomery 1981. "The structure of monologue". In M. Coulthard & M. Montgomery (eds). *Studies in Discourse Analysis*. London: Routledge & Kegan Paul.

Dubois, B. 1987. "Something on the order of around forty to forty-four: Imprecise numerical expressions in biomedical slide talks". *Language and Society,* 16: 527- 541.

van Eemeren, F. 1992. *Argumentation, Communication and Fallacies. A Pragma-dialectical Perspective*. Hillsdale: Lawrence Erlbaum.

van Eemeren, F., R. Grootendorst, S. Jackson & S. Jacobs 1997. "Argumentation". In T. van Dijk (ed). *Discourse as Structure and Process*. London: Sage.

Eggins, S. & D. Slade 1997. *Analyzing Casual Conversation*. London: Cassell.

Frobert-Adamo, M. This volume. "Humor in oral presentations: What's the joke?"

Grice, P. 1975. "Logic and conversation". In P. Cole & J. L. Morgan (eds). *Syntax and Semantics*, vol. 3; Speech acts: 41-58.

Goffman, E. 1959. *The Presentation of Self in Everyday Life*. New York: Anchor Books.

Grewendorf, G. 1981. "Answering as decision making: a new way of doing pragmatics". In H. Parret, M. Sbrisà & J. Verschueren (eds). *Possibilities and Limitations of Pragmatics*. Amsterdam: John Benjamins, 263-284.

Halliday, M. A. K. 1994. *An Introduction to Functional Grammar*. (2nd edition). London: Arnold.

Ilie, C. 1994. *What else can I tell you? A Pragmatic Study of English Rhetorical Questions as Discursive and Argumentative Acts*. Stockholm: Almquist & Wiksell Int.

Jacobs, S. & S. Jackson. 1982. "Conversational argument: a discourse analytical approach". In J. R. Cox & C. A Willard (eds). *Advances in Argumentation Theory and Research*. Carbondale: Southern Illinois University Press, 205-237.

Lakoff, R. 1971. "Passive resistance". *Papers from the 7th regional meeting of the Chicago Linguistic Society, CLS, 7,* 149-162.

Lakoff, R. 1973. "Questionable answers and answerable questions". In B. B. Kachru *et al.* (eds). *Issues in Linguistics*. Papers in honor of Henry and Renée Kahane. Urbana: University of Illinois Press, 453-467.

Levinson, S. 1983. *Pragmatics*. Cambridge: Cambridge University Press.

Myers, G. 1989. "The pragmatics of politeness in scientific texts". *Applied Linguistics,* 4: 1-35.

Sacks, H., E. A. Schegloff & G. Jefferson 1974. "A simplest systematics for the organization of turn-taking for conversation. Studies in the organization of conversational interaction". *Language* 50 (4): 696-735, Variant version also in J. Scheinkein (ed). *Studies in the Organization of Conversational Interaction*. New York: Academic Press, 693-735.

Salager-Meyer, F. 1994. "Hedges and textual communicative function in medical English written discourse". *English for Specific Purposes,* 13 (2): 149-169.

Schegloff, E. & H. Sacks 1984. "Opening up closings". *Semiotica,* 8: 289-327.

Schiffrin, D. 1987. *Discourse Markers.* Cambridge: Cambridge University Press.

Shalom, C. 1993. "Established and evolving spoken research process genres: Plenary lecture and poster session discussions at academic conferences". *English for Specific Purposes,* 12: 37-50.

Shalom, C. This volume. "The academic conference: A forum for enacting genre knowledge."

Sinclair, J. M. (ed.). 1995. *Collins COBUILD English Dictionary.* 2nd edition. London: Harper Collins.

Skelton, J. 1997. "The representation of truth in academic medical writing". *Applied Linguistics,* 18 (2): 121-140.

Stenström, A. 1984. *Questions and Responses in English Conversation.* Lund: Studies in English 68. Malmo: CWK Gleerup.

Swales J. 1991. *Genre Analysis: English in Academic and Research Settings.* Cambridge: Cambridge University Press.

Swales, J. 1996. "Teaching the conference abstract". In E. Ventola & A. Mauranen (eds). *Academic Writing: Today and Tomorrow.* Yliopistopaino: Helsinki University Press, 45-59.

Tannen, D. 1990. *You Just Don't Understand: Women and Men in Conversation.* New York: Morrow.

Thompson, S. E. 1997. "Presenting research: A study of interaction in academic monologue." Unpublished PhD thesis. Liverpool: University of Liverpool.

Ventola, E. 1993. "Any Questions? – Discourse features of discussion time". Paper delivered at AILA, Amsterdam, August 1993.

Ventola, E. 1996. "Discussing discussions". Paper presented at the International Conference of Pragmatics, Mexico City, Mexico.

Ventola, E. 1998. "Interpersonal choices in academic work". In A. Sanchez-Macarro & R. Carter (eds). *Linguistic Choices Across Genres.* Amsterdam: Benjamins, 117-136.

Ventola, E. 1999. "Semiotic spanning at conferences: Cohesion and coherence in and across conference papers and their discussions". In W. Bublitz, U. Lenk & E. Ventola (eds). *Coherence in Spoken and Written Discourse. How to Create it and How to Describe It.* Amsterdam: Benjamins.

Ventola, E. This volume. "Why and what kind of focus on conference presentations?"

Webber, P. 1996. *Varieties in Medical English.* Milan: Argo.

Webber, P. 1997a. "Casual conversation features in scientific conference presentations". Unpublished MSc dissertation. Birmingham: Aston University.

Webber, P. 1997b. "Some linguistic aspects of scientific conferences". *Aston University LSU Bulletin,* 11: 3-11.

Weber, E. G. 1993. *Varieties of Questions in English Conversation.* Amsterdam: Benjamins.

Appendix

Some of the longer exchanges are given here in their original sequence.
Workshop on Hypertension (Helsinki)

First Presenter ("David")

1)   Chair: We'll open your paper for discussion. We've got about 5 minutes for questions (.) Gunther.

2)   Gunther: David, the beneficial effect of ACE inhibition on the progression of diabetic retinopathy is of considerable interest. Was this positive effect totally related to a decrease in diastolic blood pressure or could (.) be (.) other factors also be involved like modification of ?? function or other mechanisms?

3)   R: Yes, this is the question we always get asked. In the analysis which you can go and see in poster 1966 (you remember?) (you're not German, you're Austrian, aren't you?) (.) you'll see all the details of the analysis there – we have statistically sort of tried to adjust this for differences in blood pressure which occurred quite early on in the trial but some people are not happy with the way we have done that and we could probably look for other ways of analysing the data to stratify for BP response.

4)   Chair: Other questions? (.) If there are no other questions, may I ask you, when you classify, you talk about microalbuminuria and hypertension. Really, you are using categories for variables that are continually distributed and in fact that overlap that you showed, that overlap would disappear if you were to look at lower levels of blood pressure, which in the micros would still be higher than in the normoalbuminiuric patients. Would you agree with that?

5)   R: Yes, I agree, it does change with the level, of course.

6)   Chair: Any other questions from the audience?

7)   (.) R: (cont.) I would just like to make a comment on the economics again, which I skipped over, because I don't know anything about it basically. In some countries this might be an important issue, in some of the countries represented here, where drugs like the ACE inhibitors can be extremely expensive. ACE inhibitors are due to be coming off their patent in the year 2002, and if you judge from the experience with captopril, which came off patent in the US last year, within 2 to 3 months the other drugs which came in to replace it, the other captoprils, were 10% of the cost of real captopril.

8)   Chair: Thank you, yes (.) there's a question there (.) Walter

9)   Walter: David, what's the evidence base for the blood (David, I'm in the middle) what's the evidence base for the blood pressure levels that have been taken by JNCV and the ADA and so on of 130 over 85 – what hard evidence is there that these targets should be achieved, leaving aside the problem of getting there in the first place?

10)   R: Well, I think not really very much, not for cardiovascular disease, anyway. P. will no doubt tell us this afternoon that there are good reasons for getting blood pressure down even lower than that at least for renal protection, but I presume they base their recommendations on the trials that have been carried out in non-diabetic patients.

11)   Chair: I think there is another question (.) I think it is Walter – I can't quite see you very well – must be old age

12)   Walter: It is Walter. No, you're not used to seeing me wearing a tie, that's probably why. David, in- David, I'm over here- the thing is, in your intervention study apparently there was a clear treatment effect below the normal diagnostic criteria for microalbuminuria (.) erm (.) and that raises the whole issue of redefining the entity of microalbuminuria, because at least in non-diabetic individuals a much lower threshold is also predictive of development of cardiovascular disease, as we are presenting in poster 1748. So how would you like to comment on that?

13)   R: What happened in 1748, I wonder? No, I quite agree with you and we obviously do need to – we keep reconsidering these recommendations. We are, as you may know, already in the progress (process? Transcriber's note) of doing a meta analysis of all the ACE inhibitor trials that have taken part and are willing to collaborate and that may give us a better idea of whether there is a lower threshold for treatment benefit.

14) Chair: final question!
15) Dr K.: I'm Dr K. from India. These ACE inhibitors are supposed to be nephrotoxic beyond certain levels of creatinine. Can you suggest some cut-off limit beyond which we should not use ACE inhibitors in case of renal failure?
16) R: I wouldn't care, I wouldn't even attempt to answer that question, not being a person dealing with patients with renal failure, but Carlo may have more experience for that question
17) Chair: you want me to answer the question?
18) R: I-er- yeah, yeah, you answer that.
19) Chair: Well, the risk of precipitating acute renal failure is – increases as the serum creatinine increases. Usually, for serum creatinine about 300 mmol per litre one has to be very cautious starting therapy with ACE inhibitors and what you have to do is measure creatinine and electrolytes a week later after starting treatment to make sure these people don't go into acute renal failure, or their renal function deteriorates rapidly. OK, if there are no other questions, thank you very much, David, and we'll move on to the second speaker, who comes from Australia, John C., who will talk about renal protection with anti-hypertensive treatment.

Second Presenter ("John") (only the last 2 questions are given here)
1) Chair: Two more questions. One from my co-chairman
2) Co-Chair: In your presentation you have concentrated on the renal protection of course, but we shouldn't forget that most of the (.) er these NIDDM patients die of cardiovascular disease before they entered end-stage renal failure, so you have not mentioned the potential role of beta blocking agents in this highly complex field. Could you make a comment a little bit on that?
3) R: Yes, erm (.) I vaguely alluded to it at the end of my topic (.) er talk, but I decided to keep to my target (renal protection and hypertension), but I agree with you that the potential vascular protection not only of beta blockers but even of some of the anti-anginal calcium channel blockers are able in a non-diabetic context to reduce heart failure or recurrent myocardial infarction. I think this is where we're going to find the power of these agents. For example, the ACDC study involved cardiac end-points, all the new studies with ?? will involve cardiovascular end-points and I would be surprised if we don't see that these changes in renal protection are also seen with respect to cardiovascular protection.
4) Chair: Klaus
5) Smith, from the UK: John, you seem very convinced about the usefulness of micro (.) er reduction in microalbuminuria as a proxy marker for renal protection. Firstly, are you that convinced. Secondly, if you are, how do you explain that when you stop ACE inhibitors in the few studies that have been done, the proteinuria goes back to greater than pre-treatment levels, I think in some cases and er if if, given that, how do you think ACE inhibitors are actually doing their job? If it's just masking the protein excretion rather than doing something fundamental?
6) R: First of all, Klaus, I would have thought that my(.) I – obviously – I'm (.) I obviously have been misinterpreted, but it's probably my fault. I *don't* assume that reduction in urinary albumin excretion reflects improvement in renal function, particularly with an agent such as an ACE inhibitor which might have a particularly potent effect on urinary albumin excretion. I'm sorry if I didn't make that clear. One would be cautious about interpreting that. From the Melbourne diabetic nephropathy study group, that was the

most remarkable finding I think from that study. Initially it was the dramatic rise in urinary albumin excretion to levels at least that we had seen 12 months earlier when we stopped the drug. But there are now data with renal biopsies – for example, there was a study shown on Sunday, albeit a small study from another group in Melbourne which used x for 3 years and showed (.) a reduction in interstitial fibrosis, prevention of glomerular membrane thickening, and this was very similar to the data that was obtained in rodents, and I think probably there is an effect of these agents on renal structure, (.) and you're more of an expert than I am, but I would believe that preserving renal structure must be a good thing. What do you think, Klaus?

7) Klaus: Well, I agree, but I think the jury are still out to show that they do.

8) R: I think over the next few years, there are quite a few studies, biopsy studies, which (.) where I think we will find more information on that data.

SPEAKER-AUDIENCE INTERACTION:
THE CASE OF BULGARIANS PRESENTING IN ENGLISH

Irena Vassileva

South-West University of Blagoevgrad, Bulgaria

Abstract – It is often suggested that in the modern age of globalisation of academic communication and the ever-increasing multiplication of voices within it knowledge transmission may become problematic with English as the exclusive lingua franca. The paper thus focuses on the similarities and differences in conference language self-representation and speaker-audience interaction in English and 'Bulgarian English'. The investigation is based on data from paper presentations in the field of linguistics. The aim is to establish and analyse certain surface features like the employment of the *I* and/or *we* perspective, direct address, rhetorical questions, reference to previous/following speakers, fillers, etc. The instances and linguistic means of direct speaker-audience interaction are then classified according to the type of micro-speech acts they appear in – aims, focusing, reference, exemplification, advance organisers, etc. The study starts from the hypothesis that there exist certain culture-bound rhetorical variations that influence discourse production in a foreign language. The results lead to some general conclusions concerning the problems of, first, whether the established differences would hamper comprehension and lead to misunderstandings and, second, whether culture-specific rhetorical patterns should be tolerated in order to avoid total unification in the academia that may result from the spread and dominance of English as *the* international language of scientific communication, or sacrificed for the sake of unproblematic and universal mutual understanding.

1. Introduction

Gnutzmann & Lange (1990: 87) note that "a general survey of the approaches to special language description shows that they may be reduced to two main trends – the terminological one and the functional one".[1] The first of the above-mentioned trends dominated the study of special languages for a considerable length of time. With the emergence of text linguistics / discourse analysis and the present ever-increasing interest of linguists in the study of higher-level language units, however, we are witnessing a switch within the paradigm of scientific language research. The focus has gradually, but steadily, moved from the level of individual words, phrases, grammatical constructions, etc. typical of

---

[1] All translations in the text are mine.

the language of science, to the investigation of entire textual and discoursal entities, i.e. discourse rhetoric.

As far as academic communication in particular is concerned, although its principal aim is to pass knowledge from one generation to another, no less important is its function as a transmitter of discursive norms and practices. The process of production, distribution and consumption of academic discourse, however, is realised within certain cultural contexts which presuppose and reveal shared values and beliefs. The latter embody basic assumptions both as to the nature of the discipline and the subject matter, and as to the 'professional ethic' and relationships between the members of the respective community or, as stated by Bizzell (1982: 193), all academic discourse is "a form of language use that unites a particular community". Convincing as it may sound, this claim seems to need serious reconsideration in the modern age of globalisation of academic communication. How are we to define the community Bizzell refers to? And does present-day academic discourse really unite scientists of different social, economic, ethnic, cultural, etc. backgrounds, or does (or maybe should?) the very expansion of the community and the ever-increasing multiplication of voices within it result in diversification rather than unification? And if so, will this lead to communication breakdowns, considering that, as noted by Baumann (1995: 118), "some studies in cognitive psychology point to the fact that there are mutual relationships between the cultural environment, the model of thinking and the type of communication, that influence the understanding of texts."

Two contradictory viewpoints dominate the study of cross-cultural scientific discourse rhetoric at present: the universalist and the culture-specific one. The first view is probably best exemplified by Widdowson's (1984: 51) statement that

> I take it that the discourse conventions which are used to communicate this common culture are independent of the particular linguistic means which are used to realise them ... . So I would wish to say that scientific discourse is a universal mode of communicating, or universal rhetoric, which is realised by scientific *text* in different languages by the process of *textualization*.

Scientific discourse is thus treated as a common culture, as a universal mode of communication which "imposes a conformity on members of the scientific community no matter what language they happen to use." (Widdowson 1984: 61).

Widdowson himself (1984: 16), however, seems to contradict his own point of view by also claiming that "scientific discourse can be seen as a set of rhetorical acts ..., but the manner in which these acts are related one with the other and the manner in which they are linguistically realised may be restricted by accepted convention." Conventions, on their part, are culturally marked phenomena that belong to some of the most stable social systems promoting and preserving cultural identity. Thus, as Spillner (1996: 108), among others, suggests, "in spite of the tendencies towards international standardisation, there are differences in specialised discourse that may be attributed to national rhetorical tradition, law regulations, academic conventions, language- and style-teaching, [...]". It is common knowledge that cultural dissimilarity has a serious impact on intercultural communication in general and academic communication in particular. It is therefore the main task of contrastive discourse analyses to identify 'the points of collision' not only in order to facilitate the teaching of academic discourse comprehension and production, but also to raise scientists' awareness of and tolerance to the existence of various academic cultures, where each has its due place in the global exchange of knowledge.

Although written academic communication dominates cross-cultural scientific contacts and has therefore attracted the interest of linguists of late, conference language, unfortunately, still remains insufficiently investigated in spite of the recently observed intensification of face-to-face interaction due to increased mobility of scientists all over the world. Thus, it seems that the time has come for conference language to receive its due attention.

Some of the most typical surface exponents of the genre of conference presentations are *speaker self-representation* and *interactional skills* that will be in the focus of this study. The latter are, more often than not, only subconsciously perceived by the audience, as its attention is normally concentrated on the ideational aspects of the presentation. This tendency in the consumption of modern science is best described by Foucault (1969: 126) who claims that

> In the 17th and 18th centuries, a totally new conception was developed when scientific texts were accepted on their own merits and positioned within an anonymous and coherent conceptual system of established truths and methods of verification. Authentification no longer required reference to the individual who had produced them; the role of the author disappeared as an index of truthfulness.

Foucault, however, envisages primarily the written mode of scientific communication where the interpersonal function of language is realised in a very different way. Recent studies in author identity and audiences (Scollon 1995, Gee 1990, Hartley 1993 among others) take up a more interactional Bakhtinian approach that views the author not as a fully independent individual with entirely original ideas and, respectively, language means for their realisation. Rather, "the self which is constructed in discourse is a highly pluralistic and interactionally contingent conceptual entity, even where intercultural discourse is not considered" (Scollon 1995: 23). Intercultural communication, on its part, presents even greater problems and is even more demanding on the author, as s/he is required / expected to switch from one system of cultural values and beliefs to a sometimes totally alien one not only in the case of using a foreign language, but also due to the presence of an international audience. That means "going native" (Bizzel 1990: 53), or changing one's identity – the identity constructed and constituted by the national culture and society, as well as the native scientific community conventions.

The very impossibility of full identity change becomes even more severe in cases when the latter has to be accomplished by scientists coming from very different cultural backgrounds as compared to the target one or who have, for primarily political and economic reasons, spent a long time in isolation from the international scene of knowledge exchange. Thus, in this paper I shall investigate the way representatives of such a small and until recently isolated scientific culture (namely the Bulgarian one) cope with English as an international conference language in view of the features mentioned above.

2. Aim of the study

The purpose of the present study is thus to investigate several means of direct speaker-audience address and speaker self-representation in English and Bulgarian English paper presentations in linguistics, namely:

(a) the first person singular *I* perspective versus the first person plural *we* perspective;
(b) the *you*-perspective;
(c) the use of rhetorical questions;
(d) extra-textual references;
(e) jokes;
(f) story-telling elements;
(g) deixis;
(h) personal reference;
(i) cross-reference to other speakers participating in the same event.

An attempt will be made to suggest some explanations of the differences and to point to certain cross-cultural misunderstandings which may ensue from the established variations. I will also argue here that those variations are primarily due to cultural reasons by starting from the assumption that, regardless of their propositional value, the linguistic means enumerated above function along the 'speaker - audience' axis of discourse realisation and reflect relations outside the semantic scope of the text itself, i.e. social, or interpersonal in terms of Halliday (1985) relations.

As some informal interviews with colleagues show, both presenters and audience are, more often than not, unaware of the phenomena listed above, but are frequently left with a sense of dissatisfaction whose roots may be traced back to unsuccessful choice of interactive means on the part of the speaker. All that, for its part, has direct impact on the process of content comprehension and evaluation.

3. Methodology

The contrastive analysis is based on the parallel comparison of genre- and field-compatible texts, in this particular case paper presentations in linguistics. The employment of the various means of authorial presence realisation and speaker-audience interaction is statistically established in terms of overall numbers of occurrences and their quantitative distribution throughout the texts, followed by a detailed qualitative analysis of the micro-speech acts where one or another linguistic means is favoured or avoided. Since the investigation aims at gaining insight into discourse rhetoric, the analytical approach adopted here treats rhetoric as a pragmatic function "represented by sets of conditions defining such communicative acts as classification, description, explanation" (Widdowson 1984: 26) within the framework of a modified version of speech act theory (Austin 1962, Searle 1969).

Speech act theory, or at least its application to data analysis, has been predominantly oriented towards analyses of dialogical texts where segmentation does not present great problems. With monologic texts, however, the main difficulty arises when their surface linearity has to be broken down in order to identify the clusters of hierarchically organised speech acts which could serve as a tertium comparationis for the purpose of a contrastive analysis. This normalisation problem may be solved by employing Ferrara's (1985: 143) principle: "for each hypothetically identified speech act to be confirmed as a single and distinct act, we must find at least one goal that can conceivably motivate its performance." Every separate micro-speech act enters into a cluster of similar ones thus forming a macro-speech act manifesting a general goal. A change of the micro-speech act is signalled by a change of the micro-theme in terms of Functional Sentence Perspective theory.

4. Corpora

The investigation is based on data that have been excerpted from typescripts of recorded paper presentations at several international conferences, namely: "Seventy years of English and American Studies in Bulgaria", Sofia, 1-3 October 1998, "Recent Developments in Linguistic Theory", Poznan, Poland, 30 April – 2 May 1999, the 12th European Symposium on Language for Special Purposes, 30 August – 3 September 1999, Bolzano, Italy, the 31st Colloquium of Linguistics, 7-10 September, 1999, Germersheim, Germany and "LSP Forum '99", 17-19 September 1999, Prague, the Czech Republic.

The presentations are analysed in their entirety, and those made by Bulgarians are produced by some of the most prominent specialists in English in order to avoid any 'low-level' transfer and ensure author-authenticity, i.e. the fact that no translator is involved as mediator, as is frequently the case with natural sciences, for example. Ten native speakers of English were recorded (five American and five British) with a total time of five hours. The Bulgarian English speakers were twelve, with a total time of six hours.[2]

5. Data analysis

5.1. General distribution

Since, as already mentioned, there is a difference in the overall number of hours recorded in the two languages, it seems viable to first look at the frequency of usage of the linguistic means enumerated above. Thus, Table 1 shows the frequency of use of the three basic means of speaker-audience interaction (the *I*, *we* and *you* perspectives) per minute, as well as the overall frequency including all means under consideration. Speaker variation is also presented.

	English	Bulgarian English
I perspective – average	1.2	0.6
I perspective – speaker variation	0.5 - 2.1	0.05 - 1.4
We perspective – average	0.7	0.3
We perspective – speaker variation	0.06 - 1.4	0.05 - 1
You perspective – average	0.4	0.2
You perspective – speaker variation	0 - 1	0 - 0.8
all means – average	2.47	1.2
all means – speaker variation	1.4 - 4.5	0.1 - 2.4

Table 1: Frequency of use.

---

[2] For ethical reasons no list of presenters' names will be given here.

As the data clearly demonstrates, Bulgarian English (henceforth BE) employs almost 50% of the means in question as compared to native-speakers' English in terms of frequency. This striking difference can only be accounted for in purely pragmatic terms, as it is not 'language as a system' knowledge that we are dealing with here, but knowledge of discourse production rhetoric. The marked authorial presence is a comparatively new tendency that is directly related to the Anglo-American idea of 'author responsibility', commented on, surprising as it may seem, by the non-Anglo-American Michail Bakhtin (1986: 301) as follows: "*I*-authors are positioned by their discoursal choices as single authors, as independently responsible for the contents of their writing ... *we*-authors – a collaborative rather than a competitive approach". The Bulgarian tradition in this respect still adheres to the more 'objective' way of presenting scientific knowledge that presupposes avoidance of discourse personalisation. Thus, one of the high-level interlanguage features that becomes apparent here is the transfer of native-language discourse strategies (for more details on written academic English and Bulgarian, see Vassileva 1998, 2000). At the same time, speaker variation is much more pronounced in English – a fact that supports once more the claim that even in English the new tendency towards a more prominent authorial presence is not an established norm as yet.

As far as the distribution of the linguistic means discussed here is concerned, Table 2 shows the overall number of occurrences and the relative percentage of each of them in the two language data:

	%	English	N- 846	%	Bulgarian English	N- 442
I perspective	46		391	53		232
We perspective	23		196	21.5		95
You perspective	14		119	14		61
Rhetorical questions	4		33	4		19
Extra-textual reference	3		24	5		24
Jokes	1		7	0.25		1
Story-telling	1		6	0.25		1
Deixis	5		44	1.5		6
Personal reference	1		7	0		0
Reference to other speakers	2		19	0.5		3

Table 2: Number of occurrence and distribution.

I should start by noting here that while all presenters resort (although to varying degrees) to both the *I* and the *we* perspective, only seven out of twelve use the *you* perspective, i.e. address the audience directly, in BE, compared to nine out of ten in the native speakers' group. The presenters who avoid direct address are predominantly young and inexperienced. The degree of employment of a personal perspective in academic writing is also dependent on age, experience and status, as has already been indicated by other authors (Kresta 1992 among others). Insufficient, or no attention (to my knowledge at least) has, however, been paid to the same type of avoidance strategy in direct author-audience interaction.

In spite of the previously mentioned low overall frequency of interactive means, the Bulgarians show a similar distribution as the native speakers within the first basic groups. Jokes, story-telling elements, deixis and references to other speakers, however, are incidental singular cases in BE.

In the next section I shall present a more detailed analysis of the various micro-speech acts where each of the linguistic means listed in Table 2 above have been established.

5.2.   The I perspective

The micro-speech acts identified as containing the *I* perspective in the corpora are the following:

1. *'Analysis / Argumentation'* – the case when the speaker chooses to present his/her arguments in the process of the analysis from the *I* perspective.
2. *'Aims / Advance organisers'* – explicit statement of aims and/or use of advance organisers.
3. *'Personal view'* – these are clear cases of expression of the speaker's personal view about what is being discussed.
4. *'Personal experience'* – this is the case when the speaker refers to his/her own personal (mainly practical) experience in order to support his/her claims with 'real life' data and thus sound more convincing to the audience.
5. *'Focusing'* – if the speaker decides to follow the 'from general to particular' structural type of discourse development, focusing comes inevitably at the point when the exact object of the study should be clearly defined.
6. *'Self-reference'* – under this cover term I have included two cases: first, when the speaker quotes him/herself by referring to his/her previous publications from the *I* perspective and, second, when the speaker refers back to his/her own claims / statements / results already discussed in the same text.

7. *'Conclusions'* – the case of explicit marking of the speaker in concluding statements.
8. *'Terminology / Procedures'* – this is the case when the speaker refers to or clarifies terms and procedures s/he employs in the current study.
9. *'Exemplification'* – the introduction of examples from a personal perspective.
10. *'Reference'* – reference to other people's research in the field.
11. *'Back organisers'* – the term is used here to denote the opposite case of advance organisers, that is, the case when the speaker refers to the structure of the preceding text.
12. *'Permission'* – what I call 'permission' here is a case of employment of the *I* perspective which finds its linguistic expression in the phrase *let me.*

The study does not pretend to cover all linguistic resources that are 'responsible' for the interaction between the speaker and his/her audience, but rather serve as a starting point for such investigations. Thus, the elements discussed here are the most transparent, the most 'visible' ones that operate on the very surface of discourse and account for the most immediate reactions of the audience.

	English	**Bulgarian English**
Analysis / Argumentation	15%	17%
Personal experience	35%	9%
Personal view	17%	15%
Aims / Advance organisers	8.2%	15%
Focusing	6%	13%
Terminology / Procedures	4%	13%
Back organisers / Reference	4.6%	4.5%
Permission	5.7%	2.5%
Self-reference	3%	1%
Exemplification	1%	5%
Reference	0%	4%
Conclusions	0.5%	1%
Total	100%	100%

Table 3: The *I* perspective.

Table 3 presents the types of micro-speech acts where the *I* perspective is preferably employed.

Although Table 3 attempts to present the data in terms of frequency, it is obvious that the *I* perspective demonstrates a rather different distribution in the two languages – it is more or less equally employed in the micro-speech acts (henceforth MSAs) of *analysis / argumentation, personal view* and *back organisers / reference* only, but varies considerably in the rest of the cases. Thus, the native speakers use the *I* perspective mainly to relate their *personal experience* to the audience where two basic sub-cases may be observed:

a) the speaker refers to his/her immediate teaching/organisational responsibilities at his/her university or elsewhere, as in Example 1:

(1)   My particular job – I am responsible for in-sessional courses. That means the students I do with are students ...

b) the speaker refers to a specific fact/example drawn from his/her professional experience, as in Example 2:

(2)   When I did that some years ago in Germany, someone came up to me and said: "I enjoyed your talk, but ...".

It should be noted here that in written English the share of this MSA is only 4% (see Vassileva 2000: 64), i.e. face-to-face interaction brings about a necessity for the speaker to 'situate' him/herself better within the context of both his/her topic and the immediate communicative situation. The Bulgarian presenters, on their part, seem hardly eager to resort to such personalisation and do it only in order to support their claims with problematic encounters in their own professional life, as illustrated in Example 3:

(3)   I have had problems with how to make tags part of the communicative competence of my students.

The *I* perspective is equally used in the presentation of the *analysis* itself in order to put forward *arguments* in favour of authorial claims. In native speakers' English this is primarily realised by means of so-called 'metadiscoursal verbs' – *suggest, try to show, argue, propose, consider, hypothesise, assume, suspect, claim, point out, seem,* etc. – (following Crismore 1989):

(4)   I'd like to suggest, however, I have been suggesting, that if one ... while the Bulgarians are much more direct:

(5)   My argument here is that ... .

Moreover, as Example 4 shows, the majority of metadiscoursal verbs carry the flavour of uncertainty concerning the truth value of the underlying proposition and function as mitigators, or downtoners, or, even, hedges that the speaker uses strategically in order to minimise the danger of being accused of either arrogance (if putting his claims in an explicitly straightforward and dogmatic manner) or incompetence (if other studies challenge or deny his results).

The expression of *personal view* is also equally pronounced in the two languages. In practically all cases the linguistic realisation is by means of so-called 'verbs of thinking and emotions' like *think, believe, feel, hope, fear*:

(6) (English) I think there are several reasons for this: [...].

Such phrases usually appear in the *Discussion* part of the research article with the exception of *I hope,* which is predominantly reserved for the *Conclusions* and reflects the relatively lower degree of commitment of speakers to the outcomes of their study. Although phrases of this type seem to signal authorial presence to the highest extent, some authors (Myers 1989, Hyland 1997) treat them as hedging devices, i.e. downtoners rather than boosters in the sense that they indicate authors' personal evaluation of a problem and the truth value of a proposition without any pretentions for expression of universal truths. Thus, by using such phrases, the author implies that this is the way s/he sees things and leaves the door open to other, alternative suggestions, interpretations and ideas. The pragmatic effect is therefore not so much that of mitigating claims, but rather of personalising them without necessarily involving the audience at all costs. The overuse of hedging devices, on the other hand, is considered by some linguists (Graefen 1997 among them) as endangering the author's prestige and reliability, especially in cases when s/he admits possible gaps in his/her knowledge of the problem.

The Bulgarian speakers under investigation seem also to demonstrate overuse of *advance organisers* and *statements of aims*, most probably due to the influence of the written 'standard' of English academic writing:

(7) (BE) I'll talk a little bit about the theoretical framework, then I'll show you ..., then I'll talk about ... .

One could treat this phenomenon as an interlanguage-specific overgeneralisation strategy, since such MSAs rarely appear in written Bulgarian academic discourse (see Vassileva 2000: 66). More or less the same could also be said about the MSAs of *focusing* and the introduction of *terminology and procedures*, especially as far as the latter is concerned, as Bulgarians, by tradition maintained through peer advice, feel much more secure in operating with a term after a strict definition of it rather than take it for granted that the audience shares their understanding of operative terminology:

(8) (BE) At this point I'll make some terminological clarifications: first, ...

Back organisers are utilised to the same extent in the two languages and are in themselves accounts of the various steps the particular study has gone through. They refer not so much to the results of the investigation – those are discussed in concluding statements – but point back to and remind the listener of the structure of the text itself. Back organisers usually appear before the concluding part of the presentation and, together with advance organisers, provide some kind of a structural frame of the text. They therefore serve as a means of creating textual cohesion and coherence, demonstrate author's consistency in building up the text and facilitate the listener in referring back to the text:

(9)   (English) Very briefly, let me summarise what I've been saying. I have made an attempt to ... .

The MSA of '*permission*' is much more frequent in native speakers' English and is obviously not sufficiently internalised by the Bulgarian speakers. This may be explained by the fact that there exists no one-to-one translation equivalent of this MSA in Bulgarian, so native language discourse transfer could be suspected:

(10) (English) Let me try to sum up what I think I've been saying.

Considering the context these MSAs appear in, I cannot fully agree with Swales *et al.* (1998) and accept such forms as 'imperatives'. I have tentatively called this micro-speech act 'permission' since, at least on the surface of discourse, it has the propositional structure of 'you – the audience – allow me to'. In practice, however, such phrases seem to have a purely organisational function, namely to draw the reader's attention to change of theme and signal a new direction of textual development. In other words, these forms are a specific type of advance organisers on a micro-textual level and facilitate the creation of textual cohesion and coherence.

I will not dwell in detail on the rest of the MSAs where the *I* perspective is also used, as these are cases with a relatively low frequency, but I have to mention the fact that even there BE shows deviations from the native speakers' standard.

5.3.   The **we** *perspective*

A comparison of the sub-headings used in Table 3 and Table 4 (the *we* perspective, below) would show certain similarities as well as differences. Instead of *reference to personal experience* we observe cases of *reference to common experience*, respectively *reference to terminology* is substituted by *reference to common knowledge* of theories and terminology, *permission* - by *invitation*. One additional category is also included here, namely the reference to *team work*. Moreover, it is only natural that the use of certain MSAs from the *we* perspective, such as the expression of *personal view* and *self-reference,* is avoided. At the same time, while *concluding statements* from the *we* perspective have their due place in written academic English (see Vassileva 2000), this function is fully dominated by the *I* perspective in paper presentations. However, most of the speech acts where either of the two personal perspectives is used coincide. This means that authors show a similar and more or less stable preference for realising certain rhetorical functions by more personalised linguistic resources.

	English	**Bulgarian English**
Analysis / Argumentation	48%	68%
Team work	36%	5%
Common knowledge	6%	4%
Common experience	5%	13%
Invitation	3%	4%
Aims / Advance organisers	1%	4%
Focusing	1%	1%
Exemplification	0%	1%
Total	100%	100%

Table 4: The *we* perspective.

One could, of course, argue here that this is a rather subjective categorisation which can hardly be objectively justified. It is true that the methodological problem of establishing the actual scope of the authorial *we* has not, unfortunately, been solved yet: "it is not quite clear whether *we* is used simply as a synonym of *I*, or whether it is an exponent of modern authors' bias to represent their own statements as belonging to a team" (Panther 1981: 235). All in all, there appear to be four possible interpretations of *we*: 1. the royal *we* (*pluralis majestiae*), 2. the humble *we* (*pluralis modestiae*), 3. the authorial *we* (*pluralis auctoris*) and 4. the collective *we* (*pluralis communis*). The collective *we* may further be differentiated into the 'inclusive' (in relation to the audience) or the 'exclusive' one. In the following, an attempt will be made to match the categories (contexts) used in the present study with these much more general cognitive categories in the two languages under discussion. I believe that, without a second thought, one can dismiss the interpretation of the academic *we* as equal to the royal *we* since, as Myers (1989: 4) points out, "the community as a whole is supposed to be vastly more powerful than any individual in it. Thus we will often see the relations between one researcher and another requiring little deference, while one researcher must always humble himself or herself before the community as a whole" – a fact practically all experienced researchers are aware of.

As the data shows, both languages demonstrate a well-pronounced preference for the *we* perspective where the speaker aims at engaging the audience in the process of *argumentation* (inclusive collective *we*). In written English meta-discoursal verbs like *hypothesise, assume, accept, consider, recognise*, etc. are, more often than not, accompanied by the most tentative modal verbs (*may, might*), which mitigates the author's demand for co-operation (Vassileva 2000). In conference language, however, this is not the case. Speakers' demand for co-operation is much stronger there and is linguistically realised by modal verbs like *need, have to, should*, thus expressing the author's conviction that there is an 'objective common necessity' for the audience to agree with his/her assumptions:

(11)   There is a distinction we have to make between [...] we need to make a connection to social practices ... .

As for BE, this MSA is more frequently used in the context of *data analysis* where the *we* perspective seems to be exclusive rather than inclusive:

(12)   In the meaning of the direct object we have neutralisation of this element ... .

The employment of *we* in native speakers' English is also very frequent in references to *team work*, which seems only natural:

(13)   When we try to produce testing procedures for those programmes, it's very important for us that we ...

BE, however, shows a considerably lower percentage of employment of this speech act. A very probable explanation of this, at first glance, strange phenomenon might be that nowadays team work in linguistics is not very widely spread in the country and researchers tend to focus on individual projects due to various (including financial) reasons.

Reference to *common knowledge* entails the case when the speaker expects the audience to share his/her understanding, interpretation and/or evaluation of certain background knowledge (inclusive *we*):

(14)   Since then, of course, we have seen the rise of contrastive rhetoric.

Reference to *common experience* comes second in frequency in BE, where speakers seem to prefer to include the audience in the discussion by relating the issue(s) under study to common, mainly practical experience, thus assuming shared problems and areas of interest:

(15)   Now, we see, and we look at this, and at the next conference we will have another perception of these things, we are not always conscious of this all our lives, ...

In native speakers' English these are cases of reference to common professional rather than every day-life experience:

(16) We don't tell our course participants what the faculty says about literature reviews ... .

Swales *et al.* (1998: 107) treat the phrase *let us* + *VP* in English as "the less imposing counterpart of the prototypical second person imperative" which shares "the illocutionary force of '*invitation*'" and, depending on the verb, may have various rhetorical functions like 'initiating a new subtopic', 'beginning the explanation of a point', 'initiating an argument' and the like. '*Invitation*' forms are mainly used to initiate a new topic:

(17) Let's take another case, the third one here.

This micro-speech act normally occurs in the main body of the text where argumentation takes place and is used by speakers as a milder substitute of the imperative *per se* that is perceived as demanding, presumptuous or imposing for the listeners, as implying that the speaker is in full control of the communicative situation and the audience has no choice but to comply.

The rest of the MSAs play a minor role in terms of frequency, so they will not be discussed here.

5.4. The you *perspective*

Table 5 presents the quantitative and qualitative characteristics of direct address by means of the *you* perspective:

	English	Bulgarian English
You = 'one'	41%	49%
Reference to OHP/Handouts	16%	11%
Common experience	12%	0%
Common knowledge	5%	13%
Commands	10%	5%
Reference to data	8%	5%
Exemplification	5%	7%
Focusing	1%	2%
Others	2%	8%
Total	100%	100%

Table 5: The *you* perspective.

As the data shows, *you* is most frequently used in the meaning of 'one' which, in general, is considered to be one of the means of 'objectivising' or 'depersonalising' academic discourse. Is this, however, exactly the case here? To my mind at least, the very fact that *you* is avoided in written communication, but so frequently employed as an alternative of 'one' in oral presentations, means that the author, although still trying to maintain a certain distance, also tries to engage the audience in the process of argumentation:

(18) (OBE) In other words, if you say you have read the book, you cannot continue with it, you go on ...

Next as to frequency comes the use of *you* in order to make the audience pay attention to data, examples, graphs, tables, etc., presented in the form of *handouts* or *OHP* transparencies:

(19) (OBE) So, if you look at those examples you'll see that ... .

I have to note here that almost all presenters (both native speakers and Bulgarians) resort to handouts and/or transparencies for illustrating their research results, approaches, sources, etc. Very few of them, however, present their studies without having a full text in front of them. This observation reveals that in spite of the attempts at visualisation, a higher degree of 'interactiveness' and a freer form of presentation, speakers still do not feel comfortable enough to fully 'improvise' their talks. On the other hand, as the example above demonstrates, requests to the audience to refer to visual materials are often realised in the form of a conditional sentence, which mitigates the speakers' demand for co-operation and functions as a hedging device.

The data concerning the use of *you* in *reference to common knowledge* and *reference to common experience* in the two languages shows that while the native speakers expect the audience to share the same professional experience, the Bulgarians assume shared knowledge:

(20) (English) You know that in order to advise their clients about what might be the best mode of action, lawyers ...

(21) (BE) In contemporary English, as you know, there are two verbs that by definition ... .

The latter, I believe, is a perfect exponent of a Face Threatening Act – avoiding strategy on the part of the speaker who presupposes and explicitly states the existence of common knowledge and beliefs which are shared by the audience. In contrast to written discourse, where preference is given to the 'we' perspective in this case (see Vassileva 2000), in oral communication the author takes advantage of the real time face-to-face communication context to address his/her audience directly.

Under '*commands*', that are much more frequent in native speakers' English, I have included imperative sentences which are practically non-existent in written communication, but are usually used in conference presentations in order to attract the attention of the audience to a particular fact:

(22) Notice what I'm saying!

or to introduce arguments:

(23) OK, consider the possibility of X, so, ... Suppose that ... .

Reference to data and *examples* by addressing the audience directly is actually a sub-case of *reference to handouts* and/or *transparencies*, where presenters do not explicitly mention the source, as it is clear from the context of the current situation:

(24) (English) If you look at the data, then you discover that the metaphors are ... .

The MSA of *focusing* is very rarely realised from the *you* perspective. Under '*others*' I have included here cases of direct address that appear mostly in BE and are difficult to classify under any of the above-mentioned categories. This, for example, is a case when the speaker says,

(25) So you can see what I'm aiming at.

at a point when, judging by the expressions on the faces of the listeners, none was really able to follow the presenter's line of thought (this fact became clear in the subsequent discussions).

5.5. Other means of speaker-audience interaction

In what follows I will present the rest of the linguistic resources used for the realisation of speaker-audience interaction as listed in Table 2.

5.5.1. Rhetorical questions

Surprisingly, a rhetorical strategy well-known from ancient times, namely the use of *rhetorical questions*, is rather infrequent in conference presentations in both languages. The question 'why' remains open, i.e. whether this is a typical characteristic feature for the discourse of linguistics in English, or a more or less universal property of conference language in other fields of science as well. Rhetorical questions, as a rule, are used to present a problem to be followed by a solution suggested by the speaker:

(26) (English) What is the stylistic effect of beginning a sentence like that?

What I call here '*extra-textual reference*' is a really interesting phenomenon and encompasses a variety of cases where the speaker addresses the audience in various ways seemingly not in relation to the presentation itself, but actually employing some kind of a rhetorical strategy aimed at winning the audience's good disposition and insuring against possible future criticism:

(27) (BE) Please excuse my voice, I'll do my best ...

(28) (BE) So, I am the last one. This reminds me that I should thank you for being here. I'd like to make clear that this (paper) is an appeal to help. So please have mercy. (a very young presenter)

The native speakers investigated here often refer to sources of materials, contacts, etc., or simply use the occasion for promoting products/publications of their own:

(29) If you are interested in this, you can't buy it here, you should be able to look at it on our web-site where you can also download it.

Sometimes they mention something related to the immediate context of the presentation:

(30) I started about quarter past, I will go on till eleven or so, I tell you that now so you can dispose yourselves and if you need to leave you can leave, OK?

Jokes and *story-telling* elements (practically non-existent in BE) are of basically two types. They are either directly related to the immediate context of what is being said, as in Example 31, or relate indirectly to some 'practical background' of an investigation, as illustrated in Example 32:

(31) Notice what I'm saying – it's about the time – this was an intertextual insertion, it's not a remark, and linked to a discursive practice which is called 'knocking the professions when you have the chance'.

(32) I was talking to my uncle, my mother's brother, who was born in the North of the country in ... .

The latter type usually appears in the form of an 'everyday-life story' that is, assumingly, related to the issues under consideration and is supposed to 'bring the discussion down to Earth', so to say, as well as to point to the practical importance of the problem. The very existence of such story-telling elements is in contradiction with the widely accepted belief that these do not belong to the language of science. In fact, this has been formulated by Weinrich (1989: 135) as one of his 'bans': "Ban: a scientist does not tell stories". Clyne (1991, 1993) treats such excurses as deviations from the straight line of development of the research article. In spite of that, however, it appears that story-telling in the language of linguists is not a taboo and, to my mind at least, contributes to the creation and maintenance of a friendlier, more egalitarian relationship between the speaker and audience.

Deixis concerns here direct reference to data on primarily OHP transparencies:

(33) I will particularly focus here on this area. (the speaker points)

This is, of course, only possible in case the speaker is using transparencies with which s/he operates actively, that is, they are not just exhibition pieces left there for the audience to try and fight its way through. Since the latter is, unfortunately, frequently the case in BE, this accounts for the low frequency of employment of deixis there.

While *personal reference* (the case when the speaker refers directly to him/herself) is rather seldom in native speakers' English and non-existent in BE, *reference to other presenters* within the same event is used to create a feeling of belonging, of common interests, but may also be treated as a Face Threatening Act – avoidance strategy in cases when confirmation is pursued, especially when outstanding names in the field are concerned:

(34) I hope that nothing I've said this afternoon here is inconsistent with what Christopher (Candlin) was saying this morning.

Another phenomenon to be mentioned here is the use of a large number of fillers for the purpose of gaining time. They occur typically in oral presentations. The most frequent fillers are: *now, you know, so, OK, right, well,* where individual speakers show different preferences for one or another of them. They are far more frequently observed in BE where they are actually exponents of hesitation and insecurity rather than a kind of 'frame' (which is the case in native speakers' English). It is also interesting that almost all Bulgarian presenters use repetitively one and the same filler, i.e. variety is seldom observed in the speech of a single person. This fact might also be considered to be a 'deviation from native-speaker standards'.

6. Conclusions

To sum up, I would like to emphasise the following: Bulgarian linguists who use English as a means of international communication employ far fewer means of direct speaker-audience address and in spite of the more or less similar internal distribution of those means still demonstrate a high degree of variation in their use in individual micro-speech acts. Most of the 'deviations' from native speaker standards can be traced to native-language rhetorical patterns of discourse organisation and presentation since the Bulgarian standard of academic writing still resist complying with the new tendencies dictated by the Anglo-American rhetoric. One of the reasons is that this standard has formed over the years under the dominant influence of Russian, French and German, where there is a more or less stable tendency of avoidance of scientific discourse personalisation. Another aspect to be mentioned here is the notable difference between the educational systems in Bulgaria and in the English-speaking world. The focus in Bulgaria is on reproductive forms of both teaching and evaluation, and good writing is considered to be more of a personal talent than something liable to instruction. Thus, as far as academic writing is concerned, no courses are offered at Bulgarian universities as yet, and novices are compelled to learn from reading, from practice, by copying the style of experienced colleagues, and the like. The teaching of rhetorical skills necessary for oral presentations of any kind, on its part, is practically non-existent either in the mother tongue or in any foreign language.

Hence, it was surprising to find that Bulgarian authors, at least in the field under investigation, have, to a large extent, mastered the Anglo-American standard of interpersonal communication in academic discourse. The deviations that are observed could hardly be expected to hamper cross-cultural comprehension in spite of the great differences between Bulgarian and English academic rhetoric. Further research concerning the psychological and psycholinguistic aspects of the phenomenon is necessary in order to confirm or reject the hypothesis suggested here. Whether the strict adherence to the Anglo-American rhetorical patterns should be evaluated positively, however, is another question - i.e. whether this would not lead to intellectual unification to the point of loosing cultural identity. For the time being I will leave this question open, but I would personally rather side with those pleading for tolerance and mutual understanding of intercultural specificities.

The latter brings us back to the more general question posed at the beginning of this paper, namely the validity of the traditional understanding of the notion of 'academic discourse community' as 'shared conventions'. This view has recently been challenged by Raforth (1990: 149, 145) who claims that

> the conventions of a discourse community, to the extent that they serve established interests of a particular group, are deliberately or tacitly imposed by members of this community on initiates or outsiders. ... Whose language is being shared, and what function does this sharing serve? Both questions address matters of personal and social identity, ownership and authority, dominance and subordination.

Thus, to my mind at least, in order to avoid the negative effects of such a position, and especially in view of the total dominance of English as the academic lingua franca, one should strive to reformulate the notion of 'academic discourse community' in the direction of shared *knowledge* conventions, views, ideas, etc., rather than shared deeply culturally bound *language* conventions. In other words, a switch within the paradigm of discourse community research is necessary, where the focus should prevailingly be on the *content* rather than on the *form* so that to account for the above-mentioned growing globalisation and multiplication of voices in the academia.

Such an approach would also lead to the re-establishment of the 'disappearing author' who would feel free and unrestricted to reveal his/her real cultural and social self without the fear of being ousted from the academic community and/or stigmatised as an outsider.

In view of the above, it seems inviable to make attempts at teaching the interpersonal linguistic means discussed here since, as Gee states (1990: 171) "people do not acquire Discourses by overt instruction and explanation". Instead, contrastive studies of this type should facilitate intercultural awareness raising and thus encourage variation and multiculturalism in the world of science.

References

Austin, J. 1962. *How to Do Things with Words*. Oxford: Oxfrod University Press.

Bakhtin, M. 1986. "The problem of speech genres and the problem of the text in linguistics, philology and the human sciences: An experiment in philosophical analysis." In C. Emerson & M. Holmquist (eds). *Bakhtin: Speech Genres and Other Late Essays*. Transl. V. McGee. Austin: University of Texas Press, 250-317.

Baumann, K. 1995. "Die Verständlichkeit von Fachtexten. Ein komplexer Untersuchungsansatz". *Fachsprache*, 3-4: 116-126.

Bizzell, P. 1982. "Cognition, convention and certainty: What we need to know about writing". *Pre/Text, 3*: 213-241.

Bizzel, P. 1990. "Beyond anti-foundationalism to rhetorical authority: Problems defining 'cultural literacy'". *College English, 52*: 661-675.

Clyne, M. 1991. "The sociocultural dimension: The dilemma of the German-speaking scholar". In Schröder, H. (ed). *Subject-Oriented Texts*. Berlin: de Gruyter, 49-67.

Clyne, M. 1993. "Pragmatik, Textstruktur und kulturellle Werte. Eine inter-kulturelle Perspektive". In H. Schröder (ed). *Fachtextpragmatik*. Tübingen: Gunter Narr, 3-18.

Crismore, A. 1989. *Talking with the Readers: Metadiscourse as Rhetorical Act*. New York: Peter Lang.

Ferrara, A. 1985. "Pragmatics". In T. van Dijk (ed.). *Handbook of Discourse Analysis, Vol. 2, Dimensions of Discourse*. London: Academic Press, 30-45.

Foucault, M. 1969. "What is an Author?" In D. Bouchard (ed.). *Language, Counter-Memory, Practice. Selected Essays and Interviews. 1977.* Oxford: Basil Blackwell, 113-138.

Gee, J. P. 1990. *Social Linguistics and Literacies: Ideology in Discourses.* London: Palmer.

Gnutzmann, C. & R. Lange. 1990. "Kontrastive Textlinguistik und Fachsprachenanalyse". In C. Gnutzmann (ed.). *Kontrastive Linguistik.* Frankfurt/M.: Peter Lang, 85-116.

Graefen, G. 1997. *Der Wissenschaftliche Artikel – Textart und Textorganisation.* Frankfurt/M.: Peter Lang.

Halliday, M.A. K.1985. *Introduction to Functional Grammar.* London: Edward Arnold.

Hartley, P. 1993. *Interpersonal Communication.* London: Routledge.

Hyland, K. 1997. "Scientific claims and community values: Articulating an academic culture". *Language and Communication,* 17: 19-31.

Kresta, R. 1992. "Interpersonale Sprachmittel in Fachtexten der Linguistik". *Deutsch als Fremdsprache,* 4: 239-244.

Myers, G. 1989. "The pragmatics of politeness in scientific articles". *Applied Linguistics,* 10, 1: 1-35.

Panther, K.-U. 1981. "Einige typische indirekte sprachliche Handlungen im wissenschaftlichen Diskurs". T. Bungarten (ed.), *Wissenschaftssprache.* München: Wilhelm Fink Verlag, 231-260.

Raforth, B. A. 1990. "The concept of discourse community: Descriptive and explanatory adequacy". In Kirsch, G. & D. Roen (eds), *A Sense of Audience in Written Communication.* London: Sage Publications.

Scollon, R. 1995. "Plagiarism and ideology: Identity in intercultural discourse". *Language in Society,* 24: 1-28.

Searle, J. 1969. *Speech Acts. An Essay in the Philosophy of Language.* Cambridge: Cambridge University Press.

Spillner, B. 1996. "Interlinguale Stilkontraste in Fachsprachen". In B. Spillner (ed.). *Stil in Fachsprachen.* Frankfurt/M.: Peter Lang, 105-137.

Swales, J. M., U. Ahmad, Y. Chang, D. Chavez, D. Dressen, & R. Seymour 1998. "Consider this: The role of imperatives in scholarly writing". *Applied Linguistics,* 19,1: 97-121.

Vassileva, I. 1998. "Who am I / who are we in academic writing?" *International Journal of Applied Linguistics,* 8,2: 163-190.

Vassileva, I. 2000. *Who is the Author? (A Contrastive Analysis of Authorial Presence in English, German, French, Russian and Bulgarian Academic Discourse).* Sankt Augustin: Asgard Verlag.

Weinrich, H. 1989. "Formen der Wissenschaftssprache". *Jahrbuch 1988 der Akademie der Wissenschaften zu Berlin,* 119-158.

Widdowson, H. 1984. *Explorations in Applied Linguistics, 2.* Oxford: Oxford University Press.

TITLES OF CONFERENCE PRESENTATION ABSTRACTS: A CROSS-CULTURAL PERSPECTIVE

Tatyana Yakhontova

The Ivan Franko L'viv National University, Ukraine

Abstract - Titles are significant components of research reporting, whether writing or presentation, 'responsible' for gaining readers'/listeners' attention and facilitating successful perception of any kind of research communication. The role of titles as the 'labels' of research texts that ensure their dissemination and circulation is further increasing in the information age and, thus, makes scientific titles an interesting and up-to-date object of inquiry. Despite their recognized importance, titles can still be considered an understudied area of discourse analysis; for example, possible culture-specific aspects of research titles have not been analyzed, although the influence of cultural contexts on research communication has already been demonstrated in the intensively developing field of contrastive rhetoric and textlinguistics. This paper investigates the differences in the titles of conference presentation abstracts in English versus two related Slavic languages (Ukrainian and Russian) in two fields of knowledge (linguistics and applied mathematics) and the possible correlation of such proclivities with the generic features of the conference abstract. The corpus analyzed consists of 400 titles equally representing the languages and fields of inquiry compared. The results of the investigation reveal some preferences of the titles of different language groups for various structural patterns; for example, the Ukrainian and Russian corpus includes a considerable amount of nominative constructions, whereas the English one obviously favors "colon"-titles. As to semantic and pragmatic features, the most conspicuous difference consists in the strong tendency towards 'interestingness' and self-promotionalism revealed in the English titles and in its notable absence in the Slavic group. This feature of titles as the structural elements of the conference presentation abstract seems to correlate with the major rhetorical characteristics of this genre in the languages compared. The revealed differences are explained in the paper from cognitive linguistic, socio-historical, and socio-ideological perspectives. The pedagogical implications of the explicit teaching of English titles to non-native speakers are also briefly discussed.

1. Introduction: Research titles as objects of investigation

Titles are significant components of research reporting, whether writing or presentation, 'responsible' for gaining readers'/listeners' attention and facilitating successful perception of any kind of research communication. The role of titles as the 'labels' of research texts that ensure their dissemination and circulation is further increasing in the information age and, thus, makes scientific titles an interesting and up-to-date object of inquiry. Furthermore, the investigation of structures and rhetorical functions of research titles may find its practical application in academic skills pedagogy by helping students to master the art of composing successful titles appropriate for their research themes, fields and academic communities.

Despite their recognized importance, titles can still be considered an understudied area of discourse analysis, although a certain amount of research into the different aspects of academic titles and the regularities of their production and functioning has already been elaborated. Dudley-Evans (1984), for example, described the processes of composing Master's thesis titles that take place in a team consisting of a student, a language teacher, and a subject lecturer. Swales focussed on the pedagogical importance of discussing the successes and failures in writing titles claiming that they may require "an inordinate amount of time, discussion and mental effort" and even have rather serious effects (1990: 222). He also recognizes that "there may be *national* rather than disciplinary propensities operating in this area" (1990: 223). Berkenkotter and Huckin (1995) point out that the structure and content of titles change with the flow of time. According to their data from the field of biology, titles are becoming more informative and tend to be syntactically fuller and semantically richer acquiring at the same time advertising, self-promotional features. Posteguillo (1997), in turn, detected serious cross-disciplinary variations in computer science titles versus titles in chemical engineering, business and applied linguistics.

Titles (of research papers in particular) have been also investigated on the basis of Russian and English languages in the Soviet school of functional stylistics and text linguistics. Within these analytical paradigms, titles have been treated as the tokens or "strong positions" (stylistically marked, relevant elements) of texts (Arnold 1990) that perform nominative, informative, persuasive and text-compressing functions (Kharchenko 1968). However, possible culture-specific aspects of research titles have not yet been analyzed, although the influence of cultural contexts on research writing, its essential elements and the structural parts of scholarly texts has already been demonstrated in the intensively developing field of contrastive rhetoric and textlinguistics (Bloch & Chi 1995, Clyne 1991, Connor 1996, Mauranen 1993, Vassileva 2000).

While the major focus of research has so far been on the titles of written work, oral forms of academic communication such as conference presentations nowadays play an equally important role in disseminating research findings within academic communities. Proceeding from these considerations, I will attempt to find out whether there are any special preferences for the structures of titles in different languages and cultures and whether such proclivities correlate with the generic features of the texts to which the titles belong. The investigation will compare the titles of conference presentation abstracts in English and two related Slavic languages (Ukrainian and Russian) in two fields of knowledge from both linguistic and sociocultural perspectives.

As important components of conference presentation abstracts, titles may be presumed to share with them certain pragmatic characteristics including those that are shaped culturally. This relationship seems to be rather subtle, as far as titles are concerned, since the 'universal' elements of various texts have strong common features and thus support the phenomenon of intertextuality — as recombination of genres and discourses in the process of historical development (Fairclough 1995:134) — more overtly than any other textual element. However, consideration of the correlation between the structure and rhetoric of abstract titles and the communicative features of the genre may help us better understand cultural preferences in the construction and use of titles. For the purposes of such a comparison, it is necessary to discuss the dominant features of the genre of the conference presentation abstract and the instances of their cultural variation.

2. The genre of the conference presentation abstract

The conference presentation abstract as a genre has been recently investigated by a number of researchers (Berkenkotter & Huckin 1995; Faber 1996; Swales 1996; Yakhontova 1998, in press). The major findings in this area are as follows.

According to Swales (1996), conference abstracts are stand-alone texts that enter into competition for the available slots on the conference program. In contrast to journal abstracts, which directly relate to the papers themselves, they are independent texts communicatively oriented at impressing a review committee and, further, appealing to a broader audience of professionals of the same area. Comparing conference abstracts with the so-called 'homotopic' journal ones, Swales and Feak note that the former are "much more of a 'selling job'" (1994: 214).

Berkenkotter & Huckin (1995) investigated a large number of abstracts submitted to a US conference (convention) on composition and communication and came to a conclusion that a dominant rhetorical feature of conference abstracts is 'interestingness' created by the appropriate selection of a topic, convincing problem definition and novelty. 'Interestingness' also implies the manifestation of the 'insider's' knowledge of terminology, special topoi, and references.

Faber (1996) extended this study by considering the abstracts submitted for the same conference from the viewpoint of their ability to recognize and replicate the forms of discursive power developed within the conference organization. He arrived at a conclusion that along with the several distinguishing discursive features associated with the convention, the abstracts possess formal qualities relating them to the hybrid genres that combine elements of self-promotion and job application. In fact, all the above-mentioned authors are consistent in treating conference presentation abstracts as types of promotional texts discursively constructed in an interesting and appealing way.

Nevertheless, it has been shown (Yakhontova, in press) that the genre of the conference abstract, or rather some of its rhetorical features, are subject to certain cultural variation. The comparison of English versus Ukrainian and Russian abstracts in the field of discourse analysis and testing has revealed certain essential differences that concern the above-mentioned notion of 'interestingness' and the variability of how this is created in the texts. While the discourse in English abstracts is framed "in an interesting and interestingly problematic way" (Swales 1996: 47) – with preliminary scene-settings that show the importance and novelty of the research, intriguing conclusive parts, ready-friendly format and appealing language – formal, serious, and article-like Ukrainian and Russian abstracts look rather uninteresting, at least to an outsider. The promotional English texts do their 'selling job', whereas their Slavic counterparts seem to appeal to their addressees by 'telling'. It is natural to assume, therefore, that the titles of abstracts may be also sensitive to the rhetorical feature of 'interestingness' and its reflection on their structure and content. The data and their discussion below will provide some further insights into this assumption.

3. Corpus and the approach to its analysis

The cross-cultural investigation of the titles of conference presentations abstracts has been carried out on the basis of the titles of abstracts belonging to humanities and hard sciences – linguistics and applied (industrial) mathematics (for the names and dates of the conferences, see the Appendix). The choice of these fields has been motivated by the following reasons.

To begin with, different fields have their own writing conventions (that are likely to have impact upon titles) and, therefore, the investigation of one field will not yield generalizable enough results. At the same time, cultural contexts may be presumed to influence writing in all spheres to a greater or lesser degree. From the viewpoint of the validity of results, therefore, the consideration of a larger number of fields would be more desirable. However, the choice of the above-mentioned areas (made with due regard for the task of representing quite different fields of inquiry) as well as the amount of data, was determined by the limited availability of the texts themselves. As Swales (1996: 46) notes, the conference abstract is one of those 'occluded' academic genres, neither highly visible nor that easily obtainable, exemplars of which rarely appear in print.

The corpus analysed consists of 400 titles chosen at random. Half of these are linguistic titles and the other half are mathematical ones. Out of each 200, 100 are written in English (by native speakers), and 100 in Slavic languages; of these, approximately 50% are written in Russian, and 50% in Ukrainian. Both languages, although lexically different, have close syntactic features and, more importantly, share common rhetorical patterns developed under the influence of certain socio-historical circumstances. This allows us to consider them as one group, at least in contrast to English titles.

While the corpus is relatively small, quantitative data, however modest, are necessary as far as they verify the observations and intuitive assumptions of the investigator. In this particular analysis, the validity of generalisations to be stated is also supported by the choice of titles belonging to two different fields and, furthermore, to two fields of enquiry that methodologically oppose each other – more theoretically oriented (linguistics) and applied (industrial mathematics).

In addition, it is necessary to note that there may be other research limitations caused by the selected material and the specificity of its cultural contexts. The titles chosen for the analysis belong to the abstracts of individual accepted panel presentations. However, the Slavic abstracts have been written for a national (bilingual) audience in Ukraine, while the English texts available for analysis address an international audience. Overall, the conventions of research writing in the English language seem to be more diverse due to certain differences between British and North American writing traditions, whereas the academic culture in Ukraine ideologically and physically isolated for many years from any outer influences still preserves certain discursive homogeneity (despite the use of two languages). Additionally, the choice of certain title structures and their semantic and rhetorical features may depend upon the professional status of a research writer (on whether, for example, he/she is a scholar with an established reputation or a beginner). For the purposes of this study, these differences arising from certain historical and socio-professional circumstances were not taken into consideration. The general approach to the comparative analysis of titles is, therefore, predominantly qualitative, and aimed at revealing the broad regularities in their structures that will be treated in this paper only as the *prevailing culture-specific tendencies.*

The syntactically determined structure of a title has been chosen as a major parameter for comparison. After the patterns had been identified, all titles were divided into the groups with respect to the languages and fields of knowledge they represent. The titles of the coinciding dominant groups in English and Slavic languages were additionally compared. Further, the semantic features of the titles were analysed and appropriate comparisons were made.

4. Results: Structural types of titles and their semantic peculiarities in English versus Ukrainian and Russian languages

4.1. Types of title structures revealed

According to their syntactic structure, the titles in both languages and fields fall into six groups. A distinctly identifiable character of these five types of constructions allows us to treat them as the models of titles that have been crystallized in the course of historical development and may be lexically 'filled in' in various ways.

1. Nominative constructions (a noun/nominalised verb phrase in the nominative case). This group includes some sub-types that will be exemplified and discussed further.

2. Verbal constructions (containing a non-finite form of a verb as a bearing element), e.g. 'Solving short wave problems using special finite elements'.

3. Incomplete sentences modified by the prepositions 'on' (Ukrainian *pro*, Russian *o, ob*), 'to', 'towards' (Ukrainian *do*, Russian *k*), e.g. 'On 'with' in language acquisition'.

4. One-sentence constructions (that is, titles consisting of complete sentences of different syntactic types), e.g. 'Does cognitive linguistics live up to its name?'

5. 'Colon' constructions consisting of two parts (either nominative/verbal constructions or sentences) separated by a colon, e.g. 'The rotor-tip vortex: structure and interactions'.

6. Other types of two-part constructions consisting of the parts of different syntactic types (nominative or verbal constructions, various types of sentences), which are separated by an interrogation mark, comma, semicolon or dash. As far as their total number is small, they will be

regarded as one group; e.g. 'Beyond BE and HAVE – foundational semantic concepts and the grammaticalization of auxiliaries'.

The last two title models may be called compound, while the first three are syntactically simple.

The number of titles in English and Slavic languages representing each model in two fields is shown in Table 1.

Titles	Nominative constructions	Verbal constructions	Incomplete sentences	One-sentence constructions	'Colon' constructions	Two-part constructions	Total
English titles (linguistics)	55	3	1	3	34	4	100
English titles (applied mathematics)	75	9	0	3	9	4	100
Total (number/ percent)	**130/65**	**12/6**	**1/0.5**	**6/3**	**43/21.5**	**8/4**	**200/ 100**
Slavic titles (linguistics)	75	—	14	1	8	2	100
Slavic titles (applied mathematics)	93	—	4	—	3	—	100
Total (number/ percent)	**168/84**	**0/0**	**18/9**	**1/0.5**	**11/5.5**	**2/1**	**200/ 100**

Table 1: Structural types of titles

As can be seen, nominative constructions dominate both groups. However, among the Slavic titles their prevalence is overwhelming (a total of 168) comprising 84%. In the English group, their number (130) constitutes only 65%. In contrast, the average percentage of colon titles for two fields – 21.5% (forty-three occurrences) is essentially higher in English titles than in Slavic ones with their low 5.5% (11 occurrences). At the same time, one may notice a considerable cross-disciplinary variation in the use of these types of constructions: both English and Slavic titles in linguistics favour nominative and colon constructions more than their counterparts in mathematics.

The titles based on a construction with a verbal are entirely absent from the Ukrainian and Russian groups, while they are represented (with 12 occurrences) in the English group. One-sentence constructions, though not numerous, also prevail in the English group (6 against 1). Another notable difference consists in the use of prepositional structures (incomplete sentences) that make up average 9% of Slavic titles (18 occurrences), whereas there is only one such a construction in the English group. Two-part constructions, which are infrequent in the data, are more numerous among English titles – 8 occurrences against 2.

As seen, English titles have revealed six models across two fields and thus appear to be more diverse than the Ukrainian and Russian ones that represent fewer models, especially in the field of mathematics. However, the most important conclusion that can be drawn here is that within each language group there is obviously enough similarity in the structures that seem to over-ride the proclivities of the fields.

A closer look at nominative titles and their structures reveals three variations:

1. Nominative constructions with one noun as a principal element that can be extended by attributes, adverbial groups, or prepositional objects, e.g. 'Network models for workforce allocation'.

2. Nominative constructions with two or more nouns as principal elements that can be extended by attributes or adverbial groups, e.g. 'Cultural and conceptual relativism, universalism, and the politics of linguistics'.

3. Nominative constructions with the conjunction 'as' (Ukrainian *yak*, Russian *kak*) introducing an apposition to the principal noun, e.g. 'Writing as language'.

The number of occurrences of these constructions is shown in Table 2. Both the English and Slavic titles exhibit preference for the nominative constructions with one noun as a principal element (92, or 70% of English nominative titles versus 138 occurrences, or 82% of Ukrainian and Russian similar constructions). However, it is important to be aware of the differences across the fields: mathematical nominative titles are much more frequently based on one noun than the nominative headings in linguistics. In the field of linguistics, the essentially larger number (as compared to Slavic titles) of English nominative constructions has two nouns as principal elements (26 versus 9). The Ukrainian and Russian headings, in contrast, show much stronger preference for the use of the 'as'-construction (16 occurrences in both disciplines against 6 instances in the group of English nominative titles).

Titles	Constructions based on one noun	Constructions based on two or more nouns	'As'-constructions	Total
English titles (linguistics)	24	26	5	55
English titles (applied mathematics)	68	6	1	75
Total (number/ percent)	**92/70**	**32/25**	**6/5**	**130/100**
Slavic titles (linguistics)	51	9	15	75
Slavic titles (applied mathematics)	87	5	1	93
Total (number/ percent)	**138/82**	**14/8**	**16/10**	**168/100**

Table 2: Types of nominative constructions

4.2. Summary of structural features of titles in two language groups

Summing up, the following major conclusions about the differences in the structure of Ukrainian and Russian versus English research titles can be formulated.

1. Ukrainian and Russian titles show more preference for nominative constructions.

2. English titles show much more preference for 'colon' structures.

3. In both language groups, there are constructions that are not found (or found occasionally) in the compared group: prepositional constructions (incomplete sentences) present in the group of Slavic titles do not actually occur among the English titles; verbal and one-sentence constructions appearing in the English group are almost absent (with insignificant exceptions) from the Slavic group.

4. Ukrainian and Russian nominative titles tend to use 'as'-constructions much more frequently.

5. In the field of linguistics, English nominative titles are more frequently based on two nouns as principal elements.

6. English research titles are more diverse from the viewpoint of their structural variation.

4.3. Semantic features of titles in the languages compared

Considering the semantic features of the titles, I will compare how and to what extent the titles in English and Slavic languages indicate the theme and scope of research to be presented at a conference as well as the generic feature of 'interestingness' they possibly reveal. To simplify the discussion, the findings will be presented according to the fields, although the main research focus remains, as in the previous section, on the relevant differences in the languages compared. These differences will be summarized in 4.3.3.

4.3.1. Semantic features of titles in the field of linguistics

The largest sub-group of linguistic titles, nominative constructions, indicates the theme and scope in two ways depending on their structure. The nominative titles with two or more principal elements (nouns) in both language groups do not show any noticeable differences. The nouns in these constructions indicate two themes that are actually related (often the first noun indicates the field, while the second one – the sub-field or the theme belonging to it with some additional specifications), or, in many cases, the themes that are claimed to be shown by an author as related (this, however, is clear only for an insider). In the latter case, the title emphasizes the novel character of the research or the contribution to the field indicated by the first noun, for example:

(1)   'Linguists and public linguistics in the 21st century',

or:

(2)   *Yazykovaya nominatsiya i kulturnyje stereotipy* ('Language nomination and cultural stereotypes').

However, as mentioned above, such titles appear in the English corpus two and a half times as often as in the Slavic group. At the same time, 'as'-constructions, which are prominent in the Ukrainian and Russian group and underrepresented in the English one, produce a somewhat comparable effect, e.g.:

(3)   Sobstvennoye imia kak komponent obrazno-khudozhestvennoj tkani literaturnogo
       proizvedeniya ('Proper name as a component of image and artistic systems of a literary
       text').

The part of this title type introducing an apposition to the principal noun
indicates a new aspect of a research theme or its rethinking and so emphasizes
the novel character of the investigation.

The constructions with one noun as a principal element differ in some respects
in the language groups compared. In the English titles of this kind, the noun
(usually modified by an adjective) indicates the theme of the presentation, while
the attributive or adverbial groups following it point at the scope of the study,
e.g.:

(4)   'Prosodic patterns in African American English'.

Similar headings can be found among Ukrainian and Russian titles, although
they often show preference for a much wider use of adjectives attributed to both
principal and secondary nouns. Often, a principal noun is modified by two
adjectives:

(5)   Nominativnoye I referentnoye razvertyvaniye syntaksicheskikh tsepochek ('Nominative
       and referential expansion of syntactical chains').

Such titles foreground not so much the theme of the research itself, but rather
emphasize its aspects (new or important) investigated by the author who, thus,
contributes to the field or research theme.

A similar rhetorical effect can be found in the group (consisting of 9 titles) of
one-noun nominative constructions in Slavic languages that have, as a principal
element, the words *osoblyvosti* (Ukr.) – *osobennosti* (Rus.) ('peculiarities',
'features'), *rol'* (Ukr.and Rus.) ('role'), *problemy* (Ukr. and Rus.) ('problems'), or
the words that denote the character of research, for example *doslidzhennia*
(Ukr.) – *issledovaniye* (Rus.) ('investigation'), e.g.:

(6)   *Vyyavlennia osoblyvostej diyeslivnoyi chasovoyi systemy frantsuz'skoyi movy pry analizi
       ofitsiynykh dokumentiv* ('The investigation of the peculiarities of the French language
       tense system in the analysis of official documents').

This example that may be regarded as an extreme case of this title type has,
along with the word *osoblyvostej* ('peculiarities'), even two words specifying the
character of the research (*vyyavlennia* – 'investigation' and *analizi* – 'analysis').

It should also be added that the constructions with the word 'problem(s)' as a
bearing element are, according to my observations, extremely popular in the
Ukrainian and Russian titles of various fields, especially in humanities. This

may be attributed to the key pragmatic role played by the word 'problem' in Ukrainian and Russian research writing, where a particular study is usually presented as a problem which is to be tackled or solved by the author.

In contrast, such types of one-noun nominative structures are almost absent (with the one exception) from the English group. As compared to another types of nominative titles, they are more semantically 'closed', in so far as they denote a specified type and theme of an investigation, while, for example two-noun structures leave space for conjectures of a potential reader about the character or details of the research.

The same can also be said about the Ukrainian and Russian titles with the pattern 'preposition *do, k* + dative case of *pytannia* (Ukr.) – *voprosy* (Rus.) / *problemy* (Ukr., Rus.) '(Towards the question/problem of ...), or 'preposition *pro* (Ukr.) – *o* (Rus.) + prepositional case of a noun' ('On ...). For example:

(7) *K voprosu o reforme nemetskoj orfografiji* ('Towards the question of the reform of German orthography');

or:

(8) *O nekotorykh nominatsiyakh v kontseptosfere russkogo yazyka* ('On some nominations in the conceptual sphere of the Russian language').

This model, absent (with the one exception) from the English group, has an impersonal character and presents a particular study as a contribution to the research theme or problem that is assumed to be known for the members of the research community. In Example 8, the word *nekotorykh* ('some') – another popular element in Slavic headings – specifies the scope of the research adding a less assertive intonation to the formulation of the title.

Another peculiar feature of the Ukrainian and Russian titles of this type is a rather detailed description of the research they provide in many cases. This is achieved (in six titles) through an additional specification given in parentheses, e.g.:

(9) *Do pytannia pro utvorennia neologizmiv u suchasnij ispans'kiy movi (na osnovi tekstiv z informatyki)* ['Towards the question of the formation of neologisms in modern Spanish (on the basis of the texts on informatics)'].

The parenthetical indication of the scope of research demonstrated by the above example can also be occasionally found in nominative constructions, e.g.:

(10) *Leksychna structura tekstu (na prykladi opovidannia E.T. Hoffmana 'Pishchanyj cholovik'* ['The lexical structure of text (by the example of the short story 'Sandman' by E.T. Hoffmann)'].

To a certain extent, these constructions may be compared to 'colon' structures in the sense that they both separate ideas in the relation of 'general-specific'. However, prepositional titles emphasise more the generalizing aspect of research (by enclosing in parentheses a more specific part and thus attributing to it secondary importance), while 'colon' constructions foreground both aspects of investigation.

The differences observed in the semantics and rhetoric of 'colon' titles are indeed remarkable. The infrequent Ukrainian and Russian titles of this type strictly follow a 'general-specific' pattern with the first part indicating a research area and the second one naming an object/aspect of investigation, both parts having the form of nominative constructions:

(11) *Angliys'ka ekonomichna terminologiya: problemy pravyl'nogo rozuminnia ta perekladu* ('English economics terminology: problems of adequate understanding and translation').

The English titles observing the same pattern nevertheless show a much greater variety in the structures of their parts. Within this set of titles, we may note all three types of nominative constructions described above plus a new model consisting of two nouns coordinated by conjunctions *or* and *versus*, e.g.:

(12) 'Heaviness and Difficulty: 'Image content' vs. 'response content' in conceptual metaphors',

(13) 'Adjectives or Pronoun: The status of prenominal possessives',

as well as the constructions with verbals, questions and relative clauses:

(14) 'Defining linguistics: E.H. Sturtevant and the early years of the Linguistic Society of America',

(15) 'English dialectology: where to in the year 2000?',

(16) 'Semantic overlap and spatial blending: How different conjunctions can (sometimes) build the same mental spaces'.

The titles representing this model are obviously longer and indicate content in more detail than their Slavic counterparts. These English titles frequently specify not only the object of investigation (in an after-colon part of a title), but also the type or aspect of the research as in the following example:

(17) 'Case semantics as an illustration of threshold phenomena in language: the case of the genitive'.

Here the first part of the title redefines a research area from a new angle of vision.

However, the most dramatic difference between English and Ukrainian-Russian 'colon' titles consists in presence of vivid outward features of 'interestingness' in the English group and their absence in rhetorically neutral Slavic constructions of this type. The English 'colon' titles obviously have an 'eye-catching', appealing and therefore self-promotional character, which is created by: i) the structural variety of the constitutive parts of titles, as shown in (12)-(16), ii) the emphasis on a novel character of the research to be presented (as in Example 16), and iii) the use of different stylistic devices, e.g.:

(18) 'Philistines, Barbarians, Aliens, et al: cognitive semantics in political 'otherness'',

or

(19) 'A new metaphor for metaphor: evidence for a single dynamic metaphorical category'.

The interestingness of these titles is created, in case of (18), by the biblical allusions, and in (19) – by the tautological repetition of the word 'metaphor' resulting in the interplay of meanings that attracts the attention of a reader. Additionally, if we have another look at Examples 12 and 13, we may notice that the opposition (in Example 11) and possible choice (in Example 12) of linguistic notions contributes to the expressiveness of the titles by making them slightly intriguing, this stylistic effect being reinforced by the periphrasis in (12) based on the use of semantically related abstract nouns.

Nothing similar, however, can be found in the Ukrainian and Russian 'colon' constructions. The only exception is one quite 'English-looking' title based on a mythological allusion:

(20) *Parfyans'ki strily intertekstualnosti: pole tekstiv Vilyama Sefaera* ('Parthian shafts of intertextuality: the field of texts by William Safire').

Another Slavic title that differs from the rest of the group – a one-sentence construction – possesses not so much interestingness but rather the rhetorical strength of explicit persuasion:

(21) *"Neponyatnoye – ne znachit "plokhoye"* ('"Incomprehensible" does not mean "bad"').

At the same time, the interestingness of the English titles under investigation is supported additionally by three one-sentence and four two-part constructions (the latter being very close to 'colon' structures as to the type of meaning and rhetorical effects), e.g.:

(22) 'Does cognitive linguistics live up to its name?';

(23) 'When the mind trips into the wrong language';

(24) 'Why can't the dog bark the postman hoarse? On fake objects in resultative constructions.'

The impressive structural form of these titles (in the form of questions in (22) and (24), or of a sentence, as in Example 23) obviously aims at gaining the reader's attention. A certain dynamism to the English corpus is also added by three titles with the non-finite verbal forms, one of them being especially intriguing due to the eye-catching form of presenting unusual content:

(25) 'Relatively speaking, turning Americans into absolute Tenejapans'.

It is worth mentioning that in these and similar constructions, interestingness seems to outweigh the informative aspects of a title.

4.3.2. Semantic features of titles in the field of applied mathematics

The titles in the field of applied mathematics reveal a somewhat different picture, although the general tendencies indicative of the features of both language groups can still be observed here. For example, five English titles display the signs of interestingness similar in their nature to the described above:

(26) 'Why bubbles rise anomalously in water with air present',

(27) 'Stirred, but not shaken, mixing the stretched and torn'.

Example (26) is attractive to a reader because of its inquisitive character expressed via the sentence with an interrogative meaning, while (27) is appealing due to the allusive reference to the popular J.B. film series.

In contrast, the Slavic titles avoid any self-advertising, promotional features, although this corpus shows the limited presence (as shown in Table 1) of prepositional structures (syntactically incomplete sentences), which are found neither in English titles in linguistics nor in mathematics, e.g.:

(28) *Pro odyn pidkhid do pobudovy variatsijnogo formulyuavannia zadach teplomasoperenosu* ('On one approach towards the variational formulation of the problems of heat and mass transfer').

These four constructions present in the Slavic mathematical corpus share semantic and pragmatic characteristics with their linguistic counterparts.

The English 'colon' titles and two-part constructions (the total number of which is four times greater than that of the Slavic titles of this type) do not possess any additional features of interestingness and do not seem to differ very much semantically from their few Ukrainian and Russian counterparts, e.g.:

(29) 'The rotor-tip vortex: structure and interaction.'

(30) *Nelokalna teoriya pruzhnosti: problemy ta perspektyvy* ('Non-local theory of elasticity: problems and prospects').

The nominative titles that dominate the applied mathematics group have much more proximity in their structure and semantics. The overwhelming majority of them (as seen in Table 2) are based upon one noun modified by an attribute(s) that indicate rather specifically the theme of the presentation, while the adverbial groups or prepositional objects following the principal noun point at the scope of research, e.g.:

(31) 'Quantitative measures of topological complexity for fluids and magnetic fields',

(32) *Heterogenni matematychni modeli v chyslovomu analizi konstruktsij* ('Heterogenous mathematical models in the numerical analysis of constructions').

Both English and Slavic titles similarly tend to be informative and often indicate precisely the character of the research to be presented. This is achieved, in particular, by the use of such nouns as 'application', 'method', 'approach', 'investigation' in the role of the principal elements, e.g.:

(33) 'Applications of cohesive theories to dynamic fracture and fragmentation',

(34) *Primeneniye teoriji potentsiala v zadachakh gidromekhaniki so svobodnoj granitsej* ('Application of the theory of potential in the problems of hydromechanics with a free boundary').

However, this is more characteristic of the Slavic mathematical (and also linguistic, as it was shown above) headings, thirty of which reveal this model, while it is found in twelve English mathematical titles only. In addition, another four Slavic titles use the word *osoblyvosti* (Ukr.) – *osobennosti* (Rus.) ('peculiarities'), which specify research by emphasising the aspects/features investigated:

(35) *Osoblyvosti proektuvannia ta optymizatsiyi obolonkovykh pruzhnykh elementiv vibrozakhysnykh system* ('The peculiarities of designing and optimization of the shell elastic elements of the systems protecting against vibration').

The nominative constructions based on two or more nouns are not numerous in either group. Those analysed differ to some degree – compare Examples 36 and 37:

(36) 'Mathematics of impact and friction problems',

(37) *Nelinejnoye deformirovaniye i ustojchivost' sfericheskikh obolochek pri termosilovom nagruzheniyi* ('Non-linear deformation and the stability of spherical shells under thermal and force loading').

Five (out of a total of 6) of the English titles of this type follow the pattern shown in (36). As with the linguistic titles, they indicate two (or more) research themes or areas, while all their Slavic counterparts (5 in number) indicate two aspects of one topic. In rhetorical terms, English titles of this type produce a stronger impression, since, by relating different themes, they make more claims.

Another difference, which can be observed in the mathematical titles, is the presence of non-finite verbal forms in the English titles that emphasise the dynamic, process character of the research described in it. These forms are not found in the Slavic group, although somewhat comparable meanings are conveyed by the nominalised verbs used in twenty-seven headings of the Ukrainian-Russian group, cf.:

(38) 'Calculating contact pressures from strain and deflection',

(39) *Postroyeniye sootnoshenij svyazi dlia mnogofaznykh anizotropnykh tel* ('The building of the correlations of connection for multi-phase anisotropic bodies').

Such nominalised verbs are strongly characteristic of the Russian and Ukrainian grammatical systems.

4.4. Summary of semantic and pragmatic features of titles in the two language groups

As has been seen, the semantic and pragmatic features of the investigated titles are different in two language groups compared. The whole picture, however, is rather complex, mainly because opposed language groups contain structurally different sets of titles that nevertheless reveal similar pragmatic features, while those equivalent in their form may produce different rhetorical effects. For example, two-noun nominative English titles in linguistics that tend to reveal some claims for novelty or originality strongly outweigh their Slavic counterparts in number. However, the latter show rhetorical counterbalance in the presence of the 'as'-constructions (emphasising the new vision of a research theme), which are not widely represented in the English group. For the same reason, it is not possible to compare the amount of informative features in the two sets of titles. It is therefore important to be cautious in making inferences from the analysed data and in generalising the observations and findings. With this in mind, three major conclusions may be formulated, which are supported by quantitative data and qualitative interpretation:

1. The English titles demonstrate a tendency towards 'interestingness' and, consequently, advertising and self-promotionalism revealed via structural diversity and appropriate discursive features. The Ukrainian and Russian titles do not seem to show similar inclinations.

2. The English and Slavic titles in applied mathematics are closer to each other semantically and pragmatically than their counterparts in linguistics.

3. At the same time, the semantic and pragmatic features of the English titles on the one hand, and the Ukrainian and Russian headings on the other tend to reveal a cross-disciplinary character.

With a lesser degree of confidence, it may be stated that:

4. The Ukrainian and Russian titles tend more than the English headings to foreground the aspects of a research theme investigated (rather than the theme itself) and, thus, to emphasize the contribution of the author to a field or a research area.

5. The Ukrainian and Russian titles also tend to illuminate more the theoretical or general aspect of the investigation to be presented (at least, in the constructions of a certain structural type).

5. Discussion and tentative explanation of the observations and findings

The visible enough differences in the titles of the two groups compared and, more importantly, their cross-disciplinary character can be attributed to the influence of cultural factors. It may be assumed that certain structures of titles with inherent semantic and pragmatic features were developed in each culture under the impact of social and historical circumstances. In the process of cultural evolution, these structures have also been shaping the existing and developing writing traditions that, in turn, leads to their (structures) further crystallisation. On the other hand, a dynamic, developmental character of social and cultural practice constantly creates and maintains space for the modification of thinking and writing patterns and their linguistic representations, and, consequently, for the everlasting two-way process of the interaction of culture and discourse.

However, some differences in titles seem to reflect more visibly 'pure' cultural (social, ideological) factors, while the others may be deeper rooted in the languages themselves (although in this case they are not less 'cultural'). A rather subtle observation in this respect has been made, for example, by Nichols (1988) who claims that certain inventories of Russian grammatical categories are consistent with such features of Russian academic discourse as the uniform style, expository strategy consisting in generalisation followed by illustration, the use the depersonalising editorial *we* etc. Also, Kassevitch (1997) mentions the relationship between the rigid word order in the French language and a highly ordered, formally transparent and clear-cut structure of the French discourse. Taking up this joint linguistic and cultural perspective, it is possible, for instance, to assume that the absence of the titles based on the non-finite form of a verb in the Slavic group and their presence in the English one is due rather to the language-specific grammatical phenomena (to the ways they construe and present the content) than to the other cultural factors. Such an assumption, certainly, needs separate consideration with the involvement of appropriate frameworks and data from comparative linguistics. I would like to emphasise here only that the investigators in the field of contrastive rhetoric need to be aware of the interplay of the cultural influences of different 'depth', in particular, of the overlapping character of language and culture that has been recently emphasised by cognitive linguists (see, for example, Langacker 1994, Dirven & Verspoor 1998, or the work of Kassevitch (1997) mentioned above).

Considering the possible socio-historical explanations for the revealed differences, I will turn to the findings in the sphere of the cross-cultural comparative investigations of intellectual discourses. The majority focus on the differences between Anglo-Saxon versus European traditions of intellectual thinking and writing (Galtung 1985, Clyne 1991, Čmejrková & Daneš 1997, Duszak 1997) and provide generalized observations that may be extended to the case of titles. Thus, the features of European style include a special emphasis on theoretical issues, a relatively greater significance of the content of writing (than of its form) and rather weak interactive properties of written texts, whereas Anglo-Saxon culture shows an inclination towards empirical pursuits and an interactive, writer-responsible style of presentation. Some data from this research point to direct proximity between the Ukrainian-Russian and German academic writing, which, as the above mentioned authors claim, has had an impact on East European intellectualism, scholarship, and appropriate discourses due to the circumstances of historical development. For example, Čmejrková and Daneš (1997: 52) mention that the practice of using prepositional titles of "Towards/on ..." type in Russian in Czech corresponds with the German usage of the prepositions *über* and *zu*, and old Czech purists even demanded this prepositional form as a norm.

Apart from this instance of structural coincidence, we may trace other features in the group of the Slavic titles on the one hand, and in the English on the other that may be explained from the perspective adopted by the studies mentioned above. The theoretical profile of European culture may possibly reflect on such peculiarity of the Ukrainian and Russian titles as the foregrounding of the more general, usually theoretical, aspect of research and the inclusion of the empirical part into parentheses (which is the case of the same prepositional titles and some nominative constructions); the complete absence of such a pattern in the corpus of the English titles signals that it is quite alien for this group. Another important explanation that stems from the domain of culture may be connected with the degree of the *self-prominence* (Kassevitch 1997) typical of the specific culture. While some cultures tend to highlight the ego and favour individualism, others are inclined towards the lesser degree of self-prominence. The Anglo-Saxon culture known for its orientation towards individualism may be referred to the former, while the Slavic one may be treated as relatively more conformist. Respectively, it is possible to attribute the tendency to bring into prominence the novelty and originality of individual research in the English titles and to present the research as a modest contribution to the field in the Slavic ones to the impact of this significant cultural factor.

However, we need to be cautious when estimating the rhetorical effect of this or that writing pattern within or outside of its culture and discourse community. Čmejrková & Daneš (1997), for example, note that the prepositional titles of the "Towards/on ..." type have an obvious hedging effect consistent with the low assertiveness of Czech scientific style. Having no intention of contesting this observation, I would like only to mention that the degree of rhetorical strength of this title structure is not the same if viewed from different cultural standpoints. It is, certainly, a rhetorically low-key construction when it is treated against the background of the Anglo-Saxon writing preferences. But, from the insider's perspective, the claim of making a research contribution formulated explicitly and modestly at the same time, establishes or emphasizes the scholarly credibility of the author as a worthy member of his/her research community. As in this case, rhetorical persuasion often expands beyond the level of surface features and may exert its influence in various ways within different communities.

The same caution is necessary when we attempt to see any interconnection between the stereotypes of writing and the ideology prevailing in this or that society. As Fairclough (1995) states, dominant ideologies shape and determine the modes of discourse. Thus, the communist ideology, which suppresses the individual in favour of the communal, may be presumed to still leave imprints on the writing of scholars in Ukraine, where it dominated for more than seventy years. In particular, the rhetorical strategy of entitling research as a contribution that fits a broader scholarly context in a non-conflicting way may be attributed to this recent strong ideological influence. However, it is not always easy to distinguish between cultural and ideological factors that seem to be intertwined and entrenched in each other. For example, Vassileva (2000:108), who compared the 'I' versus 'we' perspective in the research texts produced by scholars of East and West Germany and did not find any differences, assumes that cultural traditions can be more powerful than ideologies.

Much more evident than all the previous mentioned factors are, however, the combined social and ideological influences (or their absence, as relevant for the case of titles) of the promotional culture and consumerism that has already become a distinctive feature of the Western society. I have already referred to Berkenkotter & Huckin (1995) who showed the increase of advertising features in research genres and their structural parts, including titles. Fairclough (1995) still more overtly describes the processes of marketisation and commodification that have started to affect discursive practices in different public spheres, including universities and academic conferences. This reality of the Western life most plausibly explains the specific 'eye-catching' features of the English titles that include claims for novelty and originality and versatile types of title constructions with the appealing and intriguing framing of discourse. Not less salient is the absence of such properties in the Slavic group, which may be unambiguously attributed to the weakness of market ideology influences in Ukraine and its scholarship. Again, there seem to be two reasons for this: one is more 'social' and more obvious, – it is limited market experience of the former Soviet states that affects academic spheres in these countries mostly indirectly (if at all!). Another explanation, which is more deeply entrenched in culture and history, is possibly connected with the elitist attitude in Ukraine and Russia towards science and scientific writing that have been barred from the 'lower' spheres of life and appropriate discourses and communication styles.

Whatever the explanations might be, it is quite obvious that the 'interestingness' of titles in one group and its absence in the other is the most conspicuous feature of the corpus analyzed. However, it is also a peculiar difference that is likely enough to become less distinct (than, perhaps, other revealed features) due to the intensive social processes that partly cause and partly make possible the importation of market ideologies, values and discourses to Eastern Europe. Nevertheless, the data of this investigation show that the Ukrainian and Russian titles of even such a dynamic and sensitive genre as the conference abstract are still resistant to the marketisation of research discourse. On the other hand, as demonstrated, this feature of the Slavic titles is consistent with their other generic properties marked by 'seriousness', whereas impressive English headings correspond with such features of the texts as claims for novelty and originality or intriguing final parts. This allows me to conclude more theoretically that such features of titles as the structural elements of the conference abstract correlate with the major rhetorical characteristics of this genre in different languages and cultures (although this does not necessarily imply that the feature of 'interestingness', for example, will not be found in the titles of other genres).

A final point concerns the relative likeness of the English and Slavic titles in the field of applied mathematics and their more visible heterogeneity in the linguistic group. The explanation for this discrepancy seems to lie in the cognitive (rather than in the cultural) domain: sciences are much more marked by the universality of thinking paradigms than humanities and usually exhibit a lower degree of national originality, as has been demonstrated by this study.

6. Pedagogical implications: Do we need to teach titles?

Swales (1990: 224) draws the attention of teachers to writing titles considering it an important and at the same time entertaining rhetorical task. Indeed, my recent pedagogical experience of teaching English research titles to the students of the Master's program at a Ukrainian university corroborates this view. The Ukrainian students not only enjoyed discussing different types of titles but were even able to demonstrate certain background knowledge of their cultural propensities, immediately identifying, for example, 'colon' titles as the 'American' (US) ones. They also displayed their culture-rooted preferences by pointing at nominative constructions as the most preferable type of titles for them for a piece of writing in any language and motivated this choice both rationally ("These titles are informative" or "They are most explanatory") and emotionally ("Such titles sound better" or "I like them most of all").

However, as always in teaching writing in foreign languages, there is a question of whether we have the right to impose not only linguistic structures of a non-native language but also its culture-specific and often alien rhetorical patterns on a learner. In Europe, this concern has recently acquired the form of a plea for English as an International Language (EIL), the philosophy of which establishes an understanding "that non-native speakers of English do not necessarily join the native English-speaking societies in their conceptualisation of the world, but instead have a culturally distinct vision which reflects European experience" (Modiano 2000: 36). I am, nonetheless, more inclined to view this problem in a somewhat different plane that has certain affinity with the issues of critical language awareness raised by Fairclough (1995) and a critical approach to EAP teaching advocated by Pennycook (1997). Being socially constructed, but not pre-determined, writing is rather a matter of individual preferences resulting from the affiliation to particular possibilities available to writers in their social contexts. And if we wish our students to be confident and content with their choices, we need to raise their language and cultural awareness and provide them with the appropriate knowledge whether about English titles or any other relevant elements or features of writing practices and genres.

References

Arnold, I. V. 1990. *Stilistika sovremennogo anglijskogo yazyka* ('Stylistics of Modern English'). Moscow: Prosveshcheniye.

Berkenkotter, C. & T. Huckin. 1995. *Genre Knowledge in Disciplinary Communication: Cognition/Culture/Power*. Hillsdale, NJ: Lawrence Erlbaum.

Bloch, J. & L. Chi. 1995. "A comparison of the use of citations in Chinese and English academic discourse." In D. Belcher & G. Braine (eds), *Academic Writing in a Second Language: Essays on Research and Pedagogy*. Northwood, NJ: Ablex, 231-274.

Clyne, M. 1991. "The sociocultural dimension: The dilemma of the German-speaking scholar." In H. Schröder (ed.), *Subject-oriented Texts: Languages for Special Purposes and Text Theory*. Berlin: Walter de Gruyter, 49-67.

Čmejrková, S. & Daneš, F. 1997. "Academic writing and cultural identity: The case of Czech academic writing." In A. Duszak (ed.), *Culture and Styles of Academic Discourse*. Trends in Linguistics. Studies and Monographs 104. Berlin: Mouton de Gruyter, 41-61.

Connor, U. 1996. *Contrastive Rhetoric: Cross-Cultural Aspects of Second Language Writing*. Cambridge: Cambridge University Press.

Dirven, R. & M. Verspoor. 1998. *Cognitive Exploration of Language and Linguistics*. Amsterdam/Philadelphia: Benjamins.

Dudley-Evans, T. 1984 "A preliminary investigation of the writing of dissertation titles." In G. James (ed.), *The ESP Classroom. Exeter Linguistic Studies,* 7: 40-46.

Duszak, A. 1997. "Cross-cultural academic communication: a discourse-community view." In A. Duszak (ed.), *Culture and Styles of Academic Discourse*. Berlin: Mouton de Gruyter, 11-39.

Faber, B. 1996. "Rhetoric in composition: The formation of organizational discourse in Conference on College Composition and Communication abstracts." *Written Communication,* 13,3: 355-384.

Fairclough, N. 1995. *Critical Discourse Analysis: The Critical Study of Language*. New York: Longman.

Galtung, J. 1985. "Structur, Kultur und Intellektueller Stil." In A. Wierlacher (ed.), *Das Fremde und das Eigene*. München: Judicum Verlag, 151-193.

Kassevitch, V. B. 1997. "Culture-dependent differences in language and discourse structures." *Proceedings of the 16th International Congress of Linguists*. Oxford: Pergamon. Paper No. 0003.

Kharchenko, N. P. 1968. *Zaglaviya, yikh funktsiyi i struktura* ('Titles, their functions and structure'). Unpublished Ph.D. Dissertation. Leningrad: Leningrad University.

Langacker, R. W. 1994. "Culture, cognition, and grammar." In M. Pütz (ed.), *Language Contact and Language Conflict*. Amsterdam/Philadelphia: Benjamins, 25-53.

Mauranen, A. 1993. *Cultural Differences in Academic Rhetoric*. Frankfurt am Main: Peter Lang.

Modiano, M. 2000. "Euro-English: Educational standards in a cross-cultural context." *The European English Messenger,* 9,1: 33-37.

Nichols, J. 1988. "Nominalization and assertion in scientific Russian prose." In J. Haiman & S. Thompson (eds), *Clause Combining in Grammar and Discourse*. Amsterdam: Benjamins, 399-428.

Pennycook, A. 1997. "Vulgar pragmatism, critical pragmatism, and EAP." *English for Specific Purposes,* 16,4: 253-269.

Posteguillo, S. 1997. "Writing titles for Computer Science research articles in English." Paper presented at the 11th LSP Symposium. Copenhagen.

Swales, J. M. 1990. *Genre Analysis: English in Academic and Research Settings*. Cambridge: Cambridge University Press.

Swales, J. M. 1996. "Teaching the conference abstract." In E. Ventola & A. Mauranen (eds), *Academic Writing: Today and Tomorrow*. Helsinki: Helsinki University Press, 45-59.

Swales, J. M., & C. Feak. 1994. *Academic Writing for Graduate Students*. Ann Arbor: University of Michigan Press.

Vassileva, I. 2000. *Who is the Author? A Contrastive Analysis of Authorial Presence in English, German, French, Russian and Bulgarian Academic Discourse*. Sankt Augustin: Asgard.

Yakhontova, T. 1998. "Genre and writing: Methodological issues". *Proceedings of the 16th International Congress of Linguists*. Oxford: Pergamon.

Yakhontova, T. In press. "'Selling' or 'telling'? The issue of cultural variation in research genres". In J. Flowerdew (ed.). *Academic Discourse*. London: Longman.

Appendix

Names and dates of conferences

XXXI Polish Solid Mechanics Conference SolMEC. Mierki n. Olsztynek, September 9-14, 1996.

16th International Congress of Linguists. Paris, July 20-25, 1997.

The Fourth International Congress on Industrial and Applied Mathematics. Edinburgh, July 5-9, 1999.

The 6th International Cognitive Linguistic Conference. Stockholm, July 10-16, 1999.

34. Linguistisches Kolloquium. Mainz, September 7-10, 1999.

Mezhdunarodnaya nauchnaya konferentsiya "Yazykovaya nominatsiya" ('International Conference on Language Nomination'). Minsk, June 25-26, 1996.

Tretya mizhnarodna konferentsiya "Strategiji ta metodyki navchannia movam dlia spetsialnykh tsilej" ('The 3rd International Conference on Strategies and Methodologies of Teaching Languages for Special Purposes'). Kyiv, April 24-25, 1997.

Zakhidno-regional'na konferentsiya "Lingvo-dydaktychni problemy vykladannia inozemnykh mov na ekonomichnykh fakultetakh" ('The West Regional Conference on the Linguo-didactic Problems of Teaching Foreign Languages for Economics Departments'). Ternopil', May 13-14, 1997.

Mizhnarodna naukova konferentsiya "Suchasni problemy mekhaniky i matematyky" ('The International Conference on Current Problems of Mechanics and Mathematics'). L'viv, May 25-28, 1998.

Acknowledgement

Support for this research was provided through a National Academy of Education/Spencer postdoctoral fellowship.

ENGLISH AS A CONFERENCE LANGUAGE FOR STUDENTS OF BUSINESS IN BELARUS: PROBLEMS, SOLUTIONS, AND PROSPECTS

Viktor Slepovitch

Belarus State Economic University, Minsk, Belarus

Abstract – Public speaking, especially in a foreign language, has been a matter of great concern and even fear many people. Like many non-native speakers, students of business at the Belarus State Economic University (BSEU), are very motivated in mastering English as the major language of international business communication. This chapter describes work with these business students on conference language and academic speaking[1], which has resulted in a considerable increase in their presentations made both within the university and beyond. The focus in teaching English as a conference language to students of business in Belarus is on academic speaking and includes such issues as establishing contact with the audience, formal/informal style differentiation, control of pace, voice, pronunciation and eye-contact, and last, but not least, the organisation of the presentation in general. All the above, during the process of active listening in class, are subject to critique and discussion on the part of peers and instructors. Various types of presentations (summary speeches, data commentaries, research overviews, mid-term speeches, etc.) serve as an excellent environment for non-native students of business English to develop their business communication skills. These, together with general English, cultural awareness and their content course, substantially add to their business English awareness.

1. Introduction

Students of international business at the Belarus State Economic University (BSEU) have recently been exposed to the techniques of teaching conference language in English. The course in question is viewed as critical to the country's efforts in its transition to a market economy which necessitates broad research, business, and other relations with the rest of the world. Future experts in business, economics, management and other related fields, who are to become Belarus' policymakers, will want to see their country as an equal partner integrated in the international community. At this point, there is still much to be done in the transitional period of the economy to bring Belarus to the stage of comprehensive integration with the European and world community.

---

[1] The assistance of the University of Michigan English Language Institute has been invaluable in teaching conference language and academic speaking skills to the BSEU students of business.

The peculiarity of the situation lies in the contradiction between what is taught by academics following the universal economic laws of development and the pressurised business realities existing in the country. The desire of business students to contribute to the process of normalising the business environment in the country, attracting foreign investors, and promoting domestically manufactured goods, results in a considerable growth of their contacts on an international level, research in the field of business administration, and participation in international conferences with presentations reflecting the results of their research.

In this context, the issue of teaching English as an international conference language, and to be more specific, conference speaking, has acquired crucial importance.

2. General situation of teaching EFL in the former USSR

In the Soviet period, due to the country being closed, English and foreign languages in general (unless they were a major taught to university students) were generally treated as very unimportant subjects whose application was narrow and limited. Departments used to have a two-year syllabus of English as a foreign language consisting of the basics of grammar, a few topics (ideologically loyal or neutral and related to everyday life or the field of studies), which were to be memorised and presented as a monologue – in fact, almost recited – at an oral exam, and texts for translation usually taken from *Moscow News*, a weekly printed in Moscow.

Lack of exposure to English speaking cultures, contacts with native speakers, and motivation resulted in a very boring routine of learning English taught by local instructors, very few of whom had been abroad and were able to share their experience. Some of the interest shown by students in English could be accounted for by Western pop and rock songs that were mostly performed in English. Otherwise, the whole process of teaching and learning EFL was largely close to 'stagnation.' For graduate 'kandidatsky' (Ph.D.) exams, the texts for translation and summarising were selected from original sources in the field of their research that could be found in the central library or in the Academy of Sciences of a particular union republic.

The above approach to teaching EFL was broadly limited to the 'read-and-translate' scheme and contained few, if any, communicatively-based methods. Those interested in reading foreign sources in their field were able to enrich their vocabulary, which, coupled with the knowledge of practical grammar, made it possible to achieve their goal. Such aspects as academic speaking and writing were never taught even to students majoring in English. This situation caused communication problems in all spheres, and EFL practice was a burden for both teachers and students. A genuine interest in a new subject at school, a foreign language, was very soon reduced to nothing after a few weeks of a boring routine. Work was rarely combined with pleasure in English classes.

It became possible to seek and implement the solution to the above problem when Belarus became an independent country after the USSR's disintegration, and there appeared real incentives for activation of the process of teaching foreign languages on all levels, especially for university students. New tasks and aspects of foreign language education were brought in based on the demand and requirements of the time. Innovations in the methods of teaching as well as in designing a curriculum for students of international business at BSEU have become a natural outcome of the joint desire of instructors and motivated students to move ahead.

3. ESP curriculum for students of business at BSEU

The overall structure of the EFL curriculum for students of business at the Belarus State Economic University is outlined in this section. For four years (eight semesters) the students are offered the following obligatory courses:

1. Pronunciation and Listening;
2. Reading and Discussion;
3. General English Oral Practice;
4. British and American Studies;
5. Grammar;
6. Video Tapes and TV Programmes (Politics and Business);
7. English for Business Study;
8. Academic Writing;
9. Business Correspondence;
10. Translation and Interpretation;
11. Academic Speaking.

Each of the courses listed is aimed at developing students' skills in reading, writing, summarising, listening, production of monologues and dialogues, translation and interpretation through a variety of teaching approaches selected individually by the instructors. Within the framework of the goals and objectives to be accomplished in the teaching process, English language instructors are now free to choose what they consider to be the most effective methods and materials. As a result, students are able to discuss in English their professional issues freely with visiting professors and other specialists in their field of study.

Below is a short description of each of the English courses as taught at the Economic University in Minsk, Belarus (Slepovitch 1997).

Pronunciation and Listening. The goal of the pronunciation component is to instruct students at both the segmental level (i.e. vowel and consonant sounds) and the suprasegmental level (i.e. basic prosodic structures of discourse, including formal and informal intonation patterns of statements, questions and exclamations). One of the goals of the listening part of this class is basic training in listening comprehension. A second goal is to develop listening skills in the areas of articulation, usage of static and kinetic tones, pausation, etc.

The introductory pronunciation and listening course usually lasts two months and is followed by an evaluative process which includes an interview and discussion where the students can demonstrate their competence in these skills.

Reading and Discussion. The content of this course includes samples of British and American literature. The two goals of the course are to develop skills of independent reading, and the ability to discuss and evaluate the information in a text. In the class scheduling, this course immediately follows the Pronunciation and Listening course and is taught by the same teacher in order to integrate the work of these two parts of the curriculum, thus enabling students to improve their speaking, listening, reading, and writing skills in English.

General English Oral Practice. This course is based on developing oral practice skills in the form of a dialogue and a monologue on a variety of general English topics (travelling, generation gap, ecological problems, learning a foreign language, immigration, music and theatre, etc.)

British and American Studies. This class is focused on teaching, geography, history, traditions, religions, systems of education, and literature and arts in Great Britain and the United States. Visiting scholars and lecturers from the U.S. and England often contribute to this course. Individual, pair and group tasks are used to foster collaborative learning and students are encouraged to take the leading role in class.

Grammar. Grammar difficulties still being a problem for many students, English grammar is taught throughout the first two years of education. Practical grammar issues, such as the use of articles, tenses in the active and passive voice, modals and verbals, are taught through a variety of exercises, both oral and written.

Video Tapes and TV Programmes. The purpose of this component is twofold: to give students additional access to cultural information and to provide listening and viewing practice. Materials for these classes are assembled with the assistance of the laboratory of technical teaching aids. Students discuss political and business issues from the BBC and CNN news channels. The video and TV aspect is included in the final English exam for undergraduate students.

English for Business Study. The syllabus for this course features reading and discussing various materials related to the sphere of business, international trade, as well as macro- and microeconomic issues, with the use of a case study. This course is taught for two years.

Academic Writing. This course aims at teaching students to write different types of texts and appreciate text structure. Genres looked at include summaries, critiques and abstracts, while rhetorical structures involve problem-solution, general-specific, etc. The course takes into account the main considerations of academic writing: audience, organisation, style, flow, and presentation. It is taught to the third-year students of international business.

Business Correspondence. The syllabus for this course includes a variety of business letters (enquiries, replies, orders, payments, complaints, and others), memos, and miscellaneous correspondence, including CVs, cover letters and different formats of resumés.

Translation and Interpretation. The purpose of this course is to guide the students to appreciate the rendering of the original and make the reader (in case of written translation) forget that the original was written in English. This is a challenging task which is achieved by translating the meaning rather than the literal word. This aspect of the ESP curriculum includes several subcourses: (1) Fundamentals of translation techniques; (2) Lexical and grammatical issues of translation (e.g. neologisms, phraseology, differences between British and American English, translator's 'faux amis', etc.); (3) Translation in the form of a summary, abstract, etc.; (4) Interpretation (consecutive and simultaneous) skills.

Academic Speaking. The basics of academic speaking are introduced in the courses of General English Oral Practice and English for Business Study, with a special focus on conference presentations as a genre in the third year of studies. The purpose of this course is to prepare students for presenting papers in English at international conferences, and it is this aspect of ESP that is given special emphasis in this paper.

4. The course in English as a conference language

In introducing the course in question for students of business, I considered conference language as a genre following Swales' definition (Swales 1990: 58).

The importance of applying genre analysis of oral presentations for teaching purposes is said to be quite significant (e.g. Thompson 1994). Our focus of teaching English as a conference language to students of business is made on the basis of academic speaking (Reinhart 1995). Hence, at an early stage of the course, students, begin planning for their presentations.

A presentation is treated as a process of communication, meaning that it has the following components: *communicator, channel, message, audience,* and finally, *effectiveness.* It is noteworthy that information contained in a presentation is not only transferred to listeners. According to Slobodchikov & Isayev (1995: 141), it is often *formed, specified, and developed* in this interactive process.

The conference presentation as a genre, in addition to displaying a set of common communicative purposes, should also have a shared rhetorical structure: a clear rhetorical movement through a sequence of communicative moves and steps (Swales 1990: 58).

One of the most common types of structures which students practise at home and in class is a *problem-solution* speech which is considered to be very appropriate for the current economic and social situation in Belarus. Contextual differences between the West and the former Soviet Union also need to be taken into account (Stevens 2000: 55). The country's future policymakers and specialists in international business prefer to focus on the ways of solving numerous problems related to improving the investment climate, foreign exchange policy, import and export activities, monetary policy, and so on. A four-part structure of such a presentation is normally used:

1. Description of the situation
2. Identification of the problem
3. Description of a solution
4. Evaluation of the solution (Swales & Feak 1994: 59).

According to Reinhart (1995: 10), during the first part of this structure it is necessary to set the scene or provide the background to introduce the problem. During the second part, students should clearly present the problem, so that the audience can understand it. In the third part, a presenter tells the audience what his/her solution to the problem is or what could be the best solution. If the problem has already been solved, an explanation of how it was solved needs to be given. The fourth part should evaluate the solution by briefly discussing its strengths and weaknesses. In trying to prepare a presentation, a non-native speaker of English can be compared to a non-native writer, who, according to Ventola's observation:

... is in a somewhat awkward position. Often s/he is caught between two opposing poles: sometimes, due to language incompetence, s/he writes too simply and sometimes, when pursuing more complex language, the message is lost in elaborate and often erroneous attempts to construct texts in English (Ventola 1996: 154).

It is true, however, that speakers, unlike writers, may have greater freedom of rhetorical movement in their presentations due to greater variation of spoken genres as compared to written genres (Swales 1990: 182, Thompson 1994: 181). Two samples of presentations made by third year students in the 'problem-solution' format are given here to illustrate their attempts at working on English as a conference language.

1. THE EFFECT OF THE CHERNOBYL ACCIDENT IN BELARUS

As a result of the Chernobyl nuclear power station's explosion in 1986, the Republic of Belarus has been faced with a serious ecological problem.

After the Chernobyl accident, almost 23% of the country's territory is now badly contaminated with Cesium-137. Most of the Homel region has been affected by the radioactive Iodine contamination. This has led to a sharp increase of the number of people suffering from the thyroid gland cancer.

In addition, the air pollution makes the situation more complicated. Various harmful substances once discharged into the atmosphere cause even more mutations than radiation does. For example, only in Minsk 20% of all the infants are born with serious health defects. Unfortunately, the government does not seem to be helpful.

In this situation, people and local governments should take care of themselves without waiting for assistance from aside. First, badly contaminated areas should be closed, and agricultural activities in all the other regions contaminated with radioactive elements should be restricted and controlled. Second, much higher fines should be imposed on the enterprises polluting the air, water and land. It is also important to instruct and inform the population, for example, about the use of medications and food consumption.

The above measures, combined with a number of others, in my opinion, might give us a chance for survival after the Chernobyl nuclear disaster.

(Anna F.)

2. THE IMPACT OF FOREIGN FINANCING IN BELARUS

Foreign financing is a kind of financial activity concerning financial funds or assets transferred through state borders.

Normally, a state tends to attract this kind of financing when its economy is short of internal financial resources. The Republic of Belarus, however, due to unwise policy in the sphere of economic reforms, is experiencing lack of negotiable assets. At the moment, a certain amount of foreign financing is badly needed for the country.

There are three main levels of foreign financing. The first of them is the level of international financial organisations, such as the International Monetary Fund or the World Bank. These organisations were established in order to accumulate financial resources of developed countries and distribute them among the less developed ones. The second source of foreign financing an interstate agreement on credits. And the third level is direct foreign investments. It is obvious that the latter have the biggest potential. At the same time, they are the most difficult to attract.

In Belarus, for the reasons mentioned above, the IMF and the World Bank are very reluctant to deal with the government. As a result, it is almost impossible to attract direct foreign investments any longer. Moreover, the international prestige of the country has fallen after the referendum of November 24th [1996].

To improve the situation, in my opinion, our republic needs to have a constitution which will not allow to violate law and human rights as well as a realistic economic programme which will enable to overcome the crisis and implement market reforms.

My understanding is that the above solution measures will hardly be taken in the near future. As a result, the level of foreign financing will fall to zero, which is very sad to state.

(Sergey Y.)

As can be seen above, by the third year of the ESP university course the students of international business at BSEU have already accumulated sufficient background knowledge in the field of their studies as well as in ESP to be able to make the best use of the conference language classes in English. Following Reinhart (1995: 11), students are given a number of steps to follow when working on their presentations. One of them is to make sure that the description of the situation and the problem are clear. At various points during the presentation, it is a good idea to check to see whether the audience is following the presenter. One technique that good speakers use is to ask a question. The following reasons (or one of them) may guide the presenter:

1. to get the audience's attention;
2. to make sure the audience is following him/her;
3. to have a dialogue with the audience;
4. to focus the audience's attention on the topic of the presentation
5. by asking a rhetorical question.

In order not 'to lose the audience' students are taught to check for understanding, as there could arise problems of understanding the presenter's accent or even key vocabulary if it is mispronounced. In the context of a non-native English language environment, this can prove quite helpful for the communication process to be more effective. It is therefore important to pause at appropriate breaks, using one of the following expressions to check for understanding: *Are you following me? Do you have any questions? Do you understand so far? Is that clear? OK so far?*

In addition to the organisational structure the students use in their speech, transition words and sentences are another major concern when teaching English as a conference language. These normally fall into four main categories: (1) openers, (2) connectors, (3) responders, (4) closures (Imber 1991). Those transitions effectively lead the audience from one part of the presentation to the next.

As mentioned above, the audience is an important part of the communication process and so a special emphasis is placed on active listening during a classroom presentation. Note-taking activities help students listen more purposefully (Thompson 1994: 183), thus making it easier for them to ask for clarification and evaluate a presentation according to a special scheme. Additionally, both the presenter and listeners have a self-critique scheme of a problem-solution speech. An example of an evaluation sheet is given in Appendix 1.

This feed-back is extremely important for students to acquire confidence and competence in giving their presentations in an environment beyond the classroom, at conferences and international meetings.

The next stage of teaching English as a conference language focuses on *explaining a visual, graph, or a chart*. Miller (1998: 30) warns teachers of ESP against "viewing visual elements as peripheral to their real task of focusing on the message of the main verbal text". He believes that this logocentric approach (Lemke 1995) "leads teachers to ignore what may be the most important and perhaps problematic aspect of the academic article" (Miller 1998: 30). With an oral conference presentation, however, visuals are not separated from a verbal text. Therefore, they have become part of the course of English as a conference language. Visuals are often included in a problem-solution speech. The most common ways that are recommended to students to organise information are as follows:

From general to specific (say what the visual as a whole is about and then to start explaining the specific details).

Linear or spatial order (start at one point in the visual and then proceed clockwise or linearly to the next point, especially when describing a process).

Chronological order (if the graph represents years and historical changes, start from the past and move to the present; if it tells a history, use a chronological order).

Comparison / Contrast (talk about one object and then compare it with the other, or compare one aspect of the first object with one aspect of the second object, and so on).

Cause and effect (either start by explaining the action and then describe the result or effect, or begin with the result/effect and then explain what action caused it).

Combination (combine organisational types, e.g. give a chronological comparison).

In teaching how to use and discuss visuals, attention is paid to useful phrases and prepositions for discussing graphs, charts, and tables; using dates; discussing amounts, differences, and changes; making references to a visual; modifying statements about change, stability, or comparison by using adjectives or adverbs of degree – from the least to the greatest.

The proper use of the above grammar and vocabulary by non-native speakers of English is absolutely necessary for adequacy in both explaining and understanding visuals. The following is made a matter of the students' awareness when working on explaining visuals:

— Only a very limited number of prepositions fully correspond to those in other languages (e.g. *from ... to, during, between*). Most of them need to be memorised and practised.

— Special difficulties are caused by countables and uncountables when discussing information dealing with amounts (*many* vs. *much, a great deal of, a large amount of*, etc.).

— Various ways of making references to visuals are discussed with students, e.g. *The table below/ the figure above shows/illustrates/reveals ...* or *As seen in /as shown in/ as is shown in Figure / Table 1, ...* .

— When discussing charts, graphs, and tables, students find it useful to modify statements about change, stability, or comparison by using adjectives or adverbs of degree. The following are useful for discussing accuracy: *entirely, roughly, precisely, almost, approximately, nearly, completely*; or, when describing a decrease (decline) the following adjectives are helpful: *steady, gradual, slight, moderate, abrupt, steep, sudden.*

When preparing for explaining visuals, students are recommended to make use of a check list (see Appendix 2).

When working on other types of presentations, students are also provided with self-evaluation schemes that help them keep control of their organisation (introduction, body, conclusion) and keep in mind all the criteria for a successful speech. One of these is *style*, which is of special importance as far as the language of conferences is concerned. Style differentiation is constantly in the focus of attention in the course in question. The style of a particular presentation must be consistent and appropriate for the message conveyed and for the audience (Crystal & Davy 1974). Academic style is not used in all academic settings. Presentations and lectures are generally delivered in a relatively non-academic style (Swales & Feak 1994: 15). In the course of academic speaking, the students are very careful about using a particular level of formality in whatever piece of information they present:

> Level 5: very formal;
> Level 4: formal;
> Level 3: neutral;
> Level 2: informal;
> Level 1: rude and vulgar.

The students are aware of a vocabulary and grammar shift (prosodic parameters are also taken into account) required for the style they need to use when making a conference presentation.

5. Conclusion

In this paper I have tried to present the first attempts at teaching English as a conference language to students of international business at the Belarus State Economic University (Minsk, Belarus). These are also the first attempts of this kind in a country which is a new independent state with an economy in transition. Having presented the general situation of teaching English as a foreign language in the former USSR and the current curriculum of ESP for students of business, the focus was then placed on teaching conference presentations in English. The results of this course for students of international business in Belarus are encouraging. They have been successfully using the skills acquired in the course of conference English speaking through active participation in conferences both within the university and beyond, in international meetings and seminars. One of the recent examples of the students' giving presentations in English is the conference "Europe at the turn of the 21st century" held at BSEU (1999). Students presented papers at several panel sessions to their peers and native English speakers from international organisations, embassies, and joint ventures located in Minsk. The latter were favourably impressed both with the students' competence in their field of study and proficiency in making presentations. The evaluation commissions, which comprised university teachers and representatives of foreign businesses and international organisations, in assessing the students' presentations used an evaluation sheet (see Appendix 2) for their guidance. Numerous awards given at the conference provided a good incentive for other students to work on English as a conference language.

Further research into the subject aims to concentrate on key points in conference discourse which will help students as novice presenters to feel more comfortable. The pedagogic input in this field is still to be assessed in future, especially in the context of economies in transition making efforts to equal the rest of the world and establish partnership relationships with other countries.

References

Crystal, D. & D. Davy 1974. *Investigating English Style*. London: Longman.
Imber, B. 1991. (In manuscript) *Verbal Stratagems*. Ann Arbor: University of Michigan English Language Institute.
Lemke, J. 1995. *Textual politics*. London: Taylor & Francis.
Miller, T. 1998. "Visual persuasion: A comparison of visuals in academic texts and the popular press". *English for Specific Purposes* 17 (1): 29-46.
Reinhart, S. 1995. (In manuscript) *Academic Speaking Course Pack*. Ann Arbor: University of Michigan English Language Institute.
Slepovitch, V. 1997. "An ESP programme for business students in Belarus". *ESP Russia* 5: 29-32.
Slobodchikov, V. I. & E. I. Isayev 1995. *Psihologia cheloveka* ('Psychology of Man'). Moscow: Shkola-Press.
Stevens, B. 2000. "Russian teaching contracts. An examination of cultural influence and genre". *Journal of Business and Technical Communication* 14 (1): 38-57.
Swales, J. 1990. *Genre Analysis*. Cambridge: Cambridge University Press.
Swales, J. & C. Feak 1994. *Academic Writing for Graduate Students. A Course for Non-native Speakers of English*. Ann Arbor: University of Michigan Press.
Thompson, S. 1994. "Frameworks and contexts: A genre-based approach to analysing lecture introductions". *English for Specific Purposes* 13 (2): 171-186.
Ventola, E. 1996. "Packing and unpacking of information in academic texts". In E. Ventola & A. Mauranen (eds). *Academic Writing. Intercultural and Textual Issues*. Amsterdam, Philadelphia: John Benjamins, 153-194.

Appendix

(1)   Evaluation Sheet of a Problem-Solution Speech

	Good	OK	Needs work	Comments
1) TOPIC (interesting, relevant, appropriate for audience)				
2) INTRODUCTION (got audience attention and kept it, imaginative)				
3) ORGANISATION (clear, easy to follow, speech had 4 parts)				
4) TRANSITIONS (made clear transitions between the 4 parts of the presentation)				
5) EYE CONTACT (looked at everyone, didn't focus on the ceiling, windows or 1-2 people)				
6) VOICE (good volume, enthusiastic, confident)				
7) PRONUNCIATION (easy to understand, pronounced key words correctly)				
8) PACE (good pace, not too fast or slow)				
9) CLARIFICATION CHECK (checked to see if the audience was following at the appropriate time)				
10) WEAK AREA	--	--	--	

(2)   Checklist for presenters

1. Is my visual interesting, yet simple enough to explain in 2 minutes?
2. Is my visual too complex for a general audience to understand? (If so, choose another one.)
3. Is my visual big enough for all the students to see?
4. How have I organised my presentation? Does the plan fit my topic?
5. How will I make sure my audience is following me? When is a good time to stop and ask them?
6. What questions might the audience ask me about my visual?
7. Is my speech longer than 2 minutes? If so, how can I cut it?
8. Did I practise my speech twice and put it on tape?

(See Reinhart 1995: 14-16)

THE FRENCH SCIENTIST AND ENGLISH AS A CONFERENCE LANGUAGE

David Banks

Université de Bretagne Occidentale, Brest, France

Abstract – In the ESP area there seems to be a tendency to attribute opinions and attitudes to scientists purely on the basis of hearsay. This chapter[1] is a first attempt to provide a partial rectification of this situation. It presents the results of a questionnaire sent to scientific researchers in a French university. It shows that while many commonly held beliefs are confirmed, the importance of some types of presentation may have been underestimated, and taking part in debates and discussion is found to be particularly difficult. These facts need to be taken into account in the training given to future researchers and in the linguistic services set up to help them.

1. Introduction

The fact that English has become the *lingua franca* of international academic writing is no longer in dispute. It is undeniably so in the hard sciences, and the phenomenon is rapidly spreading to the social sciences and many disciplines in the humanities. This fact however presents serious difficulties for the non-anglophone researcher, who is now obliged to publish in English, not only from the academic point of view of making his or her work available to the international academic community, but also from the pragmatically pedestrian point of view which makes it necessary if he or she is to have anything like respectable career prospects. This paper will be concerned with the situation in France, and to some extent this problem has been looked at from a number of different angles. Cooke (1993) for example looks at this problem comparing the writing of fully-fledged researchers with that of students; Birch (1994, 1996) and Crosnier (1996) consider the question in the light of genre analysis (cf. Swales 1990); and Birch-Bécaas [the same person as Birch above] (1997) considers sentence level and global revisions; Sionis (1995) compares the writing of older and younger researchers, and in a second article (1997) compares both of these with their ability before and after communicative training. The importance of this question in France is indicated by two recent significant doctoral theses on this subject, Carter-Thomas (1998), and Ormrod (2000). Of course, studies have been carried out in many other language

---

[1] This is a revised and extended version of Banks 1999.

communities, and, *inter alia*, one might mention Gosden (1995) on Japanese speakers, Shaw (1991) who looked at a group of speakers of various non-European languages, and most notably the work of Ventola who studied speakers of Finnish (1992), German (1994), and compared these two language groups (1993). However, it is striking first of all that all of this work centres on the production of written text, and secondly that it examines only what the researcher produces in the way of text.

This volume is in itself an attempt to fill the first gap, in that it deals with spoken rather than written language, specifically that used in international conferences. This particular contribution is an attempt to fill the second gap: all too often what is said about what scientists feel and think of the use of English at conferences is based on hearsay, or at best on informal contact with a small number of scientific colleagues. This paper attempts to remedy that situation by attempting to find out the opinions of scientific researchers working in one French provincial university.

A questionnaire (cf. Appendix 1 for the original and Appendix 2 for an English translation) was circulated to those engaged in research in the scientific and medical faculties of a French provincial university. The number sent out was 386, though informants were invited to photocopy and pass on the questionnaire if they were aware of researchers who had not received it. The present paper is based on the first 98 completed questionnaires returned, and gives the raw data of the replies. Raw numbers are given in the Tables, but since these are based on 98 replies they can also virtually be taken as percentages rounded to the nearest integer. The questions which are discussed include: the languages used at the conferences attended by the informants, and the languages in which they spoke; the form that their presentations took; what they did to prepare for the presentation; their perception of the degree of difficulty of the conference situation; and their opinion of the language training they had received.

2. The population

Informants were asked to give their field of research. Seven fields were provided for in the questionnaire with in addition an *others* category. The results are given in Table 1 below.

In the *others* category, one was given as *oceanographical biology*, and can presumably be conflated with *biology* for the purposes of this study. Of the others, 14 are in the general area of geographical/geological sciences (*geology* (five), *earth sciences* (four), and one entry each for *geography, geoarchitecture, geochemistry, geosciences* and *geophysics*). In addition, there were three entries for *electronics,* and one each for *hydrology, oceanography* and *history of science*, while one informant marked *others*, without giving any specification. Some informants marked more than one category, e.g. *biology* and *medicine.*

Physics	11
Chemistry	8
Biology	21
Technology	0
Mathematics	2
Computer Science	5
Medicine	36
Others	22

Table 1: Numbers of informants by field of research.

As might be expected, given the population targeted, informants were rarely under 30 years of age, and few were over sixty. The age distribution is given in Table 2.

less than 30	2
30-39	19
40-49	36
50-59	32
60 and over	9

Table 2: Numbers of informants by age range.

Seventy-four of the informants are male, and twenty-three female. One did not say.

The informants are basically French speakers. Only three did not give French as their mother tongue. Two of these were regional languages, *Breton* and *Alsatian*, the third was the North African language *Kabyle*. Of the native French speakers, four said they were bilingual. Three of these cases again concerned regional languages: two were *French/Breton* bilinguals, and one *French/Alsatian*. One informant was a bilingual *French/English* speaker.

3. The problem and its extent

The hypothesis is that French scientists experience difficulty when they have to give papers in an English-speaking context. The greater the number of conferences they attend, particularly if they have to give a paper in English, the greater the problem. In an attempt to judge the extent of this problem, informants were asked how many conferences they had attended since 1 January 1997, and the number of conferences at which they had presented a paper in the same period. Since the questionnaire was distributed in autumn 1998, this represents a period of almost two years. A few informants seem to have misunderstood the question as the number given for the number of conferences attended was lower than the number at which they had given papers. The figures given here are nevertheless the raw data as supplied by the informants, and still provide some idea of the extent of the problem. The number of conferences attended by informants is given in Table 3.

In France	411
In an English-speaking country	110
Elsewhere	91

Table 3: Numbers of conferences attended by informants by geographical area.

There were large differences from individual to individual, including two informants who claimed to have attended approximately fifty conferences in the period, and one about thirty. All three of these replies came from the medical faculty, which seems to suggest that the question of conference attendance is one which has different implications in the medical sector compared with other branches of science. Nevertheless, even if one allows for a certain inflation of the figures due to these replies, it seems reasonable to say that on average the scientists in the sample attend, over a two-year period, three or four conferences in France and two abroad, of which one will be in an English-speaking country.

The number of papers presented over the same period is given in Table 4.

In France	223
In an English-speaking country	87
Elsewhere	78

Table 4: Numbers of papers presented by informants by geographical area.

These figures suggest that over a two-year period these scientists will probably present about four papers, of which half are likely to be outside France, with one in an English-speaking country.

4. The languages of conferences

Informants were asked what languages were used in the conferences, and which languages they used themselves to present their papers. The languages used are given in Table 5.

The languages used by the informants themselves for the presentation of their papers is given in Table 6. Some informants indicated languages even though they had not presented papers in the geographical area concerned within the specified period. The wording of the questionnaire is open to this interpretation. In these cases the languages indicated are presumably those that would have been used if the informant had given a paper during that period. The figures given here are those given by the informants, on the presumption that they are not distorted to any significant extent.

In France	French	77
	English	45
	Others	0

In an English-speaking country	French	1
	English	59
	Others	0

Elsewhere	French	16
	English	51
	Others	6

Table 5: Numbers of papers and language of presentation by geographical area.

In France	French	82
	English	33
	Others	0

In an English-speaking country	French	3
	English	75
	Others	0

Elsewhere	French	16
	English	57
	Others	2

Table 6: Languages used by informants for presentations by geographical area.

It will be seen that French scientists give about 30% of their papers in English even when the conference takes place in France. Some informants pointed out that this corresponds to those conferences that are international, rather than national, in nature. As might be expected, the use of languages other than English is extremely rare in English-speaking countries; even the three cases of a paper being given in French in an English-speaking country might seem strange to some. In non-English-speaking countries abroad it is still English which dominates, being used for almost 80% of the papers given. Some pointed out that where French was used abroad, this was in a country with a French-speaking tradition, e.g. North Africa or francophone Canada.

These figures also show that these scientists can expect to give 1.7 papers in English over a 2-year period. Even allowing for this figure being inflated by the phenomenon mentioned above, one might hypothesise that the average figure approaches at least 1.5.

5. The form of the presentation

Informants were asked what form their presentations took. The questionnaire provided for two possibilities, *read a written text,* and *speak from notes,* with an *others* category for those that did not fall into these two. The results are given in Table 7.

read a written text	28
speak from notes	43
others	27

Table 7: Numbers of papers by type of presentation.

As can be seen, the majority speak from notes, though a quarter find it necessary to have the text of their paper written out in advance. One person marked both *written text* and *notes.* The specifications of the *others* category supplied some interesting information. The main feature emerging from this section was the importance that presentations taking the form of a *commentary on transparencies or slides* have acquired. This was the form indicated by 17 of the in-formants. However, since this is a category not provided for in the original questionnaire, it is conceivable that the phenomenon is more extensive than appears here. Also surprising was the six who claim to *speak without notes.* It is conceivable that these are using some support such as slides or transparencies and so fall into the same category. One informant indicated that he learnt his text by heart, and one, presumably humorously, indicated his form as *poor improvisation.*

6. Preparation

When asked if they sought help in preparing their presentations in English, a surprisingly large number said they did not seek help. Some informants marked more than one category. The replies are given in Table 8.

prepare by yourself (without help)	60
seek help from an anglophone scientific colleague	20
seek help from a non-anglophone scientific colleague	14
seek help from an anglophone non-scientific colleague/friend	8
seek help from a non-scientific non-anglophone English specialist	6
others	3

Table 8: Numbers of informants by method of preparation.

While it would seem that less than half of the scientists seek help in preparing their presentations in English, where they do so there is a preference for consulting other scientists rather than non-scientists. More of them turn to a non-English speaking scientific colleague than to an English-speaking non-scientist. This may in part be due to non-availability of English-speakers, but one can still hypothesise that being able to understand the scientific content ranks higher for these scientists than linguistic competence. It is perhaps worth pointing out that this particular university has a service which helps researchers with their English writing. This service is manned by one non-anglophone scientist. Some of the entries for a non-anglophone scientific colleague were undoubtedly people using this service; two specifically said so. On the other hand, some informants seem not to be aware of this service. This is notably so in the medical faculty. Although the person running this service is a fully qualified biochemist, the official level (and remuneration) of the post is that of a temporary position for a job-seeker. Attempts to create a post of a more permanent nature have so far come to nothing. The service was initially free to researchers, but the university authorities now charge at the rate of 50 francs per hour. The quantity of work brought to the service dropped dramatically when the charge was introduced. Roughly a quarter of the work is translation, and three-quarters correction of texts already written in English. The person running the service usually works on her own initially and then with the scientist concerned in the final stages. However, in relation to the subject of the present article, the vast majority of the work is on articles for publication; the comparative lack of work on conference papers may be due to the current tendency towards poster sessions. She is also fairly frequently consulted on documents such as university contracts, and post-doctoral references and CVs.[2]

---

[2] I would like to thank Marie-Paul Friocourt for information on this point.

7. Scientists' perception of the problem

Informants were asked to grade the difficulty of three tasks: giving a paper in English, taking part in debates and discussion in English, and taking part in social events in English. They were asked to grade these as very difficult, fairly difficult, or not difficult. The results are given in Table 9.

give a presentation in English	very difficult	20
	fairly difficult	45
	not difficult	33

take part in discussions/debates in English	very difficult	37
	fairly difficult	38
	not difficult	23

take part in social events in English	very difficult	18
	fairly difficult	42
	not difficult	33

Table 9: Informants' perception of difficulty by type of task.

I have frequently heard it said that French scientists' main difficulty in taking part in international conferences is not so much the conference proper, that is the giving of papers, but in the social aspects of the event. Once outside their specialist subject matter, so the argument goes, they are at a loss. The results in Table 9 show that this is not so, at least for the scientists in this sample. Taking part in social events is perceived as being no more difficult than giving a presentation in English. What some of these scientists do find particularly difficult is taking part in debates and discussion. Almost twice as many graded this as being *very difficult*, and one added a special extra category and wrote in *impossible*. At the other end of the scale, 33 found giving papers and taking part in social events *not difficult*, but only 23 gave this grading to taking part in debates and discussions. Some pointed out that the difficulty depends on the variety of English spoken by English-speakers. Speakers of American English are frequently perceived as being more difficult to understand, and are taken to task for making little or no concession to non-native speakers. Texans are singled out by some as being virtually incomprehensible. Perhaps part of this problem is that while these informants will have come into contact with examples of both American and British varieties of written English in the course of their English training, the phonological model adopted by the vast majority of English teachers in France is that of standard British English. Consequently, the informants may well have had comparatively little exposure to oral American English, and indeed to different varieties of American English.

There is an obvious pedagogical implication in these results. Being able to take part in debate and discussion, including being able to field questions following a presentation, is a necessary part of taking part in international conferences, but it is probable that this aspect plays too little a part (if it plays any part at all) in the scientists' English training.

Finally, the informants were asked how well they thought their training in English had prepared them for the task of taking part in international conferences. The results are given in Table 10.

very well	2
fairly well	10
adequately	10
not at all	75

Table 10: Informants' evaluation of their English training.

The vast majority felt that their training in English had not prepared them at all for the task of taking part in international conferences. This should obviously be seen in relation to the age distribution of the informants, and particularly to the fact that only two were under thirty years of age. It is possible that the situation has improved in recent years, though one suspects that no substantial changes have taken place. It is also necessary to take into account certain biases of the French educational system. German is frequently used as an unofficial means of selection in secondary education; only the more-able pupils are allowed to take German as their first foreign language. The more-able are those who perform well in tests and exams in general, not necessarily those with a particular bent for languages. This is because German is popularly perceived as being a difficult language, and as such it took over the selective role previously played by Latin when the study of classical languages declined. There is also a bias towards science subjects; brighter pupils are encouraged to concentrate on science. The result is that a considerable number of French scientists will have studied German as their first foreign language at the secondary level. English will at best have been their second foreign language. Consequently they start off with a disadvantage as far as English is concerned.

Scientists will have received some training in English as part of their university education. In recent years there has been an increasing tendency to recruit teachers who are seconded from secondary education for this task. These will usually be teachers who have passed the *Agrégation*. This is the higher of the two competition exams for the recruitment of secondary teachers in France, the other being the *CAPES*. Both of these exams carry high prestige, the *Agrégation* particularly so. Those who obtain them have civil service status and are thus guaranteed employment until retirement age. Those who obtain the *Agrégation* have higher salaries, and a lower number of teaching hours than other secondary school teachers, and in general are considered the cream of the secondary school teaching profession. Those who have passed the English *Agrégation* obviously have a high degree of competence in English. On the other hand, they typically have a basically literary training, and if they have a research interest, this will tend to be of a literary nature. One might think that this situation is justified since there are comparatively few people with the necessary qualifications in ESP to take up these posts, but this only acts as a justification if one could look forward to a situation where there was an increased effort to recruit those with ESP qualifications. As the number of such people increases there would consequently be an increase of suitably qualified people able to train future scientists in the English used within their profession. Unfortunately, it seems likely that administrators see the employment of *agrégés* in these posts as a final, not as an interim, solution, and will thus continue to create posts of this type. For the administrator, the solution resides in supplying a teacher, it does not extend to supplying a teacher with appropriate specialist qualifications.

8. Concluding remarks

This study is based on 98 replies to a questionnaire sent out to scientific researchers in a French provincial university. Many of the results confirm expectations. They show that these scientists will on average attend three or four conferences in France and two elsewhere over a two-year period. Over the same period they are likely to present about four papers, of which two will be outside France, and at least one in English. English is the dominant language outside France, and at international conferences in France. The informants follow this pattern, giving most of their papers in English when abroad, and at international conferences in France. The scientists have a poor opinion of the English training they have received.

Some of the results however were less expected. While many speak from notes or read a prepared text, a significant number describe their papers as commentaries on slides or transparencies, a category not provided for in the original questionnaire. The majority prepare their papers without outside help, but where help is sought, scientific knowledge seems to rate higher than linguistic competence. What the scientists find difficult in relation to the use of English in conferences, is not so much the presentation itself, but the questions and debate which follow.

The pedagogical implications of these results seem to be that more work needs to be done on the presentation of slides and transparencies as a specific sub-

325

genre, and on the difficulties of non-native speakers in question and answer sessions and debates.

The work described in this paper is being followed up in two ways. First, it is hoped that further work can be done on the questionnaires to analyse then in greater detail; this is being done with the cooperation of colleagues in the Sociology Department. Secondly, recordings are to be made of the question and answer sessions at international conferences with a view to analysing their language.

Although the questionnaire was anonymous, informants were asked to give their name and contact details if they were willing to be interviewed in a follow-up to the questionnaire. Of the 98 who replied 56 gave their name and details. I believe that this fact indicates the extent to which the scientists concerned take this to be a serious and interesting question with important implications for them and their position in the international world of scientific research.[3]

References

Banks, D. 1999. "Becoming part of the network: French scientists and the use of English at conferences". *Anglais de Spécialité - Revue du GERAS (Groupe d'Etude et de Recherche en Anglais de Spécialité)*, 23/26: 209-220.

Birch, S. 1994. "Writing scientific articles in English: Solutions for French researchers?" *Anglais de Spécialité - Revue du GERAS (Groupe d'Etude et de Recherche en Anglais de Spécialité)*, 3: 57-64.

Birch, S. 1996. "French researchers publishing in English. An analysis of a corpus of first drafts". *Anglais de Spécialité - Revue du GERAS (Groupe d'Etude et de Recherche en Anglais de Spécialité)*, 11/14: 75-88.

Birch-Bécaas, S. 1997. "From author to reviewer to editor: Negotiating the claim in a scientific article. A study of French researchers publishing in English". *Anglais de Spécialité - Revue du GERAS (Groupe d'Etude et de Recherche en Anglais de Spécialité)*, 15/18: 397-408.

Carter-Thomas, S. 1998. "Organisation thématique et qualité textuelle. Une analyse des difficultés rencontrées par de élèves ingénieurs francophones lorsqu'ils rédigent en anglais". Unpublished doctoral thesis. Paris: Université Paris 5 – René Descartes.

Cooke, R. 1993. "Learning to publish in English: How can French researchers bridge the gap?" *Anglais de Spécialité - Revue du GERAS (Groupe d'Etude et de Recherche en Anglais de Spécialité)*, 1: 463-474.

[3] I would like to thank those scientists who took the time to reply to my questionnaire. I would also like to thank all those commented on earlier versions of this paper, and in particular Elizabeth Rowley-Jolivet, Celia Shalom, Viktor Slepovitch, and Eija Ventola. The paper has undoubtedly benefited from their advice, but they are in no way responsible for any deficencies which remain, for which I accept total responsibility.

Crosnier, E. 1996. "L'intérêt de la modélisation comme aide à la rédaction en anglais pour les scientifiques français". *Anglais de Spécialité - Revue du GERAS (Groupe d'Etude et de Recherche en Anglais de Spécialité)*, 11/14: 89-102.

Gosden, H. 1995. "Success in research article writing and revision: A social-constructionist perspective". *English for Specific Purposes*, 14 (1): 37-57.

Ormrod, J. 2000. "La rédaction de l'article scientifique par des anglophones et par des francophones : Le groupe nominal". Unpublished doctoral thesis. Brest: Université de Bretagne Occidentale.

Sionis, C. 1995. "Communication strategies in the writing of scientific research articles by non-native users of English". *English for Specific Purposes*, 14 (2): 99-113.

Sionis, C. 1997. "Stratégies et styles rédactionnels de l'article de recherche : Les ressources de l'utilisateur non-natif devant publier en anglais". *Anglais de Spécialité - Revue du GERAS (Groupe d'Etude et de Recherche en Anglais de Spécialité)*, 15/18: 207-222.

Shaw, P. 1991. "Science research students' composing processes". *English for Specific Purposes*, 10 (3): 189-206.

Swales, J. 1990. *Genre Analysis. English in academic and research settings*. Cambridge: Cambridge University Press.

Ventola, E. 1992. "Writing scientific English: Overcoming intercultural problems". *International Journal of Applied Linguistics*, 2 (2): 191-220.

Ventola, E. 1993. "English as a 'Lingua Franca' for academic writing in Finland and Germany". In J. F.-B. Martin (ed). *Actas de las Jordanes Internacionales de Linguistica Aplicada, Vol.1*. Granada: Universidad de Granada, 588-611.

Ventola, E. 1994. "From syntax to text: Problems in producing scientific abstracts in L2". In S. Cmejrková & F. Stícha (eds). *The Syntax of Sentence and Text*. Amsterdam: John Benjamins, 284-303.

Appendix 1

Questionnaire : le scientifique francais et la langue anglaise

Quelle est votre domaine de recherche?

physique	
chimie	
biologie	
technologie	
mathématiques	
informatique	
médécine	
autres (préciser)	

Dans quelle tranche d'age vous situez-vous?

moins que 30	
30 - 39	
40 - 49	
50 - 59	
60 et plus	

Vous êtes de quel sexe?

M	
F	

Quelle est votre langue maternelle?

le français	
autres (préciser)	

A combien de colloques/symposiums/congrès avez vous assisté depuis le 1er janvier 1997?

en France	
dans des pays anglophones	
ailleurs	

A combien de colloques/symposiums/congrès avez vous communiqué depuis le 1er janvier 1997?

en France	
dans des pays anglophones	
ailleurs	

Quelles langues étaient utilisée pour la présentation des communications?

en France:

le français	
l'anglais	
autres (préciser)	

en pays anglophones:

le français	
l'anglais	
autres (préciser)	

ailleurs:

le français	
l'anglais	
autres (préciser)	

Dans quelle langue présentez-vous vos communications?

en France:

le français	
l'anglais	
autres (préciser)	

en pays anglophones:

le français	
l'anglais	

ailleurs:

autres (préciser)	

le français	
l'anglais	
autres (préciser)	

Si vous présentez en anglais, comment le faîtes-vous?

lire un texte écrit	
parler à partir de notes	
autres (préciser)	

Pour préparer une communication en anglais, quelle stratégie utilisez-vous?

préparer vous-mêmes (sans aides)	
demander de l'aide à un(e) collègue scientifique anglophone	
demander de l'aide à un(e) collègue scientifique non-anglophone	
demander de l'aide à un(e) collègue/ami(e) anglophone non-scientifique	
demander de l'aide à un(e) collègue/ami(e) angliciste (non-anglophone) non-scientifique	
autres (préciser)	

A quel point trouvez-vous les tâches suivantes difficiles?

présenter une communication en anglais:

très difficile	
assez difficile	
pas difficile	

participer aux discussions/débats en anglais:

très difficile	
assez difficile	
pas difficile	

participer aux manifestations sociales en anglais:

très difficile	
assez difficile	
pas difficile	

Est-ce que votre formation en anglais vous a préparé pour la tâche de communiquer en anglais?

oui, très bien	
oui, assez bien	
adéquat	
non, pas de tout	

Si vous avez des remarques ou commentaires à ce sujet, veuillez les ajouter ici:

Seriez-vous prêt d'être interviewé à ce sujet, pour la suite de l'étude? Si oui, veuillez ajouter vos coordonnés:

    Nom:
    Adresse:
    Tel:
    e-mail:

Retourner à: David Banks, Faculté des Lettres et Sciences Sociales 'Victor Segalen', Université de Bretagne Occidentale.

Appendix 2

Questionnaire: the French scientist and the English language

What is your research field?

physics	
chemistry	
biology	
technology	
mathematics	
computer science	
medicine	
others	

What is your age?

less than 30	
30 - 39	
40 - 49	
50 - 59	
60 and over	

Are you male or female?

M	
F	

What is your mother tongue?

French	
others	

How many conferences/symposia/colloquies have you attended since 1 January 1997?

in France	
in an English-speaking country	
elsewhere	

How many papers have you presented at conferences/symposiums/colloquies since 1 January 1997?

in France	
in an English-speaking country	
elsewhere	

What languages were used for the presentation of papers?

in France:

French	
English	
others	

in English-speaking countries:

French	
English	
others	

elsewhere:

French	
English	
others	

What language do you use to present your papers?

in France:

French	
English	
others	

in English-speaking countries:

French	
English	
others	

elsewhere:

French	
English	
others	

If you speak in English, which of the following methods do you use?

read a written text	
speak from notes	
others	

In preparing a paper in English, which of the following strategies do you use?

prepare by yourself (without help)	
seek help from an anglophone scientific colleague	
seek help from a non-anglophone scientific colleague	
seek help from an anglophone non-scientific colleague/friend	
seek help from a non-scientific non-anglophone English specialist	
Others	

How difficult do you find the following tasks?

give a presentation in English:

very difficult	
fairly difficult	
not difficult	

take part in discussions/debates in English:

very difficult	
fairly difficult	
not difficult	

take part in social events in English:

very difficult	
fairly difficult	
not difficult	

Did your English training prepare you for the task of communicating in English?

very well	
fairly well	
adequately	
not at all	

If you have any further remarks or comments on this subject, please add them here:

Would you be willing to be interviewed in the next stage of this study? If so, please give your details here:

    Name:
    Address:
    Tel:
    e-mail:

Return to: David Banks, Faculté des Lettres et Sciences Sociales 'Victor Segalen', Université de Bretagne Occidentale.

SHOULD I SPEAK ENGLISH OR GERMAN? – CONFERENCING AND LANGUAGE CODE ISSUES

Eija Ventola

Paris-Lodron-Universität Salzburg, Salzburg, Austria

Abstract – Conferences and symposia today frequently turn out to be multilingual speech events, where codeswitching is a frequent phenomenon, whether the organisers want it so or not. Codeswitching at conferences has so far had little attention in either the codeswitching or discourse analysis literature. Using a conference held in Germany as an example, this chapter discusses the kinds of codeswitching issues that very often arise in conference situations where participants come from different language backgrounds. Most of the presentations at this conference were given in German, but some of the presentations were totally or partly given in English. Both German and English were used for discussing the presentations. The chapter discusses how presenters and discussants may announce which language they prefer for their papers or turns in the discussion, what kind of codeswitching seems to be happening within the presentations and discussions and how conference participants use codeswitching for making common knowledge-building possible, by construing meanings together by using different languages. On some occasions, common knowledge construction and exchange of ideas simply breaks down, when conference participants cannot manage meaning-making by means of codeswitching. Further, there will always be members of the audience who will be partly left out or simply incapable of making a contribution, because of their language skills. The onus is on applied linguists to help conference participants, by studying issues of language code and codeswitching from a linguistic perspective and by bringing these aspects to the pedagogy of conferencing.

1. Introduction

This paper focuses on *language code* and *codeswitching* issues at conferences. Conferences or symposia today all over the world are less and less frequently carried out only in the national language(s) of the places where they are held. Sometimes conference organisers invite English native speakers or other international figures as plenary speakers to national conferences, to give the meetings 'international flavour'. These plenaries and the discussions that follow them are then mostly carried out in English, which functions as a lingua franca. Although a conference or symposium held in a non-English speaking country may not have been advertised as being 'an *international* conference', it may turn out to be 'almost an international one', because foreign scholars may hear of the conference, become interested in it and want to travel to it from abroad. Other foreign scholars may already be working or visiting in the country and wish to participate, although they may not be fluent speakers of the national language(s). Today e-mail quickly and efficiently distributes invitations to small-scale seminars happening in distant places (a recent example of such an invitation received by the author of this article is provided in the Appendix). English emerges as a 'lingua franca' of these kinds of conferences and symposia, even though it may not even have initially been granted an official status as 'the language' (or one of the languages) of the conference/symposium.

Invited and visiting scholars very often give their papers in English, and the discussion of these papers is carried out in English. Discussions of other papers may also switch into English, as such scholars comment on other presenters' papers in English (provided they have been able to follow the language in which the papers are presented). English has become the language that everyone may resort to in multilingual situations. It is perceived that English ensures efficient presentation of information and exchange of ideas, since it is the language code which we presume to be more or less available for everyone in today's academia. Yet, is it so? Can we always be assured of getting the message across to our fellow conference participants in English?

Conference data offer linguists excellent material for studying the success and problems of English as a lingua franca, codeswitching between languages at conference events and the question of what happens in such speech events when construing knowledge and negotiation of meanings unfolds dynamically in two (or possibly even more) different language codes. The claim made in this chapter is that a considerable amount of linguistic and interactional trouble may take place at conferences where participants have different cultural and linguistic backgrounds and English is used as a lingua franca, especially as an 'impromptu' one.

The chapter will concentrate on three language code issues that have been observed in Conference Section Papers and their Discussions, at a conference where German was the primary language for the majority of the conference participants, but where English emerged frequently as a second presentation language and as an impromptu lingua franca for discussion among the participants.

The chapter will focus on:

(i)   English as a global language and academic lingua franca, and the role that the choice between English and German play in the data discussed here (Section 2),

(ii) codeswitching as a linguistic phenomenon and the role of codeswitching between English and German in the data (Section 3),

(iii) the dynamics and consequences of pursuing knowledge construction and meaning-making interactively using two codes (Section 4),

(iv) some implications of the examples and discussion (Section 5).

Examples that will be presented in this chapter come from a two-day symposium held in Germany on Georg Forster, an 18th century discoverer, who, among other things, accompanied Captain James Cook on his third voyage around the world[1]. The conference took place in a large conference room, and the individual presentations were both video- and audio-recorded (the papers were also later published). The symposium was not planned to be 'very international' in character, and thus it serves as an excellent 'sounding board' for looking at what happens when English 'emerges' as a lingua franca for the conference. The majority of the participants were German (some living permanently in the USA), but there were also scholars present among the speakers and in the audience from other European countries (the UK, Portugal, France) and from some other parts of the world (the USA, New Zealand). The native speakers of English gave their papers in English and the German speakers in German. The decision for the language of discussion was not made explicit for the participants in advance, and thus had to be negotiated during the conference. Some German speakers codeswitched to English both in their presentation and during the discussions, for the benefit of the English speakers. Some of the English native speakers and most of the other European participants seemed to be fluent also in German, and they, too, tended to do some codeswitching during the discussions.

The need for systematic research in this area is urgent. This chapter will not attempt to cover all aspects of English as a lingua franca of conferencing, codeswitching, nor the issues of dynamic unfolding of interaction in two languages at conferences; but rather aims to raise about where, when and why the language code becomes an issue at a conference. This paper does not aim at a quantitative analysis of such language choice issues or codeswitching, but rather discusses the phenomena from the point of view of future issues for research and pedagogic implications in the field of 'conferencing' studies.

---

[1] The data from this conference has also been used for Chapters 1 and 7 of this volume.

2. English as an international and global language and as a lingua franca for publications and conferences

The position of English as the most important language in today's world is indisputable, even without statistics (but see Crystal 1988; Pennycook 1994). Many defend its spread as a convenient 'lingua franca' in the ever-shrinking world, arguing the benefits it brings for international commerce and communication in various fields, including academic ones. Many consider the spread of English as:

> natural, neutral and beneficial ... natural ... because ... its subsequent expansion is seen as a result of inevitable global forces ... neutral because it is assumed that ... it is now a neutral and transparent medium of communication ... beneficial because ... of international communication [being assumed to be] on a cooperative and equal footing. (Pennycook 1994: 9)

Many dread its spread, especially in the non-English-speaking countries, thinking that English endangers their own national languages and thus, eventually, their own identities as representatives of a certain culture and language. The French are frequently used as an example of vehement opponents of the spread of English in all spheres of the French culture and language. The opposition is strongly expressed also on the political level. Lamy (1996: 35) quotes the following French minister's appeal against the monopoly of English in *Le Monde*:

> [W]e, as members of the European Union, must resist the blandishments of arguments promoting a single vehicular language, which would eventually demote all of our languages except one to the rank of a local dialect.

Such appeals can also be found in the media and in the political discourse of the other countries of the European Union, although one might agree with Phillipson & Skutnabb-Kangas (1999: 21) when they write that generally "language matters do not figure prominently in much political discourse, nor in much social or political science."

Both native and non-native speakers of English have also begun to wonder what is happening to English (or Englishes?)[2] in the process of globalisation. One of the very early studies on this is Kachru's (1985) *The Alchemy of English* (see also Kachru & Nelson 1996/2001). Today many wonder how they themselves in their professions should position themselves on the issue of 'internationalised and globalised English'. Among applied linguists, Pennycook's (1994) book *The Cultural Politics of English as an International Language* is a good example of a critical discussion within the context of English as a Foreign Language.

---

[2] British English, American English, Canadian English, Australian English, etc.

2.1. English in the academic world: publishing and conferencing

Within the academic world, English has long since surpassed in importance all other languages as a scientific publication language. English is also the main language for academic conferences in the world. As has been pointed out earlier in this volume (e.g. Ventola, Chapter 1), linguistic research has concentrated considerably on the features and problematics of English as a publication language (see Swales 1990). In contrast, conference genres and the role of English in them have received very little of linguists' attention (a point made also in Shalom 2001). No single study has yet captured the spread of English as a conferencing language in the world and the issues involved, but individual studies dealing with different countries have emerged. Some Danish academics, mostly natural scientists, for example, do not seem to strongly oppose the use of English as the only conference language, even within Nordic conferences, where Swedish has typically functioned as a lingua franca[3] (Phillipson & Skutnabb-Kangas 1999: 26-7). In contrast, the French government has tried to secure the position of French as publication and conference language in France, even legally (the language law securing the position of French was passed in 1995). Yet, as Bank's article (this volume) shows, French academics are increasingly using English as the language of their presentations in France and, according to Lamy (1996: 35) even,

> "the Académie des Sciences is prepared to test the law: unable to provide the resources to translate conference abstracts from English into French, it considers that 'the only alternative ... is to disobey and see what happens'" (cited in *The Times Higher Education Supplement, 1994*).

It would be even less financially viable to provide all conference participants who give their presentations in French with simultaneous interpreters. No country, however affluent, could fully support its academics in providing translation and interpreting services when they publish or participate in international conferences.

So what are the conference organisers in non-English speaking countries expected to do? To declare English as the only language for the conference or as a second language, thus allowing presenters to choose whether they want to present their papers in English or in the national language(s)? Or simply let the individuals decide? Let us now see how the choice of presentation and

---

[3] The Finns have always felt that the choice of Swedish has put them in a disadvantaged position within Nordic conferences, since their language is not related to the other Nordic languages and there is no mutual intelligibility. English is for this reason favoured by Finns as a lingua franca for Nordic conferences.

discussion language/languages was dealt with in our example conference in Germany.

2.2. Language code choice for presentations and discussions – German or English?

In Germany, English is also frequently taking over as an official conference language, alongside German, and is sometimes even used as the only conference language, even though the majority of the participants might be German or other non-English-speaking nationals. Unfortunately, I have no information as to what kind of discussions, if any, the organisers of the Forster conference had among themselves or with the speakers regarding the language of presentation during the conference. However, the data shows that *the choice of language code* becomes an issue during the conference, both in the presentation phase and in the discussions[4]. Neither English nor German (nor both) were declared official languages of the conference. Thus, on several occasions during the conference, the participants were not really sure what language they should use and had to either announce the language choice or negotiate it. Some of these occasions will be illustrated below.

2.2.1. Deciding the language for the presentation

In the Forster conference, the chair always introduced the presenters in German, even when the presenters were native English speakers. Thus it was up to the speaker to choose the language of his/her presentation and announce or negotiate this language choice with the audience[5]. In (1), the presenter is a non-German-speaking American presenter, so naturally her choice of language code for the presentation is English. It is worthwhile to note, however, how she emphasises the fact that the audience is not to consider her as a monolingual – which American presenters are often assumed to be. This is somehow intended to smooth the change of codes from German to English.

---

[4] The language code choice also becomes an issue later for the publication. The papers were ultimately published in German. Why this decision was made is unknown to me. Those papers that were given in English during the conference were then translated into German for the book, but it is very likely that the English-speaking presenters also published English versions in their own countries. As far as I am aware, the German papers were never published in book form in English. On the whole we can therefore consider that the papers by German authors received a relatively restricted readership and thus perhaps play a limited role in overall global knowledge construction, because they are not accessible to as many readers.

[5] Suggested dynamic generic structure element: NEGOTIATING LANGUAGE OF PRESENTATION, see Ventola, Chapter 1 this volume.

(1) *Chair:* **Wenn nicht würde ich vorschlagen, dass wir fortfahren er mit dem Vortrag von Frau [last name], der diesen Sektor der wissenschaftlichen Hinterlassenschaft in Form der Sammlungen ... der Biographie - also eine ganz wichtige Sache - behandelt.**

Chair: If not, then I would suggest that we go on with Mrs [last name]'s talk, which deals with that part of the scientific legacy that has been left to us in the form of collections ... of the biography, which is a very important subject matter.

Presenter: Good morning ... at first I thought I would give my talk in a Polynesian language which might be more relevant for today. However, I thought I would be a bit more intelligible and do it in English ... So I begin with Cook ...

In (2), the presenter is from New Zealand, and he, too, chooses English as his presentation language, although he is also able to speak German and could give the whole presentation in German. He announces, however, that part of his talk will be in German and promises linguistic assistance to those members of the audience, who cannot understand German, if trouble occurs. (In fact, we later see that he also uses French during his presentation, for a literature quote, see Section 3.)

(2) *Presenter:* I am going to speak in English and I hope that that does not cause a problem for too many people. Hope you can understand my somewhat convoluted New Zealand English. Um ... if there is a problem and when we come to a point where I shall go into German - for the benefit of my colleagues who do not speak so much German - we'll make a summary.

In both of the examples, (1) and (2), native English speakers are *announcing the language code* they are going to use for the presentation, without negotiating it with the audience. In (1) negotiation would not have been possible as the presenter did not speak German. But in (2) it would be interesting to know why the presenter ultimately chose English as the major language for the presentation and not German. Did he do it because he did not trust his German?

The German presenters chose German as the language of their presentation, even though two of them worked and lived permanently in English-speaking countries, and thus could also have presented their papers in English. Only one German speaker, quite unexpectedly in the middle of his presentation, announced the change in language code, when he showed transparencies, as shown in (3). He wanted to make sure that his English-speaking colleagues would understand this part of the lecture.

(3) *Presenter:* **... So jetzt möchte ich mal die Folie ... es geht weiter ...** [5 seconds pause] Now erm, as I know that there are some people especially interested in this part of my lecture, I erm think they will be glad, if I give this part in English. As far as I can now, erm there are several lists of erm herbaria published erm with Forster's specimen by all,

but all these lists are quite … are incomplete, and what I have collected I am sure is equally erm incomplete … [several minutes later] … There are other erm collections, smaller collections and herbaria and erm erm always others will turn out so … **Jetzt erm mach ich's doch mal wieder auf deutsch. Das ist die erm aus dem Reisebericht, das ist abgenommen hier aus der deutschen Ausgabe der Rezensenten von Steiner …**

Presenter: … So I'd like a transparency now … I'll continue…

… Now I'll do it in German again. This is the erm from the travel journal, this is taken here from the German reviewer's edition of Steiner…

Two other foreign speakers, a French woman and a Portuguese woman, chose to give their papers in German. Being very fluent speakers of German, they probably considered German as the best choice for the presentation, as the majority of the audience were German speakers.

The examples given so far illustrate the various strategies that the presenters may use for appealing to the audience's understanding for the choice of the code and their strategies for maximising the audience's understanding of the presentation. The fact that different presenters choose different language codes for their presentations does not necessarily facilitate understanding and complicates the discussion of issues presented in the papers, as will be exemplified below.

2.2.2. Deciding the language code for the discussion

Since the conference had announced no official language(s) for the presentations, but rather left the choice of language code to the presenter, there was no official language code for the discussion, either. At the beginning of the first speaker's discussion time, the chair thanked the presenter in German and made a comment in German first, to get the discussion going. The presenter, who had given his presentation in German, naturally answered in German. Since the opening of the conference, the first talk, and the first comment and the response to it were all in German, one could have assumed that German was by then more or less established as 'the language' for the conference. Yet it was not long, before the issue of language code was raised during the discussion. A German-speaking discussant who had worked in an English-speaking country for years raised the choice of code as an issue, as shown in (4):

(4) *Discussant:* **Ja, aber vielleicht darf ich mal etwas ganz einfaches mal fragen. Dürfen wir erm Fragen in englischer und auch in deutscher Sprache aufstellen, oder muss das immer nur Deutsch werden? Also erm ich meine, es gibt etliche hier, die Englisch besser sprechen können, erm es gibt auch etliche, die die beiden Sprachen sprechen können … erm Wir *wollen nur wissen.**

Chair: *Ja, ich glaube schon. Sie können ruhig Englisch sprechen, vielleicht bekommen Sie eine deutsche Antwort.
Discussant: **Gut. Vielen Dank. Na, das wollten wir nur fragen, nicht?** [several seconds pause]

*Discussant: Yes, but may I perhaps ask about something really simple. Are we erm allowed to present questions in English and also in German, or does it always have to be German? That is erm I think there are a few here who can speak English better, erm there are also some who speak both languages ... erm We *just want to know.*
*Chair *Yes, I think so. You can certainly speak English, perhaps you will get an answer in German.*
Discussant: Good. Many thanks. Well, that's what we just wanted to know, right?
[several seconds pause]

Example (4) shows that no obvious rules had been set for the participants as to what language code they should have used during the Discussion.

Even though the language issue had thus explicitly been cleared to favour the use of both languages during the conference, in Example (5), the discussants feel somewhat puzzled as to which code choice would actually be the most efficient one for common communication. Example (5) shows how a discussant, this time the participant from New Zealand, still felt uncertain about which code to use. The discussant had just taken a turn after the previous discussant's remarks which were in German.

(5)   *Discussant:* I guess so ... That's the same too [inaudible] not saying that the German perspective was not that there [inaudible]. **Ja also erm, soll ich Englisch oder Deutsch sprechen. I speak English.** I think erm and erm er I think er Dr. X. erm er X's [inaudible] has been er examined by...

Discussant: ... So erm, should I speak English or German ...

The discussant decided for English, as he was a native English speaker, but all the hesitation markers (*erm, er)* after the decision may be an indication of the fact that the question of deciding in which language to continue has put him slightly off the track in building up a coherent message.

Once the issue of the choice of language code has been discussed openly, the chair begins to use the code choice as a strategy for inviting questions. In (6), after the American speaker's presentation, the chair first invited questions in German and, when the audience felt reluctant to respond and take a turn, the chair then attempted to entice some questions or comments in English. An invitation to ask questions in English may naturally inhibit some of the German or other non-English-speaking members of the audience to ask questions at all, thus indicating some 'shyness' in using English during discussions. The chair tried to fill in the time by chatting on in English, and probably felt relieved when someone finally volunteered a question. Note that when this happened the chair switched back to German when realising his turn allocation duties.

(6) *Chair:* **Ja, Fragen zu diesem ausgezeichneten Vortrag. Wir haben uns jetzt, sagen wir, sehr viel von der er biografischen Wissenschaft der forsterischen Reisen hier präsentiert bekommen. Sie sollten die Gelegenheit wahrnehmen, gerade auf zu den Sammlungen Fragen zu stellen** [4 second pause] I would like to ask to do it in English of course. I have the experience that the obvious connection [inaudible]. The nearer you go to the material er the more it er becomes, it's like er an explosion of questions and thing. You come across these pieces and there you are [inaudible] ... **Ja?**

Chair: Well, questions about this splendid presentation. We have just been presented, let's say, a lot about the er biographical science concerning the travels by the Forster. You should take the opportunity to ask questions directly about these collections [...] ... Yes?

Sometimes there is no negotiation about the use of language code in the discussion, but the presenters and the discussants just launch in whatever language they feel most comfortable in, without ever really checking whether the chosen language code is actually convenient for getting the message across with the presenter and the members of the audience. In (7), the speaker was a native speaker of New Zealand English who could speak both German and English, and yet he gave his presentation in English. In the example, he had just answered the previous question in English. The chair then nominated the next discussant in German. This discussant presented his question in German.

(7) *Presenter:* I, I think that is the one of the most interesting voyages in terms of psychological interaction. Quite apart from the medical problems, say of the third voyage, that they had, 'cause a lot of these conditions are medically related ...
Chair: **Herr W., bitte.** [4 seconds pause]
Discussant: **Die Frage, ob erm ... der Vater, der den Sohn unterdrückt habe, erm ist wahrscheinlich eine, die erm zu sehr die Frage nach wer ist daran Schuld aufwirft ... erm Natürlich sieht in der Regel der Vater es nicht so, und der Sohn sieht es zumindest in einer bestimmten Entwicklungsfrage so. Die Frage ist doch, warum sich Georg aus einer bestimmten Entwicklungsphase nicht hat sich lösen können und diese hohe Ambivalenz bis zum Tode bewahrt hat [...] Es war ein schreckliches Leben.**
Presenter: Erm I'm not sure whether you want me to answer it. But I, I would agree. I think another thing is as he sees etc.

Chair: Mr. W., please. [4 seconds pause]
Discussant: The question, if erm the father had suppressed the son, is probably a the erm too much the question of who is to blame for it ... er Of course as a rule the father sees it that way and the son sees it another way at least at a particular stage of growing up. The question is really, why couldn't Georg at a particular stage of growing up detach himself and why did this strong ambivalence remain with him until his death. [...] It was a horrible life.

The discussant obviously knew that the presenter knew German (he had just at least read and translated some German quotations in his paper). Out of respect and politeness for the presenter's choice of the language of the presentation, there would have been room to negotiate the language choice for asking questions. The discussant could at least have asked whether the choice of German was fine with the presenter and said that it would have been fine for the presenter to give his comment in English. Neither did the presenter negotiate the language. Rather, in taking the responding turn, he launches straight into using English, although he could have used German for the benefit of the German discussant. He seems somewhat uncertain about whether the discussant's turn was meant as a question, or just as a comment, not needing a response. What seems interesting is that both parties rely on their own native language without negotiating the language with the interactional partner. They seem to know that each understands the other's language. They could each have shown politeness by selecting to communicate in the language of the other, but this did not happen.

3.3. Summary

This section has shown that in the conference taken as an example, the function and status of German and English were not established officially. Thus the issue of 'which language code – English or German – should I be using?' emerges again and again for the presenters and the discussants. Conference organisers are well advised to consider the language choice issues in advance, and clarify the situation to the conference participants. This may do away with some of the confusion that may arise in conference events where there is multilingualism.

4. Codeswitching from German to English and vice versa

We have so far looked at the general negotiation (or non-negotiation) of language code switches. A more detailed picture of codeswitching within the presentation and the discussion may give us an insight into what the participants are trying to achieve by switching language codes. This section first explains what is meant by codeswitching and what kind of research has been conducted in this area, before examining instances in the data.

4.1. Codeswitching - its emergence as a research field

Codeswitching is often used to refer to the switching between dialects of a language. Blom & Gumperz (1972) are considered among the first to study this

344

phenomenon. They noticed that in a fishing village in Norway, when the villagers came to an administrative office, they would typically exchange greetings and inquiries about family matters in a local dialect, and switch over to standard Norwegian when they started attending to business. This kind of codeswitching is today better labelled as 'register' codeswitching. Yet codeswitching had already, before Blom & Gumperz's study, also been referred to **as switching from one language code to another**. Gumperz & Hernandez-Chavez (1970), for example, discussed very early on how the Hispanics in the U.S.A. switch between American English and Spanish. Now there are numerous studies that cover the topic of codeswitching from one language to another. Some of the most notable studies dealing with codeswitching between languages, and its social and linguistic explanations, are perhaps Gardner-Chloros' (1991) study of codeswitching between French and Alsatian in Strasbourg (a dialect of German), Myers-Scotton's (1993) description of codeswitching in Africa, Gibbon's (1983) study of codeswitching in Hong Kong, and Heller's (1988) study of managers' codeswitching between English and French in Montreal.

Why is codeswitching used in speech communities? Linguists strive for various kinds of social and discoursal explanations. One possible reason for codeswitching is that it is simply expected in **certain contexts** and with **certain participants** - an example being a school principal addressing the guard at the gate in Swahili and the receptionist at an office in English (the example is from Myers-Scotton's (1993) work, see also Swann (1996: 313-16)). Myers-Scotton (1993) labels this as an 'unmarked' choice, whereas 'marked' codeswitching for her indicates an unexpected codeswitch. We could interpret this so that the choice of English as a conferencing language is an unmarked choice for English native speakers in British, American, Canadian, etc. conferences and German for German presenters in Germany, Austria or Switzerland. Similarly, when English, French or Portuguese conference participants give papers in German in Germany this could be considered an unmarked choice, since 'when in Rome do as the Romans do'. The choice of a German presenter to present in English in Germany would be a marked code choice, and so would be the choice of an English presenter to present in English.

A second reason for codeswitching often mentioned by linguists is the maintenance and negotiation of one's **identity**, e.g. when in Heller's (1988) work the anglophone Canadian managers want to become accepted by their francophone colleagues by using French. Striving for an identity as an accepted bilingual may be a driving motivation for one of the English speakers (a New Zealander) in the examples that will be discussed in the following sections.

Codeswitching may also signal negotiating **a change in the interactional relationship** and may be used to show power. In Heller's (1988) data, for example, a francophone Canadian manager changes from casual talk with an anglophone to French when opening a meeting. This kind of codeswitching is probably found more in during the social events at conferences, rather than in the actual conference talk during the sessions.

Codeswitching has further been noticed to be used for **characterising someone else's speech in a narrative** (Sebba's work on switching between London English and Creole, in Swann 1996: 315). It is plausible that conference participants might use this kind of codeswitching strategically.

Although these reasons listed above are just a few to be found in the codeswitching literature, they may function as an indication of how we ought to be perceiving and interpreting codeswitching in conference events. The next section gives some examples of codeswitching from the Forster conference data and discusses their possible functions.

4.2. Codeswitching between English and German while conferencing

So far, literature dealing with codeswitching in conference data is practically non-existent. Yet, as conference participants in multicultural and multilingual situations, we know it is happening – perhaps more extensively in the social events of conferences than in the actual 'business' events of conferences. Since no data so far have been collected from social events in multilingual conferences, let us begin this exploration by looking at codeswitching in the presentations and the discussions which follow them. The focus of the section will now move beyond the 'language code announcement' (or non-announcement), which was exemplified in Section 3.

4.2.1. Codeswitching during presentations

Why would a presenter want to codeswitch during a presentation? As we have seen from the preceding examples in Section 3.2.1, the conference language was fixed neither as English nor as German nor both. The chair, however, consistently spoke German when introducing the presenter. This caused a codeswitch when the transition was made from the chair to the next presenter, if the next presenter was a native English speaker. The presenter thus had to indicate to the audience that s/he chose to deliver his/her speech in English. German speakers chose to present their papers in German. On one occasion, a German presenter chose to switch over to English in the middle of his presentation for the benefit of the English speaking (and perhaps for the other international) members of the audience (see Example 3). This kind of codeswitch was above considered more as a **code-choice** than a codeswitch, i.e. the speaker consciously selects a language code for the whole or part of his/her presentation.

But presenters also codeswitch for other reasons than just to indicate the language preference during their presentations. First of all, there is lexical codeswitching, which will be labelled **borrowing**, after Swann (1996: 320). The term here refers to lexical items that enter the presenter's talk as whole units in the other language because they are usually names, institutions, concepts established in that other cultural context and are not easily translated. In (8) *Society of Antiquaries* and in (9) *Preussische Kulturbesitz* function as examples of this kind, here appearing in the middle of a German and English presenters' talks.

(8) *Presenter:* Eingeführt von seinem Vater, präsentierte er dieses Werk in der Londoner **Society of Antiquaries**, und diese Szene erinnert fast an ein anderes Wunderkind, das in diesen Jahren von seinem Vater in ganz Europa vorgeführt wurde, an den jungen Mozart.

(9) *Presenter:* The full title of this work runs parallel to that of the botany and is paralleled exactly in its title by the Paris botanical manuscript ... [a bit later] And is now fortunately in the **Preußische Kulturbesitz** in Berlin and deserves to be published.

In addition to borrowing, we have codeswitching when something is quoted from a source such as a book or an original letter. In (10), a German presenter quotes in English directly from the letters that Sparrman wrote to Forster.

(10) *Presenter:* Auf der einen Seite heißt es in einem Brief von Sparrman an Forster, in dem er fragt von 19- 1777: **"Will the Forstera-"** - er hat also eine Gattung nach Forster benannt, und das konnte man ja nicht selber eigentlich machen - **"Will the Forstera and descriptions of my other herbs be inserted at the same time?"** In diesem Brief ist übrigens auch die Rede von Pflanzen, die Forster an Sparrman schicken wollte, und er schreibt: **"As for the plants for me, do not hurry yourself on my account"**. Andererseits schreibt Forster 1779 an seinen Vater: "ich habe hier nur Sparrmans Papiere..."

Note that this German presenter does not provide the audience with translations of the English quotations. He more or less assumes that the audience will be able to understand English and will thus construe the meanings intended from both of the language codes. In the next example, (11), the translation is provided. The German presenter assumes that most of the audience cannot construe the meanings without a translation. The passage quoted is in Latin.

(11) *Presenter*: Er [Forster] hat sich wiederholt in die Zerteilung der Wissenschaft in getrennte und von einander abgekapselte Disziplinen gewandt, mit drastischer Bildhaftigkeit in einem Satz aus seiner Wilnaer Antrittsvorlesung, deren lateinische Sprache sie leider oder relativ unzugänglich macht. Er sagt: Egomet autem mihi fortiter persuasum habeo, sterilem fore quamli- quamlibet disciplinam dum caeleps remanserit: omnes autem tunc demum uberrimos fructus in medium prolaturas, cum mutuis amplexibus se invicem deosculaverint et veluti connubio recoaluerint. **Ich übersetze: Ich jedenfalls habe die starke Überzeugung, daß jegliche Wissenschaft unfruchtbar ist, solange sie ledig bleibt, und daß alle Wissenschaften reiche Früchte tragen, wenn sie sich untereinander umarmen und küssen und gleichsam in einer Ehe miteinander verbinden. Die deutsche Literaturgeschichte ...**

Presenter: I translate: I, at least, am strongly convinced that any science is sterile, as long as it remains unmarried, and that all sciences are fruitful, if they embrace and kiss and are somehow joined in marriage. The German literary history ...

That the translation is needed, when the quoted passages are in Latin, is today understandable. When quoted passages are in French, they may also, in today's academic world, need translations (much to the disappointment of the French language policy makers). When the presenter from New Zealand gives his speech he provides an English translation of a passage he quotes in French. Interestingly enough, and in contrast to the German speaker in (10), he also gives translations when he quotes in German, although most of the audience are German speakers. Example (12) illustrates how he gives a bit-by-bit translation of, and a commentary on, the passage in English, after he reads the quotation in German. This may be considered an example of what Sebba noted (see above) – bringing in other voices through codeswitching. Georg Forster's voice comes through his own words in German more effectively than in English translation (The quoted passage is given in bold; the translation by the speaker in bold and italics.)

(12) *Presenter*: ...On the 26th of November he wrote to Voß in Berlin, who had long been a faithful publisher of Johann Reinhold Forster, and Georg went over to him, many of you probably know the story of how they were competing for translations. Georg wrote rather wearily: "Jetzt noch eine Bitte an Sie im engsten Vertrauen. Meine Lage ist, wie Sie leicht denken können, sehr eingeschränkt. Ich bin im Haushalt ein Anfänger, habe sonst mich weit schlechter gestanden als jetzt" - we all know when that was- "und kann also auch noch nicht sagen, daß ich von vorigen Zeiten her auf dem Trockenen und Reinen wäre". **I'll briefly translate as we go. Georg is saying there, to his publisher, Voß,** "I am a beginner in setting up a household, and as you know I've had difficult times before. I don't think the situation is at the moment quite as bad as it used to be" - I guess we're referring to Johann Reinhold Forster's time. - "So rasch und eifrig ich auch seither gearbeitet habe, so wenig spüre ich doch noch Erleichterung, und dagegen zwingt mich meine geschwächte Gesundheit zu einer größeren Enthaltsamkeit im Arbeiten, wenigstens auf das nächste Jahr". **Georg is saying here,** "my health is not brilliant, although I have worked very very hard, I can see that my health is going to get

worse". It's this this scurvy. It doesn't say that here but it is clear that that's what it's going to be, so you can see his economic situation is getting worse into the next year 1792 ...

The presenter is not giving all the details in his translations. We may wonder why. We may also wonder why he bothers about the translation and does not trust the conference participants' capacity to also make meanings in German. Perhaps he feels obliged by his initial promise to help those of his listeners who did not understand German (see Example 2). Interestingly, at times, this presenter from New Zealand seems to have difficulties in giving the translations in English, as shown in (13).

(13) *Presenter:* Zimmerman may have been surprised within two weeks of the above letter to get another, complaining that no one speaks for him, that is Johann Reinhold Forster in Halle. Für meinen armen Vater spricht niemand, says Georg. He may be passed over again in preference in Halle, now that some of these professors have died and passed on. And he says, seine Wahrheitsgeist, seine Wahrheitsgeist, seine Wahrheitsgeist ist unbiegsam und störrisch, und seine Laune die eines oft gekränkten Mannes. His truth, his feeling for truth is unserving, erm, and his ... his temperament is that of an often - of a man who is often, erm - ja gekränkt, sagt er. Easily beleidigt, easily - I can't think of the English. What is the word? Pardon? Hurt! Yes, yes. I can't, sometimes I can't think of the English. Allein das hindert nicht, daß er ein guter Professor sein, und der Universität in Halle Ehre machen könne. Now that doesn't mean that he is not a very good professor, or could be, and has been, and could bring honour to the University of Halle. Georg was now determined to speak up for him in Berlin, which he did, and Johann Reinhold Forster was in Halle, as I said, was in that position for 18 years and was in the end a successful professor.

The question that arises is whether this presentation is any easier for the English-speaking audience to understand than the German presentation where English is incorporated into the presentation without a translation in German.

4.2.2. Codeswitching during the discussion

In the conference data examined, codeswitching also frequently happens during the discussion phases of papers. Similarly to codeswitching in the presentations, we find local codeswitching, where a word may be borrowed from another context. The discussant sometimes consequently continues in the code triggered by the borrowed expression. In (14), the switch is possibly caused by the term *Naturphilosophy* which comes out half in German, half in English, and from that moment onwards the discussant uses English – his mother tongue.

(14) *Discussant:* Und erm und diese, diese drei Größen, würde ich sagen, erm sprechen dafür, dass wenigstens sozusagen ein Ruck in die andere Richtung gegangen ist. (...) **Naturphilosophy,** I just like to say that erm there was descriptive methods that were

used by the (McLays) and others from about the 1820s onwards. So this whole question "Naturphilosophy" is not just a German thing. Perhaps doesn't - erm we don't have quite the same depth. But certainly from erm in London from about 1828 and 30 onwards this whole question of erm for instance economy through the circular meter, as it was called, that was very very strong *erm in -
Presenter: *Hm, hm.
Discussant: Britain.
Presenter: Ja, erm das habe ich auch gemeint. Ich meinte, die Entwicklung der Natur-
... geschichte, also die erm die Tatsache, dass die Naturgeschichte erm zu Forsters Zeit überwog und dass sie erst im Laufe des 19. Jahrhunderts abge- erm -löst wurde von erm von anderen Wissenschaftsmethoden. Das habe ich nicht auf Deutschland beschränken wollen. Das ist ganz ganz eindeutig ein allgemeiner Vorgang.

The presenter, a German scholar resident in the States, does not react to the Discussant's codeswitch, by answering in English, but rather continues with the language of the presentation; German, and his earlier replies to the other discussants. There seems to be a wish to retain his German-speaker identity.

The same New Zealand-speaker who in (14) switches from German to English, does a reverse switch from English to German in (15) and (16). The codeswitch seems to be initially caused by the technical terms of *Realpolitik und Wirtschaftspolitik (realist politics and economic politics)*, but then the speaker does not continue defining the terms. He simply relies on the audience's common understanding of these terms, as indicated by *und so weiter, und so weiter (and so on, and so on)*. The reliance is partly justified: *Realpolitik* is also a word used in English in its German form, but *Wirtschaftspolitik* is not. Similarly a little later, the codeswitch is restricted only to a nominal group, and it seems to be motivated by a mere need for a technical term, *Gründer unserer Wissenschaften von verschiedenen Richtlinien the founder of the guidelines of our sciences.*

(15) **Discussant:** ... but I, I found your, your ... very enlightening, very enlightening for those who perhaps don't appreciate quite so much the influences in Germany of between Realpolitik und Wirtschaftspolitik und so weiter und so weiter und so weiter. erm But it is important to understand that for in our part of the world, as perhaps some of us will show tomorrow, eh in the South Pacific in particular eh that Forster is seen as a person in his own right, as is Johann Reinhold Forster as Gründer unserer Wissenschaften von verschiedenen Richtlinien.
Chair: Gibt's noch Meldungen?
Chair: Are there any more comments?

It is also interesting to look at the codeswitching taking place between the conference participants during the discussion time at length. In (16), the presenter is the New Zealander, who first answers the native American discussant's (Discussant 1) question. Then the next discussant (Discussant 2) joins in. His comment shows that he has been able to follow the discussion in

English, and he simply adds to the discussion, but does it in German, to which then the presenter gives his response in English. After the chair's turn allocation, a further German discussant gets involved (Discussant 3). This discussant is the German speaker who, as has already been mentioned, is a permanent resident of the US. Thus, this discussant could have presented his comment also in English, but he does it in German, holding to his 'German-discussant' identity, and the New Zealander, on his side, holds on to his 'English-discussant' identity, although at the end he slips into German, when giving his afterthought (cf. Heller's (1988) work mentioned earlier on maintaining identity through a code).

(16) *Discussant 1:* Do you think that George was oppressed on their voyages, well that Reinhold kept him in the cabin drawing pictures, or do you think he gave him more of a free rain on the voyage?

Presenter: I think they worked as many - any scientific team worked, but I think you had two young men with a man who knew his own mind, as we've heard yesterday [...] So I think it was a close tight knit team. Whether George was oppressed by his father ... That's the question I think we've got to ...leave... open. Certainly he was a hard task master.

Discussant 1: But, but Reinhold wouldn't have thought that he was oppressing. It was George that thought he was being oppressed.

Presenter: Yeah, but he's ambivalent about that because he sends his works to him and sometimes he wants to know him, sometimes he doesn't. He knows that his view is very important. It depends what we mean by oppression. And I guess only a psychologist can answer that. I, I think that is the - one of the most interesting voyages in terms of psychological interaction. Quite apart from the medical problems say of the third voyage that they had, 'cause a lot of these conditions are medically related.

Chair: Herr R. bitte.

Discussant 2: Die Frage, ob erm ... der Vater, der den Sohn unterdrückt habe, erm ist wahrscheinlich eine, die erm zu sehr die Frage nach wer ist daran Schuld aufwirft. erm Natürlich sieht in der Regel der Vater es nicht so, und der Sohn sieht es zumindest in einer bestimmten Entwicklungsphase so. Die Frage ist doch, [...] man sollte das Georg Forstersche Leben mit Reise und Revolution keineswegs idealisieren. Es war ein sehr schreckliches Leben.

Presenter: Erm I'm not sure whether you want me to answer it. But I, I would agree. I think another thing is, as he says in a letter to Michaelis, we are almost English. ... And I think that when they came back from the voyage they intended to stay in England, and had they done so they would have published ... [the response continues quite awhile] ... They could have easily ended up like Solander, erm like many other Germans who remained in London productively erm including some of their closest friends. They could well have remained in England like so many Germans who came to the Antipodes and built up a career there. And they could have been grand gentlemen. But they would have been bloody productive grand gentlemen.

Chair: Herr U., bitte.

Discussant 3: Erm wir, wir haben vor allem über die, die, also die Tragik, wenn man so will nennen will, von Georg Forster gesprochen, aber man muss sich ja klar sein, dass erm Johann Reinhold Forster ein Mann war, mit dem niemand auskam. Und erm Georg hat in der Situation ja doch eines gelernt, dass man nämlich erm verhandeln muss und dass man erm irgendwie erm versuchen muss, irgendwie zu einem Kompromiss zu kommen [...] Und er wollte erm mit seiner Frau und deren Freund zusammen leben, und sie ist von ihm weggegangen. Also das das ist eine sehr, sehr schwierige, sehr, sehr menschlich, sehr, sehr, äußerst delikate Situation.

Presenter: At the end - the thing I would, would say is, and this is no elimination of the important years, but the last years in Halle were very mellow after George's death. Perhaps George's death taught Johann Reinhold Forster a lesson ... [the response continues quite awhile] ... Sure I think, I agree with you, the, the more important phases of his life ... but... I think perhaps Johann Reinhold Forster in the end did learn from that relationship. I - when I was writing my biography, I deliberately - mit Scheuklappen - made sure that I did not go off into the George Forster relationship. I, I, I picked up where you left it in 65 hoping that someone in Germany would, would pick that up. To me it's erm hasn't happened, may well about to be happen (he laughs). I hope that of the solutions of this, erm this, this symposium will be to look at that. If not, I guess some of us down on the deeper South. Am Ende der Welt es gibt noch ein anderes Wort am - ja das soll ich nicht sagen, nicht.

Chair: **Ja, bitte.**

This is probably the best of the examples in this conference data which shows that academic conference communication can also be successful when two languages are used. Discussant 2 continues comfortably in German after the English dialogue between the presenter and Discussant 1. The introduction he gives when beginning his turn shows that he has understood the preceding dialogue and now wants to give his interpretation: *Die Frage, ob erm ... der Vater, der den Sohn unterdrückt habe, erm ist wahrscheinlich ... [The question whether the father oppressed the son is probably...].* The native-speaker presenter shows that he has understood what Discussant 2 has argued for, but since the turn was not formulated as a question, but rather as a comment, the presenter is not quite certain what kind of a reply turn the Discussant 2 expects from the presenter: *Erm I'm not sure whether you want me to answer it. But I, I would agree.* Discussant 3 continues in German but relates his turn to what Discussant 1 has introduced as a topic in English, the character of Johann Reinhold Forster and his oppressiveness and its influences on the young Georg Forster. The presenter's response is again in English, but show that he has fully been able to develop the argument that Discussant 3 has presented in German: *Sure I think, I agree with you, the, the more important phases of his life...* Codeswitching between the languages is successfully employed in (16). For this kind of codeswitching, the participants have to understand each other's languages sufficiently, and they have to be willing to construe meanings together and exchange opinions, although they want to do that in different languages. Both parties can thus keep to their preferred languages and the language identities they have chosen for the situation.

4.2.3. Summary

This section has looked at codeswitching in more detail in the presentations and in the discussions which follow them. The examples show how frequent codeswitching can be in multilingual conference situations. It may be a means of borrowing language items useful for the presentation of the subject matter. Or it may be a means of quoting from foreign language sources, in which case it is up to the presenter then to decide whether the audience need translations and further explanations. More bilingual conference participants seem to be more likely to codeswitch during their presentations, perhaps thus hoping to enhance the audience's understanding. Yet continuous codeswitching and translation may actually confuse or irritate some of the members of the audience. In discussions, codeswitching seems also to be triggered by borrowings from another code, where the speaker then forgets to return to the original code. The discussions also show participants' considerable consistency in keeping to the language they feel closest to. In this way, conference participants who are bilingual can quite successfully participate in knowledge construction and exchanging views without losing their preferred 'language identities'.

5. Avoiding problems and aiming at successful meaning-making: intelligibility in presentations and discussions in multilingual conference events.

Many of the papers in this volume have already taken a synoptic view on the organisation of a conference paper and its discussion. According to this synoptic perspective, for instance, the discussion proceeds smoothly from a Question to an Answer or from a Comment to a Response. The chair regulates the change of turns. Most of the examples in this chapter so far have also displayed this kind of tidy turn-taking in discussions. Yet conversational reality in discussions is rarely so straightforward. Often discussions unfold much more dynamically, and the presenter and the discussant really have to work at a common understanding. Sometimes such understanding is never achieved. The examples in this section show that there is a considerable amount of checking on *meaning-making* necessary in conference discussions, especially when the discussants come from different language backgrounds and codeswitching is involved.

In (17), the discussant is a Portuguese academic who starts her turn as a discussant in German, but the presenter from New Zealand does not seem to be getting her intended meaning. Therefore, the presenter checks on the meanings she is trying to get through to him in German: *Have I understood you rightly....* Typically for him (in this data), he sticks to his own code, English. He could have performed this check also in German, because he is also fluent in German,

353

as we have seen in the previous examples. This would have been justified especially since the discussant sets German up as her language for discussion. Using German would have meant a neutral linguistic codeswitch territory, as it woud have been a foreign languge for both. But he ignores her choice of language code. The check in English is, then, interpreted by the Portuguese discussant as his difficulty of understanding her comment in German, and therefore she tries to make her meanings clear to him by codeswitching into his native language, English. The meaning negotiation is carried on in English, except right at the end, where the Portuguese participant codeswitches once again back into German, to emphasise an important point: *zu wenig revolutionär (not revolutionary enough)*.

(17) *Chair:* Ja bitte.
   Discussant: Ich wollte nur, nur eine kurze Bemerkung. Sie haben von der, erm oder, oder teamship -ship, oder, oder sagen wir nicht so, erm die enge Beziehung zwischen Vater und Sohn wissenschaftlich jetzt. Und meine Frage wäre, inwiefern man das auch so erm ... erweitern könnte, also jetzt politisch gemeint. Also ich meine, dass Georg Forster, der Sohn, dann eine völlig andere erm einen völlig anderen Weg gegangen ist, erm jetzt was seine politische Entscheidung anbelangt. Also das heißt nicht, dass der Vater da auch eine Rolle spielen erm könnte, aber ich glaube schon, dass da solche biographische Erklärung erm Klärungen nicht ausreichen, um dann Forsters politische, jetzt Georg Forsters politische Entwicklung zu erklären. Das ist wieder mein Problem.
   Presenter: Have I understood you rightly that you think that Johann Reinhold Forster had no influence on the political thinking of George?
   Discussant: No, I meant perhaps he could have *had.[6]
   Presenter: *Oh, I'm -
   Discussant: But not that much because when you erm read, when you know of erm Johann erm Reinhold's erm position after George Forster's erm, erm you said that in English erm -
   Presenter: Arrival back in Germany?
   Discussant: No, I mean in Mainz erm -
   Presenter: Yeah.
   Discussant: And after his death it's, erm it's quite complicated and, well ... I think we can't discuss about this, because it's, erm we are not, erm it's not possible to discuss what was going on in their minds.
   Presenter: *No other than -
   Discussant: *And I think that my problem is only how far, if we consider this, I, I think your task is very important. I mean, erm what concerning Johann Reinhold Forster because he's been very, erm, erm ...
   Presenter: *Neglected?
   Discussant: *neglected ...**mhm.
   Presenter: **And still is, yeah.
   Discussant: (In England) where you, you can still, - well, I'm Portuguese, so I can speak sort of erm -
   Presenter: Yeah.

---
[6] Asterisks show the beginning of simultaneous speech.

Discussant: as an outsider.
Presenter: Yeah
Discussant: But I think, if we insist on that point, I think that we forget Georg Forster as a revolutionary.
Presenter: *Yeah.
Discussant: *That's my point. It's too much -
Presenter: **Yeah.
Discussant: **scientist and ...
Presenter: Yes.
Discussant: and zu wenig revolutionär.
Presenter: Yeah. I, I, I have to say quite frankly in the Southern hemisphere that some of us here are interested in him primarily as a scientist. You can keep your revolutionary activity, if you like. I mean we are interested, but for us, erm and I'm speaking - not speaking personally - because I'm interested in the whole of the life, but here's the problem. ... They were thrown out of England, their forefathers were thrown out of England for political reasons ... [continues]

This is a good example of how dynamics break up the typical synoptic conference discussion turn-taking: chair ^ discussant's question/comment ^ presenter's answer/comment. But it also offers a challenge to current discourse analytical methods. We necessarily have to develop methods for analysing dynamic unfolding of interaction, not only in everyday interactions, but also in professional contexts. What may seem well-regulated, in a synoptic view, has in reality a possibility of extensive dynamic unfolding of interaction. This example shows the difficulties in meaning-making in native – non-native interaction and the role of codeswitching in it. The unfolding interaction is an excellent demonstration of how interactants build meanings up individually and together. The native speaker supports *(yeah)* and helps out (e.g. *neglected)* the non-native speaker in her language code formulations. Working out the dynamics of exchange in examples like these may be a challenge to our present theories of exchange and who initiates and is in control in exchanging (see Ventola 1987, Martin 1992, de Ravin 2001).

We have seen that most of the conference participants strive for construing knowledge and meaning-making together, in spite of the problems that relatively frequent codeswitching may bring. Yet, some participants will always feel linguistically disadvantaged when the presentations are not given in their own native languages and feel that they may not fully participate in the discussion. An example of this is given in (19). One of the older German discussants admits, when he finally gets a turn during the discussion, that he has not understood all of the previous discussion, since it was carried out in English: *Hm, ich konnte leider nicht alles verstehen zur Diskussion (Hm, unfortunately I couldn't understand all of the discussion).* He is thus aware of the fact that whatever he will say in his turn runs the risk of not being relevant to the discussion developed so far. Then, he launches into a long, monologic explanation of his views on the topic in German. The presenter, the New Zealand speaker, responds merely *Danke, Professor (Thank you, Professor)*. The presenter's response in its brevity raises queries. Was the response so short merely because as a younger scholar and academically in a lower position, he simply wanted to show his respect to the older discussant's views, without getting into argumentative discourse with him? Or was it the case that the English-speaking presenter got lost in the German professor's eloquent German, was unable to follow the German scholar's explanation and therefore simply 'escaped' from the situation by simply thanking the professor and thus bringing the discussion to an end?

(18) *Presenter:* ... But again anybody who was perhaps involved in [inaudible], at that time it was perhaps not a too difficult thing to do, but he certainly was involved in [inaudible] in Halle whether that was [inaudible] or they were paying him something, if, if there was money in it, Johann Reinhold Forster was usually there then. So was George [laughs] ...yeah.

Chair: Ja, schließen wir jetzt. Herr S.? Sie wollten noch mal?

Discussant: **Hm, ich konnte leider nicht alles verstehen zur Diskussion.** Jetzt ich, eh renne deswegen offene Tore vielleicht ein mit dem, was ich sagen will. Ich glaube, ich nehme an, dass eine gewisse Abnabelung vom Vater in dem Moment eingetreten ist, als der Vater nach Deutschland zurückgekehrt ist. ... Der alte Forster war in Halle wieder zu Hause, er war in seinem preußischen Vaterland [inaudible]. Der junge Forster, ein Ausländer sein Leben lang, wo er auch war. Das bedingte eine gewisse Unstetigkeit. Er wollte immer wieder entfliehen, zuletzt sogar nach Indien. Er wollte sich dauernd verändern. eh Dies - dieselbe eh -selbe Differenz zeigt sich in der, vor, in dem Verhältnis zur Freimaurerei. Der Vater war ein hoher Beamter in Halle in der, in einer Loge, eh in einer eh (strengen feudalistischen) Loge. Der Sohn drängte nach seinem Logenerlebnis in England und in Frankreich in der eh Freimaurerloge [inaudible] eh immer wieder aus dieser eh, eh streng gehorsamen Loge heraus. Nach einem kurzen Spiel in Kassel in der eh in der Loge eh hat er sich dann eigentlich zu den Rosenkreuzern, eh ist er zu den Rosenkreuzern aus dieser Loge aus diesem Grund gewissermaßen geflüchtet. eh Die Flucht ging natürlich schief, wie manche Flucht so schief geht, und eh dann fand er wieder in der josephinischen in der josephinischen Loge, zwei Logen, vor allem der einen in Wien, eh was noch in der polnischen Zeit [inaudible] Korrespondenz. Der Vater blieb aber Herr in seinem, in seinen Betrachtungen erm und lehnte ein, einen Versuch des Sohnes in die Rosen, erm den Rosenkreuzern sich anzuschließen, strikt ab. Es gab auch ein gewisses Verwürfnis, das in einem Brief (...) Severin deutlich zum Ausdruck kommt. Erm also, das wollte ich jetzt nur kurz dazu sagen.
Presenter: **Danke, Professor.**

Chair: Ja. Ja. ... Ja, wir schließen jetzt damit unsere Abteilung ab.

In the last example, (19), the discussion was carried out in English. However, both the German presenter and the native-English-speaker discussant (the New

Zealander) were constantly checking each other's meaning-making. The discussant first checked whether he had got the presenter's message right. While the discussant was explaining his understanding, the German presenter was, however, having problems in understanding what the discussant was saying because of the acoustic problems caused by the microphone that the English-speaking discussant was using. Yet the discussant did not seem to be convinced that the German presenter actually got the meanings he was putting forth.

(19) *Discussant:* ... Have you studied the English ... and the German version in comparison to ehm, and have you found any fundamental differences between George's orig-original English version and the eh German version that he translated, because I think there are differences in .... If I understand what you have done, which I would be very interested in, you are saying that in order to fundamentally understand the biography of George Forster you have to really come to grips with these ... in other words you have to understand Johann Reinhold and that Johann Reinhold ... has a lifelong influence on Georg ... If that is what you are saying, then you are one of the persons that I've heard in Germany saying that, because fundamentally I think that's the answer to understanding George as a person, that the father survived the son by four years. He had the fundamental influence, as I may say my father had, It's either symbiotic or, ... and I would maintain, ehm and I guess that is maintained in literature, that it's only in those last years ... that George became fully independent of his father. Perhaps even do you notice a difference between the English and the German text in the passages, yea excuse me [the chair indicates that he is occupying the floor for too long].
Presenter: Yes, ... it's, it's a little, a little hard I think. I think I can, could hear you better if you wouldn't, wouldn't speak into the microphone [laughter].
Discussant: Do you understand what I'm saying?
Presenter: Yes, the first question is ... eh, no, I did not, I did not compare.
Discussant: Aha.
Presenter: That would be a next eh step, eh, eh, if I would decide to, to go on with this eh thing I did not.
Discussant: I think that's ...
Presenter: Mhm.
Discussant: Did I understand exact [inaudible] the biography of Johann Reinhold ...
Presenter: I think, what is needed is a ... bio-, a double biography of the two, and, and it is quite important that eh the father lived some years longer than his son lived.
Discussant: Do you think that psychological the ...
Presenter: Yes.
Discussant: [inaudible]
Presenter: Psychologically, psychologically not ... of course in part of his thinking that ... fundamentally not.
Discussant: [inaudible]

Expressing his views in English does indeed seem to be difficult to the German presenter. Again the traditional synoptic view of turn-taking in discussions breaks down. This time it appears that even 'good will' from both sides is not able to rescue the meaning-making. These kinds of difficulties and break-downs in meaning-making are naturally face-threatening to both parties and should be avoided at all costs at conferences.

6. Conclusion

The focus of this chapter has been switching between languages at conferences. The topic has so far largely been neglected both in the codeswitching literature and in the discourse analysis literature. This data shows that such small scale events where no official language (or languages) has designated, but where the presenters and audience, nevertheless, turn out to be from various countries with different language backgrounds and language skills, are likely to be events where such codeswitching frequently takes place. The chapter has discussed how presenters and discussants may announce which language they prefer for their papers or turns in the discussion, what kind of codeswitching seems to be happening within the presentations and discussions and how conference participants use codeswitching for making common knowledge building possible by construing meanings together by using different languages. But the paper has also indicated that there will always be members in the audience who will feel partly left out or simply incapable of making a contribution, because of fear that their language skills may be insufficient for successful communication. Further, on some occasions common knowledge construction and exchange of ideas simply breaks down, when conference participants seem not to even manage meaning-making by means of codeswitching.

How can we improve the communication and knowledge-building at international conferences under these kinds of circumstances – occasions where conferences emerge as multilingual events with continuous codeswitching between participants from different language backgrounds? The papers in this volume help all conference participants and linguists involved in the pedagogy of conferencing in the sense that our linguistic knowledge about conferencing and conferencing events is increasing. This knowledge can help us all in many ways, by providing a better understanding of the social context of conferencing and the different genres in different cultural contexts. It eventually also helps future presenters to structure their presentations better according to the audience's expectations, and to linguistically fine-tune their presentations by using meta-text and appropriate interpersonal realisations. Ultimately this linguistic knowledge will also filter into the pedagogy of conferencing, and thus we shall be able to advance much further in training native and non-native conference participants than the traditional rhetorical instruction methods, whereby a good speaker is someone who "speaks clearly, is able to paraphrase, and talks at the appropriate level of the hearer in terms of proficiency, topic and speech" (Smith 1985: 333).

But in many senses, it is not just the non-native speakers who need training in international communication, as noted by Campbell & Smith (1983: 46).

> Non-native speakers need training in the use of English not just with native speakers, but with (other) non-native speakers as well. Native speakers, on the other hand, need training in the use of their own language for international communication.

Codeswitching and managing it may be the key issue in training conference participants for international communication. It is obvious that everyone, whether native or non-native, can improve their presentation through practice and experience. Yet, we have to learn to prepare future conference participants for some of the more dynamically unfolding conference genres, e.g. in discussion and social talk. During these genres, very frequently speakers resort to using their own language (if allowed e.g. during the discussion) or codeswitching back and forth with the native language and English which they see as the lingua franca for conferencing. Codeswitching can be beneficial for common meaning-making, but it may also complicate the clarity of messages, if it is used too frequently or unconsciously (the presenter not noticing that s/he remained with the codeswitch for longer than intended). It can be used as a communicative strategy for those who understand both codes. Those conference participants whose native languages are totally unintelligible for the major part of the audience, do not have an option of using their own language for delivering papers or codeswitching (e.g. Portuguese at the conference analysed). They have no other option than either giving their papers in one of the major languages of the conference and participating in the discussion in those languages (German and English at the conference analysed). The alternative is to merely take the role of 'conference listeners'. Presenters and discussants may frequently be comfortable listening to what the others say in a foreign language, but in presenting or discussing will rely on their native language or the language they feel most fluent in.

In social events, 'shying away' from using the main languages of the conference and interacting and codeswitching in those languages, means that we have representatives from one country gathering up at the dinner table or around a table at the bar and carrying on the conversation in their native tongues. Inequal participation by presenters and discussants, or leaving 'loners' in social events, certainly does not help international understanding and common knowledge building. Rather, such behaviours encourage 'islands of isolation' and also feelings of being 'outsiders'. Monolingual native English speakers may profit from knowledge construction when English is the lingua franca during the session, but they, too, may feel left out of social talk at conferences in foreign countries, and form their own islands of isolation.

A scientific community is described as a discourse community with common goals. Conferences are *meeting places* to discuss those common goals. But what we sometimes forget is that conferences are also linguistic *melting pots*. Knowledge construction and the exchange of ideas in these meeting places is for the major part achieved linguistically, as is much of the social networking which opens the inner doors to these discourse communities and makes us feel part of the community. But with which language? Is it more beneficial to rely just on one international language – today in most cases it would be English – or do we see the 'Babel' of languages in conferences as a positive phenomenon? There is no simple answer to this. However, each conference organiser should consider the linguistic challenges for the events they plan. Applied linguists may help conference organisers and participants by pursuing a better understanding of conferences as multilingual events and helping participants to better cope with the linguistic demands of conferencing, including the resource and resort of codeswitching for construing messages and exchanging views.

References

Blom, J-P. and J. J. Gumperz. 1992. "Social meaning in linguistic structures: Code-switching in Norway". In J. J. Gumperz & D. Hymes (eds). *Directions in Sociolinguistics*. New York: Holt, Reinholt & Winston, 407-34.

Campbell, D. & L. Smith. 1983. "English in international settings: Problems and their causes." In L. Smith (ed.). *Readings in English as an International Language*. Oxford: Pergamon, 35-48.

Crystal, D. 1988. *The English Language*. Harmondsworth: Penguin.

Gardner-Chloros, P. 1991. *Language Selection and Switching in Strasbourg*. Oxford: Clarendon Press.

Gibbons, J. 1983. *Code-Mixing and Code Choice: A Hong Kong Case Study*. Clevendon, Avon: Multilingual Matters.

Gumperz, J. J. & E. Hernandez-Chavez 1970. "Cognitive aspects of bilingual communication". In. W. H. Whitely (ed.). *Language and Social Change*. Oxford: Oxford University Press, 115-25.

Heller, M. 1988. "Strategic ambiguity: Codeswitching in the management of conflict". In. M. Heller (ed.). *Code-Switching: Anthropological and Sociolinguistic Perspectives*. Berlin: Mouton de Gruyter, 77-96.

Kachru, B. B. 1985. *The Alchemy of English. Functions and Models of Non-native Englishes*. Oxford: Pergamon Institute of English.

Kachru, B. B. & C. L. Nelson 1996/2001. "World Englishes". In A. Burns & C. Coffin 2001. *Analysing English in a Global Context. A Reader*. London: Routledge, 9 25.

Lamy, M. N. 1996. "Reading B". In D. Graddoll, D. Leith & J. Swann (eds). *English. History, Diversity and Change*. London: Routledge. 32-36.

Martin, J. R. 1992. *English Text: System and structure*. Amsterdam/Philadelphia: John Benjamins.

Myers-Scotton, C. 1993. *Social Motivations for Codeswitching. Evidence from Africa.* Oxford: Clarendon Press.

Pennycook, A. 1994. *The Cultural Politics of English as an International Language.* Harlow, Essex: Pearson Education.

Phillipson, R. & T. Skutnabb-Kangas 1999. "Englishisation: one dimension of globalisation". In D. Graddol & U. H. Meinhof. *English in a Changing World. AILA Review*, 13, 19-36.

de Ravin, A. 2001. *So Who's in Control Here – A Semiotic System Offering Resources for Management as Control.* Unpublished PhD thesis. Sydney: Macquarie University.

Shalom, C. 2001. *The Academic Conference: An Analysis of the Reseach Process Genres of Contrasting Academic Discourse Communities.* Unpublished PhD thesis. Liverpool: University of Liverpool.

Smith, L. 1985. "International intelligibility of English: Directions and resources." *World Englishes,* 4, 3: 333-342.

Swales, J. 1990. *Genre Analysis.* Cambridge: Cambridge University Press.

Swann, J. 1996. In D. Graddol, D. Leith & J. Swann (eds). *English. History, Diversity and Change.* London/New York: The Open University & Routledge, 301-24.

Ventola, E. 1987. *The Structure of Social Interaction.* London: Pinter.

Ventola, E. This volume. "Why and What Kind of Focus on Conference Presentations?"

Appendix

To: Professors/Associate Professors/Lecturers/University Staff/Researchers/Writers

From: Jason Lim Miin Hwa [Lecturer/Secretary, Seminar Committee, Centre for the Promotion of Knowledge and Language Learning (CPKLL/PPIB), UNIVERSITI MALAYSIA SABAH, 88999 Kota Kinabalu, Malaysia.]

Date: 4th September 2001

It is our pleasure to invite you to our Biweekly Seminar which will be held at the Main Meeting Room (Bilik Mesyuarat Utama), 3rd Floor, Centre for the Promotion of Knowledge and Language Learning (CPKLL/PPIB), UNIVERSITI MALAYSIA SABAH, from 11.00 a.m. to 12.15 a.m. on Monday, 10th September 2001.

A paper entitled "The Process of European Integration: From War to Euro" will be presented by Professor Fernando Rodrigo.

If you are an invited guest residing outside (of) Sabah, do come and join us at the Biweekly Seminar when you visit the city of Kota Kinabalu. If you are interested in presenting a paper/talk, do feel free to discuss your plan with me.

A light meal (or some refreshments) will be served. Your presence would be much appreciated.

Yours faithfully,
JASON LIM MIIN HWA

AFTERWORD

Conference language and the crucial role it plays in the professional lives of academics have been neglected over the last quarter of a century. This volume represents a start on redressing this neglect. However, much remains to be done. This afterword outlines the areas in which we, as applied linguists with an interest in conference language, still need to concentrate our efforts in the fields of research and pedagogy.

Perhaps the main reason that linguists have tended not to study conference language is its intrinsic complexity as a focus of research. We are clearly only beginning to find out about the academic conference, its genres, and the discourse communities that own them. It seems to the editors that a number of methodological and theoretical issues need to be considered in future research in the field.

A key issue concerns conference data and its collection. Those who have worked with conference data know that it is notoriously difficult to collect: collection itself is time consuming and the quality of recordings of multi-party interaction is often too poor for useful analysis. Beyond these very practical problems, there are important and complex methodological issues to address. Conference data needs to be placed in the social and academic context of any particular conference from which it has been collected. Methodologies for the collection of such data will include those of genre analysis and ethnography – they will take into account the notions of 'outsider' and 'insider' of a particular community. Case study approaches to conferences, perhaps involving interdisciplinary research groups, as well as longitudinal studies also offer ways in to the conference context. To deal with all of these problems, as a long-term goal, we would like to see the development of a database of conference language which would give researchers access to data – and situational information – from a range of academic fields. Such a venture would also encourage more collaborative research as well as providing a resource for teachers of conference language.

A second aspect that we would like to highlight concerns the description of conference genres. There is not only a lack of descriptions of the research process genres but, as far as we are aware, no one has yet attempted to describe any social genres at conferences despite the fact that many non-native academics comment on their discomfort in such situations. Further, we need to refine our linguistic tools for such description. At the global level of generic structure, old friends such as 'genre' and 'subgenre' perhaps need to be revisited and redefined while new concepts like 'macrogenre' need to be clarified and developed.

Additionally, micro-analytical categories such as 'generic element', 'move', 'step', 'act' should be revisited in the light of conference data analysis. During such a process of clarifying these Swalesian and Hallidayan categories, we would encourage dialogue between these two main approaches to describing genre and other traditions of linguistic analysis with similar aims and approaches.

A further aspect of future work on conference language relates to the fact that conference genres such as the presentation session and the academic poster involve more than one mode of expression. It is becoming clear that we need to find out more about conference genres and multi-modality and to develop our ways of studying this.

Furthermore, while it is known that the synoptic description of genre is of great benefit to the ESP situation, it is also becoming evident that we need to find out more about what actually happens when texts unfold dynamically. We need to explore the possible variations in the sequencing of elements and how they might overlap. Additionally, the interpersonal demands on participant roles such as politeness strategies, involvement strategies and repairs should be further investigated, so that we can identify and analyse situationally appropriate responses. Our understanding of the complex interaction that takes place in the discussion phase of the paper presentation session will also be developed as we have more data-driven analyses of what is actually going on. It is likely that the notion of semiotic spanning through pre-conference activities, the presentation phase to the discussion, and beyond, will help us to capture some of the inter-linking complexities.

We also need to find out more about the relationship between discourse community and genre. How do different discourse communities use these genres for positioning and power? Our concern as EAP practitioners also relates to equality in the promotion of research by academics from different cultures. Our pedagogy can be informed by further study of gatekeeping genres (and elements of those genres) such as conference abstracts and titles, and of the presentation genres themselves, particularly the paper presentation session and the conference poster. Social genres are also an important research focus from this point of view, as they are events during which community members establish bonds and continue the more public positioning that takes place in the research process genres.

The term 'cultural' has been used here in two distinct senses. Firstly, we have used it to refer to the culture of particular academic discourse communities, communities which own genre sets. But the term has also been used in its more traditional sense to talk about cultural dimensions which arise from nationalities or ethnic groupings and their languages. Future research in the field of conference language should, in our opinion, open up both these areas. More investigation into status and positioning within academic discourse communities, and how these define situationally appropriate responses, is crucial. At the same time, we need more research into cultural variation and its potential impact on generic forms, conventions and enactments in the lingua franca of English. Work such as this now urgent, not only to avoid miscommunication, but also to ensure fair and productive access for all conference contributors.

Naturally, all of the areas outlined above have important implications for pedagogy. As our knowledge of conference genres increases, we are in a much better position to construe a pedagogy of 'conferencing' which is firmly based on linguistic research. The remainder of this afterword focuses on the key issues involved.

The first obvious strand for pedagogy is developing awareness of conferencing for non-native and novice academics, based on a more extended view of the social semiotics of conferencing and detailed descriptions of various conference genres. Conference presentations should be seen as processes, whose links with activities preceding and following the presentation are made clear to novices through the notion of semiotic spanning. Novices and non-native academics should be enabled to explore the 'conference world(s)' before having to 'perform'. Such an exploration could involve actual conference visits as an ethnographic observant and discussions/interviews with experienced conference goers of the novice's own discourse community.

The next pedagogical strand is to develop novices' skills in building global generic structures for their conference papers, or other types of presentation. Emphasis should be placed on providing support when novices prepare to present their research at a conference for the first time. While many scientists' written papers roughly follow the 'IMRD' structure, novices should be aware of the difference between written and spoken genres. There are quite different demands on language and other semiotic resources during conference presentations. Presenters may, for example, include stories and humour in their presentations and during the discussion. Novices need to develop their sense of where, and for what purposes, to embed other genres within the unfolding of the presentation.

A further pedagogical strand which is necessary is awareness of the role of interpersonal factors in conference events. Linguistic research provides valuable information for helping academic presenters find the linguistic means to the right interpersonal tone with their audiences. Important for beginners are the hierarchies and social roles involved in conferences, (e.g. plenary speakers vs.

section speakers; established experts vs. novices), and how to take such these into account linguistically and semiotically during their presentations and social interaction. As indicated in this volume, it may be especially useful for novices to position themselves with respect to those who are significant in the field, since this is important for academic networking and power politics. It is essential to learn how to use the linguistic resources of modality and hedging to sound confident about one's research and its results, and to align oneself with or against other research without giving an impression of being arrogant or 'bashing' others' work.

A further, urgently needed, task for conference pedagogy is the development of skills for multimodality. Conference presentations often rely considerably on information presented through other media than the spoken word. Handouts, transparencies, slides and Power Point presentations have become the rule rather than the exception in present-day academia (although there are still some practitioners of the traditional 'read-out-loud' method). While a start has been made on researching some of the multimodal possibilities, the demands made on presenter and audience by others, such as video-conferencing, have not yet been adequately addressed, if at all. As our knowledge and understanding of modern media and the visualisation of information increases, conference pedagogy faces the challenge of developing novices' skills in combining several different modes into a useful and effective semiotic for conferencing.

Related to this issue are pedagogical issues of preparing conference participants for discussion time, and the problems of switching mode from monologue to dialogue. Normal conversational interaction rules do not usually apply in the discussion phase: turns are not freely allocated or self-selected. Rather, the chair controls both the presenter and the discussant(s) and their opportunities of speaking. The turns may be distributed politically, i.e. to the most important members of the discourse community first, ignoring novices' requests for a turn. As presenters, novices may also have to prepare themselves for some 'bashing' from established scholars. Eventually, novices may also have to take over the function of the chair and have to prepare themselves to carry out the function linguistically and non-verbally.

Last but not least, the pedagogy of conferencing must pay attention to the special needs of non-native presenters. Sometimes non-native presenters need help to become sensitive to cultural differences in ways of giving presentations. Sometimes more specific help is needed on, for example, pronunciation and intonation, lexical and grammatical problems, or discoursal and non-verbal communication issues. Conferencing pedagogy should also pay attention to raising the native or multicultural audience's level of tolerance for cultural and linguistic differences in various non-native English speakers' presentations.

Giving one's first paper in a foreign language is never easy. Native speakers who have never had to present or debate in a foreign language may have no appreciation of the manifold difficulties that foreign presenters experience in trying to get their message across effectively and appropriately. The onus of developing sensitivity towards these intercultural and language code matters is specifically heavy on those involved in the research and pedagogy of English as an international conference language. English is the number one language of international conferences. As a lingua franca, English is an opportunity for exchanging views and advancing knowledge globally. However, no-one involved in the research and pedagogy of English wants this exchange to take place at the cost of non-native speakers.

It is clear that, up to now, we have lacked a systematic approach to analysing the continuum of genres which make up conference events. The chapters in this volume point to ways in which such approaches could be developed, both in terms of research and pedagogy. We would not claim that this collection is completely comprehensive, nor that it is definitive. We are in the early stages of exploring a new and expansive area of language and communication. At this point, we are still experimenting with descriptive frameworks. These will provide support for future contextualised and data-based research, which will, in turn, feed into pedagogic practice. There is still a long way to go, but we are now in a better position to map out the conference as a macrogenre and to identify key linguistic and semiotic features of some of its component research process genres.

Sabine Gieszinger

The History of Advertising Language

The Advertisements in *The Times* from 1788 to 1996

Frankfurt/M., Berlin, Bern, Bruxelles, New York, Oxford, Wien, 2001. XIV, 363 pp., num. fig. and tab.
Münchener Universitäts-Schriften. Texte und Untersuchungen zur Englischen Philologie. Herausgegeben von Helmut Gneuss, Hans Sauer und Wolfgang Weiß. Bd. 23
ISBN 3-631-37835-1 · pb. € 50.10/US-$ 45.95/£ 29.-*
US-ISBN 0-8204-5390-0

The discourse of advertising has changed considerably over the past 200 years. This study – based on a corpus of 540 advertisements published in *The Times* between 1788 and 1996 – outlines how advertisements have developed into a distinctive text type with recurring formal, semantic and functional features. Criteria investigated are the global structure of advertisements, major topics, the use of adjectives, language play, the textual realisation of advertising functions and the emergence of the pictorial message. Although the study focuses on linguistic aspects of advertising, the discussion also includes the influence of extra-linguistic factors, such as socio-economic conditions and the development of the media.

Contents: Introduction · Historical background · Formal aspects of advertisements and text type marking · Semantic aspects of advertisements · Functional aspects of advertisements (including also aspects of politeness and politeness strategies and semiotic aspects of advertisements, such as the pictorial presentation of the product and the interrelation of verbal and pictorial message) · Summary: advertising – uniformity and singularity

Frankfurt/M · Berlin · Bern · Bruxelles · New York · Oxford · Wien
Distribution: Verlag Peter Lang AG
Jupiterstr. 15, CH-3000 Bern 15
Telefax (004131) 9402131

*The €-price includes German tax rate
Prices are subject to change without notice
Homepage http://www.peterlang.de